Play and the Artist's Creative Process

Play and the Artist's Creative Process explores a continuity between childhood play and adult creativity. The volume examines how an understanding of play can shed new light on processes that recur in the work of Philip Guston and Eduardo Paolozzi. Both artists' distinctive engagement with popular culture is seen as connected to the play materials available in the landscapes of their individual childhoods. Animating or toying with material to produce the unforeseen outcome is explored as the central force at work in the artists' processes. By engaging with a range of play theories, the book shows how the artists' studio methods can be understood in terms of game strategies.

Elly Thomas is an artist and independent scholar. She received her PhD from the Slade School of Fine Art, UCL. She has taught at UCL and the University for the Creative Arts, Farnham, UK.

HENRY MOORE
FOUNDATION

Cover Credit: Story, 1978, Philip Guston, oil on canvas, 121.9 × 152.4 cm (48 × 60 inches). Image courtesy of The Estate of Philip Guston.

Routledge Advances in Art and Visual Studies

This series is our home for innovative research in the fields of art and visual studies. It includes monographs and targeted edited collections that provide new insights into visual culture and art practice, theory, and research.

The Artist-Philosopher and New Philosophy
George Smith

Photography and the Contemporary Cultural Condition
Commemorating the Present
Peter D. Osborne

Digital Art, Aesthetic Creation
The Birth of a Medium
Paul Crowther

Geneses of Postmodern Art
Technology as Iconology
Paul Crowther

Art, Cybernetics and Pedagogy in Post-War Britain
Kate Sloan

Film and Modern American Art
The Dialogue Between Cinema and Painting
Katherine Manthorne

Play and the Artist's Creative Process
The Work of Philip Guston and Eduardo Paolozzi
Elly Thomas

Film and Modern American Art
The Dialogue Between Cinema and Painting
Katherine Manthorne

For a full list of titles in this series, please visit www.routledge.com/Routledge-Advances-in-Art-and-Visual-Studies/book-series/RAVS

Play and the Artist's Creative Process

The Work of Philip Guston and Eduardo Paolozzi

Elly Thomas

Routledge
Taylor & Francis Group
LONDON AND NEW YORK

First published 2019 by Routledge

2 Park Square, Milton Park, Abingdon, Oxon OX14 4RN
605 Third Avenue, New York, NY 10017

Routledge is an imprint of the Taylor & Francis Group, an informa business

First issued in paperback 2021

Publisher's Note

The publisher has gone to great lengths to ensure the quality of this reprint but points out that some imperfections in the original copies may be apparent.

Library of Congress Cataloging-in-Publication Data
Names: Thomas, Elly (Artist), author.
Title: Play and the artist's creative process : the work of Philip Guston and Eduardo Paolozzi / Elly Thomas.
Description: New York, NY : Routledge, 2019. | Series: Routledge advances in art and visual studies | Includes bibliographical references and index.
Identifiers: LCCN 2018046641 | ISBN 9781138054257 (hardback : alk. paper) | ISBN 9781315114583 (ebook)
Subjects: LCSH: Guston, Philip, 1913–1980—Criticism and interpretation. | Paolozzi, Eduardo, 1924–2005—Criticism and interpretation. | Play. | Creative ability.
Classification: LCC ND237.G8 T49 2019 | DDC 701/.15—dc23
LC record available at https://lccn.loc.gov/2018046641

ISBN: 978-1-138-05425-7 (hbk)
ISBN: 978-1-03-217837-0 (pbk)
DOI: 10.4324/9781315114583

Typeset in Sabon
by Apex CoVantage, LLC

Contents

Illustrations

The colour plate section appears after page 95.

Colour Plates

Preface and Acknowledgements

This book examines how Philip Guston and Eduardo Paolozzi's use of play processes enabled the artists to defer concerns with outcomes, to allow for experimental, emergent image and object making. Although I examine play specifically within the context of the work of Paolozzi and Guston, I hope the reader may find ways to apply some of the artists' strategies to their own experience, either as a practitioner or as a viewer. This project is heavily informed by my own experience as an artist. While I do not discuss my practice within the book, throughout the writing of the text I have used my studio as an experimental site to test and explore the processes discussed. I have also had the pleasure of sharing my research with art students in lectures, seminars and workshops. This book is indebted to the students' inventive responses.

I am very grateful to the Henry Moore Foundation, the Paolozzi Foundation and the Guston Foundation for their generous support. This project began during an MA at Falmouth School of Art. I would like to thank Dr Daro Montag, Dr Andy Webster and Dr Virginia Button for encouraging the research in its very early stages. The project was developed as a doctoral study at the Slade School of Fine Art. I would like to express my sincere gratitude to my supervisors: Dr Joy Sleeman, Neil Jeffries and Dr Petra Lange Berndt. I am extremely grateful to Professor Timothy Mathews for his critical guidance during the project's transition from thesis to book proposal.

I am very grateful to Musa Mayer and Sally Radic for their time and valuable support. I would like to thank Daniel Herrmann for the benefit of his expertise. Thank you to Fiona Mathison and Douglas Grierson for sharing their wonderful memories of their friendship with Eduardo Paolozzi, and for showing me their own Paolozzi archive. I greatly appreciate their kindness. I am also very grateful to Leah Lovett for putting me in contact with Fiona and Douglas.

I would like to thank archivists at the Scottish National Gallery of Modern Art, the Victoria and Albert Museum and the Tate Gallery. I am very grateful for their expertise, their time, patience and detective skills. I would also like to express my gratitude to students and staff at the Slade School of Fine Art and the University for the Creative Arts, Farnham, for their valuable insights.

I am indebted to Emma Lilley for helping the project on its way to publication. I am extremely grateful to Catherine Ingrams for her detailed reading of the manuscript. She brought a breadth of expertise together with logic, imagination and sensitivity. I was very fortunate to have enthusiastic support from my editor at Routledge, Isabella Vitti, together with the kind help of Katie Armstrong, the editorial assistant. I am also very grateful to my anonymous reviewers at Routledge. This book benefitted greatly from their comments.

This project would not have been possible without the incredible support of my family. This book is dedicated to them. Last, but by no means least, I want to thank Katy and Mathew Wheeler, whose drawings inspired this project in 2005 (when they were 6 and 8).

1 Introduction

Ageing Play

> [T]his serious play, which we call art, can't be stamped. I mean you have to keep learning how to play in new ways all the time.
>
> Philip Guston, 1972[1]

"Play" is a word one commonly hears as an artist or art student in a studio environment. It is usually used to denote the "light" and "carefree," or a stage of experimentation before the serious work of art making begins to take shape. However, by engaging with a range of play theory, one can begin to reconnect with play as an immersive activity that involves risk-taking, tension, conflict and subversion. Play as serious fun. In this book, I explore a continuity between childhood play and adult creativity. I focus on how an understanding of play can shed light on some specific creative objectives and processes that recur in the work of Eduardo Paolozzi and Philip Guston. I begin by exploring a collection of childhood play activities that develop to inform the artists' studio processes. Crucially, I will not suggest that the artists' play processes are concerned with an attempt to recapture a sense of naivety; I move in the opposite direction, to explore what continues and *evolves*.

The artists' play processes will be seen to provide tools with which to engage with the adult present. I will explore how these processes continued to be informed by the context within which they worked. While particular circumstances can be seen to have been conducive to play, the artists' use of play methods and games strategies will also be understood to have provided the means with which to subvert the status quo. As an artist, I bring an understanding of studio methods and materials. I use this to focus on the artists' studio processes. In examining the work of Eduardo Paolozzi and Philip Guston, this project does not explore performance art or socially engaged practice. While these forms may seem to be the logical territory for a study of art and play (and indeed there are already many excellent publications that explore these areas), here I focus instead on how an understanding of play can inform an approach to object and image making. My examination of these processes aims to be of use to artists, art historians, curators and creativity researchers, in addition to providing the viewer with an interactive role.

To some extent, both Guston and Paolozzi's careers have invited categorisation and myth to grow around apparent decisive, dramatic leaps in style and form. For Guston, debate has revolved around the fact that his career seems to divide into three main periods, beginning with early success as a figurative painter, followed by critical acclaim as part of the New York School of Abstract Expressionists and concluding with a dramatic and legendary break back into figuration with his late "cartoon-like" works. For Paolozzi, The Independent Group, Pop Art and Surrealism have all continued to exist as markers that define any attempt to categorise an extraordinarily multi-faceted career. Guston and Paolozzi, then, may appear to be an unlikely pairing of artists. However, in moving beyond the geographical gap and art historical labels, one can identify shared objectives and processes and thus bring a new understanding to the artists' individual working processes. I will examine both artists' distinctive engagement with popular culture as connected to the play materials available in the landscapes of their individual childhoods. Animating or *toying* with material to produce an unforeseen outcome will be understood as the central force at work in these artists' processes. It is here one discovers a continuity between childhood play and the artists' adult creativity.

Throughout the book, I explore both artists' resistance to finality. While Paolozzi is famously known as a collagist, we will see how the artist found it "upsetting" to stick things down[2] and found ways to continually reanimate "the frozen picture."[3] In parallel, I examine how Guston consistently voiced the need to treat paint as a living substance. While creating his apparently abstract works, Guston described his forms as "living presences."[4] And while creating his late figurative work, the artist described his sense that he was creating "living things"[5] that appeared to have a life of their own. This book will examine how Guston and Paolozzi's materials and processes allowed the artists to refute the conclusion of the artworks to play repeatedly with the life of form. By placing the artists' work within the messy mass of their studio material, the book seeks to continue to animate the works by placing them within an unfolding process. It is here the viewer can join the artists and play with the life of the work.

The Studio Landscape

Eduardo Paolozzi: "An Architecture From the Tools of a Child"[6]

Eduardo Paolozzi was a lifelong collector and hoarder. Over the course of his career, a towering mass of material accumulated in his studio (Figure 1.1). Among the artist's working models and cast elements were stacks of toys, books, broken machinery and printed ephemera (Figure 1.2). The artist's personal collection of popular culture, donated to the Victoria and Albert Museum as the Krazy Kat Arkive, reaches into excess of 20,000 objects. The majority of Paolozzi's printed ephemera has been left to The Scottish National Gallery of Modern Art. Looking through the hundreds of folders of Paolozzi's material held in the gallery's archives is an overwhelming experience. In the vast mass, one encounters a dizzying array of material that includes loose receipts, empty envelopes, menus, advertising, concert programmes, technical diagrams (Figure 1.3), telephone sex cards, magazine cuttings of robots, a giant picture of a flea seen under a microscope, aerial views, images of bombsites, pictures of Mickey Mouse. . . . When looking through the collection, one initially has a tendency to search for relevance, to attempt to sort the material into hierarchies of importance, to search for categories and taxonomies. But the material continually seems to fight back. Over time, one begins to see the collection in terms of action. To understand Paolozzi's processes, one has to approach all the material as equally important—the result of an activity that produced a landscape from which the work emerged.

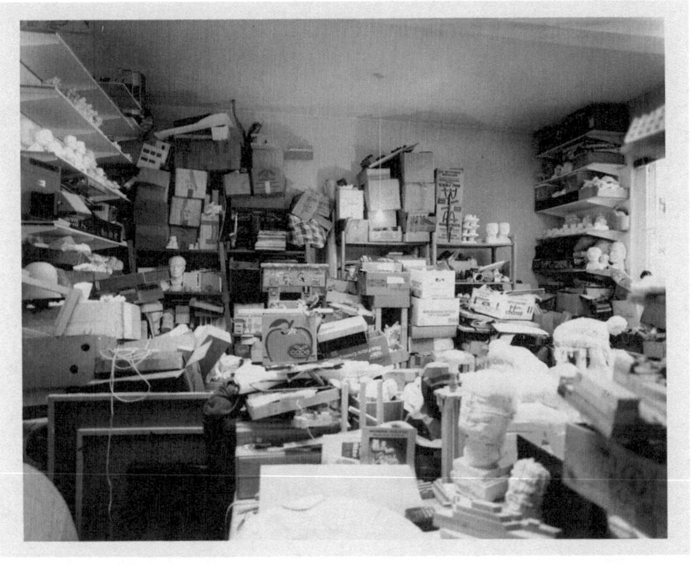

Figure 1.1 Interior of one of Eduardo Paolozzi's London studios, 1994 (View 10 of 21), Eduardo Paolozzi, National Galleries of Scotland. Scottish National Gallery of Modern Art Archive.

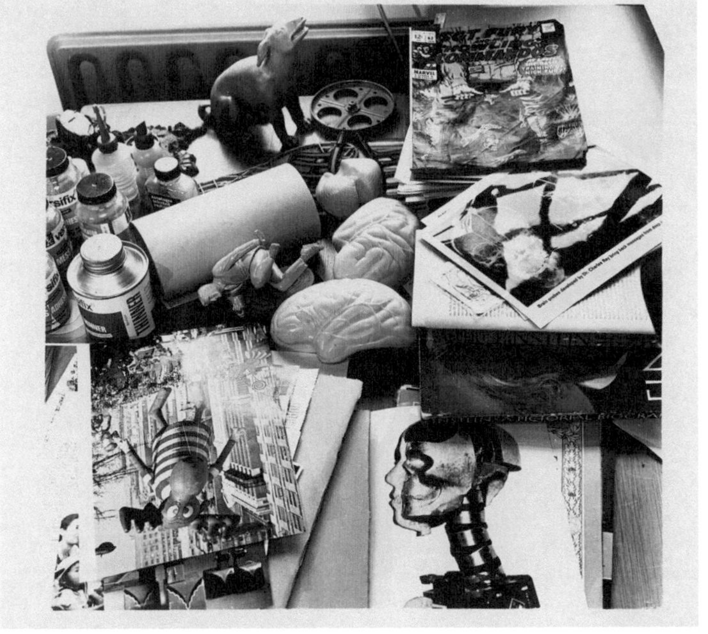

Figure 1.2 Desk with printed matter and toys/toy brains. Eduardo Paolozzi's studio at 107 Dovehouse Street, London, 1970. National Galleries of Scotland. Scottish National Gallery of Modern Art Archive.

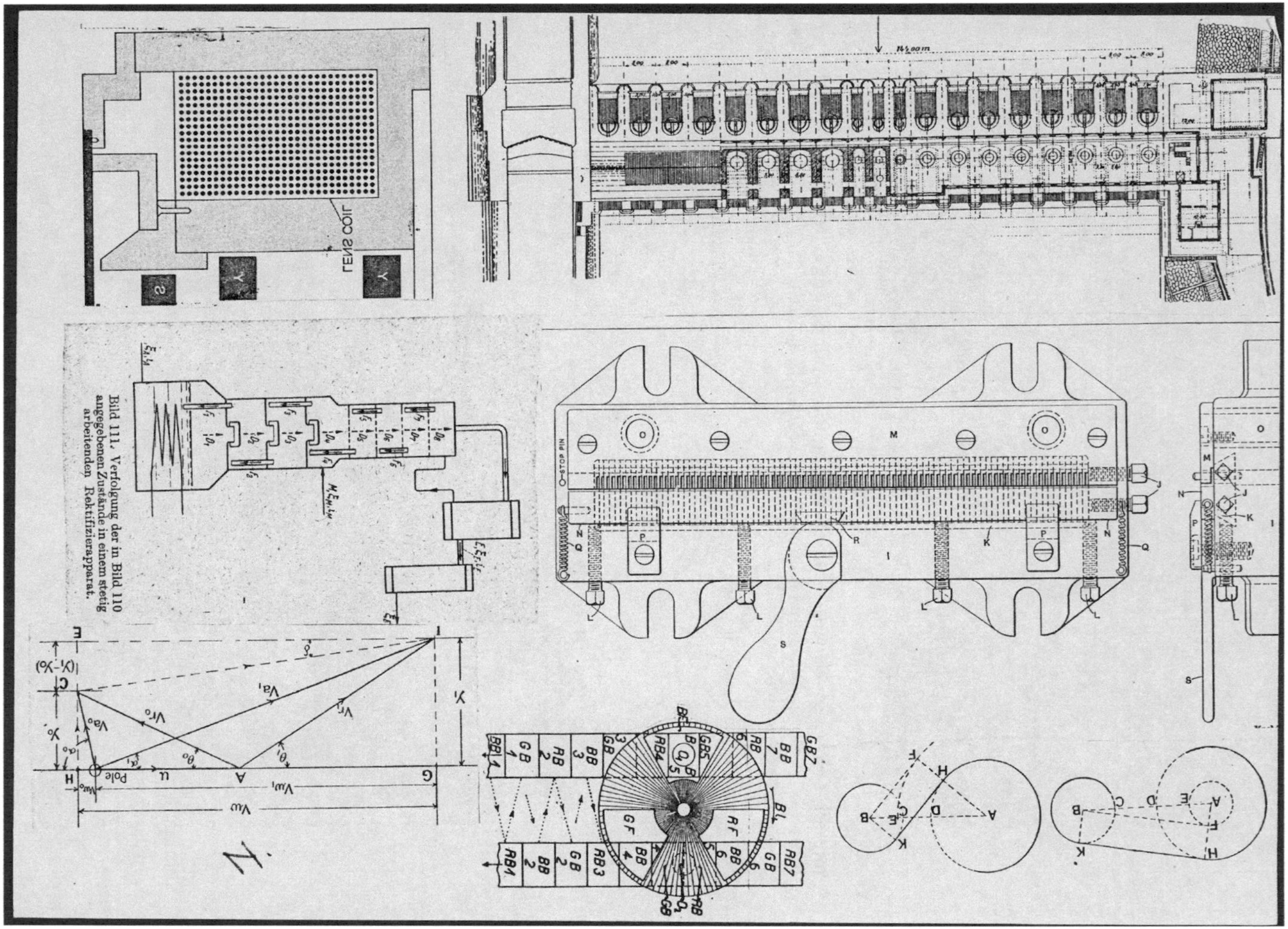

Figure 1.3 Eduardo Paolozzi Archive preliminary handlist: artwork, correspondence, papers, source material, newscuttings and printed ephemera, Eduardo Paolozzi, National Galleries of Scotland. Scottish National Gallery of Modern Art Archive.

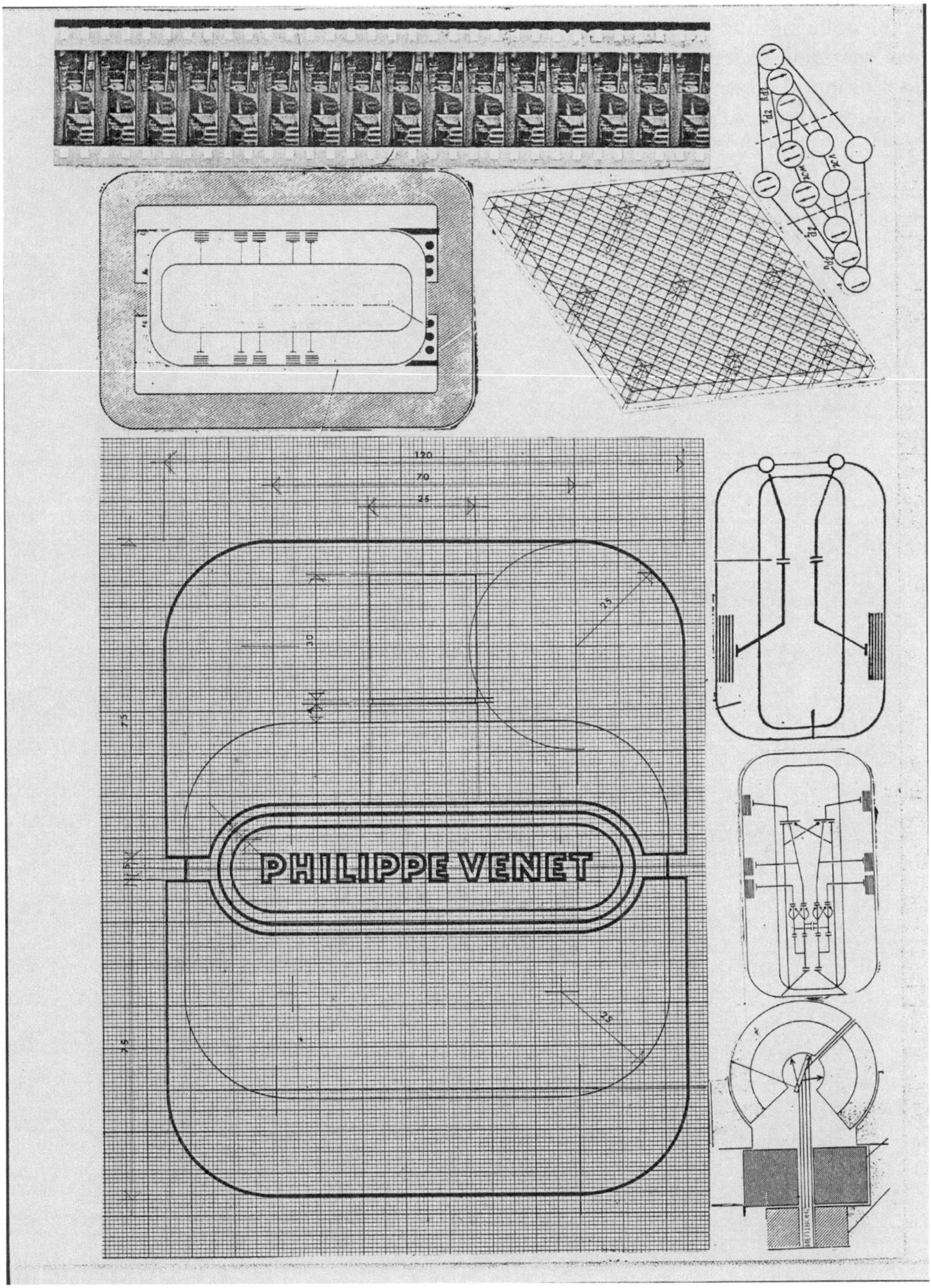

Figure 1.3 (Continued)

Throughout Paolozzi's career, the collection of printed ephemera formed the basis of the artist's collages, prints, mosaics, tapestries and films. One can see everything in the collection as held in a state of readiness, transformed from waste material to play material. Indeed, Paolozzi's avid collecting was an activity that dated back to his childhood days; making scrapbooks was a practice he had continued from childhood through to adulthood (Figures 1.4 and 1.5). Reminiscing about his early years

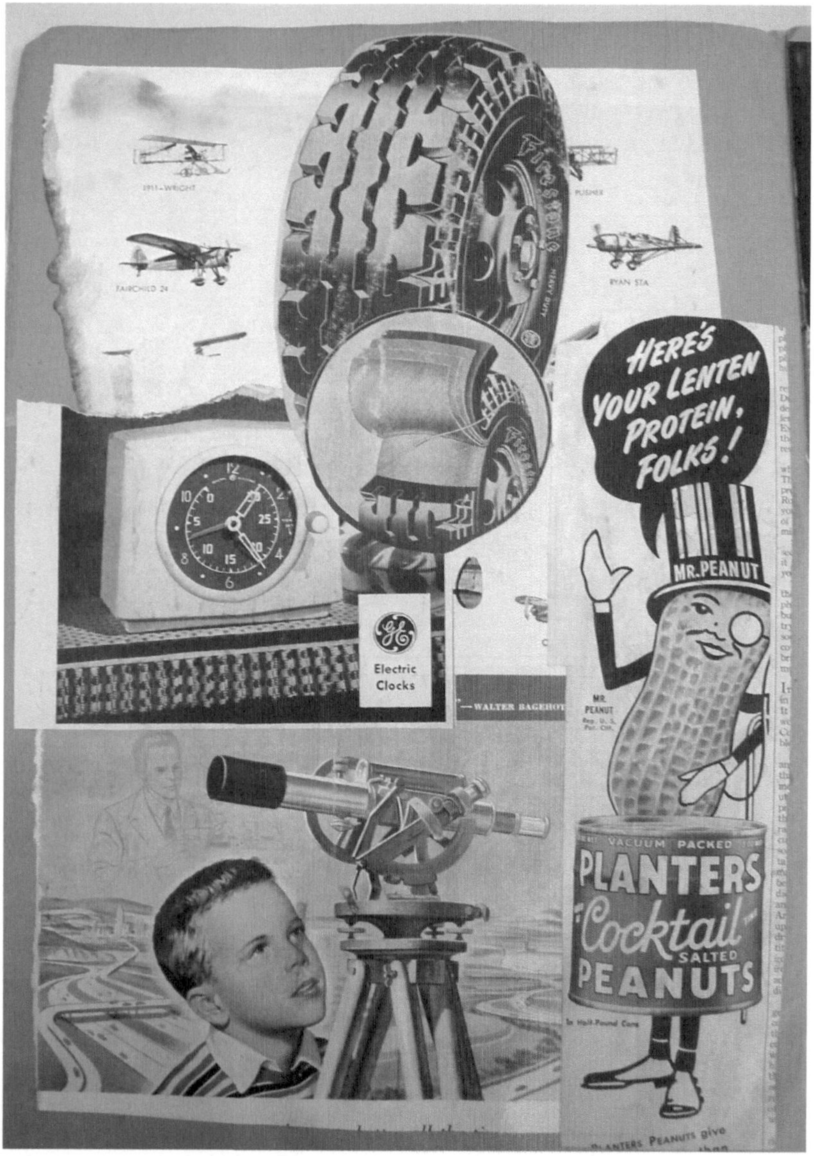

Figure 1.4 Page of a scrapbook, 1947–52, Eduardo Paolozzi, Victoria and Albert Museum Archives, London.

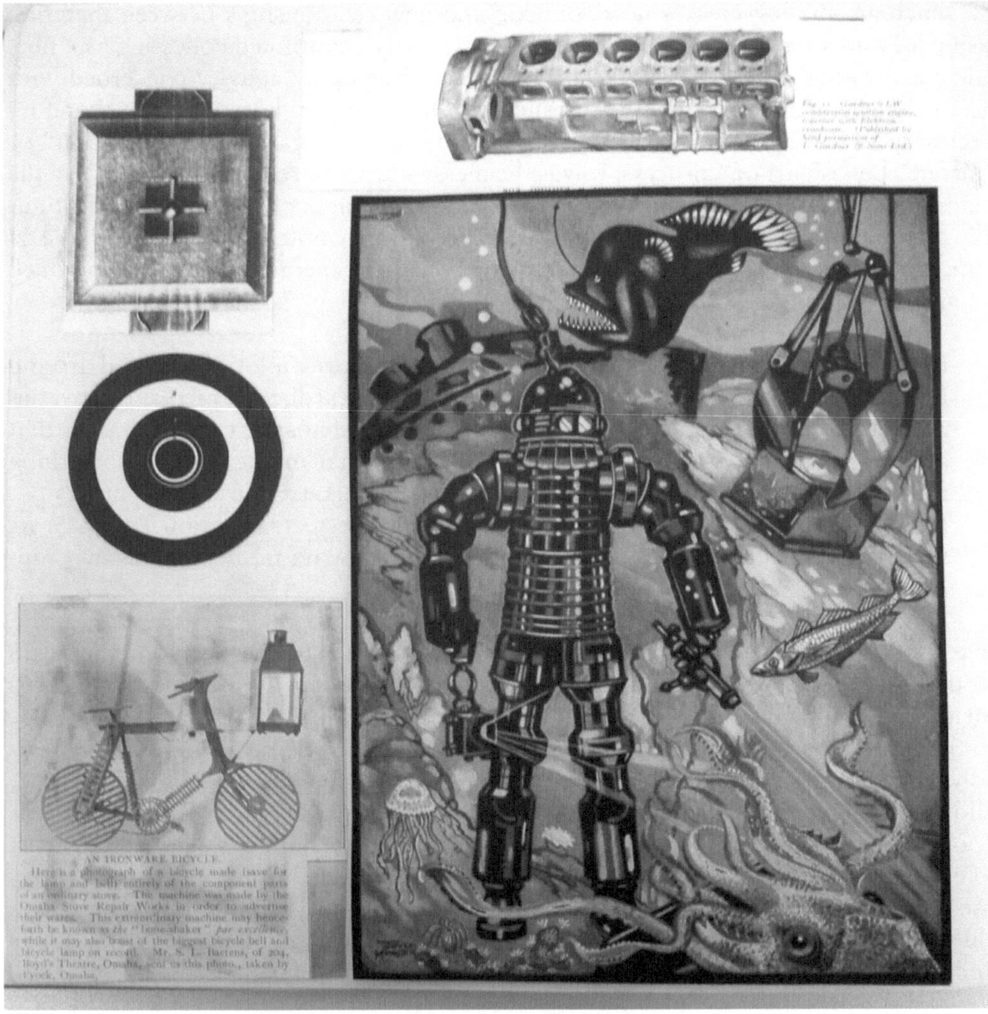

Figure 1.5 Page of a scrapbook, 1960, Eduardo Paolozzi, Victoria and Albert Museum Archives, London.

growing up in Edinburgh in the 1920s and 1930s, Paolozzi stated: "It is difficult to think of a time when cutting images out of magazines was not a daily event."[7]

The literary critic Susan Stewart defines collecting as "a form of art as play."[8] In her publication *On Longing*, Stewart provides us with a necessary distinction between the souvenir and the collection with reference to time. For Stewart, the souvenir is commonly used as an aide to memory: "This childhood is not a childhood as lived; it is a childhood voluntarily remembered . . . manufactured from its material survivals."[9] By contrast, for Stewart the collection is not concerned with a focus on the past, nor is it an attempt to restore material to an origin; rather, time becomes simultaneous within the collection. To regard collecting as a play activity is to engage with the means by which assembling creates new contexts and new relationships between material. Using Stewart's terms, we do not need to see Paolozzi's continued collecting as a nostalgic act; rather, collecting can be seen as a continued play activity concerned with inventing changing, evolving relationships within assorted material. It is therefore necessary to see the items in Paolozzi's collection not in isolation as a "diagram" or "advert" but as part of a process. It was the mess—the open relationships between the items—that was so important to their usefulness. The mass of material was continually on the move within the artist's studio. In preparatory notes for a lecture, Paolozzi himself described how this shifting landscape was the generative source from which all his work sprang:

> In the preparations for this talk I had to move endlessly a lot of material around my studio projects old and new, plaster, plywood, cardboard pieces, discoveries and long forgotten items. The room resembles in its chaos the various dramas that go into making a drawing or sculpture. What is that moment when something torn out of "Time" magazine, date unknown, reveals itself in view of others . . . meaning subject to interpolation or image subject to translation redefines its identity.—Transformation by context and last but by no means less instinct supported by obsession.[10]

In exploring Paolozzi's work in relation to the ever-growing collection, one can begin to understand how the material that formed the constituent elements of the artist's image and object making was tirelessly revisited. Reproduction techniques were key to the artist's use of found objects and imagery. Sculpture elements were cast repeatedly, while found images were photocopied and screenprinted, enlarged and reduced, allowing the material to drift further away from its original source. Throughout the book, I will explore how Paolozzi's use of reproduction techniques allowed the artist to engage with repetition as central to a play process. In addition, the artist's various use of reproduction methods can themselves be understood as connected to the artist's childhood play practices. Paolozzi described copying and tracing images from books and magazines with his friends as a child:

> Comic books and magazines for all ages were consumed hungrily and passed on until literally worn out. It was common practice for me and my friends to copy pictures from these publications and, for those of us unskilled in drawing, a piece of greaseproof paper borrowed from the kitchen drawer would be superimposed on the photo of a film star or aeroplane.[11]

It is possible to see how Paolozzi's childhood practice of tracing images evolved into the artist's use of reproduction techniques. Throughout the book, I will explore Paolozzi's engagement with mass production as driven by play processes defined by subversion, distortion and corruption.

Paolozzi's all-embracing approach to visual culture was to make the artist a key figure in the Independent Group—a cross-disciplinary group of architects, designers, theorists, photographers, painters and sculptors that met at the Institute of Contemporary Arts, London, between 1952 and 1955. The members of the group shared an interest in popular culture such as advertising, science fiction, movies, magazine imagery and comics. As if in continuity with playground swaps and the sharing of comic books and magazines, Paolozzi and the fellow members of the group would meet to discuss and analyse mass culture. Scrapbooking was a shared activity among the Group, and found imagery would form the basis of exhibitions organised by its members, including *Parallel of Life and Art* (1953). In a sense, one can see found imagery as the shared play material within the Independent Group. In the following chapter, I will examine how explorations of the Group's engagement with contemporary culture in terms of the "as found" provide significant connections with definitions of the properties of the toy.

Paolozzi credited Amédée Ozenfant's 1931 publication, *Foundations of Modern Art*, with opening up a pathway that allowed him to see "the possibility then of combining my childhood loves with the other kind of things, you know, the Bugatti wheel and the warship."[12] In Ozenfant's book, almost any aspect of the visual world appears worthy of scrutiny—from the antique to the modern, from the technological to the organic and microscopic, from window dressing to prison architecture. Importantly, for Paolozzi, Ozenfant's book provides not simply a nostalgic return to childhood but rather a way of reconnecting with "childhood loves" in order to bring them *forward*, to combine them with new interests and present concerns. Ozenfant's inclusion of such images as a shop window display allowed Paolozzi's work to engage with a non-hierarchical approach to the visual world that could embrace the popular culture in which Paolozzi had been immersed as a child in his family's ice cream and tobacco shop and bring it together with an ongoing engagement with contemporary culture. But it was most of all Surrealism that provided the young artist with an expanded definition of what art can be. One learns from Paolozzi that it was after meeting Alberto Giacometti in Paris in 1947 that he gained the confidence to see his childhood play activities as valid forms of art practice. "The world"[13] Paolozzi described as having hidden under his bed as a child in toy, junk and scrapbook form could become tools for creating artwork:

> Surrealism was a wonderful court to inch your way back to all the things that excited you in childhood, like games, secret writings; there was a lot, a great deal in Surrealism where you were able to trigger all these childhood things, which in conventional art education you were taught to forget. . . . I had to seize on Surrealism . . . it gives one enormous licence to justify certain images that I even make today.[14]

The connection Paolozzi emphasises between Surrealism and games provides a means of seeing the continued presence of childhood play not simply in terms of the play materials of childhood. The connection most crucially centres on a relationship between object and image making and game playing. Throughout the book, I will explore game strategies employed by Paolozzi that allowed contingency and the improvisational to propel a creative process. In the following chapters, we will see how the shifting mass of material in Paolozzi's studio landscape directly informed the artist's working methods. In focusing on the artist's studio processes, we can examine how the play material became placed within cycles of construction and destruction. Moreover, we will see how Paolozzi handed over the unsettled nature of the material to the viewer, to allow the audience an interactive role as players in a game of improvised narrative.

Philip Guston: "A Forgotten Place of Beings and Things"[15]

In Philip Guston's studio, reduction became the source of plenty. While Paolozzi's work emerged from a mass of collected material, the collection of forms that populated Guston's canvases were generated from limited means. From 1966 until the artist's death in 1980, Guston's painting returned repeatedly to a small collection of objects in his immediate surroundings (Figure 1.6). The objects in the artist's studio were sparse: flat irons (Figure 1.7), an old armchair and an ash tray brimming with cigarette butts accompanied the basic tools of the trade, such as canvas stretchers, paint cans, pots bursting with paintbrushes and giant cans of turpentine (Figure 1.8). All the while, rack upon rack of paintings accumulated in the studio. Through repeated engagement with the everyday objects around him, Guston created a torrent of imagery, generating a landscape that could range from eternal human conflict to absurdist

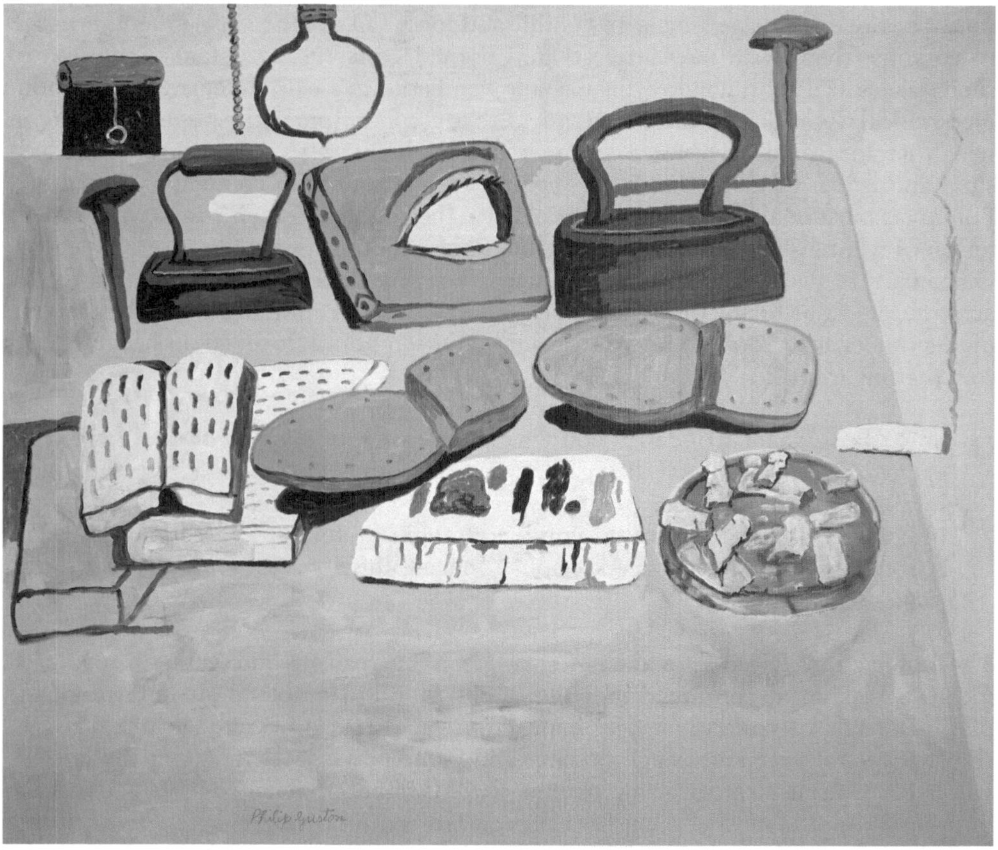

Figure 1.6 Painter's Table, 1973, Philip Guston, oil on canvas, 196.2 × 228.6 cm (77 ¼ × 90 inches) framed: 197.8 × 231.2 × 5 cm (77 7/8 × 91 × 1 15/16 inches). Gift (partial and promised) of Ambassador and Mrs. Donald Blinken in memory of Maurice H. Blinken and in honour of the 50th anniversary of the National Gallery of Art. 1991.69.1. National Gallery of Art, Washington.

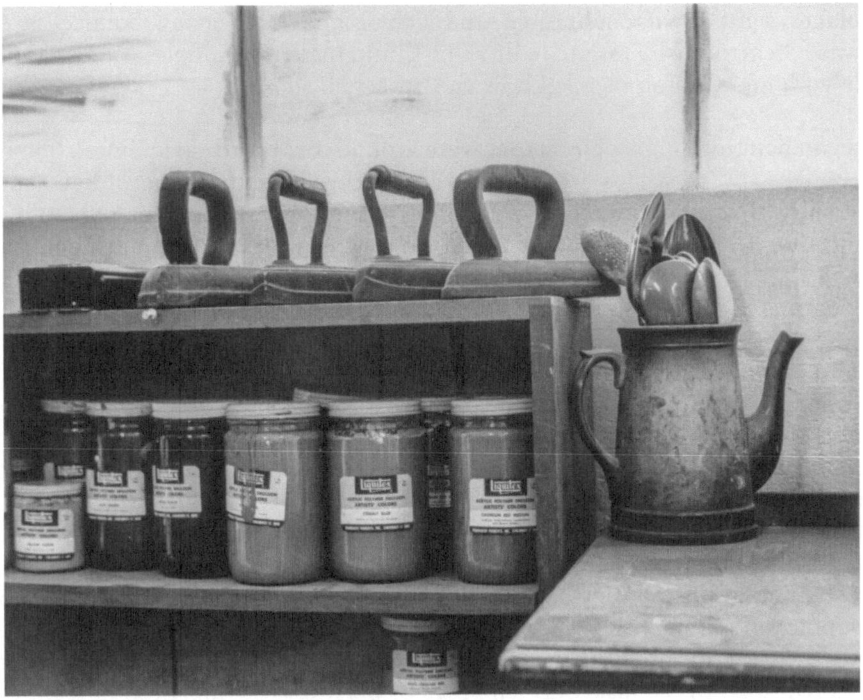

Figure 1.7 Philip Guston's studio, Woodstock, 1975.

Photographer: Denise Hare. Image courtesy of The Estate of Philip Guston.

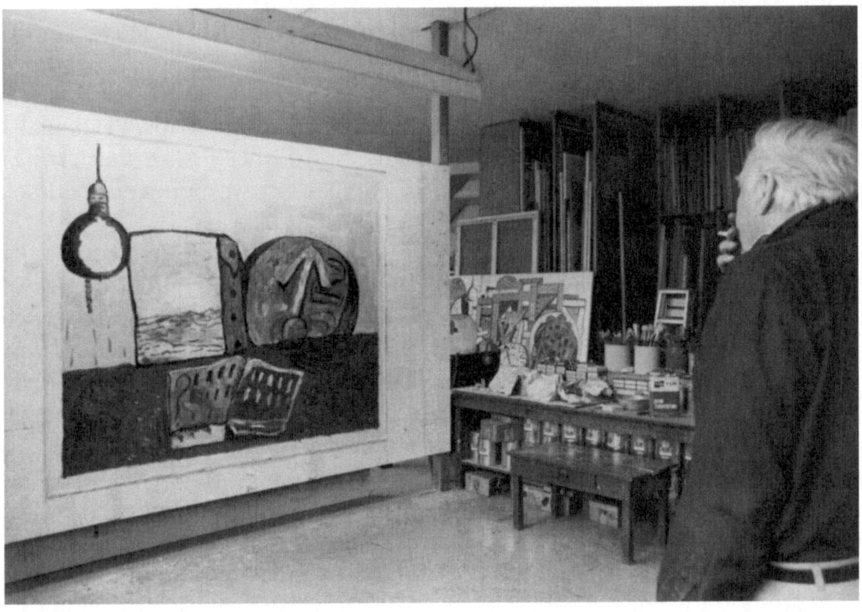

Figure 1.8 Philip Guston in his studio, Woodstock, 1975.

Photographer: Denise Hare. Image courtesy of The Estate of Philip Guston.

assemblages, right down to a humble sandwich or a pile of cherries. Connecting everything was a "cartoonish," animate line that could make the simplest object appear to tremble with life. Guston recalled how the process began:

> I began painting single objects that were around me. I read, so I painted books, lots of books. . . . It's what's around you. . . . I don't have that kind of light bulb but somehow that lightbulb recalls something to me. There's something about a naked lightbulb. Why, I don't know. If I talk too much about it I'll stop using it. . . . I do know that I enjoy the idea of unexotic objects. I like banal, simple objects, tangible, touchable. I'm doing a painting and my shoes are on the floor.[16]

It is significant here that Guston asserted a desire to remain unaware of the reason he returned to certain objects, for fear that over-determination would block their usefulness. In the following chapters, I will explore how it is the not-knowing—the unstable quality—that gives the objects their multivalent potential. In not tying down the meaning, Guston, like Paolozzi, could use variant repetition as the driving force within his process. Guston's use of repetition will also provide a means to explore notions of play and freedom. In contrast to Paolozzi, for Guston it was by pushing against the limitations of a few "banal" objects that the artist discovered multiplicity and boundless possibility.

However, if the meaning of the objects in Guston's work is unstable, the form of Guston's painting, in the last fourteen years of his life, is strongly reminiscent of Bud Fisher's comic strip *Mutt and Jeff*, Guston's favourite cartoon from his childhood days. While Guston was painting his shoes "on the floor," they strikingly came to resemble the giant, clomping clown shoes of the characters that appear in Fisher's cartoon (Figures 1.9 and 1.10). The beefy, gloved hands, roller blinds and goofy cars that recur in Guston's landscape are also borrowed directly from Fisher. Born in 1913, Guston had a childhood love of cartooning. His daughter, Musa Mayer, informs us that

> as a boy, my father loved the newspaper serials and comic strips. Particular favorites were George Herriman's *Krazy Kat* and Bud Fisher's *Mutt and Jeff*. For his thirteenth birthday, his mother gave Philip a year's correspondence course at the Cleveland School of Cartooning.[17]

While Guston recalled becoming bored with instructions on "how to draw" and quickly gave up the lessons, the love of drawing and cartoons continued. By the age of 15, Guston had won a cartooning competition run by the *Los Angeles Times*. But while the young artist's skills were lauded, they were also put to subversive ends; in 1929, for instance, Guston and his friend Jackson Pollock were expelled from Manual Arts High School, largely due to the fact that they had produced satirical cartoons that mocked the English Department. In the last section of the book, I will explore how, in the last decade of his life, Guston used the *Mutt and Jeff* cartoon form to engage with the brutality of the political climate and clown with power.

However, Guston's close friend, the poet Bill Berkson, asserted that in reconnecting with his childhood love of the comic form, "Guston wasn't quoting or taking secondary genre as subject matter; he was releasing, and in strictly painterly terms enlarging upon a way of realizing images that had long before been made second nature."[18]

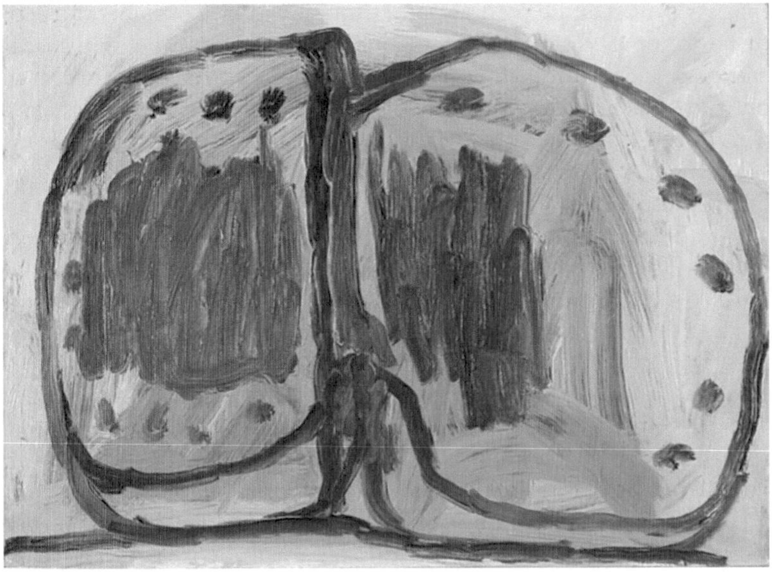

Figure 1.9 Untitled, 1970, Philip Guston, oil on panel, 30.5 × 40.6 cm (12 × 16 inches).

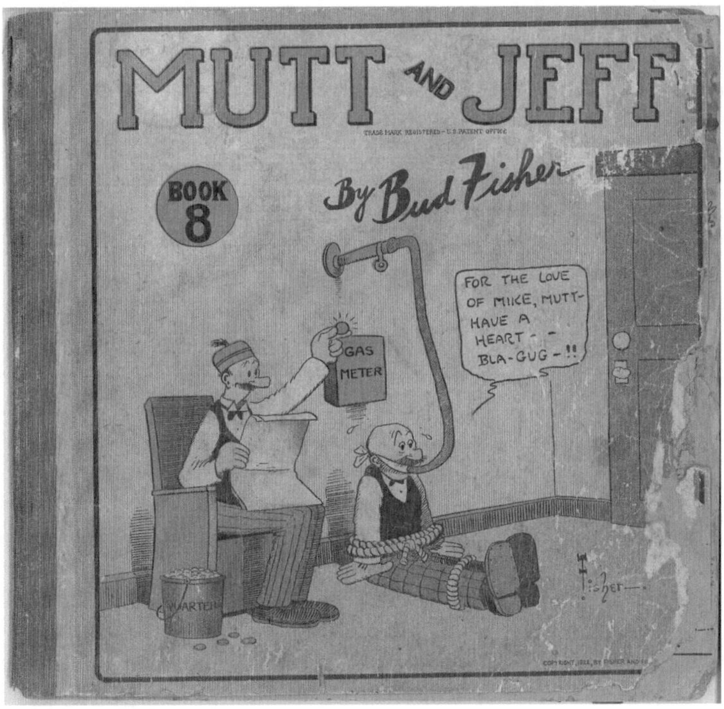

Figure 1.10 Mutt and Jeff, Book 8, 1922, Bud Fisher.

Image credit: The author.

Guston's imagery will then be seen as something far more complex and self-reflective than the late adoption of a satirical form. Additionally, in parallel with Paolozzi, Guston importantly presents a non-hierarchical approach to mass culture in his lifelong appreciation of the early cartoons. In 1972, during a lecture to students at Yale Summer School, Guston spoke directly about his continued enjoyment of the comic strip:

> Remember, those of you who love the early cartoons, Mutt and Jeff? That's my greatest love, the early Bud Fisher, not the guys who imitated him. . . . Jeff is the tall guy. Mutt was the short bald-headed one. Well, I think they were both bald headed. But Mutt in consternation would grab his head. Two fingers always appeared beside his bald head. That's great, the early Bud Fisher is really great art.[19]

Guston's love and appreciation of Fisher's comic strip as "great art" underlines that his use of the cartoon was not a form of ironic statement, delivered from a detached standpoint. Indeed, Guston's work is too ridden with anxiety and self-criticism to allow meaning to appear in certain, declamatory tones. Far from detachment, Guston's re-connection to his childhood love of the comic strip will be seen to mark a renewed, intense re-engagement with the immediacy of the world. Guston's statement on *Mutt and Jeff* also brings attention to the artist's delight in the slapstick violence that concluded each comic strip. In the following chapters, I will examine how Guston drew on the cartoon's violence and buffoonery to explore perpetual cycles of human conflict and his own troubled, self-critical enjoyment of brutal imagery.

Notions of "the battle" also become a means to engage with Guston's repeatedly stated need for a "contest" within his creative process. "The contest," understood in terms of game playing, provides a way to regard destruction as a vital, generative part of the creative process. In inviting a tussle with material, the "mistake" will be seen to become absorbed and redefined within a process to allow for an engagement with the unforeseen. Additionally, through the push and pull of material and form, one can explore difference in the repeated presence of such objects as shoes and books that recur in Guston's imagery. Where Paolozzi had created a collection from the accumulation of found objects and found imagery, Guston generated the mass, the collection, from the drawn line. Where Paolozzi will be understood to have used mass production methods to distort and corrupt the language of reproduction itself, for Guston the response of the artist's hand to material, form and the present moment provided the means to depart from idealised form. While Guston and Paolozzi pursued different approaches, we will see how both artists employed variant repetition as a way to disrupt the pre-visualised outcome. Notions of slapstick will be used to examine a process in which the artist delights in an incongruity between originating concept and the resulting artwork. Guston's daughter also informs us that the artist's father worked as junkman. For Mayer, there is a connection that can be made between her father's late landscapes, filled with images of junk and debris, and her grandfather's job. She recalled a note found in the artist's studio after his death: "I really only love strangeness, but here is another pile of old shoes and rags, in a corner of a brick wall—in front, a sidewalk. I've been there, I've seen it before, but I forgot."[20] I will not use these connections to speculate on the potential biographical meanings of the forms; rather, I want to examine the artist's use of junk or aged, battered objects as the means to create forms that appear to have lived a life. In this sense, they become connected to the artist's repeated, stated desire to create "beings"[21] or "living things."[22]

While Guston's late, cartoon-like painting most obviously shares a connection to his childhood love of the comic strip, his abstract work produced between 1951 and 1967 also reveals material connections to the early cartoons. Guston's distinctive palette of cadmium red, pastel pinks, black and muddy white remains a constant in his work for thirty years, through his apparently dramatic break from abstraction to figuration (Figure 1.11). These were the dominant colours that featured in the comic

Figure 1.11 *Beggar's Joys*, 1954–5, Philip Guston, oil on canvas, 182.9 × 172.7 cm (72 × 68 inches).

strips of Guston's youth. Guston himself declared, "Of course I've loved that color—I used to dream of having my own strip one day."[23]

The persistent presence of the cartoon strip colours in Guston's paintings across a thirty-year period appears connected to what also remains remarkably consistent in the artist's work through his shift from abstraction to figuration, namely a concern with animation. In 1962—while Guston was still creating his apparently abstract work—H.H. Arnason defined Guston's painting as "experiments with living forms and their interactions."[24] In 1966, at a time of confusion, when Guston was wrestling with two seemingly contradictory ways of working—torn between creating his "pure" line drawing and the desire to create object-based imagery—the artist nevertheless stated that at the centre of his creative concerns was a process, rather than an image. This process was the animation of paint:

> I guess, I'm not interested . . . in making a picture. Then what the hell am I interested in? I must be interested in this process that I'm talking about. . . . I don't keep the studio very tidy. You have on the floor like cow dung in the field, this big glob of paint. . . . I look down at this stuff on the floor, and it's just a lot of inert *matter*. . . . I look back at the canvas, and it's not inert, it's active, moving, and living. And that seems like some peculiar miracle that I need to have, again and again.[25]

Moving away from abstract and figurative distinctions, in the following chapters I focus on exploring Guston's process in terms of animation. I will examine how Abstract Expressionism's emphasis on an unfolding process enabled Guston's painting to depart from his highly pre-planned paintings of the 1940s that depicted children at play. Crucially, through its emphasis on action, process and the unforeseen, Abstract Expressionism will be seen to have provided Guston's painting with the means to reconnect with key characteristics of a play process.

Towards Some Definitions

Before I delve deeper into an exploration of the creative processes employed by Guston and Paolozzi, I want to outline how I will approach the key terms "toy" and "play." Left unaddressed, their meanings might slide and a framework could become impossible, especially as these terms have such broad applications. I will therefore not attempt to create an all-encompassing definition of these terms, but rather focus on processes and material properties pertinent to the book's exploration of emergent image and object making.

Paediatrician and psychoanalyst D.W. Winnicott provides this book with a model in which there is a potential continuity between childhood play and adult creativity. Moreover, for Winnicott, object play is founded on the utilisation of an object that appears to have a "vitality or reality of its own." I will employ Winnicott's concept to explore a connection between the toy and Guston and Paolozzi's attempts to animate matter, articulated by Guston as "the plane . . . acquiring a life of its own . . . it feels like you've made a living thing."[26]

In *Playing and Reality* (1971), Winnicott outlined his belief that there was insufficient consideration of the place of "cultural experience."[27] Within psychoanalysis, attention had been focused on inner psychic reality and its relation to the external environment, but for Winnicott, this was inadequate. He argued that it was necessary to introduce a third or "intermediate area of experiencing, to which inner reality and external life both contribute."[28] Winnicott claimed that this intermediate area of existence has its origins in infancy and is formed with the use of what he termed "transitional objects." According to Winnicott, these objects could bridge physical and intangible experiences, providing a means of allaying anxiety, with the meeting of object and imagination creating, for the baby, the sense of a living, autonomous being. For Winnicott, the child's relationship to these initial "comfort blankets" later evolves into an engagement with toys and the development of imaginative play, resulting in the creation of an illusionary world, controlled and animated by the player. However, Gerald I. Fogel points out that Winnicott's use of the term "illusion" can be misleading.[29] He contends that by employing the term, Winnicott was merely offering a concession to science and notions of "objective reality"; the area of concern was, in fact, the *reality* of "mental experience" and referred to "real things" out in the world.[30] Fogel's important clarification allows this study both to address common misconceptions around the term "play" and to emphasise that the project does not seek to place Guston and Paolozzi's work within the realm of frivolity. In understanding Winnicott's concept of play as concerned with the meaningful in relation to "real things," one can emphasise that both artists created a landscape of forms that drew on their interaction with the immediacy of their surroundings and their engagement with the socio-political climate.

In defining the "transitional object," Winnicott provides us with a list of what he terms "special qualities in the relationship." Crucially, for Winnicott, the object "must seem to the infant to give warmth, or to move, or to have texture, or to do something that seems to show it has vitality or reality of its own."[31] So, for Winnicott, it is the object's responsiveness that provides the child with the sense that an object has a life of its own. For Winnicott, the "area" of belief, or illusion created during infancy, may potentially have direct consequences for creativity in adult life. The transitional objects may be left behind, may have lost their personal resonance, but, for Winnicott, this is because "the transitional phenomena have become diffused, have become spread out over the whole intermediate territory between inner psychic reality and the external world."[32] Winnicott's contention becomes a means of engaging with the continuing, *evolving* relevance of Guston and Paolozzi's childhood play materials and their importance to the adult present. The connection Winnicott forms between what he describes as the "actuality"[33] of the object—the way it behaves and responds—and its perceived vitality will provide this book with the means to investigate a connection between Guston and Paolozzi's desire to create "living things"[34] and "loose characters"[35] and their use of re-active, responsive processes within their work.

Winnicott's emphasis on the responsiveness of the toy is echoed by the philosopher Hans-Georg Gadamer. In *Truth and Method*, Gadamer states that while games can be solitary, they involve interaction with play material that responds to the actions of the player with a countermove. For Gadamer, this is most clearly epitomised by the ball game: "ball games will be with us forever because the ball is freely mobile in every direction, appearing to do surprising things of its own accord."[36] The movement of the ball game reveals to Gadamer what he sees as the central characteristic of all play, regardless of who plays: that is, a repetitive "to-and-fro" movement that is potentially endless.[37] In his essay "Toys and Play," cultural theorist Walter Benjamin regards repetition as "the soul of play."[38] Throughout the book, I will use Benjamin's important emphasis on repetition together with Gadamer's assertions to explore methods by which Paolozzi and Guston returned repeatedly to a collection of forms as means to counter the finality of their artworks.

In Johan Huizinga's 1938 publication, *Homo Ludens, A Study of the Play Element in Culture*, repetition is again positioned as "one of the most essential qualities of play."[39] But, additionally, Huizinga provides this book with the concept of the contest as central to game playing. One can think of Gadamer's "to-and-fro" movement reconsidered in terms of a tension-fuelled tussle with an opponent. I will use this notion to re-imagine the "creative battle" as something that is welcomed into the creative process by both Guston and Paolozzi as a means to achieve the unforeseen result. Within the context of "game playing," material resistance, mistakes and processes of destruction will become redefined as an engagement with contingency in a battle with the "life" of the work.

However, while Huizinga's seminal publication presents this study with two key concepts, I disagree with Huizinga's contention that "one of the most important characteristics of play [is] its spatial separation from ordinary life. A closed space is marked out for it, either materially or ideally, hedged off from the everyday surroundings."[40] In the following chapters, I will explore how Guston and Paolozzi's working processes present play as an intense, critical engagement with "ordinary life," rooted in the material substance of the everyday. This position is shared by scholars who criticise Huizinga for his idealisation of play. Robert Anchor draws on the work of Jacques Ehrmann and Eugen Fink to state that "play does not take place in isolation from or in opposition to the rest of reality."[41] For Ehrmann, Huizinga had failed to see "that the interior of play can only be defined by and with the exterior of the world. . . . Play cannot therefore be isolated as an activity without *consequences*."[42] The continuity Ehrmann emphasises between context and "interior" is met by Guston and Paolozzi's rejection of art as a form of escapism. Guston famously renounced abstract painting for what he saw as its insular vision:

> When the 1960s came along I was feeling split, schizophrenic. The war, what was happening in America, the brutality of the world. What kind of man am I . . . going into a frustrated fury about everything—and then going into my studio *to adjust a red to a blue*. . . . I wanted to be complete again, as I was when I was a kid. . . . I wanted to be whole between what I thought and what I felt.[43]

For Guston, then, the perspective of the child is one not of escape and fantasy but of *connectedness*. The desire stated is for a creative process that could engage with the fabric of the socio-political environment. Paolozzi shared with Guston an approach that participated in an art–life continuum, a position he formed as a member of the Independent Group. In the following statement, Paolozzi parallels Guston's desire to see art as something more than "adjust[ing] a red to a blue." In place of purely abstract aesthetic considerations, we have, in Ehrmann's terms, the "interior" of art "defined by and with the exterior of the world."

> There was a sort of idea . . . that there were other valid considerations about art besides the aesthetic ones: and that these were basically in kind sociological,

> almost anthropological. . . . It was like trying to discern the actual culture in terms of one's actual society, one's actual surroundings. . . . It was a way of treating art on a very serious level. Because, you simply can't spend the rest of your life moving shapes and colours around, really.[44]

In asserting that his engagement with contemporary culture was driven by a desire to approach art on a "serious level," Paolozzi points to what critics of Huizinga see as a key flaw in his characterisation of play. While Huizinga had asserted that many forms of play can be serious, in separating play from ordinary life, Huizinga nevertheless places play in a distinct category. In Ehrmann's terms, play then becomes positioned as "the Sunday of life . . . play 'adorns life.'"[45] By contrast, the philosopher Eugen Fink offers this study a theoretical framework in which play is embedded in the everyday. Fink powerfully asserts that "as long as we continue naively using the popular antithesis of 'work-play,' 'frivolity-seriousness' and the like, we will never grasp the ontological meaning of play."[46] For Fink, play is fundamentally a creative confrontation with the substance of being: "We play at being serious, we play truth, we play reality, we play work and struggle, we play love and death—and we even play play itself."[47] It is the dialectical nature of play that Fink so productively brings to the fore. I have found that in communicating the work of Guston and Paolozzi in terms of play, one can sound contradictory, and that the artwork itself may appear to disagree with play's associations with freedom through its historical links to romanticism. Fink's definitions make clear that to come to an understanding of play, dualities and contradictions need to be confronted and redefined, rather than resolved.

The difficulties in grasping the contradictory character of play sharpen over the concept of open-endedness. In his publication *Man, Play and Games*, Roger Caillois sets out helpful definitions of play in relation to the unknown. For Caillois, play is an

> uncertain activity. Doubt must remain until the end, and hinges on the denouement. . . . An outcome known in advance, with no possibility of error or surprise, clearly leading to an inescapable result, is incompatible with the nature of play.[48]

Throughout this book, we will see that Guston and Paolozzi repeatedly asserted a need for the unknown outcome. Both artists employed games strategies as a means to achieve the unforeseen result. However, what will become strikingly apparent through both artists' work is that the open-ended existed in dialogue with repetition and continuity. The play theorist Brian Sutton-Smith allows us to see how this paradoxical relationship reveals a key aspect of play. Sutton-Smith develops Caillois' definition to nuance a play activity's relationship with the unforeseen. In *The Ambiguity of Play*, Sutton-Smith writes that play "engenders variable contingencies (uncertainties, risks) for the purpose of exercising selective control over them."[49] Sutton-Smith complicates play's relationship to the unknown; through his elegant formulation, play does not simply abandon control or agency to the unforeseen; rather, a play process puts the two forces in dialogue. Play, then, is not simply an activity defined by freedom and the open-ended; instead, the "free" may operate in a dialectic with ritual and the need for mastery. It is with a focus on a tussle between opposing forces that I approach the play processes of Paolozzi and Guston.

Notes

1. Philip Guston, "Talk at Yale Summer School of Music and Art," in *Philip Guston, Collected Writings, Lectures, and Conversations*, ed. Clark Coolidge (London: University of California Press, 2011), 150.
2. "One of the exciting things about collage is how things float. Sometimes it's upsetting when I have to stick it down." Eduardo Paolozzi in "Paolozzi," directed by Louise Wardle, BBC (7/12/2000), accessed via www.bbc.co.uk/archive/sculptors/12818.shtml
3. Eduardo Paolozzi, "Waste, 1982," in *Eduardo Paolozzi: Writings and Interviews*, ed. Robin Spencer (Oxford and New York: Oxford University Press, 2001), 258.
4. In 1962, H.H. Arnason stated that Guston described his work in the following terms: "The sense of his forms as living presences, composed of paint which was a living essence, and existing within the canvas which was an actual place." H.H. Arnason, *Philip Guston* (exh. cat.) (New York: Solomon R. Guggenheim Foundation, 1962), 36–37.
5. Philip Guston, "The Image, 1969," in *Philip Guston, Collected Writings, Lectures, and Conversations*, ed. Clark Coolidge (London: University of California Press, 2011), 112.
6. Eduardo Paolozzi, "An Architecture from the Tools of a Child," *Writings and Interviews*, ed. Spencer, 95.
7. Eduardo Paolozzi, "Reminiscences of Childhood, 1982," in *Writings and Interviews*, ed. Spencer, 53.
8. Susan Stewart, *On Longing* (Durham and London: Duke University Press, 1993), 151.
9. Ibid., 145.
10. Eduardo Paolozzi, "Paradox, 1989," in *Writings and Interviews*, ed. Spencer, 266.
11. Paolozzi, "Reminiscences of Childhood, 1982," 53.
12. Eduardo Paolozzi, *National Life Stories, Artist's Lives, Sir Eduardo Paolozzi Interviewed by Frank Whitford*, accessed March 2012, http://sounds.bl.uk/Arts-literature-and-performance/Art-photography-and-architecture/021M-C0466X0017XX-1600V0
13. Eduardo Paolozzi, "Paolozzi," directed by Louise Wardle, BBC (7/12/2000), accessed via www.bbc.co.uk/archive/sculptors/12818.shtml
14. Eduardo Paolozzi as quoted in *National Life Stories, Artist's Lives*.
15. Guston wrote the following note to himself in the 1970s: "If I speak of having a subject to paint . . . I mean there is a forgotten place of beings and things, which I need to remember. I want to see this place. I paint what I want to see." Quoted in Musa Mayer, *Night Studio, a Memoir of Philip Guston* (New York: Da Capo Press, 1997), 180.
16. Philip Guston, "Conversation with Harold Rosenberg, 1974," in *Collected Writings, Lectures, and Conversations*, 276.
17. Mayer, *Night Studio*, 13.
18. Bill Berkson, "Pyramid and Shoe: Philip Guston and the Funnies," in *Philip Guston Retrospective* (exh.cat.), ed. Michael Auping (London: Thames & Hudson, 2003), 68.
19. Philip Guston, "Talk at Yale Summer School of Music and Art, 1972," in *Collected Writings, Lectures, and Conversations*, 159.
20. Philip Guston as quoted in Mayer, *Night Studio*, 11.
21. Guston, "The Image, 1969," 112.
22. Ibid.
23. Guston as quoted in Berkson, "Pyramid and Shoe: Philip Guston and the Funnies," 68.
24. Arnason, *Philip Guston*, 30.
25. Philip Guston, "A Conversation between Philip Guston and Joseph Ablow," in *Philip Guston 1975–1980: Private and Public Battles* (exh.cat.), ed. Kim Sichel and Mary Drach McInnes (Boston: Boston University Art Gallery, 1994), 32.
26. Ibid.
27. Winnicott's paper "Transitional Objects and Transitional Phenomena" was first published in the *International Journal of Psycho-Analysis* in 1953 and later formed the foundation of his seminal text *Playing and Reality*, first published in 1971.
28. D.W. Winnicott, *Playing and Reality* (Oxon: Routledge, 2005), 3.
29. Gerald I. Fogel, "Winnicott's Antitheory and Winnicott's Art, His Significance for Adult Analysis," *The Psychoanalytic Study of the Child*, Vol. 47, No. 1 (1992).
30. Ibid.

31. Winnicott, *Playing and Reality*, 7.
32. Ibid.
33. Ibid., 6.
34. Guston, "The Image, 1969," 112.
35. Eduardo Paolozzi, "Artificial Horizons and Eccentric Ladders," in *Eduardo Paolozzi: Artificial Horizons and Eccentric Ladders* (exh.cat.) (London: British Council, 1996), 11.
36. Hans-Georg Gadamer, *Truth and Method* (London and New York: Continuum, 2006), 105.
37. Ibid., 104.
38. Walter Benjamin, "Toys and Play: Marginal Notes on a Monumental Work," in *Walter Benjamin Selected Writings Volume 2*, ed. Michael W. Jennings, Howard Eiland and Gary Smith (Cambridge: The Belknap Press of Harvard University Press, 1990), 120.
39. Johan Huizinga, *Homo Ludens* (Boston: Beacon Press, 1955), 10.
40. Ibid., 19.
41. Robert Anchor, "History and Play: Johan Huizinga and His Critics," *History and Theory*, Vol. 17, No. 1 (February 1978): 89.
42. Jacques Ehrmann, "Homo Ludens Revisited," *Yale French Studies*, No. 41, Game, Play, Literature (1968): 42.
43. Philip Guston as quoted in Andrew Graham-Dixon, "A Maker of Worlds: The Later Paintings of Philip Guston," in *Philip Guston Retrospective* (exh.cat.), ed. Michael Auping (London: Thames & Hudson, 2003), 56.
44. Eduardo Paolozzi, "About the Prints: The Artist Talking at an Interview, 1973," in *Writings and Interviews*, ed. Spencer, 225.
45. Ehrmann, "Homo Ludens Revisited," 45.
46. Eugen Fink, "The Oasis of Happiness: Toward an Ontology of Play," *Yale French Studies*, No. 41, Game, Play, Literature (1968): 19.
47. Ibid., 22.
48. Roger Caillois, *Man, Play and Games* (Urbana and Chicago: University of Illinois Press, 2001), 7.
49. Brian Sutton-Smith, *The Ambiguity of Play* (Cambridge: Harvard University Press, 2001), 229. In *The Ambiguity of Play*, Brian Sutton-Smith examines the difficulties of negotiating through the diverse rhetorics surrounding cultural definitions of play as applied to both adults and children.

2 Kits and Building Blocks

In this chapter, I will explore how conflict between the static image and the imagined "life" of form led Eduardo Paolozzi and Philip Guston to create a very particular working method. I will use a notion of the "kit" as a means to interpret some specific studio strategies employed by both artists. This "kit of forms" will be seen to function as a collection of building blocks with which the artists could play repeatedly to produce "never ending possible combinations."[1] For both Walter Benjamin and Johan Huizinga, repetition was seen as a central characteristic of play. By employing Benjamin and Huizinga's analyses as a way of reading Paolozzi and Guston's approach to form, I will show how this allows us to view Guston and Paolozzi's forms as part of a continuum, recurring in various combinations across a number of works, rather than locked into one configuration.

In the following two sections, I will consider how Paolozzi's enduring obsession with toy kits informed a distinctive working approach to sculpture and collage. In the final sections, I examine specific recurring forms in Guston's painting to explore how variant repetition allowed Guston to re-engage with the object quality of the everyday.

"Meccano Work": Eduardo Paolozzi's Kits

In an interview with Eduardo Paolozzi in 1965, Richard Hamilton suggested that the logic of the toy kit might have made its way through to Paolozzi's construction methods:

RH: I mean in your most recent works you make separate elements and then assemble them—it's Meccano work, whether it's drawing or sticking bits of paper together or making bronzes . . .

EP: Yes, that's true. But the ship, the aeroplane . . . are made from . . . component parts. They have to be constructed and one uses this same means. But there is also the other idea in collage . . . it is a very direct way of working. . . . One is able to manipulate, to move and use certain laws that are blocked off if you do a pencil drawing.[2]

Hamilton and Paolozzi's exchange suggests how we might employ the idea of the "toy kit" as a way to revitalise and re-engage with Paolozzi's methods that, in the present literature, so often seem to stop short in their characterisation as collage.[3] The two terms—"collage" and "Meccano"—are already aligned in the Hamilton interview, and it is almost as if collage and "component parts" have become the grown-up equivalent of their parallels in the toy world. But in taking Hamilton's characterisation literally, one need not simply swap one term for another, or remain on the abstract level of concept. A direct look at the toy kit provides a way to engage with a substantial quantity of Paolozzi's collected material, now housed in the Krazy Kat Arkive, together with the means to explore how these objects, through their accumulation in Paolozzi's studio environment, followed through into his working methods. Indeed, the Krazy Kat Arkive—Paolozzi's personal collection of popular culture housed in the Victoria and Albert Museum—points to an "obsession"[4] with the toy kit through a vast range of examples that seem to offer a world in kit form, from Japanese robots to *The Sense of Taste* (Figure 2.1).

The art historian, curator and critic Wieland Schmied highlights that

> toys play an important role in Eduardo Paolozzi's studios. They are virtually everywhere. Each and every assemblage seems to be streaked with them. They are the dominating finds. They change all other things and give them back elements of toys.[5]

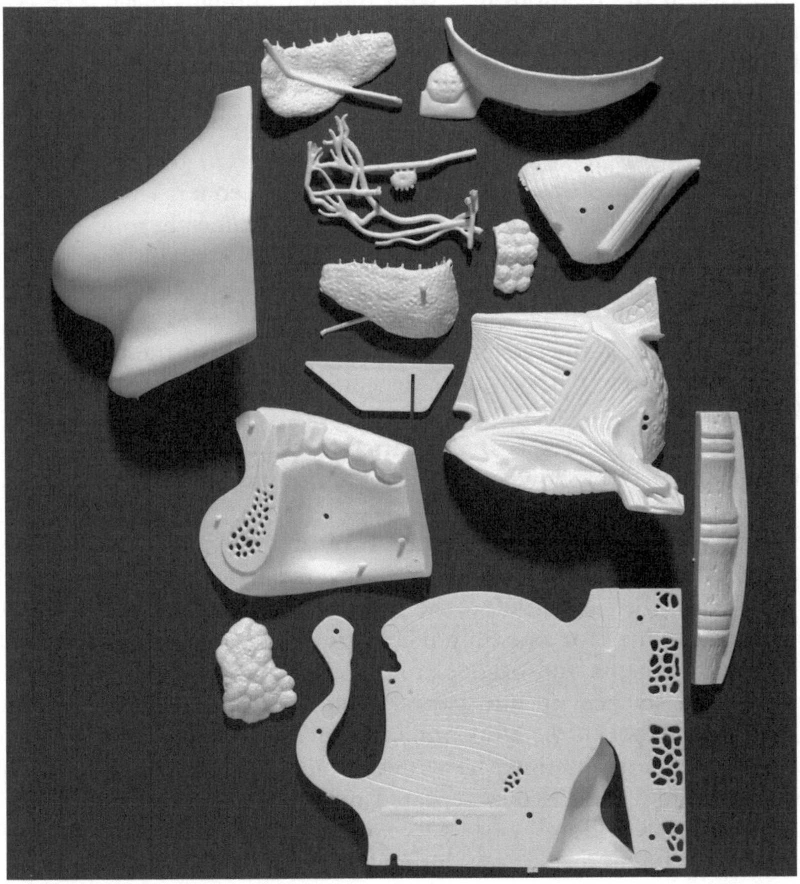

Figure 2.1 *The Sense of Taste*, 1973. Dimensions of the box: 20.5 cm × 18.6 cm × 5.8 cm, Lindberg Line—Natural Science Series, Krazy Kat Arkive, Victoria and Albert Museum, London.

Image credit: © Victoria and Albert Museum, London.

In light of Schmied's comments and Hamilton's characterisation, this chapter will begin by considering how Paolozzi's enduring love of toys—particularly the toy kit—informed a distinctive working approach to mass culture and the "as found."

D.W. Winnicott provides a way of thinking about the paradox of the toy. According to Winnicott, transitional objects[6] present the necessity to accept a paradox in that "the baby creates the object, but the object was there waiting to be created."[7] Or perhaps one could say, in the context of the work of Paolozzi, waiting to be found. The "as found" is a term that has been attributed to architects Alison and Peter Smithson and has come to stand for a particular approach to contemporary culture, exemplified by the work of Paolozzi, Nigel Henderson and their fellow members of the Independent Group. In their publication *As Found, The Discovery of the Ordinary*, Claude Lichtenstein and Thomas Schregenberger describe the "as found" as "a matter of process, and it cannot be achieved with a formal reductionism as a goal."[8] For Lichtenstein and Schregenberger, the "as found" is "the technique of reaction."[9] Significantly, it is possible to draw parallels with Schregenberger and Lichtenstein's characterisation of the "as found" as a "process" of "reaction" and Winnicott's description of the "special qualities in the relationship" with the transitional object. The connection Winnicott draws between perceived vitality and the responsiveness[10] of the object appears to resonate with what Schregenberger and Lichtenstein identify as the question posed by the "as found":

> The approach leads from the static object of the *Bild* to the dynamic process of imagining. When do images come alive for someone? This is the process of imagining, which refers to a conscious process and goes beyond simply looking at something. For the exponents of the As Found movement (to call it that for a moment), the reality of images was a central prerequisite for their work.[11]

Winnicott's description of the seemingly "vital" properties of the transitional object, together with the apparent parallels in Schregenberger and Lichtenstein's characterisation of the "as found" approach as a "dynamic process," offers a means to explore Paolozzi's use of found objects as an animating force whereby material becomes toy. In return, the conjunction allows us to reflect on the toy kit as a found object that activates the "process of imagining."

To return to Hamilton's interview with Paolozzi, the recent work that Hamilton characterised as "Meccano work" had emerged from the sculptural technique Paolozzi adopted in the early 1960s. The process began with the creation of a store of metallic units designed for assembly. These "building blocks" combined both pre-existing machine elements and original forms designed by the artist (Figure 2.2).[12] The elements were stacked up into various combinations to create works such as *Konsul*, *The Twin Tower of the Sfinx-State II* and *Town Tower*.[13] In Paolozzi's notes and artist statements of this time, he writes about creating "An Architecture from the Tools of a Child"[14] and makes repeated mention of "Building Blocks,"[15] "Toy Plummage," a "Toy Kingdom" and "Meccano."[16] These references start to appear in Paolozzi's painted sculptures made during the 1960s, which share clear similarities with the toys that would have been available to him as a child (Figure 2.3). Meccano is a toy we know Paolozzi played with during childhood, and it seems to re-emerge in the form and colours of the sculptures *The City of the Circle and the Square* (1963/6) (Figure 2.4) and *Four Towers* (1962).[17] "Toy Plummage" also appears to adorn *The*

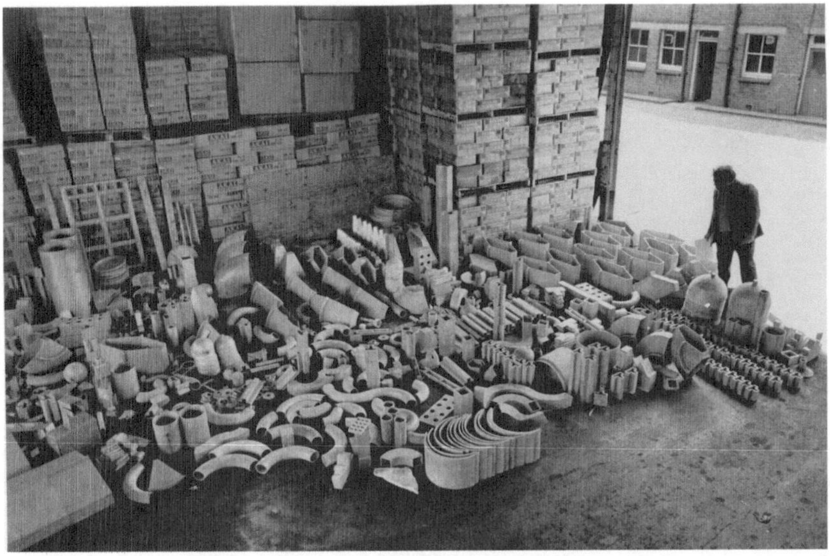

Figure 2.2 Eduardo Paolozzi at Juby's engineering works, c. 1973–4.

Photographer: N.J. Cotterell.

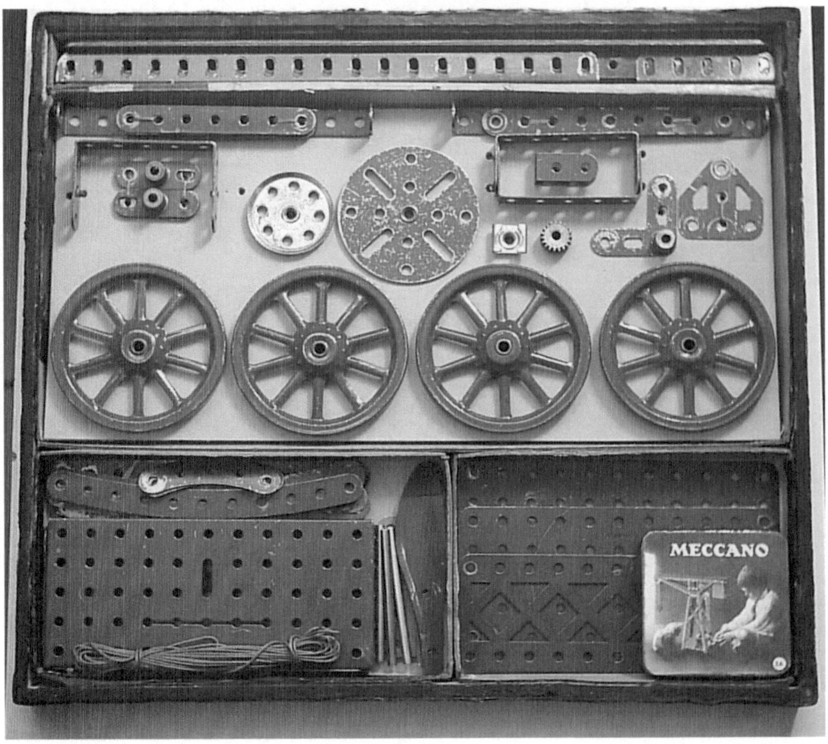

Figure 2.3 Meccano set, c. 1920.

Image courtesy of Peter Sullivan.

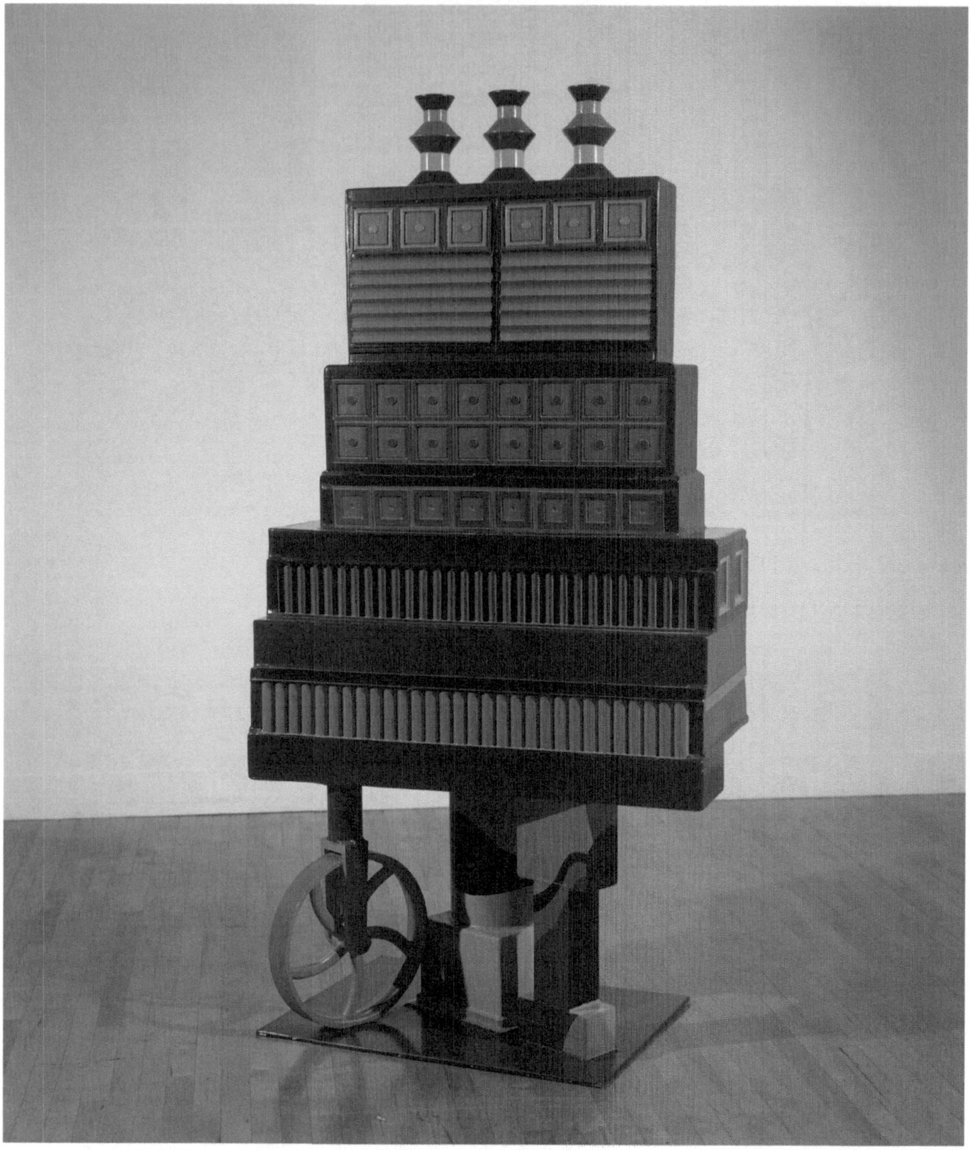

Figure 2.4 *The City of the Circle and the Square*, 1963/6, Eduardo Paolozzi, painted aluminium, 210.8 × 102.2 × 66.7 cm, Tate Gallery, London.

Last of the Idols (1963) (Figure 4.6), a sculpture that wears the colour combinations found in tin toys from the 1930s. However, Winnicott provides a means of looking at the relevance of an artist's biography in a way that moves beyond the anecdotal. For Winnicott, object play during infancy may evolve to inform creativity and cultural experience during adult life. We can, therefore, examine childhood play and adult creativity within a continuum and connect the material qualities of an object with the process it affords. This allows us to reach through and beyond aesthetic comparisons to engage with method. Specifically, the toy kit possesses properties additional to the capacity to stimulate "reaction," already proposed through Lichtenstein and Schregenberger's definition of the "as found" and its links to the transitional object. The defining elements of the play process presented by the toy kit are repetition and reconfiguration, with toys such as building blocks or Meccano providing a means for individual elements to exist in any number of combinations. Paolozzi's use of metallic units parallels this method. By combining mass-produced items with multiple casts of original elements designed by the artist, Paolozzi could create a kit of forms and play with these to create numerous configurations.

Daniel Herrmann points out that "re-combination is at the heart of Paolozzi's work."[18] In discussing Paolozzi's aluminium sculpture *Towards a New Laocoon* (1963), Herrmann asserts that Paolozzi's

> fascination with the 'Laocoon' lay not in its mythological narrative, but in the group's visual legacy. With its history of various reconstructions and respectively varying reproductions in print, cast and copy, the group served as a catalyst for Paolozzi's interest in the variation and re-combination of images and forms.[19]

Among the aluminium units that are welded together to form *Towards a New Laocoon* (Figure 2.5) one finds many elements that recur across numerous Paolozzi sculptures of the period, resurfacing in pieces such as *The City of the Circle and the Square* (1963/6), *Mechanik's Bench* (1963) (Figure 2.6) and *Four Towers* (1962). Although each sculpture exists as a complete work, by bringing them into relation, a sense of uncertainty and impermanence is introduced, as if each element had only temporarily found a resting place. The solidity of the welded metal appears at counterpoint with a configuration that, in the scheme of things, may appear to be provisional.

Here, then, is one of the key propositions in this chapter: through the addition of the term "kit" to the existing characterisation of "collage" as a description of Paolozzi's methods, a vital distinction is revealed. Collage describes the found recombined, while the Meccano kit invokes a collection of objects that are played with *repeatedly* in varying combinations. Writing in 1928, in *Toys and Play: Marginal Notes on a Monumental Work*, Walter Benjamin described repetition as

> the great law that presides over the rules and rhythms of the entire world of play. . . . We know that for a child repetition is the soul of play, that nothing gives him greater pleasure than to "Do it again!"[20]

By focusing on Paolozzi's repeated use of a kit of forms, we are able to consider the "rules and rhythms" of play and in so doing move beyond the finality of a sculpture to engage with the continuity of a process. By adopting this view, we detect how the units that comprise a work have the potential to be released from a "static object" to be animated within a flow of change.

Paolozzi's first works made with the multiple metal components were highly symmetrical and predetermined due in large part to practical restrictions—Paolozzi was living in Germany and sending sketches and plans to an engineering works in England, where technicians would assemble the sculptures. However, by 1963 Paolozzi

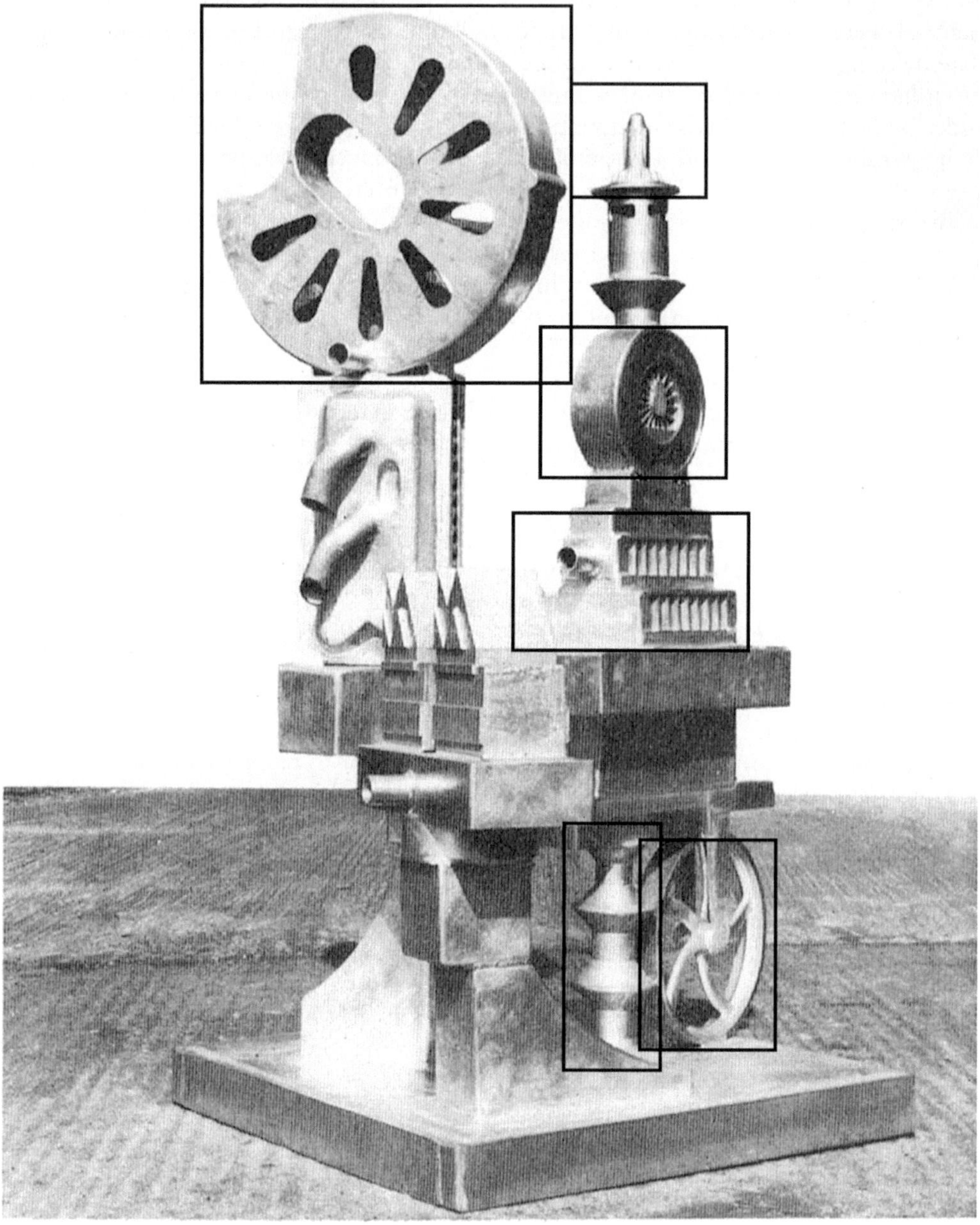

Figure 2.5 Towards a New Laocoon, 1963, Eduardo Paolozzi, aluminium, 243.8 × 127 × 91.4 cm.

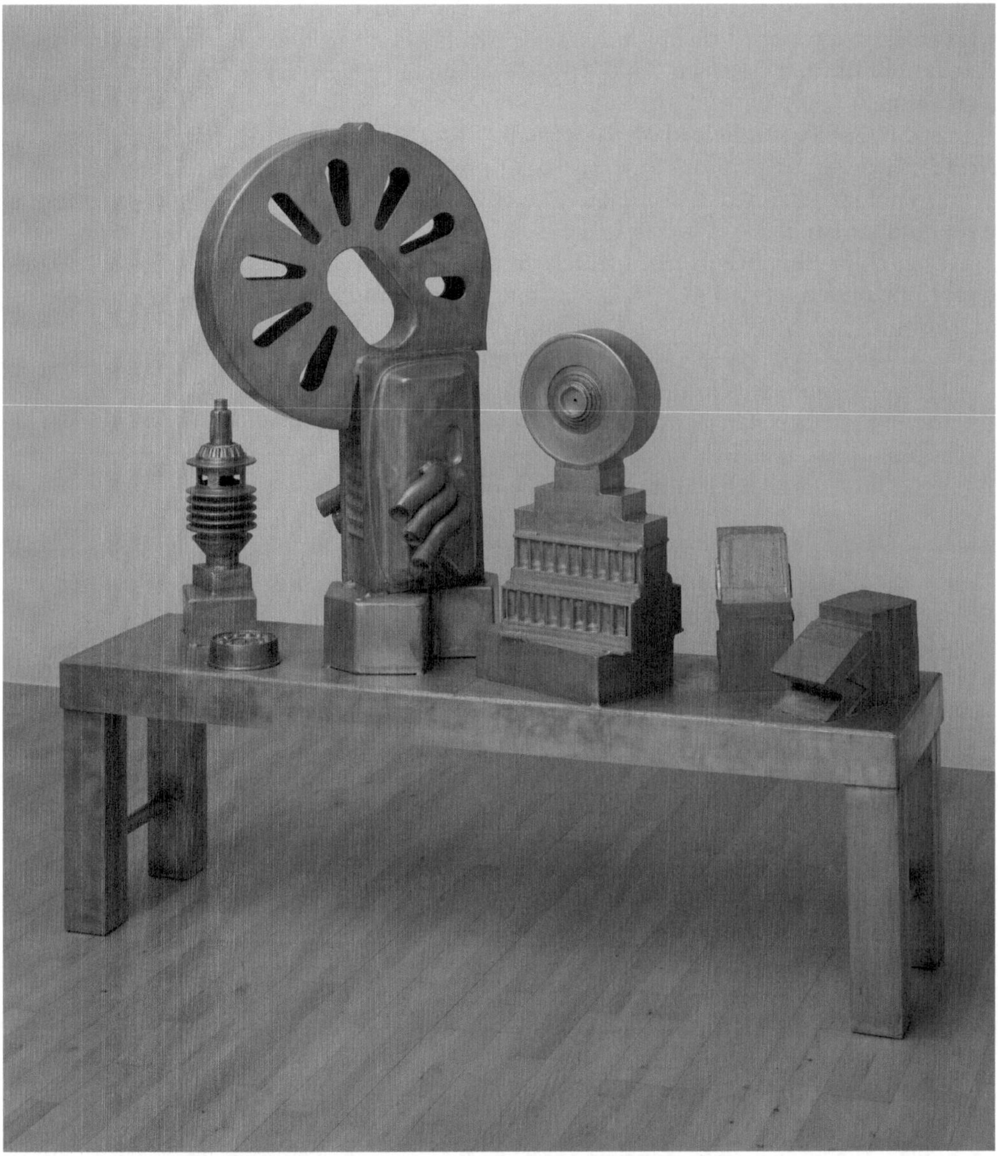

Figure 2.6 *Mechanik's Bench*, 1963, Eduardo Paolozzi, aluminium, 176.5 × 183.8 × 48.3 cm, Tate Gallery London.

had returned to England and was able to work with the technicians during the process; this allowed for the development of a more spontaneous working method. The possibilities for directness and fluidity, which Paolozzi described to Hamilton as being the appeal of a collage technique, now became realisable. The process became one that made room for a "technique of reaction."[21] This increasingly allowed Paolozzi's repeated use of the units to bring less predictability to a structure. Diane Kirkpatrick has explained that during this period Paolozzi collaborated with technicians who were able to work from imprecise drawings. For Kirkpatrick, this also led to "a new compositional freedom" and "the development of a freer approach to the final assembling."[22]

In 1980, Paolozzi reflected on the assembly process by asserting that "prefabricated elements are welded without any specific or preconceived idea about the end result."[23] While Paolozzi claimed a complete openness for the method, Kirkpatrick offers a more nuanced analysis. Writing in 1970, Kirkpatrick allows us to consider Paolozzi's drawings as starting points from which the sculptures could diverge. Paolozzi's assembly of the units operated in relation to contingency, and the artist even welcomed the unforeseen.

> He thinks out ideas in the form of free drawings and prepares "final" preliminary ideas. . . . Then he works with professionals to create the work of art. Always he is open to suggestions about new ideas. . . . Always the process must retain the precious element of spontaneity in the assembly of the works.[24]

On a page from a notebook dated 1964, Paolozzi provides a contemporaneous "analysis of *Lotus*." Here Paolozzi asserts a willingness to work with the aluminium elements using a method that departs from the limits of a plan. For Paolozzi, "proportions become a matter of necessity rather than a predetermined course."[25]

This engagement with a more responsive, collaborative process soon became apparent in the work itself. Gone was the cohesive totality of the earlier aluminium sculpture. The rigid, unitary, impervious towers that Paolozzi described as "multi-useful fort like presences" were replaced by the dynamic complexity of pieces such as *Karakas* (1964), *Crash* (1964) (Figure 2.7) and *Hamlet in a Japanese Manner* (1966).[26] Elements from *Towards a New Laocoon* recur once again. However, here the parts are not reduced to a stable, unified oneness; instead, they begin to exist as individual elements operating and interacting as part of a crowd. We see a fascination with the explosive and the unresolved. The parts connect and interrelate in such a way that they are not subsumed within the totality. The result, in a piece such as *Crash* (Figure 2.7), is that although the elements are welded together, the sculpture seems caught in a continuing, unfolding process. In a later piece titled *Domino* (1967–8) (Figure 4.2), the engagement with the unresolved becomes literalised as each element of the work remains as a separate, moveable unit, the relation of the elements now open to an endless reshuffling by the viewer. *Mechanik's Bench* (1963) prefigured the later works' concern with the unresolved. The piece features a collection of machine parts seemingly in the early stages of assembly. The elements appear to stand caught in a state of expectation. Paolozzi, in literally elevating the units on a metal table, points the way forward by establishing the importance of the parts as distinct entities.

In an interview in 1995, Paolozzi (then 71) discussed his continued interest in toys and the toy kit. The artist questioned what he saw as a false dichotomy between the "child" and the "grown-up"; in place of this distinction, Paolozzi allows us to position subjectivity and the artist's recurrent concerns within a continuum. Significantly, the interview also provides an insight on Paolozzi's thinking on the tension between the made and the unmade, the part and the whole.

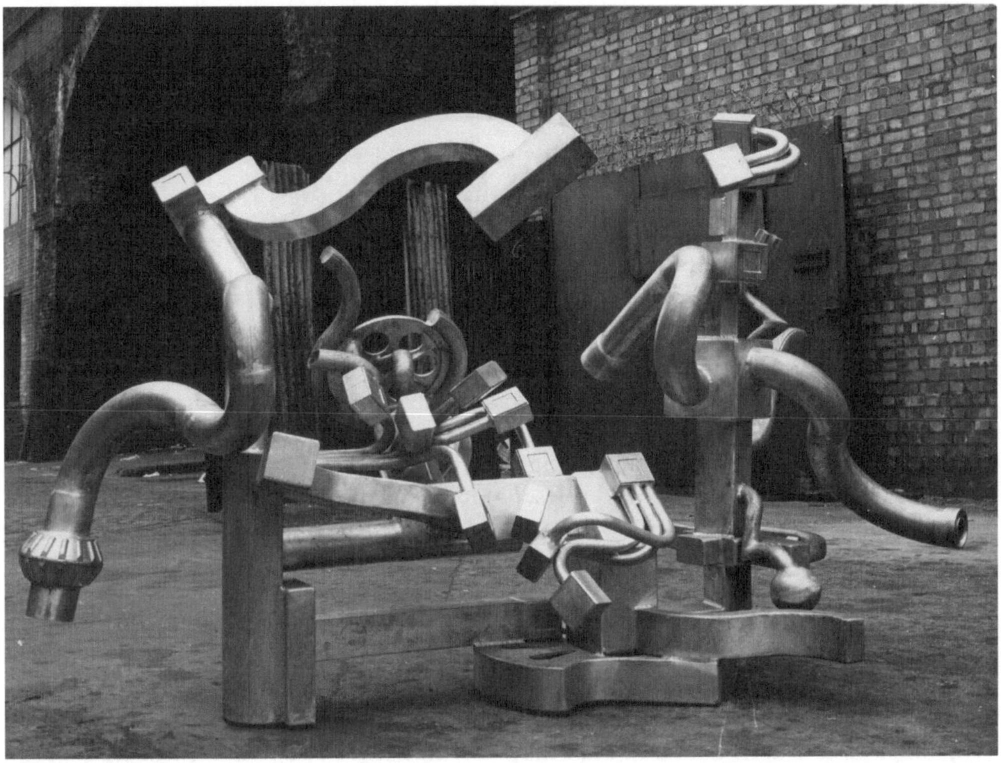

Figure 2.7 *Crash*, 1964, Eduardo Paolozzi, aluminium, 243.8 × 149.9 × 91 cm, Ulster Museum, Belfast.

> What I don't understand is when people decide that they're no longer a child and they've become a grown-up . . . why you can't still make simple toys. . . . When I used to buy aeroplane kits I'd find it difficult to make them up sometimes because I just loved looking at the details. They always seemed to lose a certain kind of potency when it was all put together. I still like making model aeroplanes.[27]

As the Krazy Kat Arkive reveals, it seems that Paolozzi's enjoyment of the unmade model kit more often than not won out over the pleasure of putting them together. In the vast collection, the proportion of unmade models considerably outnumbers the assembled. The plastic model kit differs distinctly from Meccano. While metal Meccano pieces can be screwed together and then disassembled to begin the process again, plastic model pieces, when glued together, become finalised in one configuration. In a sense, the unmade model kit continues the logic of Meccano or building blocks by stalling finalisation in favour of the multitude of possibilities presented by a collection of units. Paolozzi's love of detail and his regret at the loss of "potency" when the aeroplane parts were connected seems, then, to reveal something beyond the toy kits themselves. Paolozzi's recurrent interest in the unmade toy kit becomes a means of framing wider creative concerns.

The ready potential present in a collection of individual units, together with a pregnant sense of the unresolved, points to a key creative strategy for Paolozzi. While the aluminium sculptures of the mid-1960s appear to overtly state a concern with the incomplete, Paolozzi's vast, multi-media output offers an array of methods by which the use of the part as a distinct element develops the logic of the kit in pieces.

Repetition and Distortion: Corrupting the Mass-Produced

In Paolozzi's interview with Hamilton, Paolozzi's methods, whether in sculpture or on paper, are all characterised as "Meccano work." Hamilton points out that for Paolozzi everything begins with "separate elements" that are assembled, regardless of medium. Hamilton's description vividly lends physicality to all of Paolozzi's processes. Picture elements are something tangible that can be manipulated and toyed with. But the fact that Paolozzi's image work was constructed from separate elements also brought with it another important factor. Paolozzi's use of reproduction techniques, such as photocopying and screenprinting, parallels his use of the mass-produced in his aluminium sculptures and allowed the separate elements in his print work to exist in multiple configurations.

While discussing the assembly of the elements that made up his screenprints in a documentary in 2000, Paolozzi reflected on the enjoyment of the fluidity of the process: "One of the exciting things about collage is how things float. Sometimes it's upsetting when I have to stick it down."[28] Paolozzi's use of repetition and reproduction techniques in his print work allowed the artist to, in a sense, remove the glue, un-stick the pieces and once again allow the elements to "float." One is reminded of Benjamin's assertion in *Toys and Play* that "nothing gives . . . greater pleasure than to 'Do it again!'"[29] Johan Huizinga later echoed Benjamin's emphasis on the centrality of repetition to an understanding of play. In *Homo Ludens* (1938), Huizinga asserts that

> in this faculty of repetition lies one of the most essential qualities of play. . . . In nearly all the higher forms of play the elements of repetition and alternation (as in the *refrain*), are like the warp and woof of a fabric.[30]

By way of exploration, if one were to focus on just one detail from Paolozzi's print work, a revealing example would be the reproduction of a periodic table from a children's textbook. This oval-shaped diagram appears in Paolozzi's screenprints on at least three occasions. It appears in *B.A.S.H.* in 1971 (Figure 2.8) followed by *The Children's Hour* from 1974 to 1976 (Figure 2.9), and lastly *Turing 7*, created some twenty-six years later in 2000 (Figure 2.10). When one compares the three prints, it is clear that each time the diagram crops up it appears changed. The colours differ and its position within the composition shifts. There is a restlessness in the way the diagram returns, as if the artist is reluctant to let it settle. Each time the diagram surfaces, it seems to have drifted further from its original source. When the diagram first appears in the screenprint *B.A.S.H.*, it is clearly recognisable as a periodic table. But by the time it resurfaces in *The Children's Hour*, the distinctive letters and numbers have been removed. It becomes familiar, but hard to place. Importantly, with this loss of context and recognisable identity, something else appears to happen. The diagram ceases to function as a representational tool and starts to exist more forcefully as form. While the concepts the original diagram illustrated have been lost, the diagram

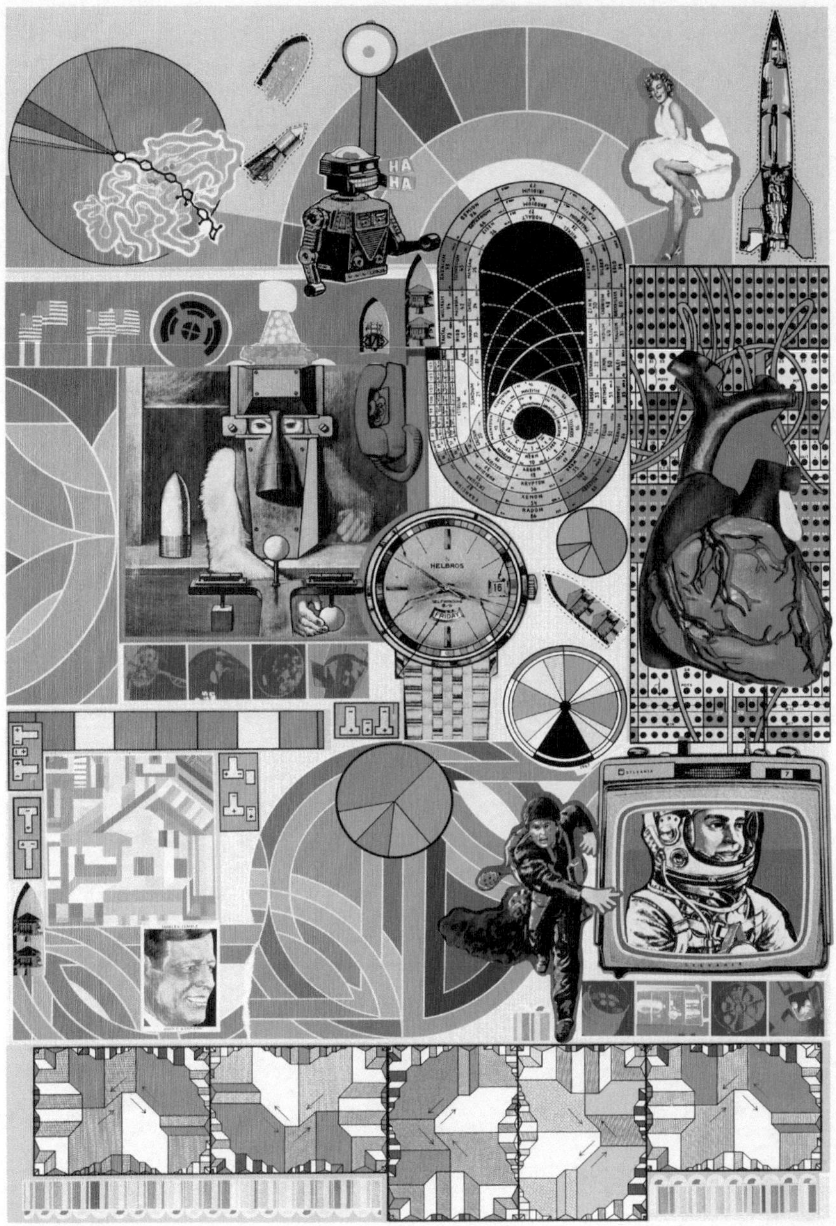

Figure 2.8 B.A.S.H., 1971, Eduardo Paolozzi, screenprint, 85 × 70 cm.

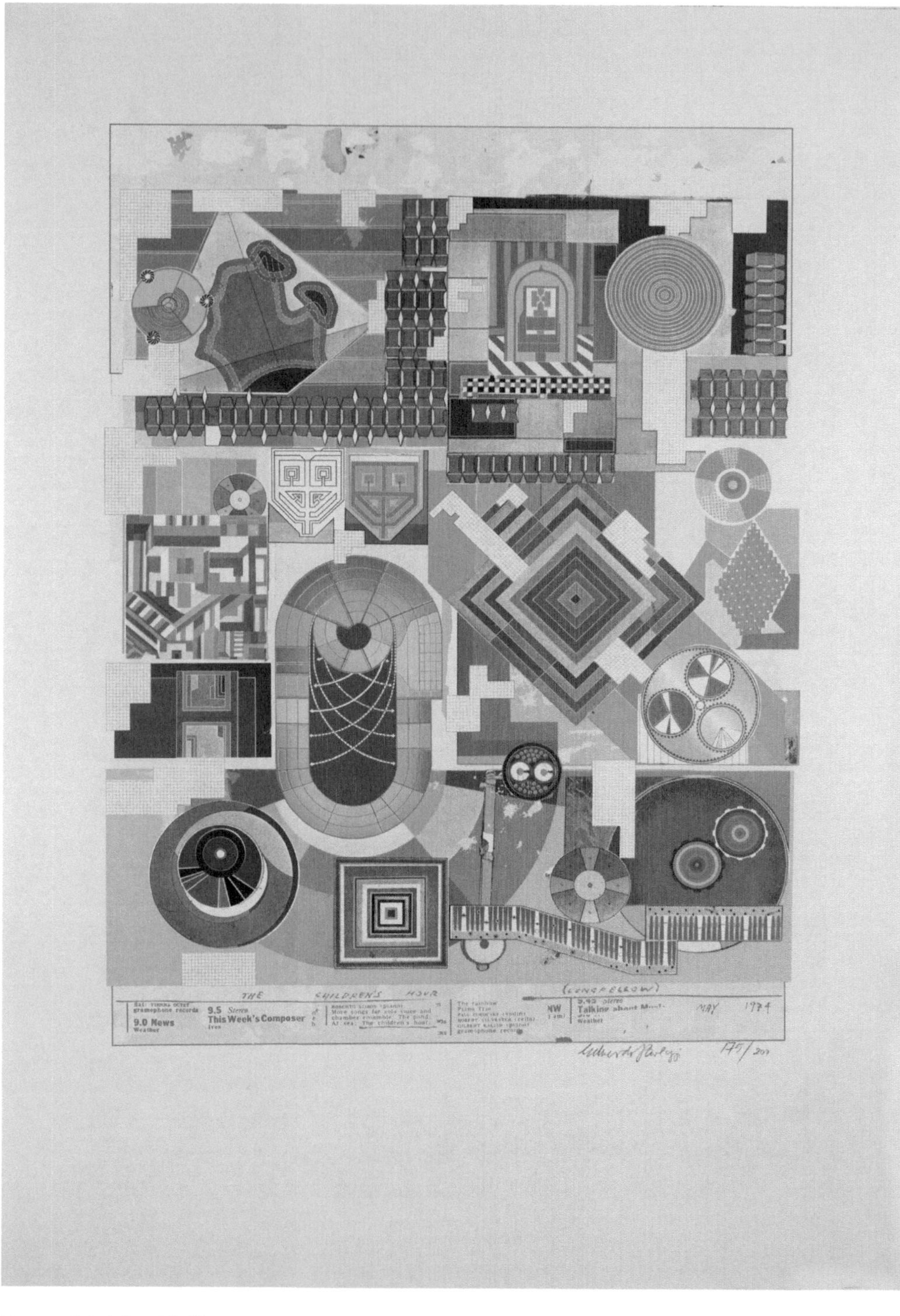

Figure 2.9 The Children's Hour, 1974–6, Eduardo Paolozzi, screenprint, 99 × 69 cm.

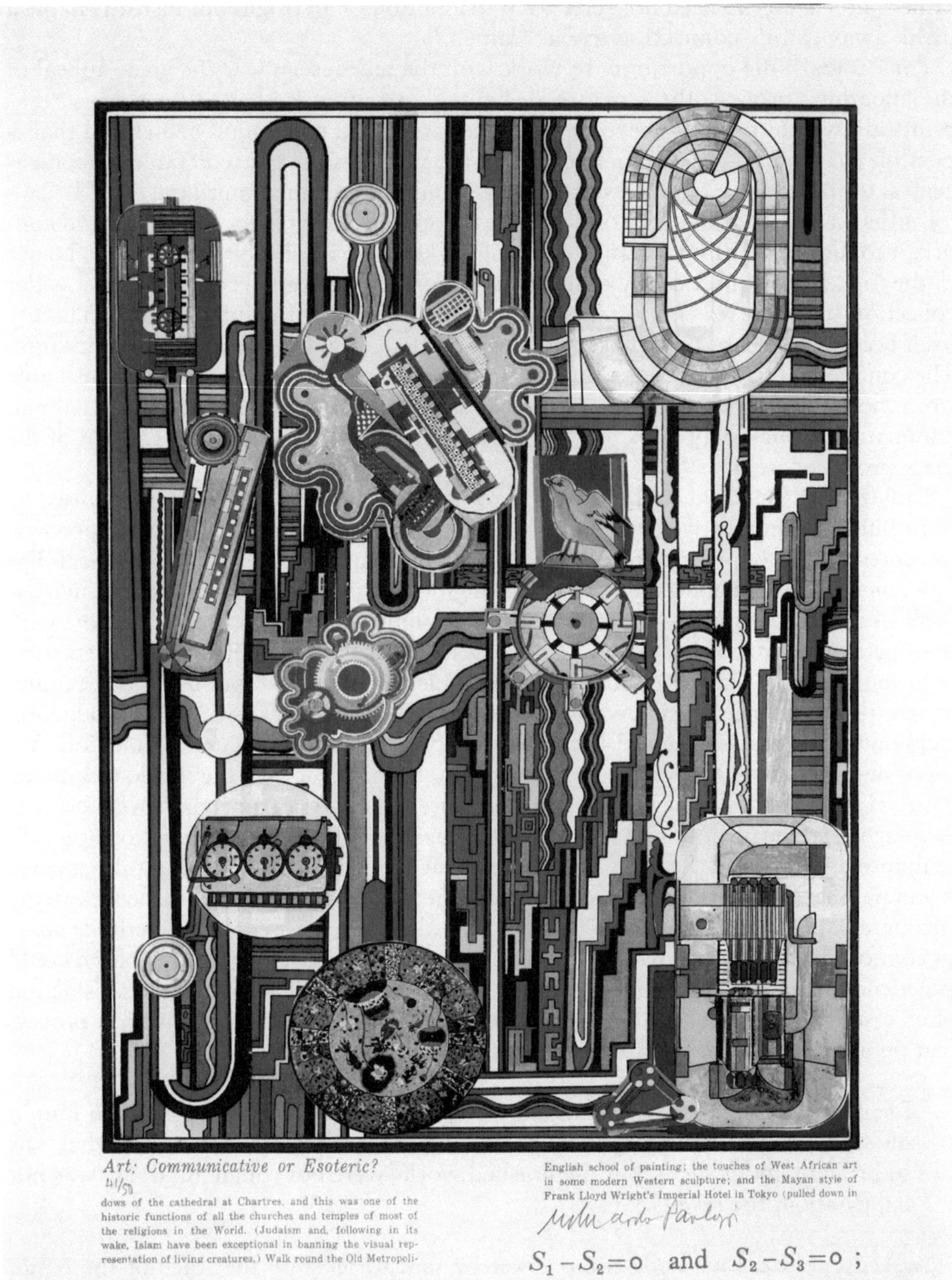

Figure 2.10 *Turing* 7, 2000, Eduardo Paolozzi, screenprint, 76 × 56 cm.

itself has begun to gain an independent life. In this sense, Paolozzi's repeated use of the same source material need not refer back to a notion of an origin but instead enable a break away from a connection to the "same."[31]

For Paolozzi, the opportunity to work with the unforeseen was the great appeal of the "floating" process; the separate elements that came together to form his screen-prints allowed him to "go beyond preconceptions, you go beyond something that is possible to imagine."[32] Here, one recalls that for Caillois the unpredictable outcome is central to the notion of play, asserting that "doubt must remain until the end."[33] Caillois offers a way to frame Paolozzi's desire to "go beyond preconceptions"[34] and connect it to the artist's return to an ever-changing kit of forms. In this sense, the influence of the toy kit is not necessarily reducible to an object, but can become part of a wider collection of processes connected to the lasting presence of childhood play. The toy itself becomes a means to explore Paolozzi's particular relationship with mass culture. The commercial toy, an object that begins as a mass-produced item, indistinguishable from thousands of others created from the same mould, becomes individualised and "animate" through play. This process finds its parallel in Paolozzi's corruption of the mass-produced item.

Paolozzi's engagement with the world of mass culture has long been recognised as one of his most innovative contributions, evident in the artist's all-embracing approach to contemporary popular culture, the everyday, the expendable and the ephemeral. For Lawrence Alloway, Paolozzi conveyed through his "mixed style" "the urban environment of shared communications, of mass entertainments which possess a rapport with both personal and group fantasy."[35] However, as we have seen, Paolozzi's interaction with the world of mass production can be understood to go beyond the objects and images that the artist considered worthy of scrutiny. Through the use of reproduction techniques, the mass-produced becomes incorporated and integrated as method. Yet this is never as straightforward as it sounds. For although Paolozzi borrowed technique, material and form from the world of mass culture, his work corrupts or "toys" with the language of sterile repetition. As Alex Kitnick has suggested, with reference to Paolozzi's sculpture of the 1950s, "using mass culture as his ground, he attempted to push against it and pull back the surfaces in order to show the impulses behind it."[36] One repeatedly encounters this "push" "and pull" that Kitnick identifies; with Paolozzi, methods never sit comfortably together. Edward Allington has spoken of the frustration Paolozzi could experience when working with fabricators. According to Allington, this dissatisfaction often resulted from the "cleaning up" that occurred through the reproduction process that on occasion altered Paolozzi's original working models:

> I had seen quite a few of Eduardo's collages and maquettes when I visited him in his studio in 1976 and they were quite rough and to my mind that was what was so brilliant about them. But the finished works were not rough at all. He was not happy about the results.[37]

However, Paolozzi's methods could never be said to fetishise the trace of the hand. Rather, it is as if for Paolozzi the work lay in slipping and sliding between techniques, corrupting the borderlines and setting one process off against another in a productive friction. In 1954, when Paolozzi and Nigel Henderson set up their own commercial printing company, Hammer Prints (to create designs for ceramics, textiles and wall-papers), it was with the intention "that an attack be made on the craft field using the silk-screen as the media to be exploited."[38] And yet this "attack" might equally have been described as an extension or expansion of craft. "Attack" offers a sense of youthful radicalism both artists would have been keen to evoke, but belies the respect that Henderson and Paolozzi had for both the applied arts and skilled craftsman. As Robin Spencer has pointed out, what was under attack was the "arty" or "crafty"[39]—a certain blinkered, backward looking romanticism of the English Arts and Crafts movement of the 1950s. Paolozzi and Henderson had wanted to expand their vocabulary to embrace what might be described as the language of the street through the use of chance, found imagery and photography. Henderson and Paolozzi screenprinted the designs themselves in what Lesley Jackson has described as a "provocative and assertively hands-on approach."[40] And yet, once again, this radical aspect comes from within a tradition—the tradition of cottage industry (quite literally in this case; Hammer Prints was based in a collection of cottages in Thorpe-le-Soken). The hand-made again becomes a means for Paolozzi to play with the forms and conventions of mass production. Paolozzi's collage *Insect Wings* (1951) (Figure 2.11) presents one of the clearest examples of this play with reproduction and distortion, his experimentation with this design pre-dating Hammer Prints. In the collage, a collection of screenprinted elements are laid out in a formation that evokes a Meccano kit stored ready for use in its box. Many of these elements later reappear repeated and overprinted in *Collage Mural for Drew and Fry* (1952), together with screenprinted designs that feature in Paolozzi's pattern book c. 1952, only to re-emerge again that year in screenprinted ceiling paper for the offices of the engineering design company Ove Arup (Figure 2.12). Here, as with the aluminium

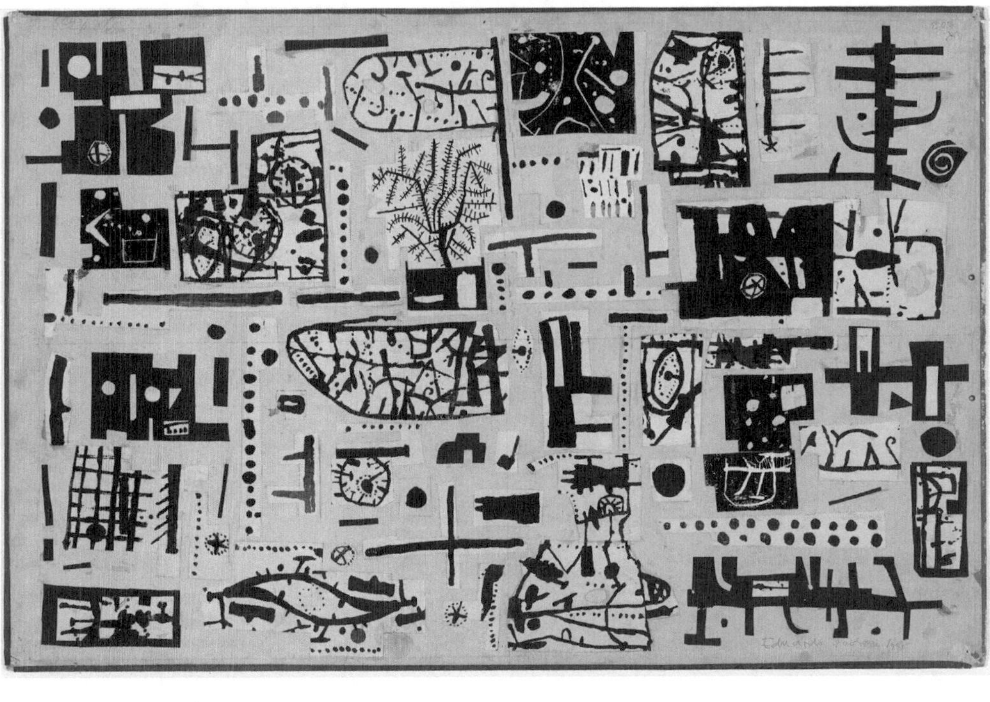

Figure 2.11 *Insect Wings*, 1951, Eduardo Paolozzi, collage, 66 × 96 cm, Arts Council Collection, Southbank Centre, London.

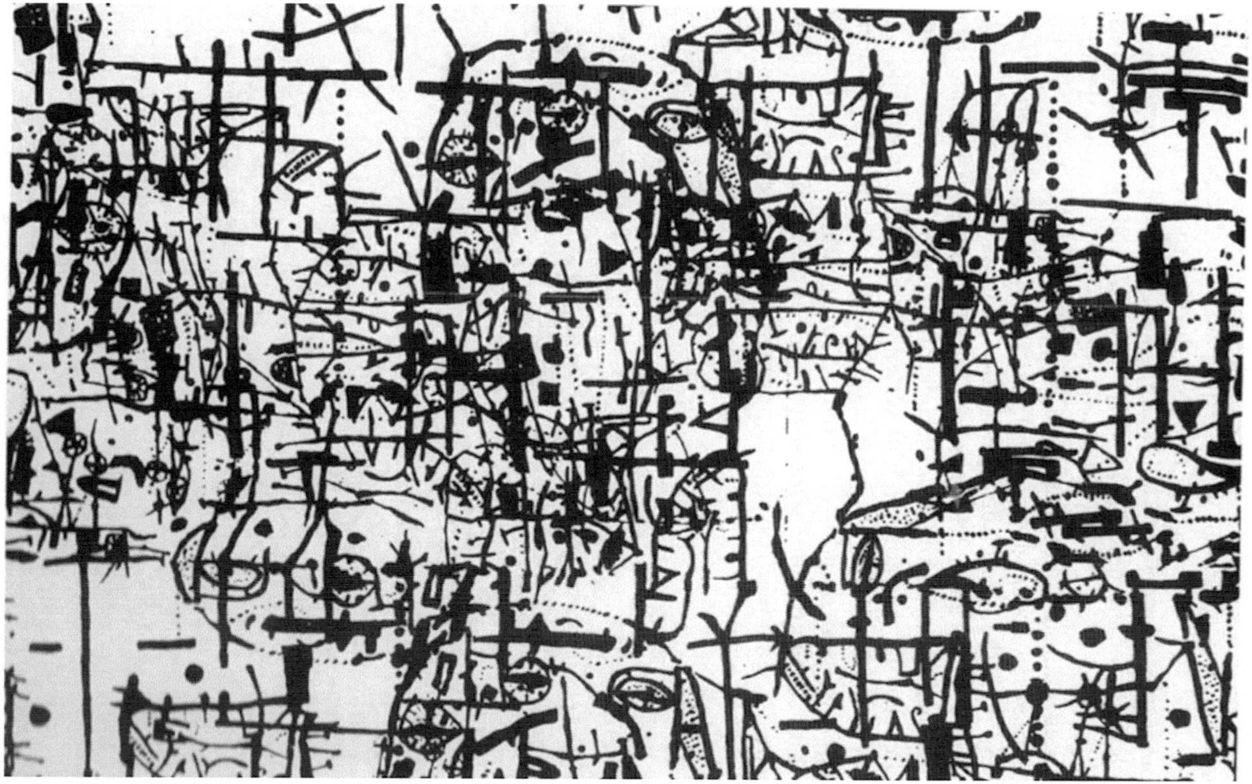

Figure 2.12 Ceiling paper design commissioned by R.S. Jenkins for the offices of Ove Arup & Partners, 1952, Eduardo Paolozzi, reproduced in Anton Ehrenzweig's book *The Hidden Order of Art*. Permission granted by The Orion Publishing Group, London.

sculptures, Paolozzi's desire for the unpredictable outcome is achieved through a game of collaboration. If, for Caillois, any play activity demands that "doubt must remain until the end," Paolozzi was able to place the screenprinted wallpaper within a play process by leaving the final configuration to workmen, asking them to paste "the rolls of ceiling paper at random so that accidental joints were produced."[41] While the 1951 collage pronounced the totality as a collection of individual elements with the "potency" of potential, the later ceiling paper allowed the kit of design elements to crowd together in a manner that appears to resist the resolution of a unified oneness.

The ceiling paper features in Anton Ehrenzweig's publication *The Hidden Order of Art* together with two of Paolozzi's aluminium sculptures: *Towards a New Laocoon* and *Medea* (1964). Ehrenzweig taught Paolozzi the techniques of silkscreen printing when they worked together in the Textile Department at the Central School of Arts and Crafts. Beth Williamson has written extensively on the collaborative nature of Ehrenzweig and Paolozzi's working relationship and their shared common ground. In examining Ehrenzweig's theory of art, which was founded on British Objects Relations theory, Williamson emphasises that in "his thinking and writing Ehrenzweig presented ideas of risk, accident, chaos and disintegration. His collaborative working with Paolozzi might be taken as paradigmatic of the way in which he theorizes the creative act as a whole."[42] Significantly, in addition to emphasising the unexpected outcome, Williamson's analysis highlights the importance of destruction as a creative force for both Paolozzi and Ehrenzweig. Williamson points to an untitled collage (1951) found in Ehrenzweig's collection and asserts that "in this instance sheets of paper have been deliberately printed with a variety of . . . patterns then cut up, only to be reassembled in a different order."[43] With the introduction of "destructive" processes, the singular becomes multiplied. Separate elements are, in a sense, set free from the pattern. Here destruction becomes as much a part of the continuity of a play process as assembly, with structures assembled only to then be broken apart into separate elements, stored ready for future use so that the process can begin again. In Paolozzi's play with pattern and mass production through a design such as *Insect Wings*, we see the reproduced break away from the identical copy; instead, multiple variations and combinations emerge through a repetitive, looped process of printing, cutting and assembly.

Ehrenzweig's *The Hidden Order of Art* was informed by the work of D.W. Winnicott. Williamson makes clear that "Ehrenzweig's central thesis in this book is that: 'any work of art functions like another person, having independent life of its own.'"[44] With this, one returns to the argument that began this chapter. In Ehrenzweig's thesis, one hears echoes of Winnicott's description of the transitional object that must seem to show it has "vitality . . . of its own," together with the question Schregenberger and Lichtenstein suggest lies at the centre of the As Found movement: "When do images come alive for someone?" In these terms, one can interpret Paolozzi's processes as creating a multifarious "life" for a kit of picture or sculpture elements through processes of collaboration, recombination, repetition and corruption. As a viewer, the notion of the kit allows us to exchange the finality of a sculpture or print-work for the continuity of a play process. In a sense, we can remove the glue from collage to engage with Paolozzi's experimentations with (in his own words)

> a portfolio of loose characters [that] contains an exhilarating brew of never ending possible combinations. . . . To finally harness this set of free spirits is like an act of betrayal, imprisoning these individuals, condemning them to a life of frozen violence.[45]

"I Got Stuck on Shoes": Philip Guston's Forms

In 1966, Philip Guston began creating hundreds of images of mundane tangible objects: shoes, books, hands, paint cans, cigarette butts. . . . This repeated engagement with a small collection of objects, most of which could be found in his immediate environment, continued well beyond 1969, the point at which they finally succeeded in bursting through into his painting with such dramatic effect. Shoes became a particular obsession: "I got stuck on shoes," Guston recalls.[46] "My shoes. You know, the shoes you wear in the country. It felt good to do that" (Figure 2.13).[47] It was not enough to simply record an object; the pleasure lay in revisiting the object time after time. But the obsessive repetition was not without function. Guston discovered that repeated scrutiny did not serve to familiarise but rather produced the opposite effect; the mundane was rendered strange. In a lecture to students in 1978, he explained, "the more I did the more mysterious these objects became."[48]

After repressing his need for images of the tangible for nearly a decade, under the appearance of what he was to describe bitterly as the "mask" of "American Abstract Art,"[49] Guston had wanted to return to "paint things as if one had never seen them before, as if one had come from another planet."[50] The painter repeatedly stated a desire to begin again, to strip things back and paint as if he were seeing things for the first time as a child or "the poet in Eden."[51] Repetition can be seen to have played a central role in a process to re-build an engagement with the everyday. Here, Guston allows us to expand how one might understand the "pleasure" of repetition described

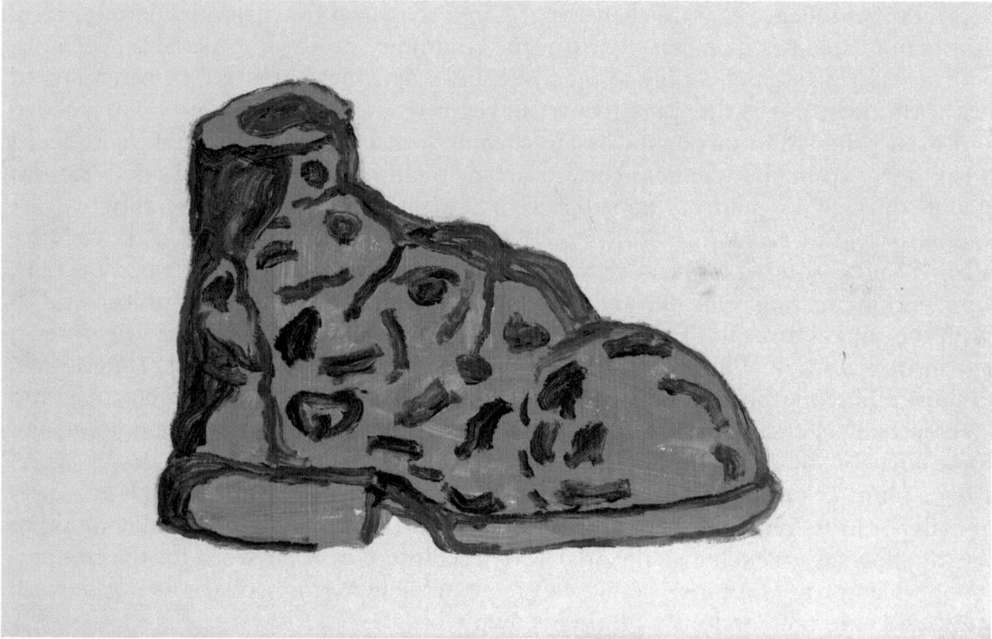

Figure 2.13 *Untitled (Orange Shoe)*, 1971, Philip Guston, oil on paper, 49.5 × 70.4 cm (19 ½ × 27 ¾ inches).

by Benjamin and extend how one can engage with its "rules and rhythms" as play. Where Paolozzi's use of repetition can be seen to lie primarily in recombination, Guston's tight focus on single objects allows us to examine repetition as a game of difference and distortion in a process to re-imagine the mundane. This is a method already suggested by the example of Paolozzi's return to a diagram of an atomic table, but with Guston this process is placed centre stage. If one looks at one of Guston's shoe paintings from 1971, it appears almost as if the object identity has been stretched from shoe to figure. The shoe is not a fragment, then, but a body. Through the vitality of the brushwork, one can almost sense Guston's relish in transforming a shoe into yet another poignant, dopey character, seemingly burdened with the weight of a life. Talking to students at Yale Summer School of Music and Art in 1973 Guston allowed the audience into this process, explaining that

> it seemed to me that just by restricting myself to a single object, a great deal opened up. . . . You know, when you really close in on a form, it seems to change, it seems to metamorphose. I mean, a book can become a tablet can become a hunk of stone.[52]

For Guston, shoes would continue to become the most enigmatic of his objects: "it changes. I don't know what the hell it looks like. It doesn't look like a shoe, but I don't know what."[53] Guston's delight in the creation of confused object identity points to a key underlying principle of play as defined by the philosopher Eugen Fink. For Fink, play produces a crucial point of emphasis, one that favours process and variation over imitation or predetermined content:

> What ought to be asked in the first place is not what is varied and portrayed, but rather what variation, what playful portrayal as such is. For if we only keep in view what the original model for the playful imitation is, then we can indeed characterize play according to its intended content, but we move thereby in a vague and incautious pre-understanding of playing in general, and then we precisely do not experience play as what is genuinely questionworthy.[54]

Fink's analysis of playful portrayal would demand a reading of Guston's shoes that follows the painter's confusion through the painting process in a drift away from their nameable identity as "shoe." As the artist and critic Robert Storr suggests, "unlike Magritte or Johns, whose elegant linguistic puzzles confound the distinction between verbal and pictorial naming, Guston was not toying with codes of representation. On the contrary, he painted as if speaking directly in the language of "things."[55] Effectively, with Guston the representative concept seems in the process of being left behind, jettisoned in favour of an engagement with variation and animation. But Fink's emphasis on an engagement with the forms of playful variation (rather than a focus on the original model) as a means to understanding where a play process resides allows us to further explore the possibilities opened up by processes of variant repetition. Fink asserts that it is through variation that play opens onto another creative sphere, one that moves beyond imitation and reproduction to create a play reality:

> The image, although it is still a reproduction, already provides a "variation" on actuality; it does not mirror, it interprets. And finally, an image can also free itself

> entirely from every reproductive function, can present a combination of colors and figures without an objective sense. . . . Does not play itself here enter into the image-character of the image.[56]

In stressing the importance of processes of variation as a means of understanding play, Fink provides a way of focusing on Guston's painting processes that allows us to consider the "how" over the "what" of Guston's shoes. Here one can start to explore how, in choosing to focus on humdrum objects, or even just the most immediate studio debris such as canvas stretchers and cigarette butts, Guston was, paradoxically, displaying an extraordinary act of bravado. The painter effectively casts himself in the role of magician or alchemist, challenging his methods and processes to conjure art out of the banal. The repetitive return to central motifs, such as shoes and books (Figures 2.14 and 2.15), augments the challenge in declaring that the artist's sorcery

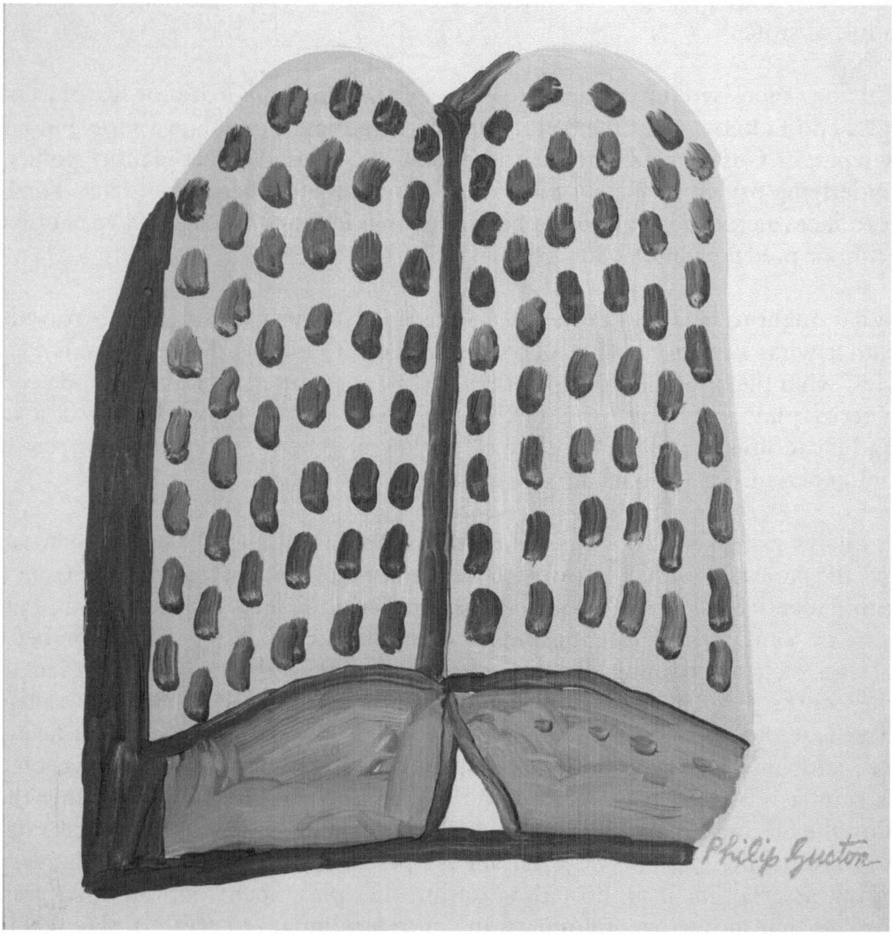

Figure 2.14 Tall Book, 1968, Philip Guston, acrylic on panel, 50.8 × 45 cm (20 × 17 ¾ inches).

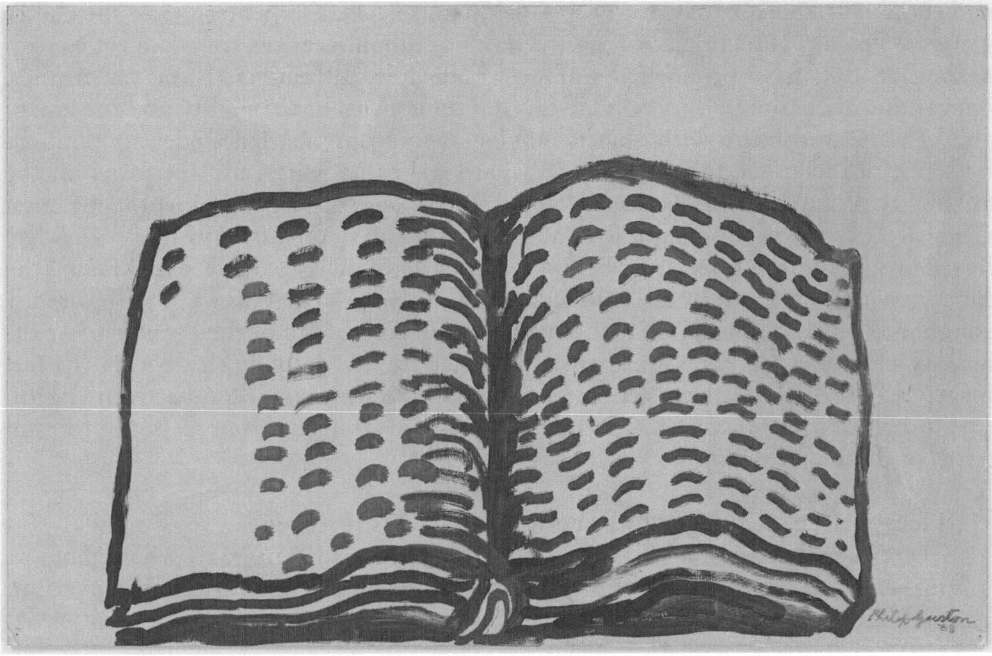

Figure 2.15 *Untitled (Book)*, 1968, Philip Guston, gouache on illustration board, 50.8 × 76.2 cm (20 × 30 inches).

enables him to return tirelessly to an object and continue to find something new, something strange.

In conversation with Guston in 1972, the writer Clark Coolidge discusses magical thinking at work in Guston's painting, to the artist's delight, contrasting it with the separation or arbitrary connection between signifiers and the signified. Turning to a "book picture," Coolidge says to Guston, "there's a kind of graspability factor that should be brought up, too, which isn't just a matter of identification."[57] Coolidge goes on to compare Guston's approach to objects to that of Samuel Beckett: "It's boooooook. Like in Beckett's *Krapp's Last Tape*, he takes the spool of tape and he says, 'spooooooool,' and he says it over and over again, so it's like an incantation."[58]

Word repetition, or echolalia, is described by Jean Piaget in his publication *Language and Thought of The Child* as a phenomenon that occurs during early infancy. Piaget observes how "in the first years of his life, a child loves to repeat the words he hears, to imitate syllables and sounds, even those of which he hardly understands the meaning."[59] For Piaget, this form of imitation operates when there is no clearly delineated concept of self, and as a consequence repetition becomes a game in which the word begins to be seen as a product of the child's own creation. Just as Krapp appears as a lone figure in Beckett's play, addressing his words to no one, Piaget observes that "echolalia is simply . . . a game; the child enjoys repeating the words for their own sake, for the pleasure they give him, without any external adaptation and without an audience."[60] It appears that, for both Guston and Beckett, repetition (like the child's game of echolalia) functions to sever the flow of communication, to reconnect us with perception at its most primordial and most bodily. For although Guston was creating images, his discussion with Coolidge centred on notions of tangibility and the graspable. There is a concern with objects moving away from a flattened identity imposed by semantics in order to gain a fleshy, material reality. But Guston's focus on the tangibility of humble objects was also an implicit, fervent revolt against the art critic Clement Greenberg's dogmatic formalism. In Guston's conversation with Coolidge, this is brought to the fore, described in terms of a creatively starved man craving the food provided by the material and substance of things. For Guston, "the everyday common objects . . . [were] almost counter to the whole idea of the flatness of painting, which I detested. Because there's a hunger for touchability. It's touch. To feel form."[61] The comments have echoes of an earlier discussion in 1966 between Guston and Joseph Ablow, in which Guston describes his relationship to process and form in terms of those of a sculptor.

> I feel as if I'm shaping something with my hands. I feel as if I've wanted always to get to that state. If a blind man in a dark room had some clay, what would he make? . . . I always thought I was a very spiritual man, not interested in paint, and now I discover myself to be very physical, and very involved with matter.[62]

In Guston's late paintings, the physicality of the paint and the limited amount of illusionary technique readily lend themselves to a sculptural reading. Although there are clearly multiple reasons for this emphasis on the haptic, one suggestion by Robert Storr was that it allowed him to work "at a pace commensurate with the rush of images through his mind."[63] Time and speed are possibly central factors. Not only was the technique economic, allowing Guston's productivity to keep up with a flood of ideas, but, I would suggest, it also allowed every line to become an articulation or physical manifestation of a thought in the present moment. Speed, then, may have operated in two directions simultaneously by increasing productivity while helping to prevent thought from operating ahead of action. Indeed, in the conversation with Coolidge, Guston describes this need for a coming together of thought, action and image, to the point that if denied the painting process becomes unsatisfactory: "if the image locks itself in there too quickly, or if I'm aware of it too much before I do it, then it's boring and I wipe it out."[64] And it is here, in this emphasis on *action* operating in the present tense to produce images that change and unfold on the canvas, that one discovers a marked connection with Guston's work of the previous decade. If Guston's emphatic return to the tangibility of things appeared as a repudiation of Greenbergian formalism and a dramatic rupture with his abstract work of the 1950s to mid-1960s, there was nevertheless a significant continuity in Guston's desire for a process that allowed for urgency, change and the unforeseen. Guston's desire for a process that allowed images to unfold through the act of painting remained closely connected to the art critic Harold Rosenberg's definition of Action Painting. A rival of Greenberg, Rosenberg continued to be a supporter of Guston even after his break back into figuration. Indeed, amid the largely damning response to Guston's first exhibition of late figurative work at the Marlborough Gallery in 1970, Rosenberg was one of the few to write a favourable review. In 1952, in his essay "The American Action Painters," Rosenberg had declared that the canvas had become an

> arena in which to act—rather than . . . a space in which to reproduce, re-design, analyse or 'express' an object, actual or imagined. What was going to go on the canvas was not a picture but an event.[65]

Despite the fact that Guston's paintings were by the late 1960s comprised of objects "actual or imagined," the continued urgency of the "act" of painting, so clearly apparent in the pronounced brushwork, emphasised the process as central to the formulation of the image. This was the act of painting re-imagined. The changing, unfolding process was now not read "purely" as artist's gesture but as here giving life to form and character as Guston sought painting methods that allowed images "to metamorphose," finding "a book can become a tablet can become a hunk of stone."

Rosenberg's declaration that the canvas for the Action Painter was not a site to "reproduce" but a site to "act" provides a significant parallel with Fink's description of play as freeing an image from its "reproductive function." Additionally, according to Rosenberg, for the Action Painters "there is no point to an act if you already know what it contains."[66] This statement clearly provides a continuity with Guston's comments to Coolidge about the need for a unity of thought, action and image. Of course, one can question whether this process was occurring in the manner presented by Guston, or if the statement was more a manifestation of the still lingering vestiges of what Guston believed qualified oneself as a modern painter. However, in their emphasis on change and the unforeseen, Guston and Rosenberg outline a process that is not only connected to Fink's notion of play as a departure from reproduction but also significantly allows us to explore the emphasis on the act of painting as contiguous with Caillois' definitions of play as predicated on the unpredictable outcome.

However, how might one understand the importance Guston places on change and the unforeseen in conjunction with processes of repetition? Surely there is a contradiction between the desire for the unpredictable and a repeated return to forms such as shoes and books? The contemporary play theorist Brian Sutton-Smith advocates that "an understanding of play must be rooted in ritual as much as it is in innovation."[67] We could understand this tension, then, between repetition and the unknown, as a part of the pull within the dialectical character of play. But, crucially, we can also see innovation as built on ritual. In this sense, we can understand Guston's repeated return to central motifs such as books and shoes as comparable to the process by which a musician gains an ability to improvise by spending countless hours practicing chord progressions, or the way in which a sportsman prepares for the unknown quality of the game by practicing an action until it almost becomes a reflex. Guston stated to students on a number of occasions that his greatest ideal was Chinese painting from the Sung period. Significantly, it was the painting method that fascinated Guston more than the paintings themselves. This is a method that is built on repetition, allowing the painter to combine a state of knowing and not knowing, as Guston outlined:

> Sung period training involves doing something thousands and thousands of times . . . until someone else does it, not you, and the rhythm moves through you. . . . I have had it happen to me. It is a double activity, when you know and don't know.[68]

Almost echoing Fink, Guston also describes how repetition allows for a break away from "mirroring"[69]; attention is not split between the sheet of paper and the object one wishes to depict. Instead, for Guston, there is "just you, the subject, the ink, the paper, it, the object. No separation."[70] With all attention given to the image unfolding in the present, a sheet of paper can be treated as a play reality where every element can build through a responsive process. In the next chapter, I will look at the structures that emerged through the improvisatory. Here, my focus is on the means by which repetition and variation generated a responsive process that made way for improvisation.

The ability to engage with the improvisatory in order to allow action and image to unfold in the present tense returns us to Storr's comments on the "pace" of Guston's image making. Guston's rapid brush marks, which form his books and shoes, do not describe action; they embody action. The physicality of the paint and the actions of the painter are laid bare within the images that at times only just hold together as recognisable forms. Guston told Coolidge that the process of applying paint was "quick. It's very quick."[71] And that "images always come, very rapidly."[72] The speed with which Guston could apply paint and render images allowed for a responsive, improvisatory process and revealed another significant definition of play, in this instance as outlined by Huizinga. In exploring the semantic roots of play-words, Huizinga discovered that in numerous languages the origins of the term lie in concepts of "rapid movement," such as leaping, dancing and even the movement of waves.[73] Prior to Guston's abstract work of the 1950s, the painter could spend up to a year on a painting. Paradoxically, the subject matter of these carefully planned and constructed works was primarily children's play, as in the case of *If This Be Not I* (1945), the most ambitious work of the series. While in the late 1960s a book or shoe had become a site of action and movement through the vibrancy of the brushwork, Guston's past engagement with play as subject (rather than process) in *If This Be Not I* presented children caught suspended in stillness in their games of masquerade.

With Guston's return to figuration, he brought a process that did not depict play, but that rather through its emphasis on the improvisatory seems to embody its key characteristics. The draftsmanship itself owes a great deal to Guston's childhood love of the comic strip and his long-standing admiration for its masters, such as George Herriman (Figure 2.16) and Bud Fisher. Guston had continued to enjoy creating cartoons throughout adult life, even during the mid-1950s; at the height of his most

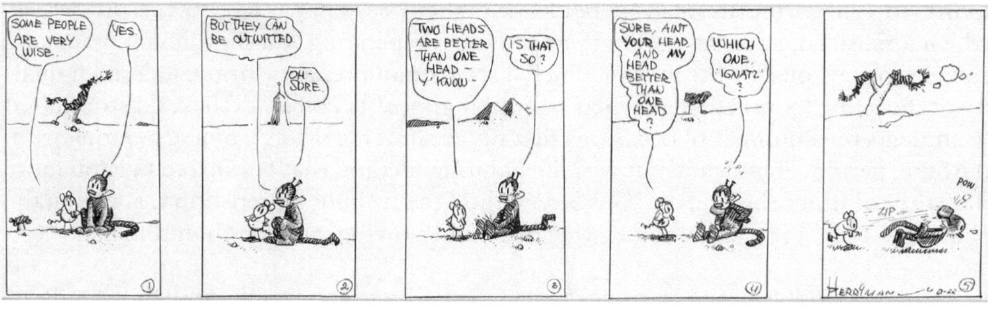

Figure 2.16 Krazy Kat, 1920s (undated), George Herriman (King Features Syndicate).

Image courtesy of Heritage Auctions, HA.com.

celebrated abstract painting, Guston was creating caricatures of his friends, such as Harold Rosenberg, Franz Kline and Willem de Kooning. It was almost as if, just as Paolozzi's continued love of childhood play material had been given validation as art through his meeting with Giacometti, Guston found in the late 1960s a climate that allowed him to re-engage with a love of cartooning that up to that point had been left at the margins. While Guston's return to figuration may have shocked and appalled many of the high priests of abstraction, Pop Art provided a landscape where the cartoon was no stranger to the canvas. And in Guston's celebration of the quotidian, he found considerable affinity with the work of Claes Oldenberg, even rather humorously telling students at a lecture in 1969 "I like Oldenburg. . . . Show me a person who doesn't like a twenty-foot ice cream cone made of plastic, I don't want to know that person. . . . He's a kind of poet too."[74]

But even before the creation of Guston's overtly cartoon-infused painting, the impact of a childhood love of Herriman's imagery could be felt. Guston's distinctive heavy black line could, through the simplest means, convey a poignancy that weights the forms within the world of experience rather than abstraction. It is here, beneath the imagery, at the level of the line, that one finds the most profound connection to Herriman. In their essay "Krazy Kat: The Art of George Herriman," Patrick McDonnell, Karen O'Connell and Georgia Riley de Havenon highlighted that

> Herriman's drawing has a spontaneity and looseness that imbues each pen stroke with a life of its own. A *Krazy Kat* page has a wholeness in its design that you can enjoy from a distance of ten feet without reading a word or recognizing a character.[75]

The life of Herriman's line, present even at a distance at which it becomes abstract, provides an illuminating means of reading Guston's apparently abstract or "pure" drawing, as he ironically termed it, created between 1966 and 1968 (Figure 2.17).

Figure 2.17 Statement, 1968, Philip Guston, charcoal on paper, 44.45 × 58.42 cm (17 ½ × 23 inches).

Image courtesy of The Estate of Philip Guston. © The Estate of Philip Guston.

Guston's final break from abstraction into the world of tangible forms had come after a two-year tussle, fought between a need for objects and a continued desire for "pure" line drawing. This "pure" drawing was created simultaneously with what Guston seems to have playfully thought of as the crudeness or dirtiness of his cartoon-like object-based imagery (describing it on occasion as "toilet drawing"). While Guston's object-based drawing was engaging with the messiness of life, his "pure drawing" was at times comprised of an element as spare as a single line. But Guston's use of the word "pure" can be misleading; as Isabelle Dervaux argues, "Guston himself did not believe in such a thing as purity in art. "Painting is 'impure'" he declared as early as 1960. "There are no wiggly or straight lines."[76] Speaking specifically of the "pure" drawings, Guston had said: "The drawings that didn't work . . . were just lines, in the ones that were good the whole space was activated."[77] In Guston's *Suite of Ten Lithographs* (1966) (Figure 2.18), there is something almost conspiratorial about the groupings of seemingly "pure" lines. The weighty, bodily presence of the congealed forms appear as if they are turned away from the viewer, wrapped deep in discussion. The groupings can be seen both as a continuation of the cluster of forms that had been a recurring force within his abstract painting of the past fifteen years in such works as *The Evidence* (1957)

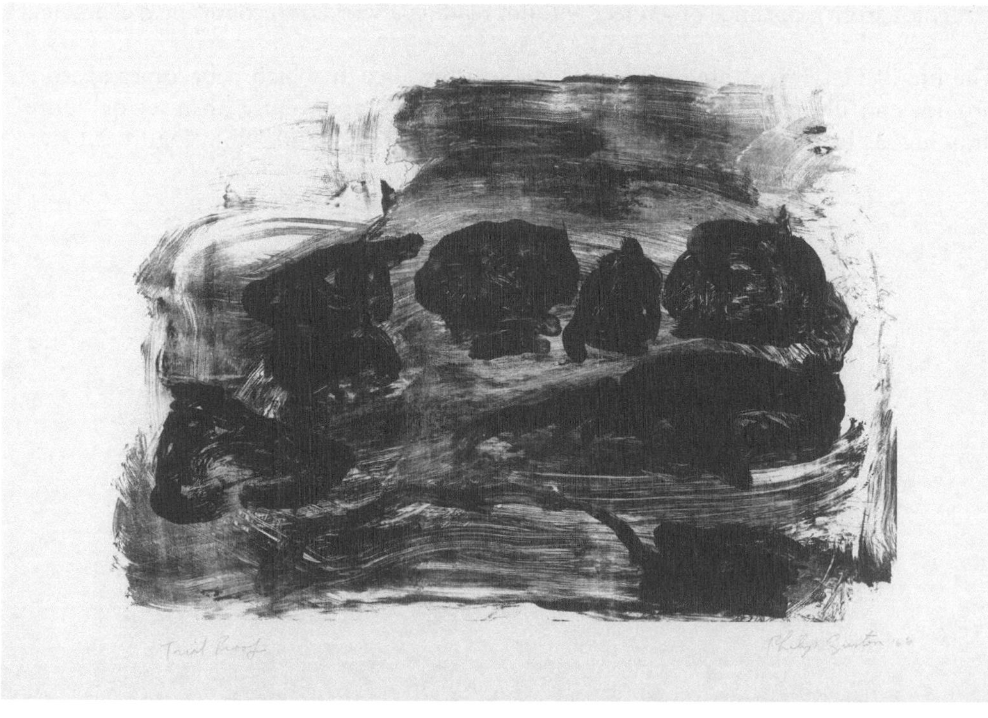

Figure 2.18 A Suite of Ten Lithographs: No.2, 1966, Philip Guston, lithograph on paper, sheet: 565 × 762 cm (22 ¼ × 30 inches).

and *Beggar's Joys* (1954–5), but also appear to predict the compressed configurations that resurface in the 1970s in such works as *Cabal* (1977) and *Group in Sea* (1979). The composer Morton Feldman visited Guston in his studio at a time when he was surrounded by dozens of drawings comprised of just one or two ink lines. Feldman recalled that Guston pointed to a drawing and said "You see that line? And you see that line a little bit on top of it? Well, that line . . . is talking into the ear of that bottom line, telling him its troubles."[78] This is more than just an amusing anecdote; it allows us to engage with a process in which a line is imagined as a character carrying a history. And importantly, the lines are then placed in dialogue with other lines equally considered as form and character. In effect, the pure drawing begins to operate like a *Krazy Kat* page, where each brush stroke "has a life of its own."

The distinction, then, between the "pure" and object-based drawing was not as irreconcilable as it had seemed. Storr highlights the fact that

> the short downward stroke frequently used in his 'pure' drawings as spatial inflection became in his new paintings the sign for windows in the blocky buildings of a city skyline. Two such blocks paired together became the symbol of an open book.[79]

The "pure" drawings had allowed Guston to reduce drawing to its most basic elements, and there he had discovered not abstraction, but rather a renewed engagement with matter in the animation of each and every mark across a surface. With each line existing as a commitment in the present moment, an object like a shoe becomes a microcosm of "living" lines. Each dot or dash, although perhaps recognisable as a button or lace, does not strive towards the creation of an abstract whole. Through the discoveries made from the artist's so-called pure drawing, each line or detail resists being subsumed into a unified oneness to remain in a state of animation. Rather than working with a gradual accumulation of brush marks to create a sense of volume, Guston allowed each line, as far as was possible, to operate as an "animate" form. This would be a process more akin to building than painterly illusion, a concern with a sense of tangibility, rather than surface.

By 1968, the "pure" drawings had been fully integrated into Guston's world of objects as an elemental form of building block. But the initially limited collection of objects was about to come together as a cast of characters that would surface in innumerable dramas played out on Guston's canvases throughout the 1970s. But, much like Paolozzi's collection of units, Guston's kit of forms first began as a group of "loose characters" without a destination.[80] Shoes and boots remained a recurring feature throughout the last decade of Guston's career. Giant, clunky shoes are a dominating presence in the comic strips Guston loved as a child. However, in Guston's works, shoes and legs take on an independent existence. Just as the pure drawing had generated a process in which Guston treated each line as a character, so too the initial focus on single objects examined in isolation had created an approach to form in which each element could be considered as a totality in itself. We see this presented through the disembodied shield wielding hands engaged in battles that recur in Guston's paintings of the 1970s in such works as *Plain* (1979) and *Aegean II* (1977) (Figure 3.2), and the feet and legs that have gained an independent life in works such as *Feet on Rug* (1978) and *Pile Up* (1980) (Figure 3.8).

Guston's approach to objects connects us to Paolozzi's methods, by which component parts are treated as distinct elements. But more than this, one can draw parallels between Paolozzi's engagement with the logic of the toy kit and Guston's use of the comic strip. The toy kit and the comic strip offered both artists a model in which a collection of forms can move through a seemingly endless series of configurations. However, it is important to emphasise again that it is the unmade kit, the kit in pieces, that most excited Paolozzi, because here there is another significant parallel with Guston's use of the comic strip. While Paolozzi asserted that the elements seemed to lose "a certain kind of potency when it was all put together,"[81] Guston's paintings refuse the inevitable conclusion of the punch line. Berkson has observed that Herriman "runs his stylized characters through infinite permutations of the same routine; although vantage point and setting may vary, the flying brick connects with Krazy's noggin every time."[82] By contrast, Guston's bricks "don't fly, they levitate and hover."[83] Held in a state of tension, Guston's objects resist resolution.

Where Paolozzi's aluminium sculpture of the 1960s had revealed a preoccupation with the incomplete, exemplified by a work such as *Crash*, Guston's late painting similarly defies conclusion. In works such as *Flatlands* (1970) (Figure 2.20) and *Story* (1978) (Figure 5.21) the elements remain as a discontinuous group of elements, while the recurring presence of heaps or clusters of forms in works including *Summer* (1980) (Figure 3.7) and *Pile Up* (1980) (Figure 3.8) allow the elements to come together as an argumentative crowd. This recalls how Paolozzi's kit of forms in a work such as *Insect Wings* (1952) (Figure 2.11) are brought together within structures that appear to fight against totalisation. The recurring presence of the pile or cluster in both artists' work is a structure that will be considered in depth in the following chapter. We can first see the structures that thwart resolution, as predicated on a process that establishes the importance of the parts as complete characters. Here, we find that both Paolozzi and Guston created works that acknowledge this process directly. While Paolozzi's sculpture *Mechanik's Bench* (1963) (Figure 2.6) had drawn attention to the importance of the individual units, Guston's painting *Painter's Table* (1973) (Figure 1.6) also focuses squarely on the component parts as distinct characters. On the table depicted, we see the familiar landscape of Guston's studio: shoes, books, flat irons, cigarettes, nails, a palette and a wide-eyed canvas. Here the objects are cast as a group of actors waiting stage-left for their cue. In *Painter's Forms* (1972) (Figure 2.19) and *Painter's Forms II* (1978), the focus is again on the role of the painter's elements. Guston's kit of forms are first seen emerging as a splutter from the painter's mouth in the 1972 version; by 1978, they pour out as an uncontrollable torrent, the painter overwhelmed by his own expressive force. Guston, in using his working methods as the very subject of the painting, expresses something that can almost be read as an act of gratitude from the artist towards his kit of forms for the flood of works they have enabled.

The creative fecundity provided by the "painter's forms" needs to be considered as founded on the instability of the meaning and identity of the forms themselves. In *Telling Stories, Philip Guston's Later Works*, published in 2010, David Kaufmann discusses Guston's late works in relation to notions of allegory, taking into consideration a term Guston had applied to the work. Kaufmann turns to *Flatlands* (1970) (Figure 2.20) to explore how the concept of allegory is predicated on discontinuity and the irresolvable.

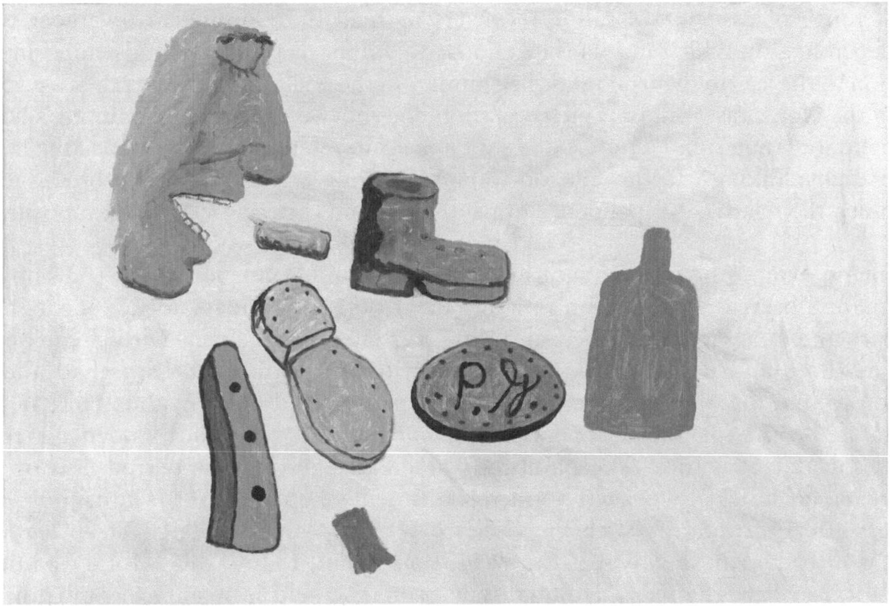

Figure 2.19 *Painter's Forms*, 1972, Philip Guston, oil on Masonite, 121.92 × 152.4 cm (48 × 60 inches).

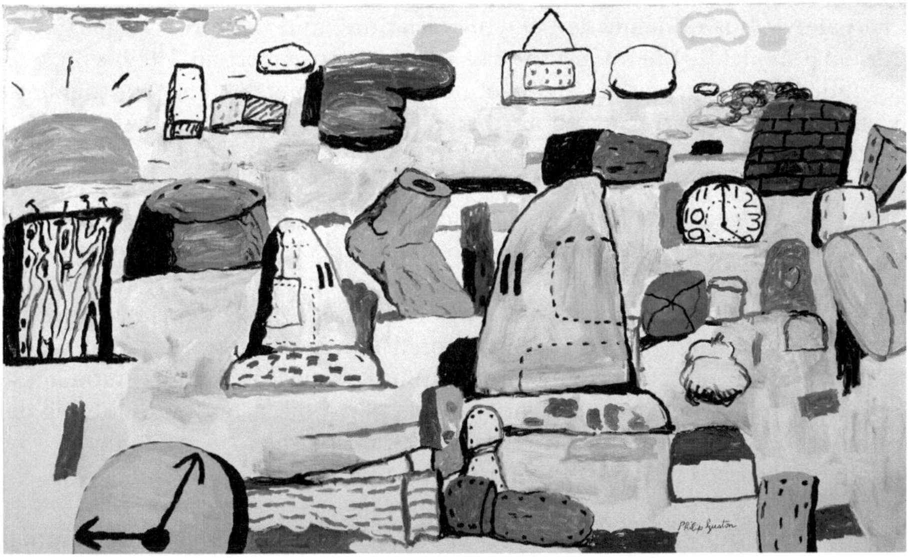

Figure 2.20 *Flatlands*, 1970, Philip Guston, oil on canvas, 177.8 × 290.83 cm (70 × 114 ½ inches), San Francisco Museum of Modern Art, fractional and promised gift of an anonymous donor.

> A range of associations allows viewers to read the painting in divergent ways, depending on which motifs they choose to emphasize. If the Hoods stand in relation to the legs in the front and the chimney in the back, they can be taken as ciphers of the Holocaust. But that interpretation does not account for the painting's books, hand, or rising sun. *Flatlands* does not appear to refer to a stable preexisting matrix of signs. Taking it as an allegory requires paying attention to its profuse lack of unity, the relative independence of its objects, and their associative juxtaposition.[84]

Kaufmann extends how one might understand the independence of Guston's objects. Kaufmann observes that Guston's picture elements retain independence through disjuncture and a lack of prescribed meaning. Repeated engagement with single objects such as shoes and books in the two years prior to creating *Flatlands* had allowed Guston to find the objects increasingly "mysterious" and unknowable. Here in *Flatlands*, they come together as a collection that retains object independence through an irresolvable structure. The painting was created during the period Guston was producing his series of works of hooded Klansmen, where meaning is at its most overt in Guston's confrontation with the violence of the political climate. But in *Flatlands* there is already a push towards the work that would follow the "Hood" paintings from 1972, where the narrative quality is primarily held in a state of ambiguity. In a lecture to students in 1972, Guston discussed painting *Flatlands* and explained: "I think what I wanted was what a friend of mine said: 'It looks like you put all forms, all the props, in a paper bag and then spilled it out.' I wanted that feeling."[85] *Flatlands* predates *Painter's Table* and *Painter's Forms*, predicting their focus on a condition of potentiality, provided by the unmade kit, with all its multitudinous possible connections and dramas. This multiplicity is founded on Guston's engagement with what Fink had allowed us to define as "playful variation" and the forms' departure from the "original model." When Guston was asked by Rosenberg in 1974 why soles of shoes continue to recur within his painting, Guston replied: "That's a tough one. I don't know. What would I say about that?"[86] It is this "I don't know" quality that keeps the shoes in play, enabling the shoes to continue to be of use.

In effect, Guston's repeated examination of a limited collection of objects may have not only forced a loss of representative concept but also allowed the artist to redefine their "function." Repeated scrutiny transformed a shoe from the flattened identity of an item that is perceived in terms of prescribed utility to a condition where "use" becomes an activity through which meaning emerges. Effectively, Guston transformed the concept of use from one of a defined, predetermined nature, to what we could understand as "use" as it appears within play, as outlined by Sutton-Smith. This is a form of "use" that reinvents the identity of the play object. Sutton-Smith highlights for us that a child's play is not restricted and defined by the toys available. In *Toys as Culture*, published in 1986, Sutton-Smith states that

> the toy car, first used as a car, may soon begin to be used as a ship in the sandbox, if that is what is needed. . . . For children it is their motivated action with these symbolic vehicles (cars and dolls) rather than the things themselves, which constitutes the nature of play.[87]

For Sutton-Smith, then, it is a mistake to think of play as simply imitative. In accordance with Fink, Sutton-Smith asserts that play can be full of actions and processes that depart from their original reference points. For Sutton-Smith, this means that a toy is an object for which the original signification very often becomes corrupted. Sutton-Smith's analysis of the flexible uses for a toy provides a way to complicate a reading of Guston's repeated use of shoes. In the duality possible within play, these would be both shoes and not shoes.

In Michael Blackwood's film *Philip Guston: A Life Lived* (1981), Guston offers us an alternative reading for the tangle of legs and shoes in the 1976 painting *Monument*. Guston begins by stating, "I was thinking about, *not* legs, they're just the excuse." When asked, "It's got nothing to do with feet and shoes?," Guston emphatically replies "Nothing! I've been hearing enough about people talking about feet, even legs, shoes, aagh . . ."[88] Of course, it is an inevitable part of the life of an artwork, that once it goes off into the world it will acquire interpretations other than those intended by the artist, and these interpretations may well be defined by cultural readings, despite the artist's thoughts to the contrary. But, if one wants to think in terms of process and use, the repeated presence of legs and shoes could be seen to function as the artist's own collection of building blocks, or "painter's forms." In this guise, we can see the forms as capable of multiple identities and multiple *uses* that need not be tied to a pre-defined representational meaning. For Guston, the legs, feet and shoes in the painting *Monument* are a means to create "forces." In the film, he discusses the painting in terms of an event unfolding in front of the viewer; some legs are seen to be charging. while others are dangling. For Guston, this collision of forces accumulates into the emergence of an invented being, a creature that appears to have acquired a life independent of the artist, as Guston states: "the idea of a completely separate organism . . . which has its own energy, energies, diverse energies."[89] But, Guston's restless knot of forms with their contrary states—stamping, charging and dangling, yet going nowhere—unavoidably reads as a collection of humanoid legs and clunky shoes, however much the artist might protest otherwise. But, if they cannot leave this identity behind, perhaps we can allow for a dual reading: an alternative in which they become something less nameable and yet more specific, a being of multiplicity yet to be generalised and classified.

For Fink, play ultimately presents an exploration of the nature of being. Through interaction and experimentation within play, a play object connects to the world beyond, to become a symbol:

> Playing is always a confrontation with beings. In the plaything, the whole is concentrated in a single thing. Every instance of play is an attempt on the part of life, a vital experiment, which experiences in the plaything the epitome of resistant beings in general.[90]

Through processes of repetition, Guston's shoes move through difference and distortion to become, in Fink's terms, "a world profound symbol." It is in their resistance to singular meaning, through repetition and variation, that Guston's shoes gain an ability to retain an unknowable quality. In allowing for the unknowable, by focusing on Guston's studio processes as play, we can explore how Guston's forms open out from the singleness of a "shoe" to the wholeness of "being." Guston stated that he had wanted to leave abstraction to return to paint the "thickness of things."[91] It is in the thickness of things that a play process accumulates, leaving a representative concept behind in order to build not simply a "shoe" but a being.

In emphasising action, variant repetition and use over prescribed meaning, Guston's objects can, like Paolozzi's sculpture and picture elements, gain a changing, evolving, multifarious "life." Here we can begin to connect with studio processes by which Guston generated form that, in Winnicott's terms, appears to show it has "reality of its own."[92] It is this desire for a sense of object independence that Guston returns to tirelessly, repeatedly stating that "when I leave my studio and go in the house I like to feel that I left people there, like throbbing beings. Golems are there. Otherwise, why paint? I mean, who wants pictures? I want living things."[93] Through an emphasis on process rather than meaning, we as an audience can bring a perspective in which an object is not fixed and finalised but rather, in Fink's terms, engages with "being itself, which structures and destroys."[94] In the next chapter, I will explore how Paolozzi and Guston's forms are placed in structures that exist within creative cycles of construction and destruction.

Notes

1. Eduardo Paolozzi, "Artificial Horizons and Eccentric Ladders," in *Eduardo Paolozzi: Artificial Horizons and Eccentric Ladders* (exh.cat.) (London: British Council, 1996), 11–12.
2. Eduardo Paolozzi and Richard Hamilton as quoted in "Interview between Richard Hamilton and Eduardo Paolozzi, 1965," in *Eduardo Paolozzi: Writings and Interviews*, ed. Robin Spencer (Oxford and New York: Oxford University Press, 2001), 138.
3. As early as 1963, Michael Middleton asserted that from the 1950s "the collage conception now came to dominate the whole of Paolozzi's thinking." Michael Middleton, *Eduardo Paolozzi* (London: Methuen, 1963), 36.

   The characterization of Paolozzi's methods as collage still dominates analyses of Paolozzi's multi-varied output. In 2013, a retrospective at Pallant House Gallery brought together 150 of Paolozzi's works under the title Collaging Culture. In the catalogue to accompany the exhibition, Simon Martin stated that "collage was central to Paolozzi's creativity as an artist . . . Arguably, rather than sculpture, it is collage that underpins all his work." Simon Martin, *Collaging Culture* (exh.cat.) (Chichester: Pallant House Gallery, 2013), 12.
4. "Obsession" is a term Paolozzi applied to his working processes and recurrent interests: "it's all got to do with layers of obsession.' *Paolozzi*, Louise Wardle, BBC (7/12/2000), accessed via www.bbc.co.uk/archive/sculptors/12818.shtml
5. Wieland Schmied, "The Artist in the Museum," in *Arche Noah* (exh.cat.) (Münich: Münchner Stadtmuseum, 1990), 58.
6. See the Introduction for a definition of transitional objects.
7. D.W. Winnicott, *Playing and Reality* (Oxford: Routledge, 2005), 119.
8. Claude Lichtenstein and Thomas Schregenberger, *As Found, the Discovery of the Ordinary* (Baden: Lars Müller Publishers and the Zurich Museum für Gestaltung, 2001), 10.
9. Ibid.
10. See the Introduction for a more comprehensive definition of the properties of the transitional object.
11. Lichtenstein and Schregenberger, *As Found, the Discovery of the Ordinary*, 10.
12. Diane Kirkpatrick, *Eduardo Paolozzi* (London: Studio Vista, 1970), 47.
13. Eric M. Stryker even makes a connection between the collage-like process used for Paolozzi's bronzes of the late 1950s and Paolozzi's collection of toy building blocks: "In the 1957–8 series of sculptures titled *Saint Sebastian*, Paolozzi's sculptural method is particularly masterful. His vertical assembly of separate trays of wax is fully visible. Stacked one against another like pieces in a collage, they also echo building blocks, another mass-produced item collected by the artist." Eric M. Stryker, "Parallel Systems: Lawrence Alloway and Eduardo Paolozzi," *Tate Papers*, No. 16 (Autumn 2011).
14. Eduardo Paolozzi, "An Architecture from the Tools of a Child," in *Writings and Interviews*, ed. Spencer, 95.
15. Ibid., 106.

16. Ibid., 100.
17. Eduardo Paolozzi, *National Life Stories, Artist's Lives, Sir Eduardo Paolozzi Interviewed by Frank Whitford*, accessed March 2012, http://sounds.bl.uk/Arts-literature-and-performance/Art-photography-and-architecture/021M-C0466X0017XX-1600V0
18. Daniel Herrmann, "Paolozzi and the Laocoon Group," in *Towards a New Laocoon* (exh. cat.), ed. Penelope Curtis and Stephen Feeke (Leeds: Henry Moore Institute, 2007), 53.
19. Ibid.
20. Walter Benjamin, "Toys and Play: Marginal Notes on a Monumental Work," in *Walter Benjamin Selected Writings Volume 2*, ed. Michael W. Jennings, Howard Eiland and Gary Smith (Cambridge: The Belknap Press of Harvard University Press, 1990), 120.
21. Lichtenstein and Schregenberger, *As Found, the Discovery of the Ordinary*, 10.
22. Kirkpatrick *Eduardo Paolozzi*, 49.
23. Paolozzi, "Neorema-Leoend," in *Writings and Interviews*, ed. Spencer, 146.
24. Kirkpatrick, *Eduardo Paolozzi*, 57.
25. Notebook page dated 1964 held in the archives of the Scottish National Gallery of Modern Art, reproduced in Judith Collins, *Eduardo Paolozzi* (Farnham: Lund Humphries, 2014), 152.
26. Eduardo Paolozzi as quoted in Kirkpatrick, *Eduardo Paolozzi*, 54.
27. Eduardo Paolozzi, "Glynn Williams Talks to Eduardo Paolozzi, 1995," in *Writings and Interviews*, ed. Spencer, 329.
28. "Paolozzi," directed by Louise Wardle, BBC (7/12/2000), accessed via www.bbc.co.uk/archive/sculptors/12818.shtml
29. Benjamin, "Toys and Play: Marginal Notes on a Monumental Work," 120.
30. Johan Huizinga, *Homo Ludens* (Boston: Beacon Press, 1955), 10.
31. Paolozzi's use of Hugo Meier-Thur's print *Stille Nacht* (a visual interpretation of organ music) is another key example of repetition and variation in Paolozzi's use of found material. Meier-Thur's print (originally published in *Kosmos* in 1927) recurs across Paolozzi's prints and reliefs of the 1970s, forming the basis of works such as *Mr Peanut* (1970), the Cleish Ceiling Panels (1972), the *Calcium Light Night* print suite (1974–6), the *Charles Rennie Mackintosh suite* (1975) and the Hunterian Art Gallery Doors (1976).
32. Paolozzi, "Paolozzi."
33. Roger Caillois, *Man, Play and Games* (Urbana and Chicago: University of Illinois Press, 2001), 7. See the Introduction for a more extensive definition.
34. Paolozzi, "Paolozzi."
35. Lawrence Alloway, *Eduardo Paolozzi, the Metallization of a Dream* (London: Lion and Unicorn, 1963), 62.
36. Alex Kitnick, "Another Time," *Art Journal*, Vol. 71, No. 2 (Summer 2012): 42.
37. Edward Allington in correspondence with the author (April 2014).
38. Eduardo Paolozzi as quoted in Robin Spencer, "Henderson + Paolozzi = Hammer Prints," in *Nigel Henderson & Eduardo Paolozzi Hammer Prints Ltd, 1954–75* (exh.cat.), ed. Michelle Cotton (Colchester: Firstsite, 2013), 61.
39. Robin Spencer, "Henderson + Paolozzi = Hammer Prints," in *Nigel Henderson & Eduardo Paolozzi Hammer Prints Ltd, 1954–75* (exh.cat.), ed. Michelle Cotton (Colchester: Firstsite, 2013), 61.
40. Lesley Jackson, *Inside Out–Outside In: The Guerrilla Fabrics of Hammer Prints*, (Hammer Prints Ltd., 1954–75), ed. Cotton, 109.
41. Anton Ehrenzweig, *The Hidden Order of Art* (London: Phoenix Press, 2000), 148.
42. Beth Williamson, *Between Art Practice and Psychoanalysis Mid-Twentieth Century: Anton Ehrenzweig in Context* (Farnham: Ashgate, 2015), 89.
43. Ibid., 81.
44. Ibid.
45. Paolozzi, "Artificial Horizons and Eccentric Ladders," 11–12.
46. Philip Guston, "Philip Guston Talking," in *Philip Guston* (exh.cat.) (London: Timothy Taylor Gallery, 2004), 27.
47. Philip Guston, "Talk at Yale Summer School of Music and Art, 1973," in *Philip Guston, Collected Writings, Lectures, and Conversations*, ed. Clark Coolidge (London: University of California Press, 2011), 221.

48. Guston, "Philip Guston Talking," 27.
49. Philip Guston as quoted in Andrew Graham-Dixon, "A Maker of Worlds: The Later Paintings of Philip Guston," in *Philip Guston Retrospective* (exh.cat.) (London: Thames & Hudson, 2003), 54.
50. Guston, "Philip Guston Talking," 28.
51. Philip Guston as quoted in "Interview with Mark Stevens, 1980," in *Collected Writings, Lectures, and Conversations*, 303.
52. Guston, "Talk at Yale Summer School of Music and Art, 1973," 221.
53. Philip Guston, "On Drawing," in *Collected Writings, Lectures, and Conversations*, 263.
54. Eugen Fink, *Play as Symbol of the World and Other Writings* (Bloomington: Indiana University Press, 2016), 118.
55. Robert Storr, *Philip Guston* (New York: Abbeville, 1986), 64.
56. Fink, *Play as Symbol of the World*, 110.
57. Clark Coolidge as quoted in *Philip Guston, Collected Writings, Lectures, and Conversations*, ed. Clark Coolidge (London: University of California Press, 2011), 207.
58. Ibid., 208.
59. Jean Piaget, *The Language and Thought of the Child* (London: Routledge & Kegan Paul, 1959), 11.
60. Ibid., 12.
61. Philip Guston, "Conversation with Clark Coolidge, 1972," in *Collected Writings, Lectures, and Conversations*, 193.
62. Philip Guston as quoted in "A Conversation between Philip Guston and Joseph Ablow," in *Philip Guston 1975–1980: Private and Public Battles* (exh.cat.), ed. Kim Sichel and Mary Drach McInnes (Boston: Boston University Art Gallery, 1994), 33.
63. Storr, *Philip Guston*, 52.
64. Guston, "Conversation with Clark Coolidge," 184.
65. Harold Rosenberg, *The Tradition of the New* (New York: Da Capo Press, 1994), 25.
66. Ibid.
67. Brian Sutton-Smith, *The Ambiguity of Play* (Cambridge: Harvard University Press, 2001), 171.
68. Philip Guston, "Talk at 'Art/Not Art?' Conference, 1978," in *Collected Writings, Lectures, and Conversations*, 284.
69. Philip Guston, "The Image, 1969," in *Collected Writings, Lectures, and Conversations*, 136.
70. Ibid.
71. Guston, "Conversation with Clark Coolidge," 185.
72. Ibid.
73. Huizinga, *Homo Ludens*, 32, 37.
74. Guston, "The Image, 1969," 127.
75. Patrick McDonnell, Karen O'Connell, and Georgia Riley de Havenon, "Krazy Kat: The Art of George Herriman," in *Krazy Kat, the Comic Art of George Herriman* (New York: Harry N. Abrams, Incorporated, 2004), 27.
76. Philip Guston as quoted in Isabelle Dervaux Schreier, "Baffling Drawings: Philip Guston, 1966–8," in *Philip Guston Works on Paper*, ed. Christoph Schreier and Michael Semff (Ostfildern: Hatje Cantz Verlag, 2007), 91.
77. Ibid.
78. Morton Feldman, "Conversation with Morton Feldman, 1968," in *Collected Writings, Lectures, and Conversations*, 89.
79. Storr, *Philip Guston*, 66.
80. Paolozzi, "Artificial Horizons and Eccentric Ladders," 11.
81. Eduardo Paolozzi as quoted in "Glynn Williams Talks to Eduardo Paolozzi, 1995," 329.
82. Bill Berkson, "Pyramid and Shoe: Philip Guston and the Funnies," in *Philip Guston Retrospective* (exh.cat.), ed. Michael Auping (London: Thames & Hudson, 2003), 70.
83. Ibid.
84. David Kaufmann, *Telling Stories, Philip Guston's Later Works* (London: University of California Press, 2010), 56.

85. Philip Guston, "Talk at Yale Summer School of Music and Art, 1972," in *Collected Writings, Lectures, and Conversations*, 159.
86. Philip Guston, "Conversation with Harold Rosenberg, 1974," in *Collected Writings, Lectures, and Conversations*, 276.
87. Brian Sutton-Smith, *Toys as Culture* (New York: Gardner Press, 1986), 250.
88. Philip Guston, *Philip Guston: A Life Lived*, directed by Michael Blackwood. New York, NY, Michael Blackwood Productions Inc., 1981.
89. Ibid.
90. Fink, *Play as Symbol of the World*, 24.
91. Guston, *Philip Guston: A Life Lived.*
92. Winnicott, *Playing and Reality*, 119.
93. Guston, *Collected Writings, Lectures, and Conversations*, 112.
94. Fink, *Play as Symbol of the World*, 135.

3 Creative Battles

The creative struggle has become something of a cliché within the biography of an artist, particularly when framed and romanticised as suffering and torment. However, in this chapter I want to examine what happens when the "battle" is a process that is actively encouraged and embraced. Both Philip Guston and Eduardo Paolozzi emphasise destruction as a vital creative force within their studio methods. Furthermore, Guston articulates "the contest" as the most engaging quality of a creative process. I will use the notion of contest as a way to explore Guston and Paolozzi's studio methods as game playing. The artists' kits of forms, explored in the last chapter, will here be seen as game elements going into battle with the unknown. In this context, the "mistake" will be re-imagined as an adversary within the artists' game playing processes, challenging the artist or "player" to produce an unforeseen response. In the final sections of the chapter, I examine significant connections between Paolozzi's 1950s sculptures—formed with junk and bombsite debris—and the discourse surrounding post-war junk playgrounds established on bombsites and waste ground. These connections will be seen to centre on play materials that enable elements to be placed within cycles of construction and destruction.

Philip Guston: Game Playing Painting

During the installation of his retrospective at the San Francisco Museum of Modern Art in 1980, Philip Guston was filmed reflecting on a life spent painting. While analysing the recurring driving forces behind his work, Guston asserted that he seemed to need a battle to unfold during the painting process if the work was to be engaging:

> My temperament seems to need . . . or is not involved unless I have a contest between a subject and the plastic form it will result in. And the reason I enjoy the contest is that this contest between the means of painting and its scale, distance, locations . . . and so on, leads to, since I constantly change on a single painting, I mean scrape out, repaint a lot as you know, leads to structures that are surprising.[1]

Guston here allows us to make a direct connection between his need for a contest and the unforeseen result. According to Huizinga, "contest means play . . . there is no sufficient reason to deny any contest whatsoever the character of play."[2] With Huizinga, we have the means to explore Guston's studio processes as game playing enacted on the canvas. However, the contemporary play theorist Brian Sutton-Smith importantly warns that although Huizinga's history of play still offers hugely valuable insights on the subject, it is also a particularly reductive, "machismo" approach to play. Sutton-Smith informs us that there are many critics of Huizinga that have pointed to "cooperative, solitary, or mental play that are not always based on contest and which he does not consider."[3] It is by focusing on the notion of the contest as central to the *game* specifically rather than play more generally that we might be able to connect Guston's emphasis on the term with contemporary play studies and games scholarship.[4] And, significantly, if the contest is considered a particularly macho approach to play, we can explore how Guston's painting undermines or plays with notions of the heroic and the "noble game" as set out by Huizinga. Through his discussion of chivalry, Huizinga asserts that "all fighting that is bound by rules bears the formal characteristics of play."[5] Guston's painting will be seen to ridicule notions of chivalry and masculinity, while also engaging in self-mockery.

In 1994, an exhibition at Boston University Art Gallery explored the battle as a recurring theme within Guston's late painting. *Philip Guston 1975–1980: Private and Public Battles* explored the artist's images of eternal human conflict in paintings such as *Aegean* (1978), together with the artist's images of the private battleground of the studio in works including *Division* (1975). In the catalogue essay, Mary Drach McInnes brilliantly brought together the paintings' subject of war and aggression with Guston's own personal narratives to see the battles as multivalent. Drach McInnes describes Guston's images of battlegrounds as meeting points that act as metaphors for the creative act and the artist's wider socio-political concerns. For Drach McInnes, "the artist's individual struggle is the starting point for all his narratives."[6] In this chapter, I want to explore this convergence between the subject of Guston's paintings and the processes behind their creation that Drach McInnes so insightfully identifies. However, here I want to bring another emphasis, to see what happens when we consider the contest as a force that is actively encouraged as enabling, satisfying a desire to push beyond the predictable. This is not to make the conflicts within Guston's work benign or lessen the artist's personal struggles—Guston unquestionably did suffer a great deal of personal conflict and self-doubt—but rather to explore the dialectic within the battle, to see it as a force within Guston's creative processes that could be as productive as it was inhibiting.

Guston's recurring images of battles in his work of the 1970s marked a return to older themes, first explored in his paintings of the 1930s and 1940s. The artist had, in his own words, "made a circle, you might say. All my older interests in painting, the children fighting with garbage cans and all that stuff."[7] Created within the context of two world wars, paintings such as *Martial Memory* (1941) (Figure 3.1) and *Work and Play* (1940) reflect war through the games of the child, enacted with dustbin lids, wooden swords and paper hats. In later works, including *Aegean II* (1977) (Figure 3.2), *Plain* (1979), *The Street* (1977) and *Hinged* (1978), we see brutish, lumpen hands locked in eternal, cyclical violence. The children have, according to Guston, "grown up."[8] But if they have grown up, the work declares they have not progressed.

Guston's images of battles, fought by paw-like hands with impoverished weapons of war, make a mockery of chivalry or "war as a noble game of honour."[9] For Huizinga, chivalry had played an essential role in society as a civilising function. Huizinga contends that ideas of "play" and "battle" combine in the archaic imagination through the notion of "a struggle with fate limited by certain rules."[10] Guston's paintings appear to imply that if these concepts are still inextricably combined, then we are forever caught in a cycle of terrible, tragic absurdity. Through his own cyclical return to children's

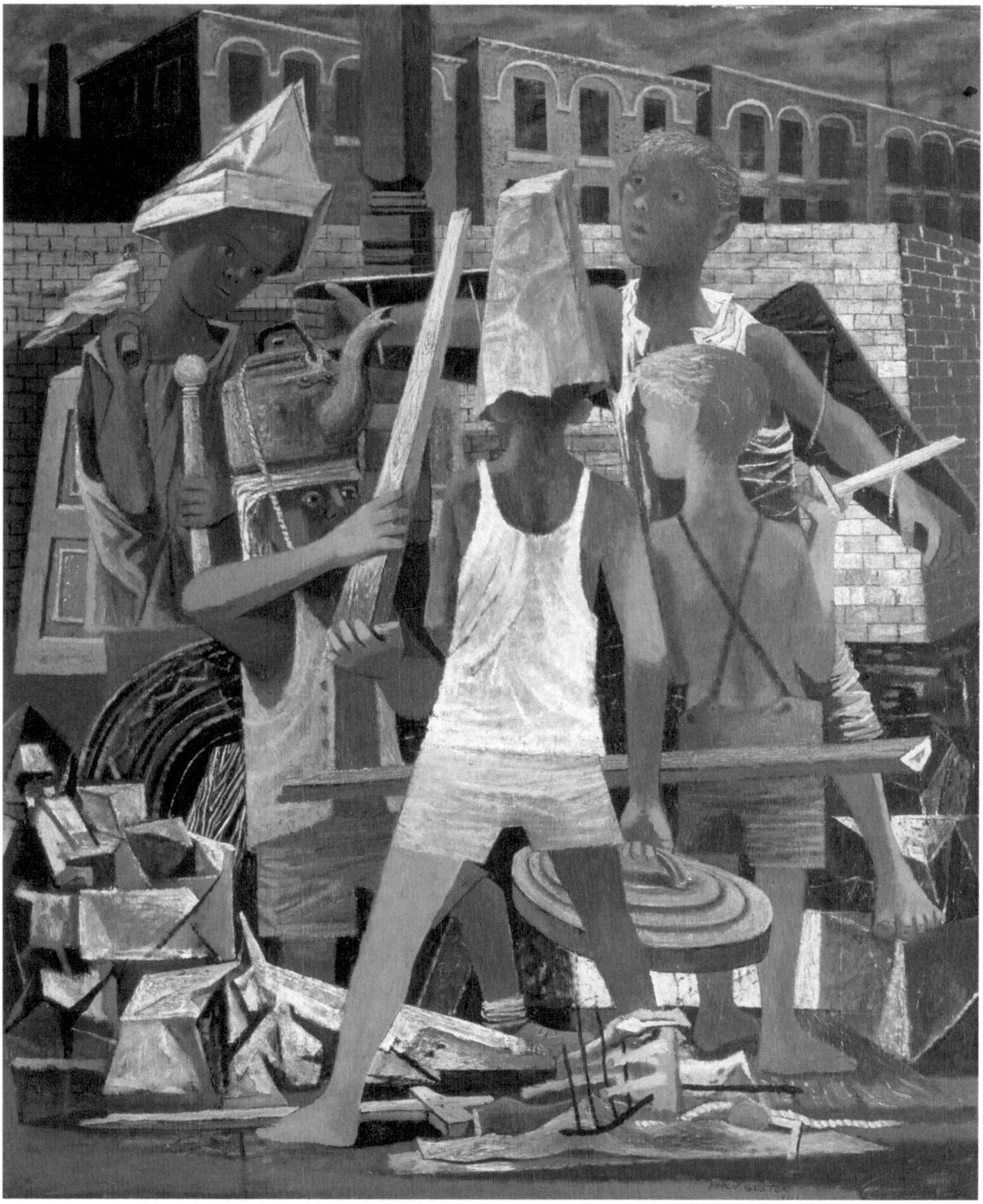

Figure 3.1 *Martial Memory*, 1941, Philip Guston, oil on canvas, 101.9 × 81.3 cm (40 1/8 × 32 ¼) inches. Saint Louis Art Museum, Eliza McMillan Trust 115:1942.

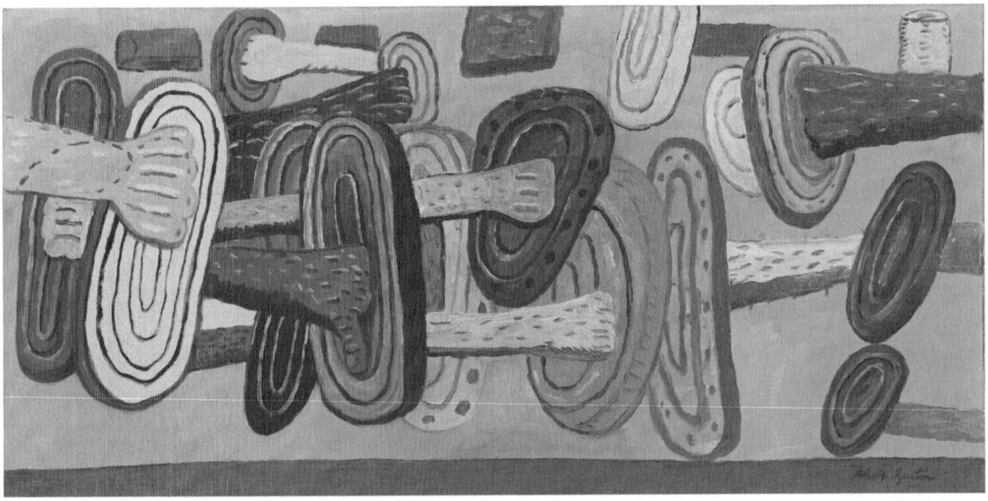

Figure 3.2 Aegean II, 1977, Philip Guston, oil on canvas, 91.4 × 177.8 cm (36 × 70 inches).

street battles, his paintings suggest that as life is generated, it is gifted with all the seeds of its own destruction. Play in the painter's hands is an activity that plays with its own absurdity, lampooning its own motivating forces with their connections to eternal human failings, vanities and hubris. In his struggles and his need for "contest," Guston's paintings of battles seem to state an almost Huizingian recognition of a connection between the impulses behind eternal human conflicts and specific creative impulses, driven by play's need for conflict, contest, drama and an engagement with chaos and the unknown. This connects us to what Sutton-Smith describes as play's metacommunicative nature. Sutton-Smith cites Gregory Bateson and outlines that

> Bateson (1972) . . . points to the paradoxical and metacommunicative nature of play, showing that play is not just play but is also a message about itself (a metamessage), being both of the world and not of the world (paradox).[11]

We can see this metamessage within Guston's painting as a play process that formulates a mocking of its own generative processes through the forms it finds and the narratives it draws. Guston openly stated his guilty pleasure in violent imagery during a talk at Yale Summer School of Music and Art in 1972. Guston explained that his love for frescoes depicting images of hell was one of the primary reasons for returning to Italy in 1970:

> I wanted to see early frescoes of Last Judgements and end-of-the-world paintings . . . marvellous frescoes of the damned, all the tortures in hell, and so on. Heaven is always very dull, just a lot of people lined up. . . . But when they're going to hell

> the painter really goes to town. All kinds of marvellous stuff. That's when they really enjoyed painting. So I feel we live in comparable times. Oh yeah, and I want to paint that. I don't want to copy, but I feel that's the big subject matter.[12]

In clearly outlining a connection between the pleasure gained in painting violent imagery and his desire to address the political climate, Guston does not stand apart in judgement, but implicates himself within the violence. Guston points towards painting that embraces destruction and chaos, while relishing the dynamic structures found. We could see this as connected to Paolozzi's sculpture *Crash* (1964), discussed in the last chapter. Again, we have a cacophonous structure in which each element is pronounced as an individual, rather than "all lined up" in a quiescent unity to create what Guston describes as a "dull" heaven.

Before I delve beneath the battle imagery to explore Guston's painting processes in more detail, I want to first suggest how an artist might be able to develop an ability to embrace the battle with the unknown (rather than suffer the confrontation with uncertainty and failure). I want to propose that we can see this ability as enabled through a form of role-play. By adopting a persona, an artist acts "as if," to use both Caillois' and Fink's formulation. This "as if," in the face of the unknown, can be imagined as a persona infused with the bravado of the heroic, enabling an artist to fight off, or at least suspend, crippling self-criticism when confronted by uncertainty, mistakes and potential failure. In a sense, we could think of the adopted persona as daring the artist on through the unknown. Guston's writings and lectures are full of such allusions. He compares artists with actors,[13] imagines himself as Lenin or Trotsky "plotting the revolution"[14] and in conversation with Rosenberg in 1974 states that

> part of my process of working is almost to pretend. But, you know, pretense becomes real after a while, and then I'm really in it, and there is no way back. I would imagine what it would be like to paint as if there had never been any painting before. Now, that's an impossibility.[15]

Guston here describes a paradoxical state of absorption and awareness. The role-play, or pretence, provides a guiding logic or narrative that allows for immersion in a created reality, but it is not delusional; it is always aware of its own "impossibility." Here, Guston describes the grandiose daydream of imagining being the first painter, unencumbered by history and the weight of one's painting heroes, while always aware that this is a strategy of pretence. It is this doubling activity that Fink sees as essential to understanding play. Role-play is at the centre of play's potential to expand the player's experience, providing the means to move out of the realm of the known. But Fink emphasises that it is always predicated on the ability to hold two realities side-by-side: the imagined and the everyday.

> Within the internal context of the sense of play, however, he takes on a *role*. . . . The player "conceals" himself by means of his "role"; in a certain measure he vanishes into it . . . he lives *in* the role—and, yet again, not like a person who is deluded. . . . The player can call himself back out of the role. . . . This doubling belongs to the essence of playing.[16]

In Guston's paintings of the 1970s, the epic struggles on the battleground of the studio and the vast planes of uninterrupted horizon are always aware they are playing *at* the heroic. Duelling and mocking their own bluster, the paintings produce an ever-present recognition of their own absurdity through the pitifully brutish. The beefy, paw-like hands locked in battle in paintings like *Aegean II* (Figure 3.2), *Hinged* (1978) and *The Street* (1977) dismiss any associations with valour. The desire for heroism in confrontation with the battle is something comic to be pitied. Guston's giant-scaled canvases embrace the need for bravado while lampooning that very need as a sign of frailty. The cartoon landscape they are informed by is populated not by the superheroes of Marvel Comics, but rather by the clowning of Mutt and Jeff: two characters that are forever the victim of their own ineptitude as they enact an unending cycle of slapstick violence.

In the final chapter of this book, within the context of processes of absurdity, I will further examine these contradictions at play in the adoption of a persona. There I will focus on Guston's recurring use of the mask. This includes the "mask" of Abstract art as Guston described it, and the mask as imagining "being under the hood" in his paintings of the Ku Klux Klan. For now, I want to focus on role-play as a studio strategy that is aware of itself as such. I think we can see this operating at perhaps the most critical point in Guston's career, allowing the artist to make the radical shift in his painting from the apparently abstract to the cartoon-like. It even enabled the artist to battle against the need for the approval of those closest to him, particularly three people whose critical validation he had relied on in the past—the composer Morton Feldman, his wife Musa and the painter and founder of the New York Studio School, Mercedes Matter. Guston describes this period of transition in theatrical terms as "my drama on the stage." Crucially, this drama is characterised by Guston as productive conflict: "you develop an 'I'll-show-them' attitude, which does give you a lot of energy. . . . I remember thinking: 'These few people who are the closest to me and think they know me well, they don't know me at all.'"[17] Significantly, this is not just a biographical anecdote or an exercise in self-dramatisation, but was given as advice to students during a talk in 1967 at the New York Studio School. Guston describes the benefit of having something to fight against and warns against the need for approval from teachers or friends. But, again, Guston casts the adversary in playful, dramatic terms as a "protagonist" that is as much as anything "a subjective creation."[18]

From Adversity to Adversary

A game requires an opponent; even solitary puzzle games can be understood as an encounter with an absent opponent in the form of the challenge set by the game designer. While Guston's "I'll-show-them attitude" clearly points towards identifiable, external adversaries, his greater contests were taking place on the canvas alone in the studio. However, I want to go beyond considering these battles simply in terms of a psychological struggle with self to propose that Guston had found a way to embrace the mistake as an engagement with the other. In this sense, accidents, changes and erasures were elements to be welcomed as part of a departure from a pre-visualised ideal. But, more than this, we can think of the "mistake" as something that is personified as a willing adversary in a desire for a contest with the unforeseen. For Fink, play is always a social activity that takes place within a community. According to Fink, it is no contradiction to acknowledge that many games are played alone. Play always involves a reaching out to others, whether real or imaginary:

> Playing is, structurally, not an individual or isolated activity—it is open to one's fellow human beings as fellow-players. It is no objection to point out that frequently, though, the ones playing carry out their games "all alone," . . . being open to possible fellow-players is already included in the sense of play, and, in the second place, such a solitary person often plays with imaginary partners. The community of play need not consist of a number of real persons.[19]

Fink allows us to find a way to think through and beyond the use of the accidental and the chaotic as an expressionistic outpouring of self. Using Fink's concept of play, an unfolding, chaotic structure need not necessarily be perceived only in terms of the artist's struggle with his own psyche, it can also become a site of multiplicity, a space that reaches out to the social, revels in the messy, unpredictable nature of the world to play games with contingency. However, crucially, Guston described how it was after getting to know many of the painters of the New York School of Abstract Expressionists that he was able to discover a process that departed from the carefully preplanned structures of his paintings of the 1940s. In a talk to students in 1972, Guston gave a detailed account of how in the 1950s he began to create paintings in which the structures were found through the painting process itself. The artist described how the abstract work evolved from dispelling notions of right or wrong and rejecting preconceptions about the final work. Guston articulated a responsive painting process that recalls Lichtenstein and Schregenberger's definition of the "as found" as "the technique of reaction."

> not knowing whether it's right, or not even caring about whether it's right. . . . And then it spoke to you, and then you reacted . . . the feeling that you're making marks, and leaving yourself open enough, or nimble enough so that things happen as you work. . . . I found it very exciting in contrast to my . . . former pictures of the forties where they're very consciously structured and planned . . . another great lesson of extreme attention while you're doing it. I mean, split-second timing. Like the whole field becomes an electrified field where every mark is magnetized.[20]

Guston's language here is full of sporting expressions; like an athlete, he talks of being "nimble enough," while employing "split-second timing" on "an electrified field."[21] It is, of course, an emphasis on action and process rather than image, returning us to Rosenberg's definition of Action Painting, outlined in the previous chapter. Importantly, Rosenberg had proclaimed in 1952 that for many American painters the canvas had become an "arena in which to act." An arena is obviously a site in which a sporting contest takes place. And indeed, Rosenberg's essay "The American Action Painters" is shot through with sporting rhetoric, as he describes the painters' processes in terms of "tension," "risk" and "skirmish."[22] If Rosenberg's allusions to sport and battle start to sound reminiscent of Huizinga's definitions of play, then his emphasis on a process that embraces "tension" and "risk" further draws significant parallels with Huizinga's definition of the "play spirit":

> To dare, to take risks, to bear uncertainty, to endure tension—these are the essence of the play spirit. Tension adds to the importance of the game and, as it increases, enables the player to forget that he is only playing.[23]

Through Surrealism, it is possible to chart a current of influence that runs from Huizinga's definitions of the game through to Rosenberg's sporting definitions of Action Painting. Claudia Mesch informs us that

> Huizinga apparently prompted Breton, in the interviews that make up his memoirs (*Entretiens*, 1952) . . . to reclassify almost the entirety of surrealist practice as the playing of games. Breton claimed that while the group (that is, he) first understood games merely as a kind of social glue and collective entertainment, and in embarrassment concealed their games as "experimental" activities, he only later realized the epistemological "discoveries" it could generate.[24]

The painter Robert Motherwell described the impact Surrealism had made on him and his fellow painters in the New York School of Abstract Expressionists. Motherwell explained the importance of the Surrealist techniques of free association (or games, as Breton would come to define them) such as "doodling," "splashing on a picture" and "putting . . . words together at random." For Motherwell, these methods opened the way towards making a work "without any a priori moral or aesthetic considerations . . . in the absolute conviction . . . that it's not possible, no matter what one does, not to have some kind of structure."[25]

Motherwell's analysis of Surrealist games as a model for the Abstract Expressionists points to two key factors that first emerge in Guston's painting in the 1950s. The artist discovers a process that allows him to dispense with the notion of the mistake and instead trust that he will discover a structure. Guston gives an illuminating account of the process behind his breakthrough work *White Painting, I* (1951) (Figure 3.3). The artist talks of setting himself the challenge of not stepping back from the canvas while painting the work. The strategy, as it is recalled by Guston, contains all the elements of the game: the rules are set, producing tension, risk and the unknown result:

> The desire for this direct expression finally became so strong that even the interval necessary to reach back to the palette beside me became too long; so one day I put up a large canvas and placed the palette in front of me. Then I forced myself to paint the entire work without once stepping back to look at it. I remember that I painted this in an hour.[26]

By "forcing" himself to create the painting without stepping back, Guston had imposed on himself the rules of a game; even the timing of an hour is reminiscent of the duration of a match as the painter steps back to see the final "score." This strongly prefigures statements Guston makes in the 1970s about the need "to eliminate, as much as possible, the time span between thinking and doing."[27] In both cases, the objective is to dispense with the analytical, to cease removing oneself from a work in order "to

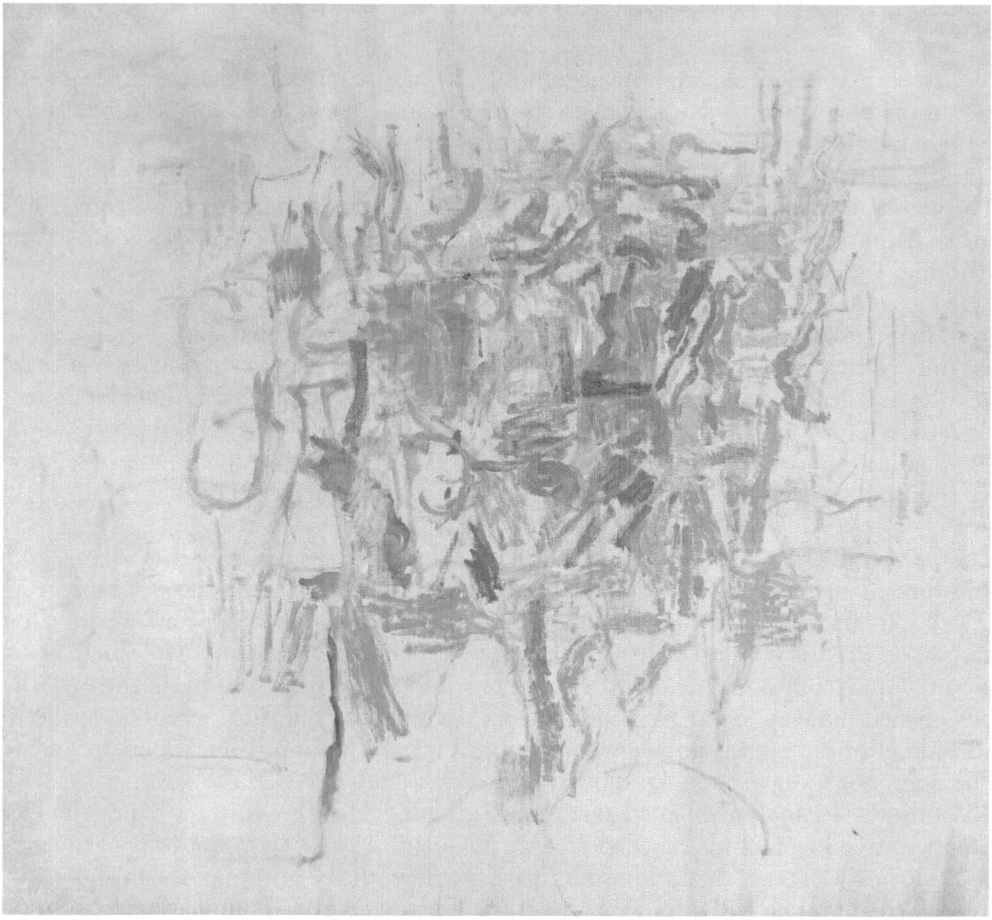

Figure 3.3 *White Painting, I*, 1951, Philip Guston, oil on canvas, 147 × 157.16 cm (57 7/8 × 61 7/8 inches). San Francisco Museum of Modern Art, T.B. Walker Foundation Fund purchase.

make judgements"[28] and instead focus on events as they unfold on the canvas. It is doubtful as to whether this "pure" state can ever be achieved without the nagging interruption of self-criticism. However, we can think of the adoption of studio tactics as functioning like the rules of a game, providing an emphasis on process rather than image, to refocus attention from inhibiting questions about how a work looks to ask instead what a strategy will *do*. This is an emphasis that would come to the fore in sculpture produced in the following decade. In 1967–8, Richard Serra would create a list of eighty-four verbs—to roll, to crease, to fold, etc.—that would act as instigators for works, to put a concern with action, material and process centre stage.

In a sense, then, we could think of the rules of the "game" of painting as being given priority over the artist's "judgements" in order to push forward through uncertainties.

It is the game, or the "verb," that provides the guiding rationale. Here Hans-Georg Gadamer's discussion of the game provides a way to take this possibility further. Gadamer emphasised that

> all playing is being played. The attraction of a game, the fascination it exerts, consists precisely in the fact that the game masters the players. Even in the case of games in which one tries to perform tasks one has set oneself, there is a risk that they will not "work."[29]

Gadamer's assertions about the all-consuming quality of the game return us to Huizinga's proposition on the role of tension as a central factor within the game, creating an immersive condition for the player.

In the rest of this chapter, I will continue to explore studio strategies employed by Guston (beyond the discipline of not stepping back from the canvas) that allow the "game" of painting to play the player. This will provide a way to explore recurring structures within Guston's painting. It will also offer a means to engage with certain statements made by Guston about his sense of absence during the painting process. Following Huizinga and Gadamer, we can view these statements as an outcome of practical methods (rather than mystical proclamations), resulting from the immersive capacity of play that pulls the player along by its own rules. Guston often liked to quote a conversation he had with John Cage, in which Guston stated,

> You go in your studio and everybody is in the studio—your friends, art writers and museums—they're all in the studio . . . and one by one they leave until you're really alone and that's what painting is. You prepare yourself and then ideally you leave.[30]

However, Guston's canvases are crowded spaces. If the artist sought a condition of absence, the structures he continued to find were far from desolate. *White Painting, I* (1951) (the work produced without stepping back from the canvas) is comprised of a dense knot of writhing forms. Indeed, throughout the 1950s, Guston's work was distinctive for compressing all activity into a cluster of reverberating mass. In the catalogue for Guston's mid-career retrospective at the Guggenheim Museum in 1962, the exhibition's curator, H.H. Arnason, provides crucial insights on the processes behind Guston's paintings of the 1950s. Arnason allows us to step beyond abstract and figurative distinctions to emphasise that, for Guston, paint was imagined as a living substance. This is described by Arnason as "the sense of his forms as living presences, composed of paint which was a living essence, and existing within the canvas which was an actual place."[31] If one recalls that, for Fink, games, whether played in company or alone, are not an isolated activity, then these canvases with their "living presences" become social spaces. The clusters and compressed formations that appear in paintings such as *Zone* (1953–4), *Beggar's Joys* (1954–5) (Figure 1.11) and *Untitled* (1955–6) (Figure 3.4) become swarming, dense multitudes within the "community of play" Fink describes. Arnason states that by 1959 Guston was "painting rapidly and continuously and increasingly felt that he was living in the painting."[32] This dramatic statement is matched by increasingly theatrical titles for the works, including *To Fellini* (1958), *Voyage* (1956), *Fable I* (1956–7), *Fable II* (1957) and *Actor* (1958). Although one can acknowledge a considerable amount of romanticism in the notion

Figure 3.4 *Untitled*, 1955–6, Philip Guston, oil on canvas, 192.7 × 182.9 cm (75 7/8 × 72 inches). Collection of Lyn and Jerry Grinstein.

of a painter "living in the painting," one could also view Guston's assertion as continuous with the artist's strategy of role-play, a method made overt in the following two decades when the artist compares painters with actors. But here, I would suggest one could go beyond the assumed persona for the painter to consider the artist role-playing the forms as they are drawn, a studio strategy in which the artist does not stand apart from the image but imagines himself placed within the scrummage of "living" paint forms. In this sense, Guston's feeling that he was "living in the painting" recalls Fink's contention that within play, the player "takes on a *role* . . . The player 'conceals' himself by means of his 'role'; in a certain measure he vanishes into it . . . he lives *in* the role."[33]

The play of forms that takes place on Guston's canvases unfolds through games of cause and effect. In the paintings *Beggar's Joys* (1954–5) and *Untitled* (1955–6), the marks are not so much arranged as acted out, as one form jostles against the next to create a restless, febrile crowd. Arnason informed us that Guston

> seeks a condition in which the work grows under his hand in terms of the manner in which forms come into existence and begin to act upon, to have an effect on other forms, which in their turn are acting upon still others.[34]

Within the context of the game (employing Huizinga's definition as contest), each mark becomes a "player" provoking a response from another mark, which then counters with a challenge. A more contest-laden reading of the relation of forms and processes (than that provided by Arnason) comes to the fore in Guston's recollection of his drawings created in 1960. Guston describes creating the work *For M (Drawing No.29)* (Figure 3.5) by beginning simply with some drops of ink. From here, lines evolved to become what Guston characterised as "fantastic form," acknowledging

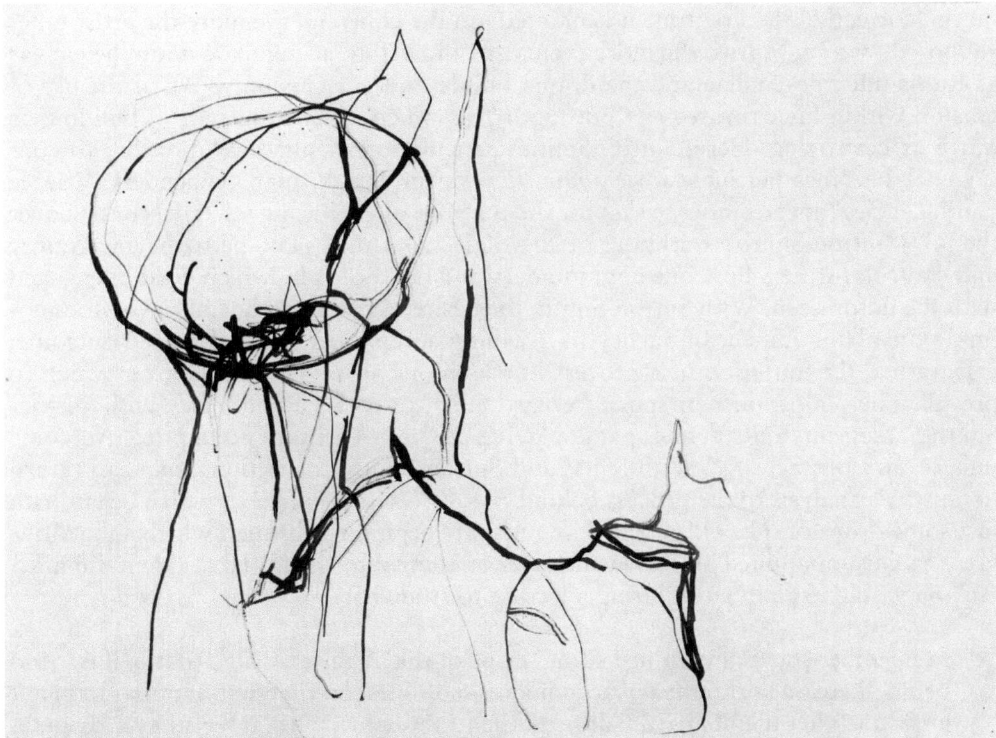

Figure 3.5 *For M*, 1960, Philip Guston, ink on paper, 45.7 × 61 cm (18 × 24 inches). Collection of A.J. Pyrch, Victoria, British Columbia.

that at this point he was becoming increasingly involved with imagery. Crucially, once again, the driving logic behind the development of the work was an imagined situation in which living forms behave and affect one another through proximity. This interaction is not a polite exchange. In Guston's imaginary, the forms push up against one another in a drama that forces a dynamic development of the elements. In a description, reminiscent of players on a pitch, Guston articulates how the "drama" unfolds on the paper through an imagined game of obstruction and attack:

> I remember being very strongly aware of forms acting on each other. Putting pressure on each other, shrinking each other, blowing each other up, or pushing each other . . . affecting each other, as if the forms were active participants in some kind of plastic drama that was going on. I . . . strove for that. In other words, if a form or a shape or a color, pattern . . . wasn't acting on another form, out it would go.[35]

Throughout the 1950s and 1960s, Guston employed methods that allowed his paintings to emerge through processes of constant change; the artist scraped forms out, moved them around the canvas, overpainted and erased. If we consider that Guston was searching for a condition of cause and effect, we can think of the "mistake" as something that is embraced. Within the context of the game, the mistake is transformed from an error, into a necessary opponent that enables, or provokes, a drama to unfold. With an emphasis on an evolving process, there is no desire to render a mark "correctly" the first time it is painted; on the contrary, the more the artist takes supposed "wrong" turns, the more events are allowed to accumulate upon the canvas as forms undergo change and the drama builds. Indeed, Guston spoke of the use of erasure within his canvases as "putting in" as much as "taking out,"[36] building as much as destroying. Here, Sutton-Smith's articulation of play's relationship to contingency becomes pertinent once again. For Sutton-Smith, play "engenders variable contingencies (uncertainties, risks) for the purpose of exercising selective control over them."[37] Sutton-Smith's outlining of the dialectic within play, between uncertainty and control, furthers how one might understand the means by which Guston engaged with the unforeseen. With Sutton-Smith, the desire to embrace the unknown does not imply the abandonment of agency to a willing acceptance of any possible outcome; it is, rather, the initiation of a process in which one seeks a challenge over which to prevail. The philosopher of sport, Bernard Suits, provides a continuity with Sutton-Smith's assertion. Suits defines game playing as "the voluntary attempt to overcome unnecessary obstacles."[38] With Suits' and Sutton-Smith's definitions, one can return to Guston's analysis of the process behind *For M (Drawing No.29)*, which began with just some drops of ink. This created an inchoate beginning through which a narrative grew as Guston applied an increasing level of control to the initial accidental marks. Guston would explain later during a lecture to students:

> I remember starting with just some drops of ink. You see where that ball is? And below there's a sort of heavy accumulation of lines. So that first happened, then it grew into that membraned ball. And then I thought, "Gee, it feels like a balloon. I'll release it from some forms down below."[39]

Drawing, as Guston describes it here, becomes a game initiated by the creation of a problem through the use of the arbitrary. The drawing unfolds as the artist works his way through the meaningless towards dynamic structuring and narrative possibility. The work then becomes a record of those actions, with all decisions embraced within the form of the work. There is no cleaning-up process; the work remains embedded within the messy process of its formation.

Guston's scraped, smeared and coagulated surfaces of the 1950s to mid-1960s emphasise mess. The jumble of forms that appear in works including *Fable I* (1956–7), *Painter I* (1959), *The Mirror* (1957) and *Dial* (1956) leave the work animated within process. In his publication *Cooking with Mud*, David Trotter puts forward an examination of "a poetics of mess, whose topic is the practice . . . of a degree of 'formlessness': the invention of complicities with and figures for contingency."[40] One could understand mess, then, as an invitation to the unknown, through a condition that implicitly offers the sense of a lack of resolution, or, in other words, an engagement with a continuing process rather than a drive towards a static object. For, unlike a game, Guston's paintings remain in a state of unresolved possibilities. In works such as *The Room* (1954–5) and *Beggar's Joys* (1954–5), there is no movement from tension to resolution that Huizinga outlines as structuring the course of a game. Instead, the works are held in a state of agitation, as if we are caught in the midst of a drama.

While Guston's process-led paintings clearly exist within the wider context of Abstract Expressionism, there is a significant point of emphasis that continues to recur in Guston's statements through the transition from abstract to figurative painting. This revolves around the position of the painter in relation to his work. As previously quoted, as early as 1962, Arnason informs us that Guston is imagining forms that "act upon, to have an effect on other forms, which in their turn are acting upon still others." Significantly, Arnason allows us to view the forms as acting upon *each other*. This returns us to the argument that opened this section of the chapter, in which I argued Fink's concept of play provides a means to regard the use of contingency as an engagement with *multiplicity*, rendering Guston's paintings social sites, rather than expressionistic outpourings of self. This is not to fail to acknowledge that the work is clearly ultimately an expression of subjectivity. It is, rather, that Fink provides a way to re-orientate the guiding narrative behind the work. The engagement with contingency (or a messy process) can then be seen primarily as a means to animate form. In 1978, during a lecture to students, Guston read the following from one of his letters, written to the poet and novelist Ross Feld:

> Perhaps the image being presented is really a *natural* one. And I have learned a primary lesson after traversing a vast circle of thoughts and impulses . . . if forms are to be represented in a painting, this is the way they would behave and affect one another.[41]

Written at a time when Guston's canvases were now crowded with heads, shoes, arms, legs and "crapola" (as the artist would describe it), Guston's "primary lesson" is nevertheless still remarkably consistent with his concerns of the 1950s and early 1960s. The artist once again seeks a condition in which the *forms* "behave and affect one another." In effect, the painting now clearly declares itself to be driven by a process in which an imagined drama is populated by the "they" of the forms rather than the expressionistic gestures of the artist. This is not to deny the increasingly biographical nature of Guston's late work; indeed, in acknowledging the artist's use of role-play, one can consider the painter absorbed within his collection of forms. The emphasis,

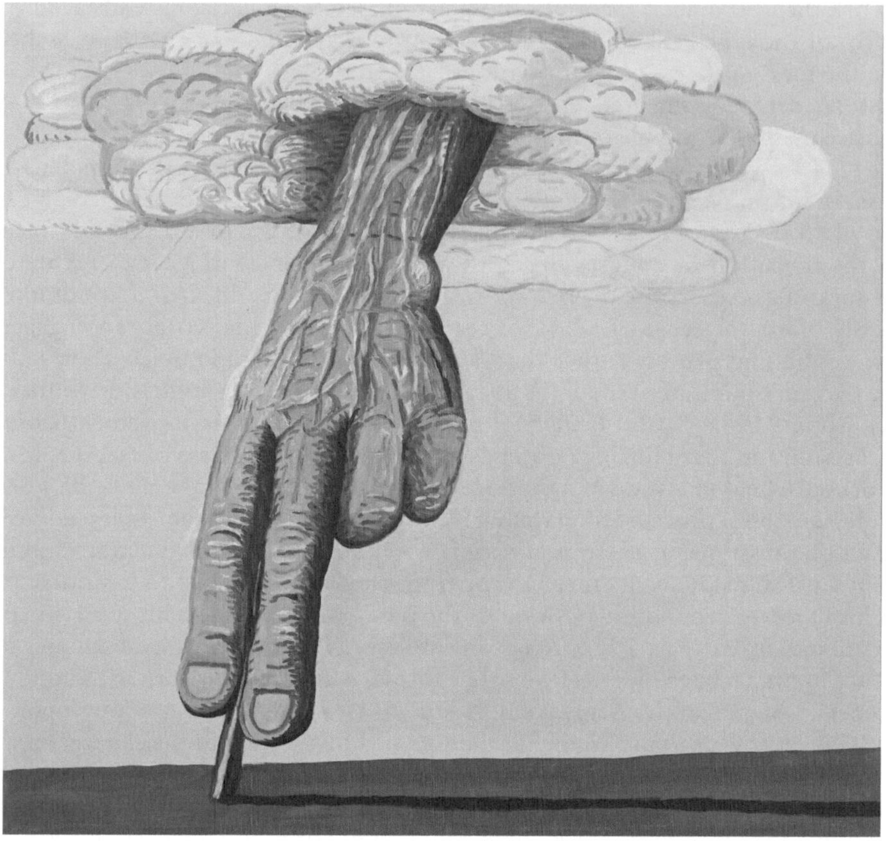

Figure 3.6 The Line, 1978, Philip Guston, oil on canvas, 180.3 × 186.1 cm (71 × 73.3 inches).

then, is on the canvas as an immersive site that operates as a field of reality, or "parallel world," as Guston was to describe it, in which the forms are rendered "as if" they have the power to affect each other. In a sense, the painter casts himself in a god-like role as the creator, bestowing forms with independence and sentience. This is a self-characterisation Guston would address and mock in the painting *The Line* (1978) (Figure 3.6), in which a varicose-ridden hand reaches out from a cloud to scrape a charcoal line across a cadmium-red ground.

Building Up and Knocking Down

> A pile of junk between two telephone poles. The itch to kick it, disperse it.[42]

In Guston's paintings of the 1970s, compressed clusters of mass recur once again. However, here they take shape as shoes, legs, heads and even cherries, piling together the "painter's forms" into a seemingly infinite series of dramas. The contests that take place on the canvas now combined process with narrative form. The jostling clusters of marks that appeared in paintings such as *Beggar's Joys* (1954–5) (Figure 1.11) and *Untitled* (1955–6) (Figure 3.4) prefigure works including *Aegean II* (1977) (Figure 3.2), *Red Sky* (1978) and *Plain* (1979): paintings in which Guston's forms emerge from the abstract to come together in battle. By this time, Guston had denounced abstract painting as "ridiculous," reasoning that "the rules of the game are drawn too quickly and they begin with where you should finish up."[43] Significantly, in Guston's characterisation of the creative process, the term contest has become interchangeable with the "game." Guston's dramatic rejection of abstraction for an engagement with the object quality of the everyday in many ways provides a parallel with contemporary criticisms of Huizinga. For Huizinga, play distinguished itself from the everyday in its apartness, or one might say *abstraction*, from the immediacies of its environment. He contends that "play is distinct from 'ordinary' life both as to locality and duration. This is the third main characteristic of play: its secludedness, its limitedness."[44]

Recent scholarship has found Huizinga's idealised view of play greatly problematic. For the political historian Jason Edwards, play is rooted in the material and economic conditions of its environment, and thus an activity that draws within it the dynamics of the social:

> What constitutes play and the character and role of playful activity is given not by a set of formal characteristics but what I have referred to as the economy of agonism, that is, the economic, social, and political relations and space through and in which play takes place.[45]

While Edwards acknowledges that Huizinga importantly emphasised that play is not simply "a contest *for* something" but may also be "a representation *of* something"[46] that is socially meaningful to the player, for Edwards, Huizinga nevertheless undermines the value of play by separating it from ordinary life: "Despite himself, Huizinga devalues play in rendering it a mere reflection (or abstraction) of an immutable and unquestionable reality, the realm of seriousness from which play is no more than a break or relief."[47] In arguing with Huizinga's conclusions as to the "autonomy" of play, Edwards provides a significant connection with Rosenberg's remarkably insightful article "Liberation from Detachment." The essay championed Guston's then controversial paintings of the Ku Klux Klan. Written in response to Guston's now legendary 1970 exhibition at the Marlborough Gallery—the show that first unleashed Guston's late figurative work on the New York art world—Rosenberg read the works not simply as political statements on the violence and brutality of the political climate, but more specifically as damning indictments of Abstract art's *separation* from the social conditions of its time. Through Guston's desire to return to objects, or "tangibilia," the artist's wrestling forms that first appear in *White Painting I* (1951) could reach beyond the paint and the canvas to engage with the substance of their material and social environment. In effect, Guston began to play a more complex game.

Guston characterised the return to figuration as being forcefully motivated by a lack of contact with "the thickness of things," declaring, "I wanted things to come from things, the graining of wood, the feeling of stone, the corruption of the world, the violence in the world."[48] Here, Guston provides a potent equation, connecting an involvement with the "thickness of things" to an engagement with the material of one's social context, and ultimately to conflict and the abuse of power. "Thickness," then, is an accumulation of layers, piling up material, associations, conflict and meaning. Now, Guston's forms battle and buffet not only one another but also the multiplicity of potentially contradictory meanings as the paintings reach out to the world beyond. An earlier critic of Huizinga, Robert Anchor, allows us to further how one might understand Guston's "thick"ened use of play processes. Anchor draws on the writing of Fink when he asserts that play "always has to do with real objects, which fantasy transforms into play objects."[49] He quotes Fink's contention that

> the play world is not suspended in a purely ideal world. It always has a real setting, and yet it is never a real thing among other real things, although it has an absolute need of real things as a point of departure.[50]

Guston's return to "things" had begun simply, with an engagement with the immediacy of his surroundings, drawing hundreds of images of his shoes, his books, hands, canvas stretchers and lumps of wood. However, by the 1970s, his canvases rapidly became vortexes, drawing in the substance of the everyday as play material with which to create epic dramas and images of eternal conflict that not only reflected on the wider political context, but also increasingly became the means to create intensely personal images of a painter battling with his own failing health as he faced his own mortality.

If in Abstract art "the rules of the game are drawn too quickly," for Guston the involvement with objects created a process in which tension was heightened as forms moved through changing structures and associations during the painting process to reach unforeseen sets of relationships, furthering the key element of the game, the unknown outcome. Guston declared that

> the engagement of a subject . . . with tangibilia and with pressures together with plastic pressures . . . that engagement which is the most hair raising . . . impossible and anxiety ridden engagement you can think of, produces the most unpredictable structures.[51]

However, if Guston was seeking the unpredictable structure, he was also able to acknowledge a great deal of repetition and continuity. In conversation with Clark Coolidge in 1972, Guston recognises the pile-up as the persistent, distinctive structure in his painting. We can see this structure repeated in countless works, including *Ancient Wall* (1976), *Summer* (1980) (Figure 3.7), *Cabal* (1977) and *Pile Up* (1980) (Figure 3.8); we are also able to note the connection to the compressed formations that appear in Guston's paintings of the 1950s. Guston describes how his forms seem caught in a cycle, crowding together into a cluster and then dispersing. With this cyclical process, Guston dispenses with the finality of a painting to imagine a continuing process in which the forms are drawn together and then pull apart, moving through his works as a continuous landscape. It is particularly striking how Guston speaks

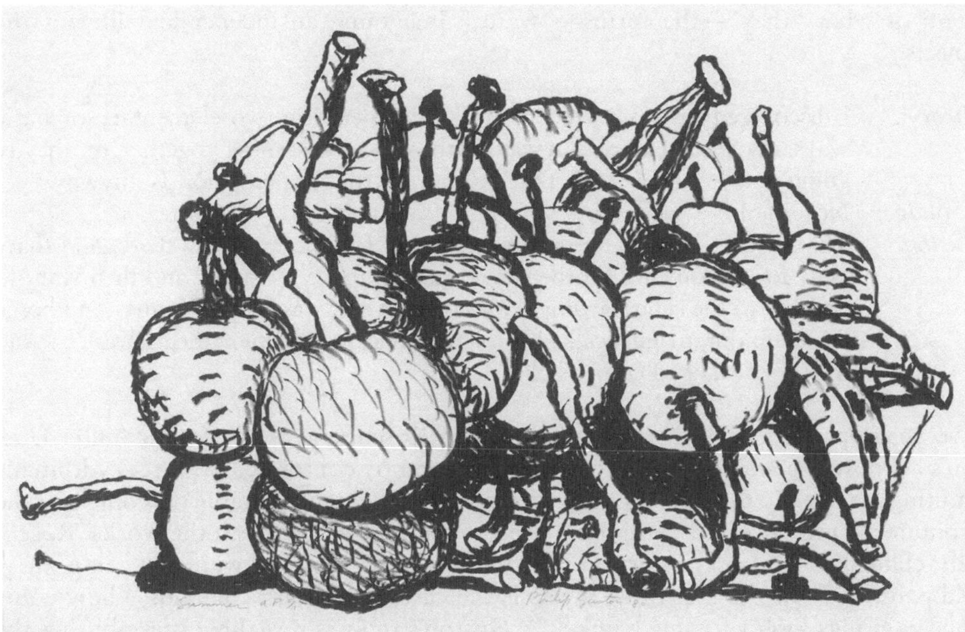

Figure 3.7 Summer, 1980, Philip Guston, lithograph, sheet: 51.4 cm × 78.1 cm (20 ¼ × 30 ¾ inches). Image courtesy of The Estate of Philip Guston. © The Estate of Philip Guston.

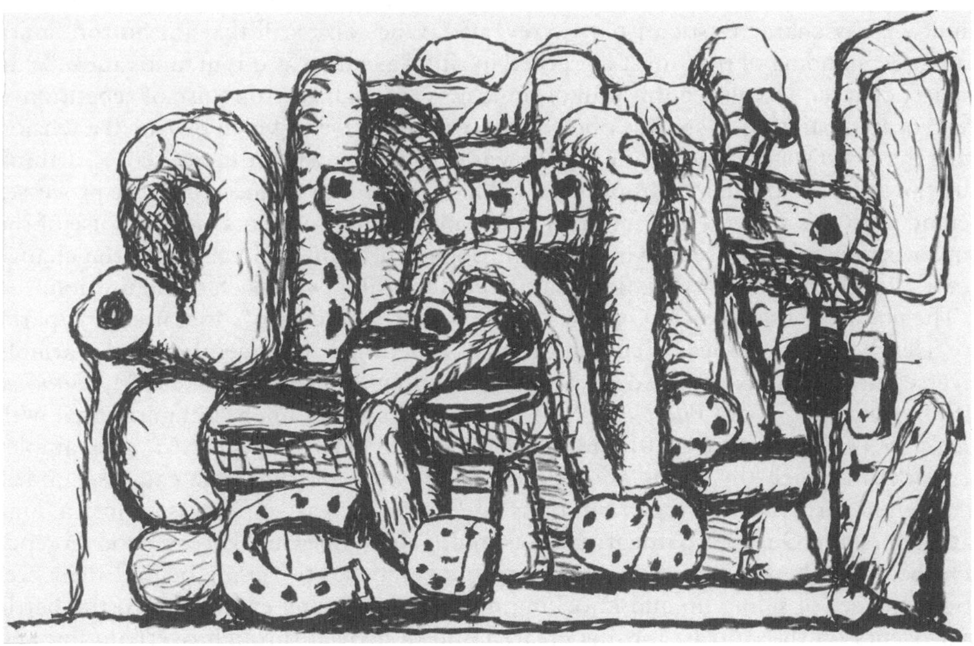

Figure 3.8 Pile Up, 1980, Philip Guston, lithograph, sheet: 50.2 × 75.6 cm (19 ¾ × 29 ¾ inches). Image courtesy of The Estate of Philip Guston. © The Estate of Philip Guston.

again of what "they"—the forms—"want," imagining an independent life for the objects.

Guston: I discovered over a period of time that there are two elementary or basic ways my forms work anyway. Either they're coming together or they're going apart. And I think that's about all that composition is anyway.

Coolidge: Never still.

Guston: That's right. They seem to want to clump together and stay there, and that's okay for a moment. But then they want to move apart . . . and then want to go back to the centre again, like a control centre, as if that's home. And home lets them out, magnetically, for a little while, just to enjoy themselves . . . And then they want to come back.[52]

Two years later, in 1974, in conversation with Rosenberg, we again encounter Guston's acknowledgement of the two central, apparently contradictory, forces within his painting, enacted in the pull between the desire for the unpredictable outcome and the pronounced presence of a continuing process that unfolds through the works. Rosenberg challenges Guston's assertion that with each painting he wants to begin anew and paint as if for the first time. If this is the case, Rosenberg contends, "how come your paintings look very much alike?"[53] Guston's reply is revealing; it establishes the distinction between the experience of being immersed within a process—full of uncertainties, unforeseen possibilities and potential failure—and the experience of standing back to observe the final work. Guston describes how during the process he feels he is "making a leap, but in truth you may be only, say, an inchworm."[54] However, in this apparent contradiction between the desire for the unforeseen and the presence of continuity, a key characteristic of play is revealed. One can recall that for Sutton-Smith "an understanding of play must be rooted in ritual as much as it is in innovation."[55] In the last chapter, I explored this pull of opposites through Guston's use of repetition—the repeated painting of specific objects, particularly shoes—which provided a tension with the artist's stated desire to engage with the unknown. In many senses, I think one can see the repeated "clump[ing] together" of form as connected to the processes behind Guston's shoes. The continuity between paintings presents Guston's use of the improvisatory as a process that occurs through repetition and variation, the change not a "leap," then, but a variation that gathers meaning with each configuration.

The paintings that present Guston's forms as either a "clump" or scattered "apart" are clearly narrative-heavy configurations, generating innumerable and variable diverse meanings, exemplified by works including *Ancient Wall* (1976), *Summer* (1980) (Figure 3.7) and *Pile Up* (1980) (as examples of clumped configurations) with *Flatlands* (1970) (Figure 2.20) and *Painter's Table* (1973) (Figure 1.6) (as examples of works in which the forms are separated). However, I think one can also understand these structures as representations of Guston's creative processes. Just as one can understand Guston's battlegrounds as multivalent, one can also see a convergence here between the subject of Guston's paintings and the processes behind their creation. Images of piling up and knocking down recur, giving expression to the battle that occurs on the canvas; form is created and destroyed through overpainting and rubbing out, layering up and scraping back. These creative processes can in turn can become metaphors for the dynamics of life—cycles of birth and death, growth and ageing, recombination and dissolution. In 1978, Guston wrote to his friend, the poet

Ross Feld, of finishing a painting that brings together contradictory forces in a contest between knowing and not knowing, building and destruction:

> a brick wall, me & Musa behind it. In *front* of the wall, a sort of scrimmage is taking place—arms, discs, etc., the abstract forces are trying to pile themselves up into a permanent mound—BUT—a hammer looming in from the top-side is definitely hitting this structure, making it seem as if it is crumbling, collapsing. Added to all of this . . . a merry mix-up of buzzing insects . . . a happy commotion. They, too, seem to be adding . . . to the general dismantling of the piled-up structure. It is a painting of crumbling—of dissolution.[56]

In Guston's extraordinarily vivid description, the artist's desire for a contest within the painting process clearly finds a subject in the struggle within life processes and both his and his wife's rapidly failing health. However, this passage can also be read as a multi-layered metaphor for the opposing dynamics within Guston's creative processes. It draws attention to the importance of destruction; through the "abstract forces" that "pile themselves up" and the "happy commotion . . . dismantling," we are able to see that, for Guston, knocking down structures was as generative as building. Repeatedly, we encounter metaphors for processes that push in opposite directions—that destroy as they build. In *The Door* (1976) (Figure 3.9), an immense pile of Guston's

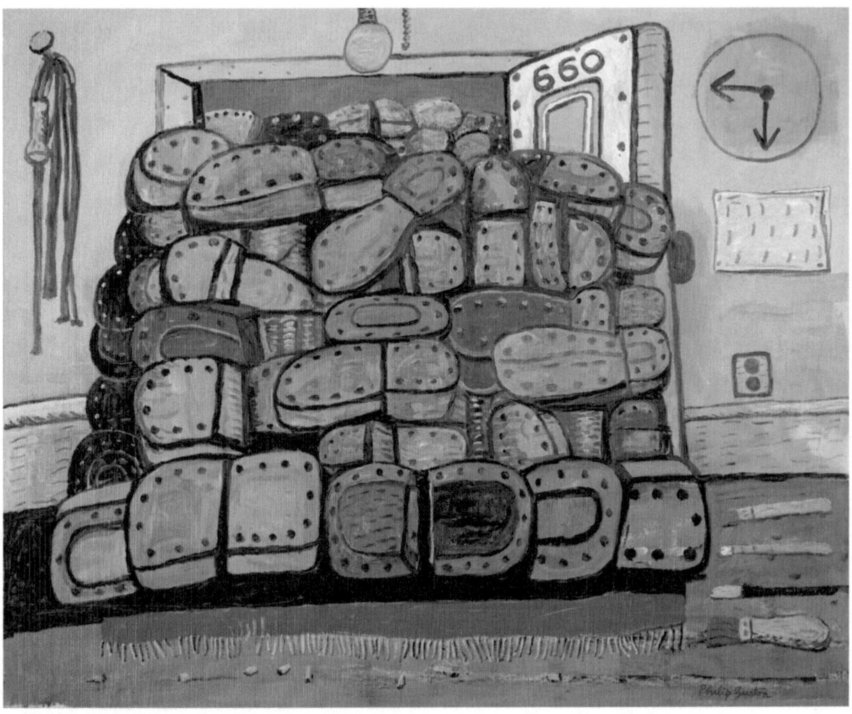

Figure 3.9 *The Door*, 1976, Philip Guston, oil on canvas, 205.7 × 243.8 cm (81 × 96 inches).

shoes has forced its way through a door that bears the number of Guston's own house, 660. High on the wall, above this avalanche of shoes, there hangs a whip, waiting as if ready to disperse the forms. Among Guston's studio notes—jottings for ideas for paintings made between 1970 and 1978—Guston had written of "a pile of junk between two telephone poles. The itch to kick it, disperse it."[57] We are continually met with the sense that structures are provisional, that form has only temporarily found a place to rest before it is "kicked" again—set off within a new cycle of recombination to form fresh relationships.

In *Red Sea* (1975), one of Guston's deluge works, subject and process combine in a re-enactment of biblical destruction. We encounter an image of legs and shoes sinking beneath red waves, an image that reflected the process by which Guston created the painting, sinking forms underneath layer upon layer of paint. Once again, processes of building and destruction, harnessed on the canvas, lead to a painting that for Guston could not have been planned out in advance, as he told Jan Butterfield in 1979: "in my triptych from 1975, the *Red Sea*. . . . Do you know how many paintings are under each one? About twenty paintings! . . . in order to get the fixation that 'feels right.' Well, I couldn't begin with that!"[58] Guston's paintings and statements frequently show an extraordinarily gleeful engagement with images of violence and destruction such as that expressed to Butterfield. Within the context of play, this becomes an important reminder of the way in which culturally we often reduce play to an activity that is light and carefree and risk marginalising it as a consequence. Here, Fink's emphasis on the "worldly," all-encompassing nature of play becomes relevant:

> the fact that play is also "worldly" . . . hardly requires closer specification and demonstration. It is thoroughly attuned by an elementary passion for life . . . a passion that is more than delight in what is delightful, useful, enjoyable, a passion for the exuberance of life that can still include in itself what is dire, evil, and horrible, as the pleasure in the play of tragedy does.[59]

Fink presents play as an activity that has the potential to relish an engagement with the full breadth of life's manifestations. One can recall here Guston's statements on Renaissance frescoes, perceiving images of heaven dull while the images of hell are, for Guston, when the painter really delights in the painting process. Just as the subject of hell allowed for dynamic structures, one can also consider processes of destruction as allowing for dynamic change and reconfiguration on the canvas. And destruction as subject matter or guiding narrative can also become a means to renew, a way to begin the process again. It is possible, then, to see each work as formulated in reaction to the last. In this sense, the new work becomes an argument, or at least a dialogue, with the previous image. During a lecture in 1973, Guston described painting the work *The Deluge* (1969) (Figure 3.10). The painter again takes on a god-like role and imagines destroying the landscape of forms he had been creating in previous works, a landscape inhabited by his hooded figures committing acts of butchery. As if in biblical judgement, Guston declared, "I sort of sank the whole world, like it was doomed."[60] In the painting, the tops of a scattering of objects can be seen peering above an immense black sea, from which a single bug crawls free. However, this appears to be not just a painting *of* a deluge, but a work that acted out a flooding and destruction of its own forms. The sea that fills two-thirds of the painting is a muddy combination of colours, clearly created when black was painted wet on wet over red, pink and white. One can

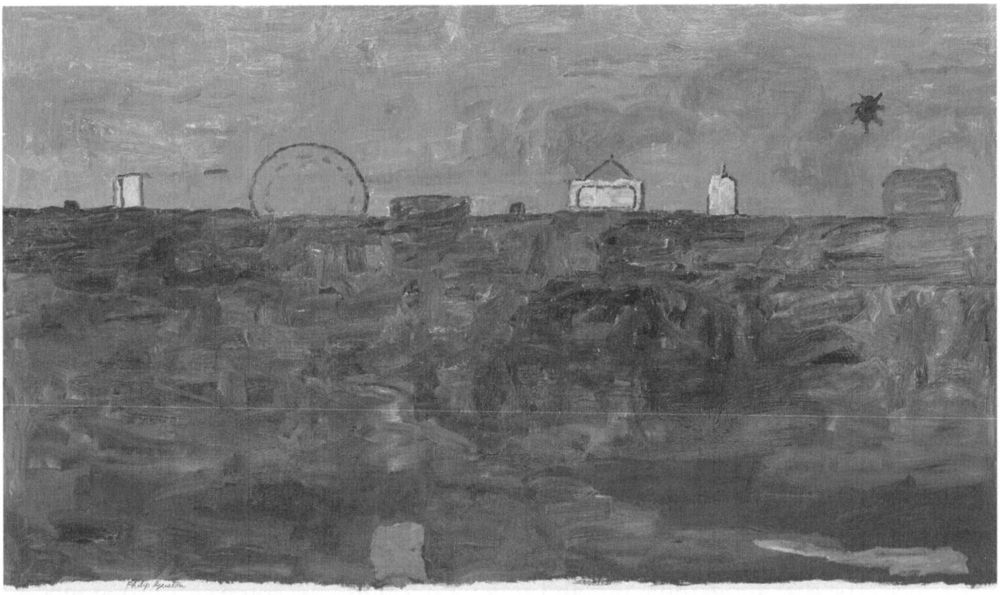

Figure 3.10 *The Deluge*, 1969, Philip Guston, oil on canvas, 195.6 × 325.1 cm (77 × 128 inches). Museum of Fine Arts, Boston. Bequest of Musa Guston 1992.509.

still see cadmium red and pink appearing beneath exuberantly painted black waves of brushstrokes that become purple patches where they "sank" another white or pink form. This work was the first in what would become a series of deluge works created throughout the 1970s.

After *The Deluge* (1969) came *Flatlands* (1970) (Figure 2.20). The work was painted uninterrupted, in one rush of activity, just as *White Painting, I* (Figure 3.3) had been almost twenty years previously.[61] However, unlike *White Painting, I*, Guston did not paint the work from one fixed position. He began the painting on the right side of the canvas, with a tight bunch of forms, and then moved out across to the left of the canvas in one burst of painting. This was again a process of discovery, to see what structure would emerge from the parameters of the "game." The physicality and the rule-setting once again give the painting a sporting element. Indeed, we are able to observe the physicality of the process embedded within the form and structure of the work. There appears to be a limited amount of overpainting. And where the fixed painting position for *White Painting, I* had produced a tightly knotted cluster of marks, we see Guston's forms unfurl in *Flatlands*, scattering out as he moved across the canvas. One can recall that a friend had told Guston that "it looks like you put all forms, all the props, in a paper bag and then spilled it out."[62] There is a very real sense in which Guston's process mirrored that action. Following the destruction of *The Deluge*, here were Guston's forms, ready to take their place in new conflicts.

Guston would frequently speak of the importance of destroying paintings. According to Guston, the paintings he destroyed were as meaningful to him as those he preserved, or even that a work that had been destroyed some years ago would reappear in a new painting. For Guston, there was "something deathlike about a painting finished"; indeed, he states that this sense of conclusion could, in itself, lead him to destroy a work.[63] I think this allows us to consider destruction once again as a means to place the creative emphasis on the "living" continuity of the process rather than the finality of the artwork. In fact, Guston's desire for a painting process that produced a contest could lead him to mistrust a painting when it developed with ease, and this in itself could provoke the painter to destroy a work. In Michael Blackwood's documentary *Philip Guston: A Life Lived*, Guston is filmed painting a work rapidly in front of the camera. When the film crew return the following day, they find Guston has erased the entire painting. Guston declared his final frustration with the work came from the sense that it was just a series of "additions." In an interview with Mark Stevens in 1980, we gain a further sense of the painter's desire for a process in which the work seems to answer back, to push against the painter's "additions":

> You want to feel resistance. Or I want to. All my pictures must be fought for. Lots of overpainting and rubbing out. You want to have lived it. The complicated problem is when you do a painting that you think looks good . . . you wake up in an hour convinced that you're kidding yourself. You haven't lived it yet. So . . . you scrape the whole thing out and stay with it until . . . you feel transparent.[64]

In Guston's need for a painting that is "fought for," one clearly hears echoes of the mythical narratives that surround Abstract Expressionism. The notion of a "struggle" played out on the canvas, was a trope the following generation of painters were keen to reject, finding the tales of existential angst laid bare self-indulgent and mannered; the artist's "torment" was a subject ripe for mockery. However, I think Guston presents a different way to frame the "fight" for a painting that allows us to extend how one might think of the contest within the context of game playing. The drama unfolding on the canvas is one that brings life to form as events accumulate, rather than the "raw" expression of the artist's emotional torment served up for a hungry public.

However, it is important to emphasise that Guston's work does not follow one pattern; one does not find evidence of overpainting and erasure in every painting; one cannot consider every work after 1947 a contest with the unknown. Guston himself acknowledged that, with his return to figuration, some paintings were quite rigorously rehearsed through drawing before he put paint to canvas. Breaking your own rules and working in a variety of ways needs to be considered as much a part of play as setting the unknown as a pre-requisite. Without this possibility for variation, a desire for the unforeseen can become self-contradictory, an ideal of its own that can paradoxically produce the predictable or even fall into an aesthetic of spontaneity. As Guston himself declared, "I do both. It's satisfying to me to know that I can have this range."[65]

Eduardo Paolozzi: "Construct, Tack, Destroy and Recombine"[66]

In 1956, Paolozzi developed a sculptural process that began with the creation of a "GRAMMAR OF FORMS."[67] This involved bringing together a collection of junk and detritus, which was then pressed into clay to leave impressions, over which Paolozzi would pour molten wax. When cold, the wax formed a skin rich in activity that could be cut into sections to create what the artist described as "sheets of an ALPHABET OF ELEMENTS awaiting assembly (Figure 3.11)."[68] These sheets

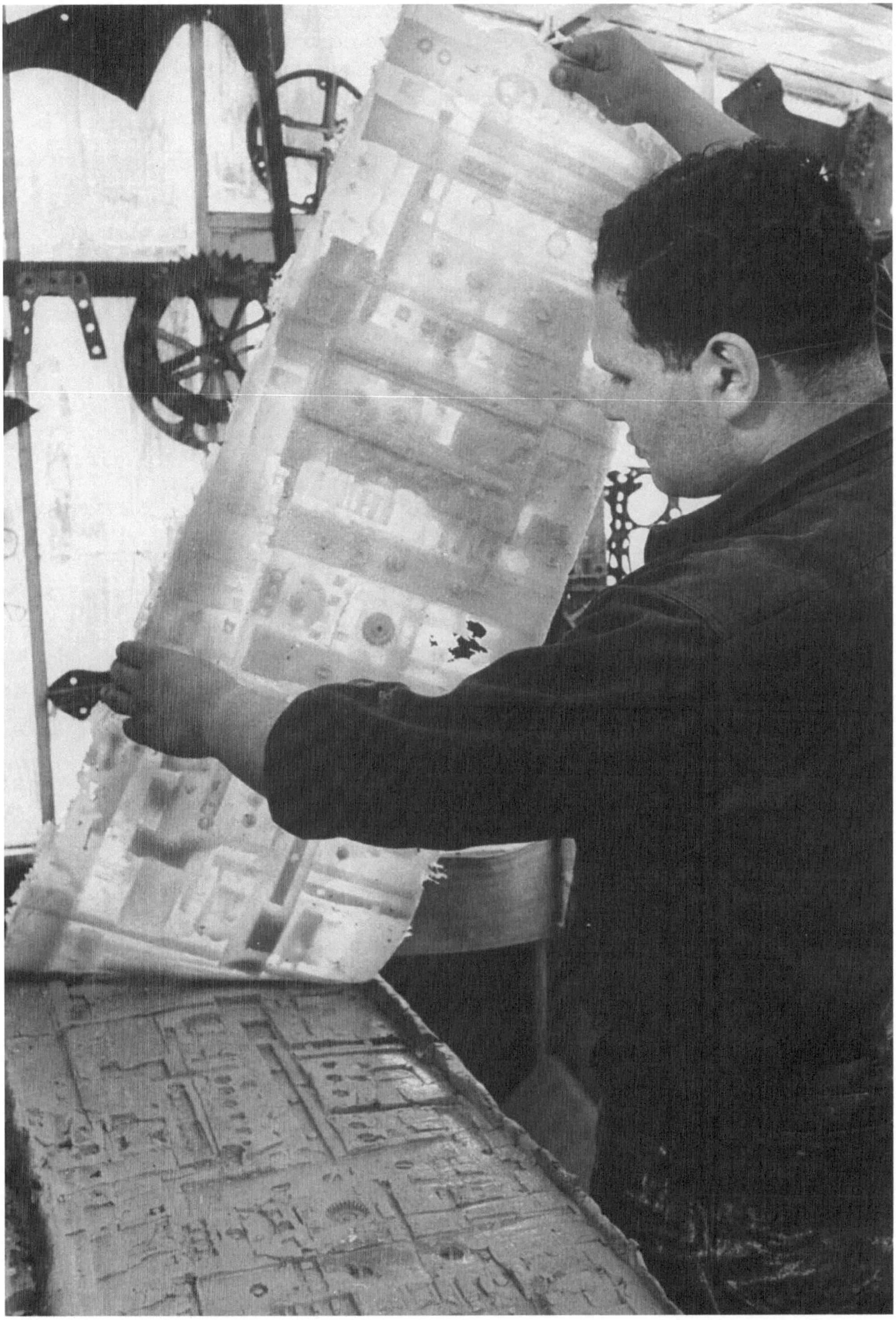

Figure 3.11 Photograph for a 1959 *Life* magazine article on Eduardo Paolozzi.

could then be burnt, bent, twisted, cut, modelled and moulded. The resulting forms were assembled into unwieldy, precarious, asymmetric structures to create figures that fused organic and mechanical realms, such as *The King* (c. 1955–8) (Figure 3.12) and *The Philosopher* (1957) (Figure 3.15). The final structures were then cast into bronze.

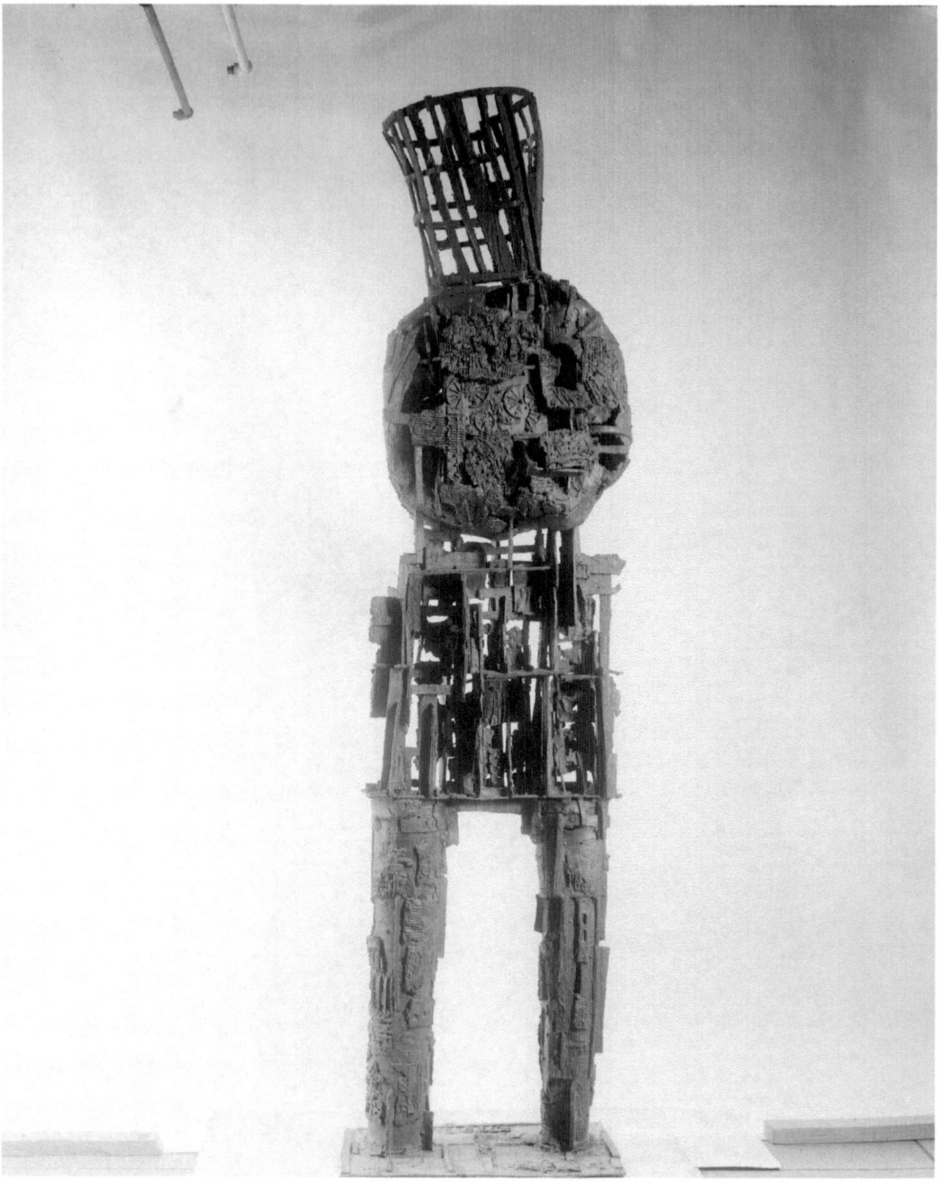

Figure 3.12 *The King* (c. 1956–8), Eduardo Paolozzi, bronze, 268.6 × 61.0 cm, Yale University Art Gallery.

Daniel Herrmann has observed that Paolozzi's 1950s sculptures employed found objects in a way that differed distinctly from other "junk" sculptors of the time, such as Richard Stankiewicz or César.[69] While Stankiewicz and César's sculptures were formed directly from objects that had been welded together, Paolozzi's collections of miscellany had gone through a process of transformation to be left as cast impressions. We can see this casting process as providing a means to re-use and recombine the "alphabet of elements," connecting the process to the methods behind Paolozzi's pre-existing print work, while also predicting the part-by-part construction of the "kit of forms" used repeatedly to create the aluminium sculpture of the 1960s. In the last chapter, I proposed that Paolozzi's enduring obsession with toy kits provides a way to read the artist's approach to printmaking and informs the methods behind his sculpture of the 1960s. While we can see the logic of the toy kit continuing through Paolozzi's bronze sculpture of the 1950s, in this chapter I contend that the artist's use of junk can also be seen as an engagement with a play material with a very particular socio-historical relevance.

Paolozzi provided an extensive list of the found material used to create his figures; while the list includes actual toys, such as a "rubber dragon" and a "toy camera," it is the detritus, such as a "broken comb," "parts of a radio," "natural objects" and "various unidentified found objects," that points towards the use of a play material that is rooted in the specific material conditions of its time.[70] In a continuation of his childhood love of collecting, Paolozzi began collecting junk and debris from bombsites in the East End of London with the photographer Nigel Henderson (with whom Paolozzi was later to form the commercial printing company Hammer Prints). Henderson and his wife, the anthropologist Judith Stephen, lived in the East End from 1945 to 1954 while Stephen conducted a sociological study in Bethnal Green. Henderson described how he created photograms from his bombsite finds: "All sorts of things had got to go down on paper, many lugged back from those gold-mines of semi-transmuted things like bomb-sites."[71] In many senses, Paolozzi's bronze figures were a sculptural equivalent of Henderson's photograms, with their surfaces printed with the shadow of the bombsite, providing a seemingly unlikely connection to the playground.

From out of the ruins, children had discovered in bombsites an extraordinary opportunity for play. In Denmark, the revolutionary landscape architect Carl Theodor Sørensen had observed children playing on bombsites and responded with the creation of junk playgrounds, the first built in Emdrup in 1943. In the post-war era, the concept was imported to Britain by Lady Allen of Hurtwood, who proposed that bombsites and wastelands be formalised into places where children could find free expression (Figure 3.13). Judith Stephen's research was sponsored by the sociologist J.L. Peterson, who played an instrumental role in the introduction of the junk playground movement to England. And beyond the photograms created with bombsite debris, Henderson's photography displays a recurring interest in children's street play. The photographer had even written to his wife during the war of "the wish to retain the 'innocent eye' of childhood, the unblinking, guileless, not self-deceived record of an eye not distorted by extraneous associations of false attitudes."[72] I think it is possible to see the processes, materials and structures within Paolozzi's sculpture created between 1956 and 1959 as sharing Henderson's concerns, revealing a landscape of the bombsite as junk playground. Indeed, in his "Notes from a Lecture at the Institute of

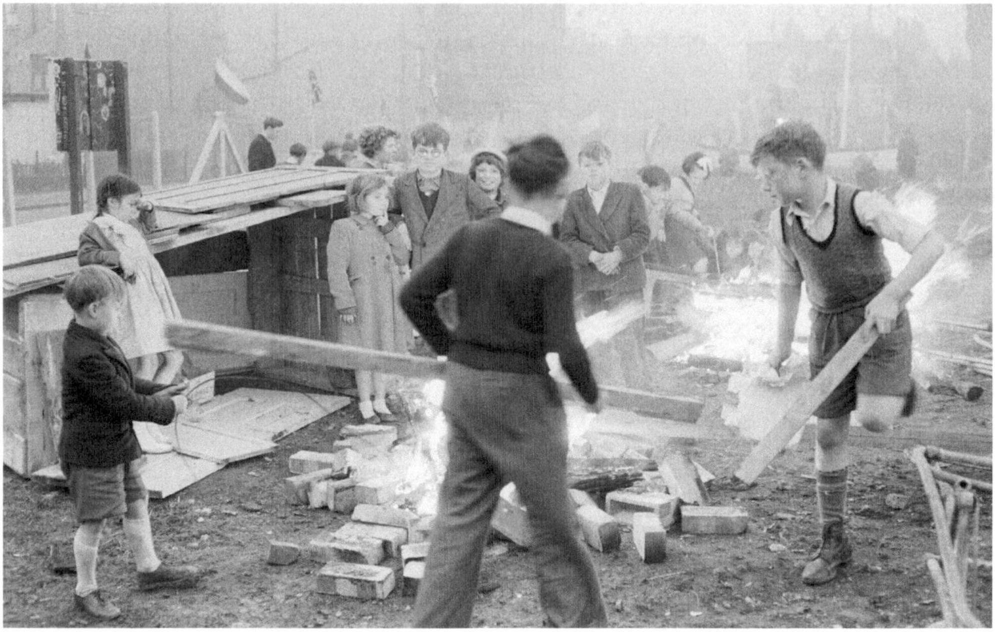

Figure 3.13 Children playing with fires, Lollard Street Adventure Playground, Lambeth, London, 1955.

Photographer: Brian Brake. Image courtesy of Museum of New Zealand Te Papa Tongarewa.

Contemporary Arts" (1958), Paolozzi invites us to see his bronze figures as a meeting point between battlefield and playground:

> My preoccupation or obsession with metamorphosis of the figure:
>
> That is a CRACKED COLUMN resembling a PETRIFIED TOWER . . .
>
> This is what I have in mind:
>
> The Clock AS A TOY
> Sites for imaginary ball games
> . . . Useful non useful Toyclock Toy Man
> . . . A fantastic project for a playground
> A Historical playground for fantastic people
> A Battlefield of ideas.[73]

Ben Highmore has described how, in the post-war era, the image of bombsite as playground became an area of contested politics. While for some the sight of children playing on wasteland was a sign of moral corruption and a breakdown in social order, for others it offered a symbol of hope, resilience, salvation and renewal in the face of death and destruction. Highmore provides a potent image of an equivalence drawn between the wildness of the bombsite and the "wild-nature of the child."[74] For advocates of the junk playground, or adventure playground as it was later termed, the site provided a space where children's destructive impulses could be directed through play, in the hope that they would dissipate, saving society from further future catastrophe.

However, Paolozzi provides a way for us to move through the polarities presented by these debates on morality that claimed the playground as a site for social reform. By focusing on the materials, processes and structures found in Paolozzi's bronzes, we are able to reflect on the play processes presented by the junk playground. Paolozzi, like Guston, repeatedly emphasised destruction as a vital productive force within his creativity. The artists allow one to view destruction within play as an element harnessed as part of the creative process, rather than simply a force of social ill that requires neutralising. Similarly, analyses of the opportunities for play provided by the bombsite and the junk playground provide a means to reflect on the processes behind Paolozzi's bronze figures and the structures that emerge. With an emphasis on studio methods, one can destabilise the symbolic meaning of Paolozzi's figures, and return to a focus on what Lichtenstein and Schregenberger describe as "the 'as found" as "a matter of process" that "cannot be achieved with a formal reductionism as a goal."[75]

In the notes for his 1958 lecture, Paolozzi goes on to provide key insights into his working methods in his "description of the creative process." Here, we understand how Paolozzi's structures are formed with elements that are seen as containing a dynamic of destruction and construction. "Design sheets"—which refer to Paolozzi's wax sheets formed over the impressions of collected junk—are described as a "broken fragment or a point of a construction (figure)."[76] Reflecting on the 1950s and their coining of the term "as found," the Smithsons provide a context for the fragments and detritus that populated Paolozzi's encrusted figures. For the Smithsons, there was

> an openness as to how prosaic "things" could re-energise our inventive activity. A confronting recognition of what the postwar world actually was like. In a society that had nothing. You reached for what there was, previously unthought things . . . how the new could re-energise the existing fabric.[77]

There is a convergence here between the Smithsons' definitions of the as found, their emphasis on renewal and what Roy Kozlovsky, in his valuable publication *The Architectures of Childhood: Children, Modern Architecture and Reconstruction in Postwar England*, has described as the "English discourse of play and ruins, in which violence is redeemed by the regenerative play of children."[78] We can see Paolozzi's junk sculptures, or "fantastic project[s] for a playground," as having grown out of this landscape. However, the battered surfaces and asymmetric structures of the bronze figures, with their holes and cavities, appear to propose that rebuilding and regeneration cannot simply seek to put the pieces back together. As children's play had discovered, the sculptures present a desire to embrace the opportunity for alternative processes and structures presented by the bombsite, to find forms that can engage with the messy contingency of the world.

Connections between the artist's studio and the junk playground were established at its very inception. Kozlovsky informs us that the use of junk as play material was not entirely due to wartime scarcity; Emdrup's first play leader, John Bertelsen, consciously aligned the playground with avant-garde anti-art movements such as Art Brut, Cobra and the Independent Group.[79] Indeed, Paolozzi, reflecting on his late 1950s sculpture in an interview in 1966, stated that "I was trying to make a kind of anti-art object . . . really trying to make something which looked horrible."[80] However, as with the Meccano kit, it is possible to look beyond aesthetic comparisons, to examine a confluence between Paolozzi's processes and those presented by the junk playground.

In Paolozzi's lecture notes from 1958, we go on to learn that Paolozzi chose objects that were "useful in flexibility & a known range of possibilities."[81] In 1994, in an interview with Frank Whitford, Paolozzi again emphasised "flexibility" as central to the working processes behind the sculptures created between 1956 and 1959: "It was kind of collage, there was a lot of sticking and cutting and immense flexibility."[82] Once again, it was the possibility for change and the unforeseen that appealed to Paolozzi about a collage process. And it is here again that one encounters the landscape of play. For Lady Allen, the adequacy of playground provision depended on its *flexibility*—on the amount to which children could change and manipulate the environment, declaring in 1953 that "the uses to which the playground as a whole are put must be flexible and be capable of being altered."[83] In her 1968 publication, *Planning for Play*, Lady Allen noted that children often rejected purpose-built playgrounds with static equipment, preferring to play on wasteland and bombsites as they could "move things around to their liking."[84] There is a repeated call to lessen the role of the designer. As Sorensen had observed, opportunities for children's play were seen to be maximised by offering raw materials and loose elements that enabled children to build their own structures and turn the playground into a landscape that could be endlessly reconfigured and re-imagined through play. The "messiness" of children's play is a force that is seen at odds with the objectives of the designer and the town planner; for Lady Allen, "they make the planners, who are mostly tidy-minded, unhappy. But they must never forget that children enjoy chaos and make their own order out of it."[85]

Lady Allen's analyses of playground provision provides a landscape with a productive set of markers with which to return to Paolozzi's sculptures of the late 1950s. The "flexibility" and "range of possibilities" Paolozzi enjoyed in the making of the sculpture is, as with the junk playground, founded on a collection of loose elements that can be recombined and reconfigured. In his lecture notes, Paolozzi places repeated emphasis on the sculptures' beginnings; we gain a sense of continual return, with the elements placed in readiness. The artist appears to take delight in listing terms for these beginnings, as if in listing a set of terminologies the volume of material possibilities accumulates and expectation builds. The wax sheets with their printed impressions of junk are referred to variously as "ELEMENTS at the ready," "DICTIONARY OF DESIGN ELEMENTS," "ENCYCLOPAEDIA OF FORMS," "GRAMMAR OF FORMS" and an "ALPHABET OF ELEMENTS awaiting assembly."[86] As with the junk playground, it is out of this mass and mess, this loose collection of miscellany, that order emerges and structures are formed. While Sorensen and Lady Allen (both landscape architects) had called for a lessening of design to expand the potential for play, Paolozzi's late 1950s sculpture also refutes the immoveable, predetermined plan. In works including the *Saint Sebastian* series (1957–8) (Figure 3.14), *Jason* (1956) and *The Philosopher* (1957) (Figure 3.15), the figures are not built around a unifying internal armature. There was no fixed end-point, no pre-planned hidden internal structure to which the wax sheets with their "Alphabet of Elements" were added that would have provided stability. Instead, Paolozzi placed the elements under the force of gravity.[87] Beginning the figures with two columns as legs at the base, planted to form a foundation, the wax sheets and moulded forms were stacked up piece by piece. As Eric M. Stryker suggests, there is a connection that can be drawn here between

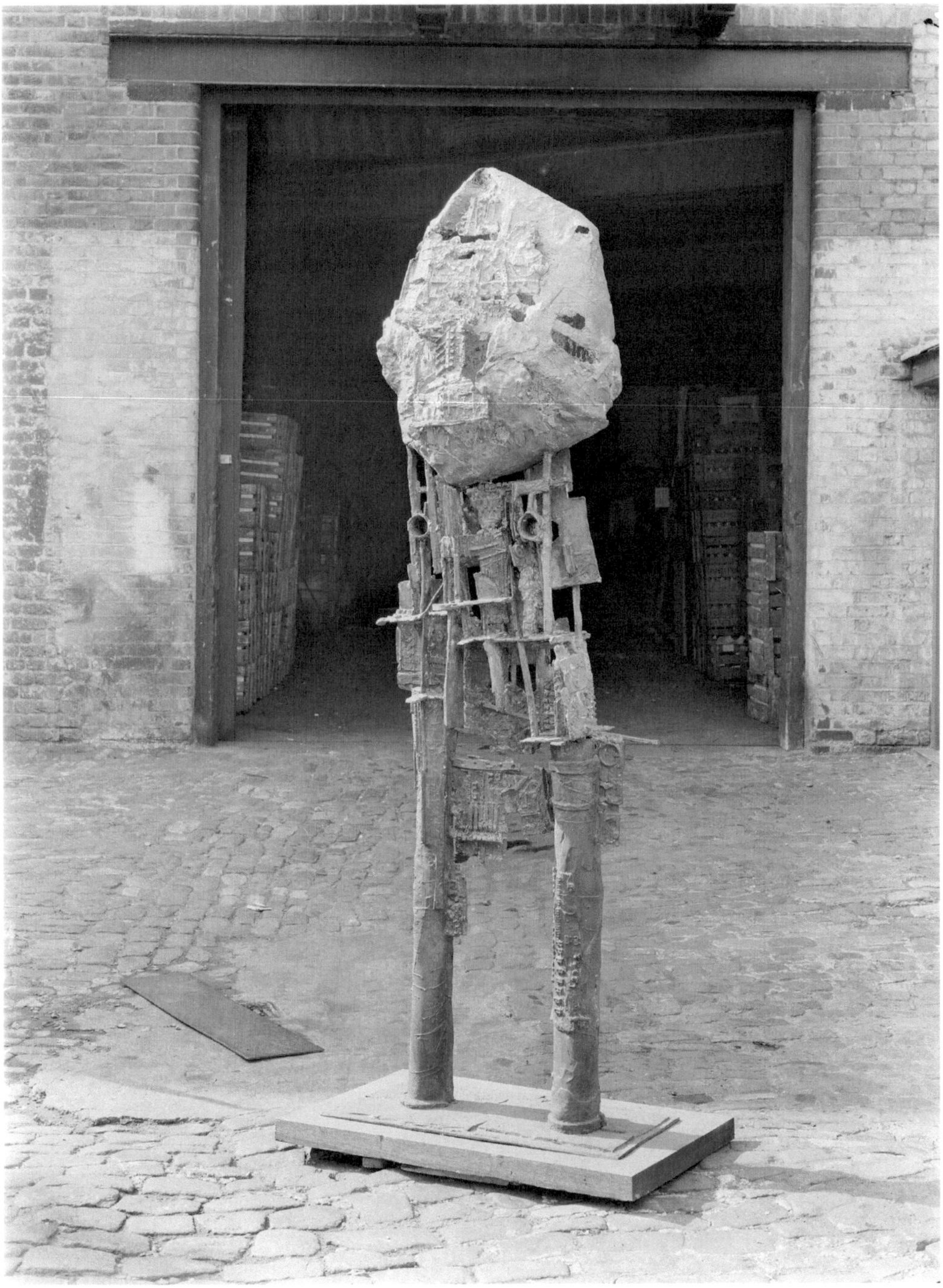

Figure 3.14 *St. Sebastian I*, 1957, Eduardo Paolozzi, bronze, height 217.2 cm (85 ½ inches), Scottish National Gallery of Modern Art.

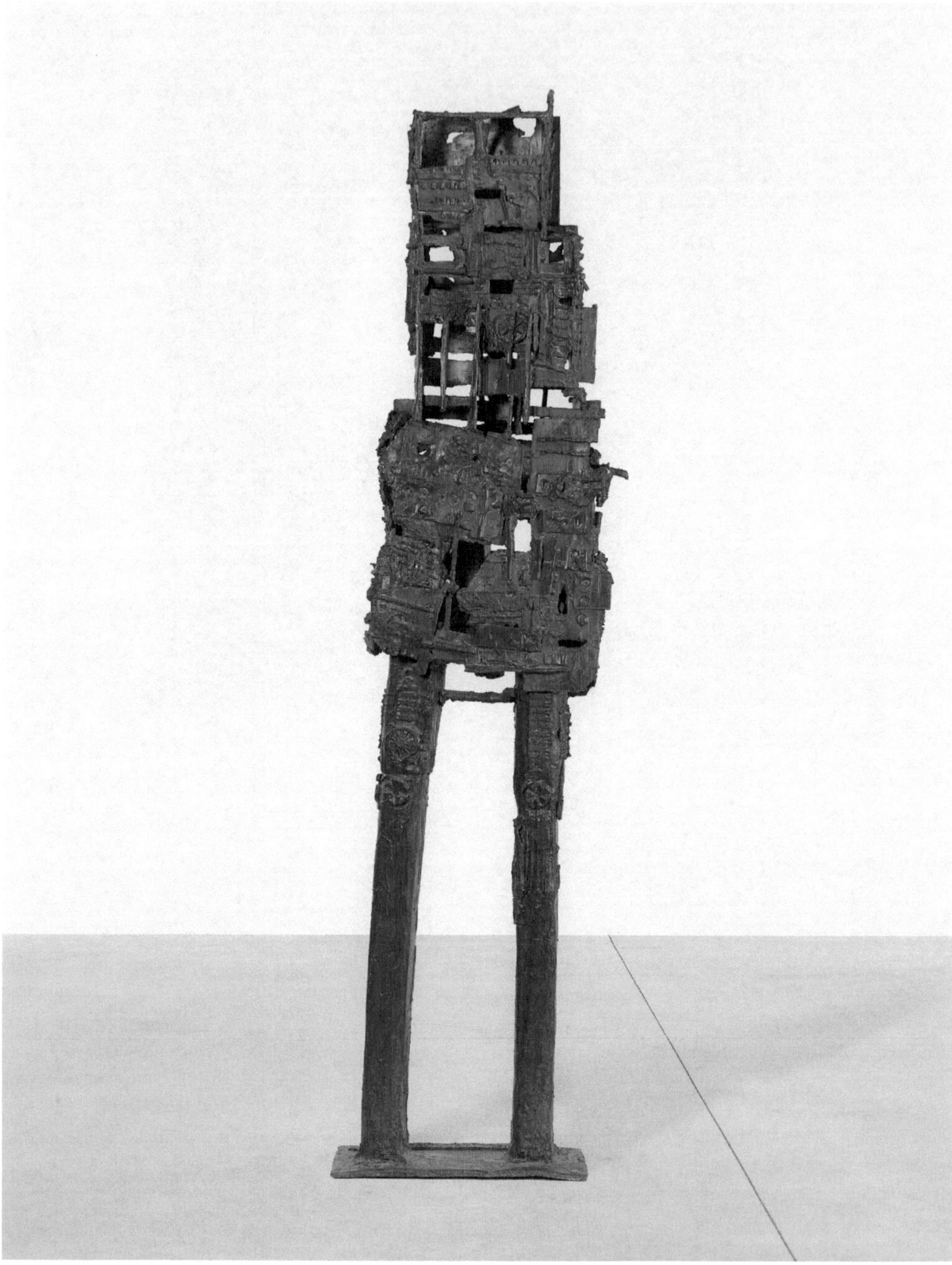

Figure 3.15 *The Philosopher*, 1957, Eduardo Paolozzi, bronze, height 188 cm (74 inches).

the collage-like process used for the figures and Paolozzi's collection of toy building blocks, some of which are now housed in the Krazy Kat Arkive:

> In the 1957–8 series of sculptures titled *Saint Sebastian*, Paolozzi's sculptural method is particularly masterful. His vertical assembly of separate trays of wax is fully visible. Stacked one against another like pieces in a collage, they also echo building blocks, another mass-produced item collected by the artist.[88]

Paolozzi's part-by-part method of assembly invited a battle with gravity. In the *St. Sebastian* series particularly, one can see the structures as games played against forces of contingency. In *St. Sebastian I* (1957) (Figure 3.14), there is no disguised internal structure that takes the strain underneath the surface "skin" (as there would be for a Henry Moore plaster sculpture, for example); instead, the body is formed as a collection of struts, attached ad hoc, that support the gargantuan head. We can see the cluster of struts and slabs that form the torso as structured as a shoring up against collapse. The resulting structure then remains, in the words of biologist and mathematician D'Arcy Wentworth Thompson, as a "diagram of forces."[89]

If Paolozzi's junk sculpture can be seen to have grown out of the ruins of a post-war landscape, then there is a very literal sense in which growth processes were a subject of focus for the artist and his Independent Group colleagues. In 1949, Paolozzi introduced Henderson to D'Arcy Wentworth Thompson's seminal book *On Growth and Form*. Henderson in turn recommended it to Richard Hamilton, who used the work as the subject of an exhibition that opened at the Institute of Contemporary Arts in London in 1951. In Thompson's study of biological processes and structures, he argued that excessively teleological concepts had been used to understand the phenomena of the natural world. Thompson argued that this "design"-led approach ignored the importance of the "ephemeral and accidental."[90] In order to further an understanding of growth patterns, Thompson contends that teleology should be seen as "interwoven" with physical causes and mechanisms. For Thompson, the form of living things can be explained in terms of a response to physical forces, such as gravity, that act on the organism.

In parallel with the junk playground, Thompson provides Paolozzi with an approach to form and process that lessens the role of design. In Paolozzi's use of part-by-part construction, he subjects the form of the sculpture to the action of gravity to allow teleology (or the artist's design) to collide with physical forces. In *St Sebastian I*, we clearly see a structure responsive to the physical demands of existing in the world through acts of contingency and necessity, enabling the structure to become a form that is found.

Paolozzi's sculptures' connection to Thompson's analyses of growth processes here becomes crucial to furthering this chapter's notion of the battle within the context of play and the creative process. The "battle" now clearly emerges for both Guston and Paolozzi as a process that is not concerned with imposing the artist's will on material in a way that would force material to conform, unaltered, to the artist's mental image. In other terms, the battle is not one in which material is subjected to a mental ideal. Indeed, to the contrary—the battle, or contest, is seen as one in which the artist enjoys inviting a push and pull between their originating concept and its material manifestation in order to discover new structures. Thompson's call to not entirely reject teleology, but rather to see it as inextricably interconnected with the accidental and the ephemeral, provides a way to think again about play and the unforeseen outcome, particularly in relation to the dialectical characteristics of play. The meta-contest can then be seen to be one in which the artist challenges their own mental ideals. Daniel Herrmann importantly provides a way to place this challenge to idealism within a post-war context. Discussing the work of Paolozzi, Germaine Richier, Marino Marini and César, Herrmann asserts that

> the disintegrating, charred and gouged bronze surfaces of their works gain their specific political and aesthetic impact from their "accusing contrast" with the flawless and eerily immaculate surfaces of fascist warrior statues in the style of an Arno Breker or a Josef Thorak. . . . The material and its deformations were pivotal to the meaning of the artwork.[91]

Paolozzi himself contrasts the "illusionary" surfaces of a Moore sculpture with his own fragmented structures. In an interview with Edouard Roditi in 1960, one hears the influence of Thompson in the parallels Paolozzi draws between his own sculptures and growth processes:

> I try to . . . suggest that matter itself is constantly undergoing some metamorphosis or evolution of its own. Everything consists of atoms or molecules or cells or fragments of other things and materials that have ceased to exist as separate entities. When we create a work of art, we try to arrest this flux, to perpetuate a single moment in this endless metamorphosis of matter. . . . The details of my sculptures try to suggest such a pause in the evolution of their materials, and the spare parts and the junk that the metal may once have been and may well become again are an allegory of the materials of which bodies of living animals and human beings are likewise constructed.[92]

Significantly, Paolozzi here imagines the structures of his sculptures as at a "pause," just as Guston had described his paintings as "pauses." With both artists, one gains the sense of a focus on the continuity of a process that places structures and their constituent elements within cycles of construction and destruction. Indeed, in Paolozzi's "Notes from a Lecture" (1958), he describes his studio as a "Devils Kitchen," and the process or "Action" as "burn cut mold model construct tack destroy and recombine."[93] The emphasis Paolozzi had placed on a repeated return to the sculpture's beginnings now meet the generative possibilities provided by destruction. Acts of destruction and ruin would continue to propel Paolozzi's studio methods; as late as 1979, Paolozzi was continuing to find terms with which to define collage. In a discussion of his creative methods that is reminiscent of Guston's rejection of a process of "additions," Paolozzi stated that:

> The word "collage" is inadequate as a description because the concept should include damage, erase, destroy, deface and transform—all parts of a metaphor for the creative act itself. Preconscious elaboration must have a relationship to chance therefore the permutations of one hundred and one figures on forty landscapes and interiors represent a process of endless destruction until finalization.[94]

In stressing the importance of the role of chance within the creative process, Paolozzi drew a connection between his creative process and the games played by Dadaists and

Surrealists that sought to release works from rational control and embrace unforeseen imagery. In fact, by this point the artist had publicly rejected the label "Pop Artist," asserting in conversation with J.G. Ballard in 1971 that "what I like to think I'm doing is an extension of radical Surrealism."[95] For both Guston and Paolozzi, then, Surrealism provided a path away from pre-planned artwork towards game playing with the unknown. Paolozzi's use of repetition, described in the statement as "permutations," returns us to the artist's use of kits of forms through which the artist played with innumerable combinations. However, through this statement one is able to appreciate the importance of the role of destruction used in conjunction with the kit. Providing an emphasis on constant beginnings, with a finalised sculpture only seen as a "pause," we gain a sense of a process in which the artist's certainties and conclusions are continually challenged and endlessly remade. From here, Paolozzi's symbols of heroic and regal power can be seen to achieve only a fleeting status.

The use of destruction, collapse and continual beginnings within a creative process returns us to a significant set of connections between Paolozzi's studio methods and the discourse surrounding the landscape of the adventure playground in post-war Britain. Kozlovsky points out that "the adventure playground . . . was not intended to have final form, as it underwent cyclic, unpredictable processes of construction and destruction; nor was it intended to be visually pleasing."[96] Kozlovsky cites George Burden, the chairman of the Camberwell playground committee and a psychiatric social worker at King's College Hospital who, in defence of the Camberwell Junk Playground established on the site of a bombed church, declared:

> We do not set out to achieve the tangible results which many visitors look for, though when showing them the playground we could sometimes wish there was something more to see! The site . . . looks like a derelict builder's yard. To appreciate what is happening an afternoon must be spent with the children.[97]

From Kozlovsky and Burden, one gains an understanding of the adventure playground as a site in which material is continually undergoing change. Lady Allen's emphasis on the importance of the provision of "flexibility," moveable elements and raw materials to maximise the potential for play transformed the playground from a landscape of fixed and finalised structures. The adventure playground was a site that placed action and process at its centre in order to allow children to continually construct and remake their environment, even if this meant that for adults there was sometimes very little visible. Growing out of the ruins, the landscape of the adventure playground could return to rubble through play processes of construction and destruction.

The structures of Paolozzi's late 1950s bronze figures imply impending collapse. In *The Philosopher* (1957) (Figure 3.15), one encounters a structure that pulls between the dynamics of construction and destruction. The part-by-part construction is laid bare; the elements and supporting struts are not silenced and concealed within a unified structure. The component parts appear to precariously hold together as a structure but refuse stable coherence. Paolozzi's "grammar of forms" remains as a collection of pieces. There are gaps and holes that not only appeal to the haptic but also reveal the trace of the hand. These are holes and openings that allowed the hands of the sculptor to reach into the structure to support it against collapse. But just as these openings reveal the method by which the work was constructed, they also present the implied possibility that a hand could grasp the elements, pull the sections apart and reassemble the structure. Rejecting resolution, the work appears placed within a process of making in perpetuum. Paolozzi himself had declared that the method involved "a lot of sticking and cutting."[98] One can see repeated cutting and assembly as a sculptural equivalent of Guston's use of overpainting and erasure. Both methods dispense with the notion of the "mistake" to allow a work to evolve through a responsive process that produces a found structure. In fact, Paolozzi even compared his methods to those found in Abstract Expressionism: "if you want an aesthetics of the *objet trouvé*, and that would be the relationship of my kind of sculpture to action painting and to some of the more recent developments in abstract expressionism."[99] Paolozzi makes this comparison based on his attempt to bring a "spontaneity" to sculpture.[100] While acknowledging that the bronze casting process is laborious and far from spontaneous, Paolozzi was keen to emphasise that his original wax models involved a great deal of immediacy. In effect, by drawing a comparison with Abstract Expressionism, Paolozzi placed action and process at the centre of the work. Made from junk and bombsite debris, Paolozzi's sculpture places the process-led artwork firmly within the material and social conditions of its time. Highmore powerfully points out how the language of the street collides with the language of American abstract painting in the collaborative commercial printmaking of Paolozzi and Henderson: "the wallpaper points . . . towards the a-formalism of 'advanced' abstraction (represented most vividly by Jackson Pollock) and to the informal practices of making, mending and messing that they found in the streets of London's East End."[101] It is this "making, mending and messing" that would predict Paolozzi's innovations in sculpture in the later part of the decade, creating an assembly technique that patched together his wax sheets bearing the impressions of recycled junk as he battled against gravity.

Through the artists' game playing with contingency, one can see Paolozzi's figures and Guston's compressed clusters as crowded social sites, in which component parts are not subsumed into a unified totality but rather appear to remain jostling within an unfolding process. The "creative battle" emerges as a contest with the unforeseen that produces a responsive process. And, crucially, in Guston's return to "tangibilia" and Paolozzi's use of junk and debris, one can see the artists' engagement with game playing as an activity that is formed through the substance of the social, material conditions of its time.

Notes

1. Philip Guston in *Philip Guston: A Life Lived*, directed by Michael Blackwood. New York, NY, Michael Blackwood Productions Inc., 1981.
2. Johan Huizinga, *Homo Ludens* (Boston: Beacon Press, 1955), 76.
3. Brian Sutton-Smith, *The Ambiguity of Play* (Cambridge: Harvard University Press, 2001), 79.
4. For a detailed survey of contemporary game scholarship see Mary Flanagan, *Critical Play: Radical Game Design* (London: The MIT Press, 2013).
5. Huizinga, *Homo Ludens*, 89.
6. Mary Drach McInnes, "Guston's Private and Public Battles," in *Philip Guston 1975–1980: Private and Public Battles* (exh.cat.), ed. Kim Sichel and Mary Drach McInnes (Boston: Boston University Art Gallery, 1994), 9.
7. Philip Guston, "On Survival, 1974," in *Philip Guston, Collected Writings, Lectures, and Conversations*, ed. Clark Coolidge (London: University of California Press, 2011), 264.
8. Ibid., 265.
9. Huizinga, *Homo Ludens*, 98.
10. Ibid., 41.

11. Sutton-Smith, *The Ambiguity of Play*, 139.
12. Philip Guston, "Talk at Yale Summer School of Music and Art, 1972," in *Collected Writings, Lectures, and Conversations*, 161.
13. Philip Guston, "Conversation with Morton Feldman, 1968," in *Collected Writings, Lectures, and Conversations*, 86.
14. Guston as quoted in Drach McInnes, "Guston's Private and Public Battles," 9.
15. Guston as quoted in "Conversation with Harold Rosenberg, 1974," in *Collected Writings, Lectures, and Conversations*, 271.
16. Eugen Fink, *Play as Symbol of the World and Other Writings* (Bloomington: Indiana University Press, 2016), 24–25.
17. Philip Guston, "On Morton Feldman, 1967," in *Collected Writings, Lectures, and Conversations*, 79.
18. Ibid.
19. Fink, *Play as Symbol of the World*, 23.
20. Guston, "Talk at Yale Summer School of Music and Art, 1972," 152.
21. Here I am deliberately misreading Guston's use of the term field and its connection to colour field painting.
22. Harold Rosenberg, *The Tradition of the New* (New York: Da Capo Press, 1994), 23–39.
23. Huizinga, *Homo Ludens*, 51.
24. Claudia Mesch, "Serious Play: Games and Early Twentieth-Century Modernism," in *From Diversion to Subversion, Games, Play, and Twentieth-Century Art*, ed. David J. Getsy (Pennsylvania: The Pennsylvania State University Press, 2011), 63.
25. Robert Motherwell in *The New York School*, directed by Michael Blackwood, written by Barbara Rose. New York, NY, Michael Blackwood Productions Inc., 1972.
26. Guston as quoted in H.H. Arnason, *Philip Guston* (exh.cat.) (New York: Solomon R. Guggenheim Foundation, 1962), 21.
27. Philip Guston, "Philip Guston Talking," in *Philip Guston* (exh.cat.) (London: Timothy Taylor Gallery, 2004), 34.
28. Ibid., 33.
29. Hans-Georg Gadamer, *Truth and Method* (London and New York: Continuum, 2006), 106.
30. Guston in *Philip Guston: A Life Lived*, directed by Michael Blackwood.
31. Arnason, *Philip Guston*, 36–37.
32. Ibid., 33.
33. Fink, *Play as Symbol of the World*, 24–25.
34. Arnason, *Philip Guston*, 33.
35. Guston, "Talk at Yale Summer School of Music and Art, 1972," 154.
36. Philip Guston, "Talk at Yale Summer School of Music and Art, 1973," in *Collected Writings, Lectures, and Conversations*, 216.
37. Sutton-Smith, *The Ambiguity of Play*, 229.
38. Bernard Suits, *The Grasshopper, Games, Life and Utopia* (Plymouth: Broadview Press, 2005), 55.
39. Guston, "Talk at Yale Summer School of Music and Art, 1972," 154.
40. David Trotter, *Cooking with Mud, the Idea of Mess in Nineteenth-Century Art and Fiction* (Oxford: Oxford University Press, 2000), 31.
41. Guston, "Philip Guston Talking," 25.
42. Philip Guston, "Studio Notes, 1970–78," in *Collected Writings, Lectures, and Conversations*, 314.
43. Guston in *Philip Guston: A Life Lived*, directed by Michael Blackwood.
44. Huizinga, *Homo Ludens*, 9.
45. Jason Edwards, "Play and Democracy: Huizinga and the Limits of Agonism," *Political Theory*, Vol. 41, No. 1 (February 2013): 108. Sage Publications, Inc.
46. Ibid., 101.
47. Ibid., 103.
48. Guston in *Philip Guston: A Life Lived*, directed by Michael Blackwood.
49. Robert Anchor, "History and Play: Johan Huizinga and His Critics," *History and Theory*, Vol. 17, No. 1 (February 1978): 92.
50. Fink as quoted in Anchor, "History and Play: Johan Huizinga and His Critics," 92.

51. Philip Guston in *Conversations with Philip Guston*, directed by Michael Blackwood. Michael Blackwood Productions. New York, NY, Michael Blackwood Productions Inc., 2003.
52. Philip Guston, "Conversation with Clark Coolidge, 1972," in *Collected Writings, Lectures, and Conversations*, 194.
53. Philip Guston, "Conversation with Harold Rosenberg, 1974," in *Collected Writings, Lectures, and Conversations*, 272.
54. Ibid., 273.
55. Sutton-Smith, *The Ambiguity of Play*, 171.
56. Guston as quoted in Ross Feld, *Guston in Time* (New York: Counterpoint, 2003), 7.
57. Guston, "Studio Notes, 1970–78," 314.
58. Philip Guston, "Interview with Jan Butterfield, 1979," in *Collected Writings, Lectures, and Conversations*, 295.
59. Fink, *Play as Symbol of the World*, 204.
60. Guston, "Talk at Yale Summer School of Music and Art, 1973," 224.
61. Philip Guston describes this in *Conversations with Philip Guston*, directed by Michael Blackwood. Michael Blackwood Productions. New York, NY, Michael Blackwood Productions Inc., 2003.
62. Guston, "Talk at Yale Summer School of Music and Art, 1972," 159.
63. Guston in *Philip Guston: A Life Lived*, directed by Michael Blackwood.
64. Philip Guston, "Interview with Mark Stevens, 1980," in *Collected Writings, Lectures, and Conversations*, 298.
65. Guston, "Conversation with Harold Rosenberg, 1974," 275.
66. Eduardo Paolozzi, "Notes from a Lecture at the Institute of Contemporary Arts, 1958," in *Eduardo Paolozzi: Writings and Interviews*, ed. Robin Spencer (Oxford, NY: Oxford University Press, 2001), 85.
67. Ibid., 83.
68. Ibid.
69. Daniel Herrmann, "Bronze to Aluminium and Back again: Eduardo Paolozzi's Use of Materials in Sculpture, c.1957–71," *Sculpture Journal*, Vol. 14, No. 1 (2005): 75–76.
70. Paolozzi, "Notes from a Lecture at the Institute of Contemporary Arts, 1958," 81–83.
71. Nigel Henderson as quoted in Victoria Walsh, *Nigel Henderson, Parallel of Life and Art* (London: Thames and Hudson Ltd., 2001), 21.
72. Ibid., 54.
73. Paolozzi, "Notes from a Lecture at the Institute of Contemporary Arts, 1958," 83.
74. Ben Highmore, "Playgrounds and Bombsites: Postwar Britain's Ruined Landscapes," *Cultural Politics*, Vol. 9, No. 3 (2013): 323–336.
75. Claude Lichtenstein and Thomas Schregenberger, *As Found, the Discovery of the Ordinary* (Baden: Lars Müller Publishers and the Zurich Museum für Gestaltung, 2001), 10.
76. Paolozzi, "Notes from a Lecture at the Institute of Contemporary Arts, 1958," 83.
77. Alison and Peter Smithson as quoted in Lichtenstein and Schregenberger, *As Found, the Discovery of the Ordinary*, 40.
78. Roy Kozlovsky, *The Architectures of Childhood: Children, Modern Architecture and Reconstruction in Postwar England* (Farnham: Ashgate, 2013), 58.
79. Ibid., 53–55.
80. Eduardo Paolozzi, "Interview with William Lipke, 1966," *Writings and Interviews*, ed. Spencer, 148.
81. Paolozzi, "Notes from a Lecture at the Institute of Contemporary Arts, 1958," 83.
82. *National Life Stories, Artist's Lives, Sir Eduardo Paolozzi Interviewed by Frank Whitford*, accessed March 2012, http://sounds.bl.uk/Arts-literature-and-performance/Art-photography-and-architecture/021M-C0466X0017XX-1600V0
83. Lady Allen as quoted in Kozlovsky, *The Architectures of Childhood*, 48.
84. Lady Allen of Hurtwood, *Planning for Play* (London: Thames and Hudson, Ltd., 1968), 55.
85. Ibid., 9.
86. Paolozzi, "Notes from a Lecture at the Institute of Contemporary Arts, 1958," 83.

87. I am extremely grateful to Chris Nash of the Arch Bronze Foundry, London, for his advice regarding Paolozzi's working methods.
88. Eric M. Stryker, "Parallel Systems: Lawrence Alloway and Eduardo Paolozzi," *Tate Papers*, No. 16 (Autumn 2011).
89. D'Arcy Wentworth Thompson, *On Growth and Form* (London: Cambridge University Press, 1969), 11.
90. Ibid., 3.
91. Daniel F. Herrmann, "Eduardo Paolozzi: Pop Art Redefined," in *Eduardo Paolozzi* (exh. cat.), ed. Daniel F. Herrmann (London: Whitechapel Gallery, 2017), 17.
92. Eduardo Paolozzi, "Dialogues on Art, 1960," *Writings and Interviews*, ed. Spencer, 90.
93. Paolozzi, "Notes from a Lecture at the Institute of Contemporary Arts, 1958," 85.
94. Eduardo Paolozzi, "Collage or a Scenario for a Comedy of Critical Hallucination, 1977–9," *Writings and Interviews*, ed. Spencer, 251.
95. Eduardo Paolozzi, "Speculative Illustrations: Eduardo Paolozzi in Conversation with J.G. Ballard and Frank Whitford, 1971," *Writings and Interviews*, ed. Spencer, 199.
96. Kozlovsky, *The Architectures of Childhood*, 49.
97. George Burden as quoted in Kozlovsky, *The Architectures of Childhood*, 62.
98. *National Life Stories, Artist's Lives, Sir Eduardo Paolozzi Interviewed by Frank Whitford*, accessed March 2012, http://sounds.bl.uk/Arts-literature-and-performance/Art-photography-and-architecture/021M-C0466X0017XX-1600V0
99. Eduardo Paolozzi, "Dialogues on Art, 1960," 91.
100. Ibid.
101. Ben Highmore, "Brutalist Wallpaper and the Independent Group," *Journal of Visual Culture*, Vol. 12, No. 2 (2013): 207.

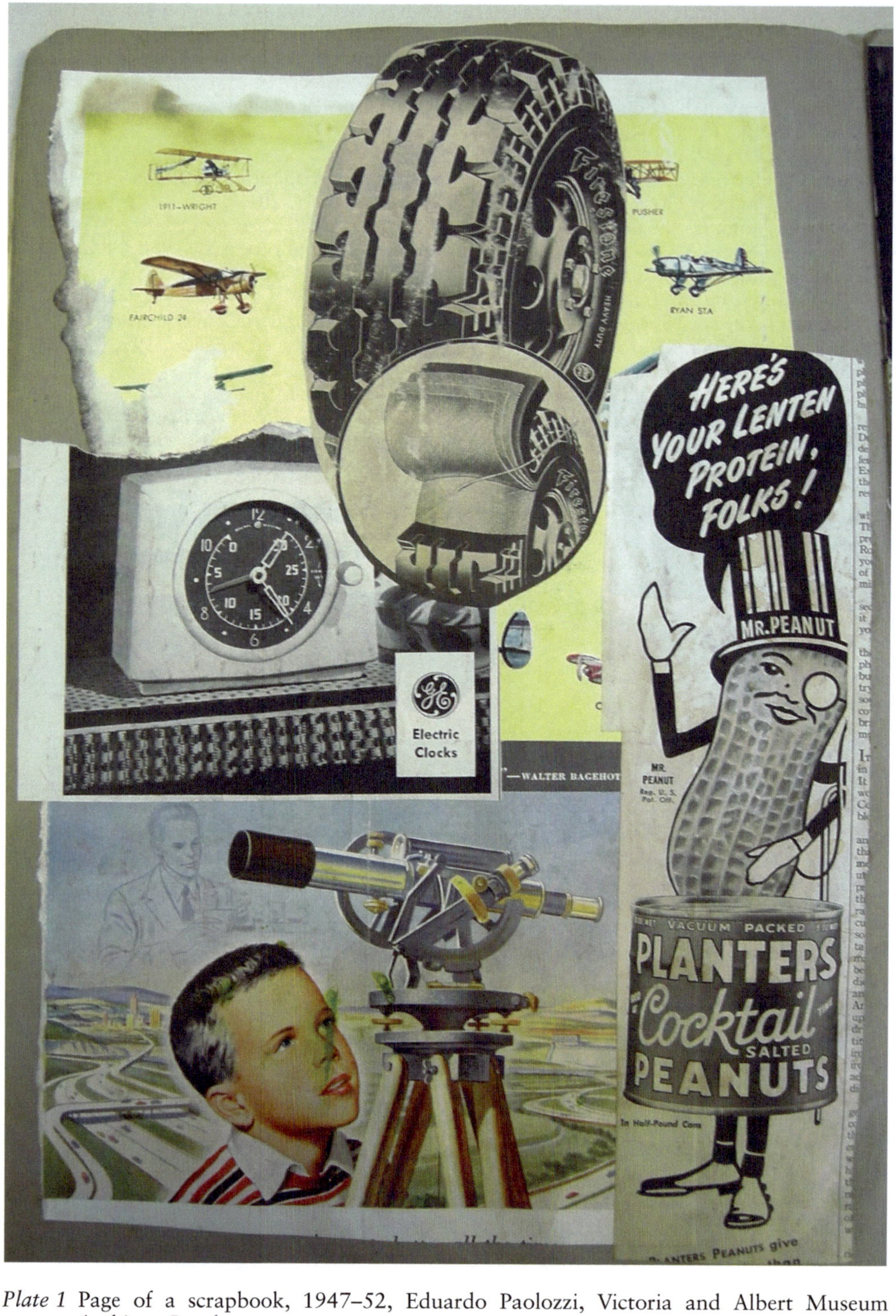

Plate 1 Page of a scrapbook, 1947–52, Eduardo Paolozzi, Victoria and Albert Museum Archives, London.

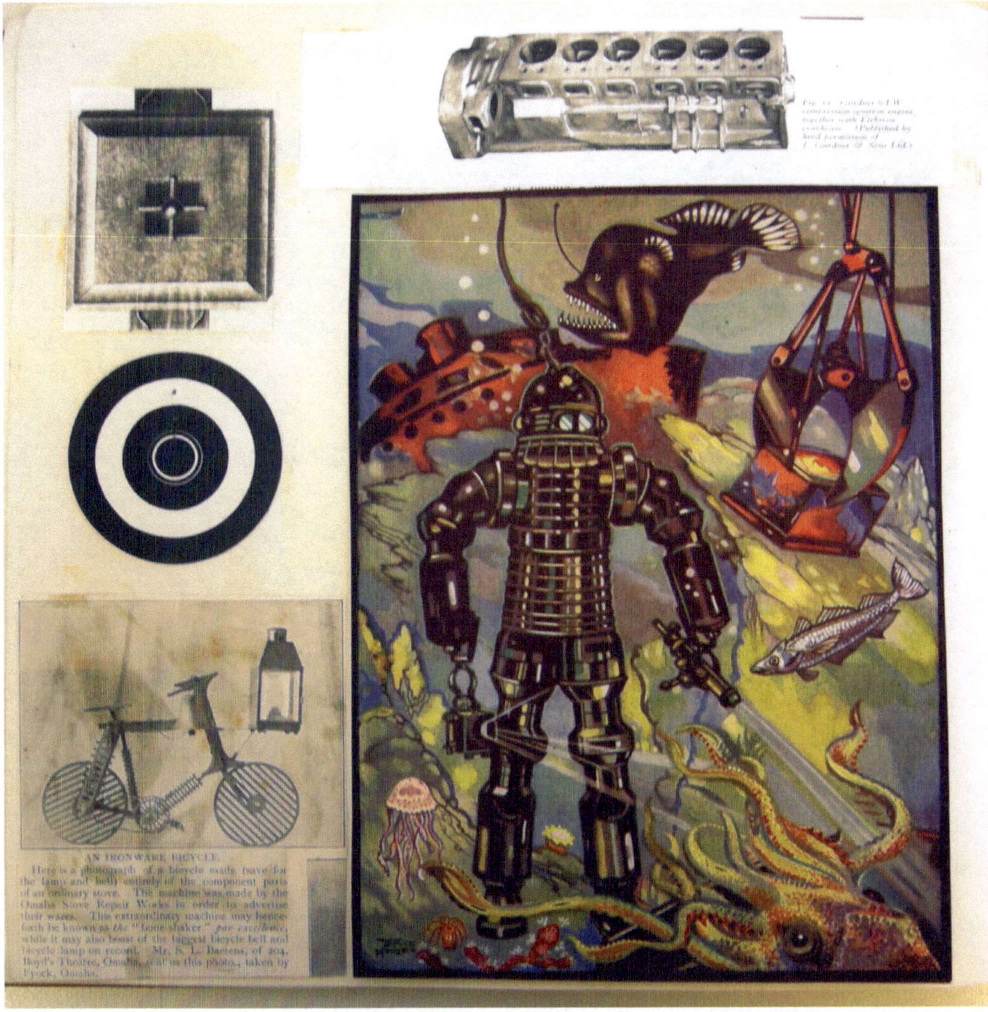

Plate 2 Page of a scrapbook, 1960, Eduardo Paolozzi, Victoria and Albert Museum Archives, London.

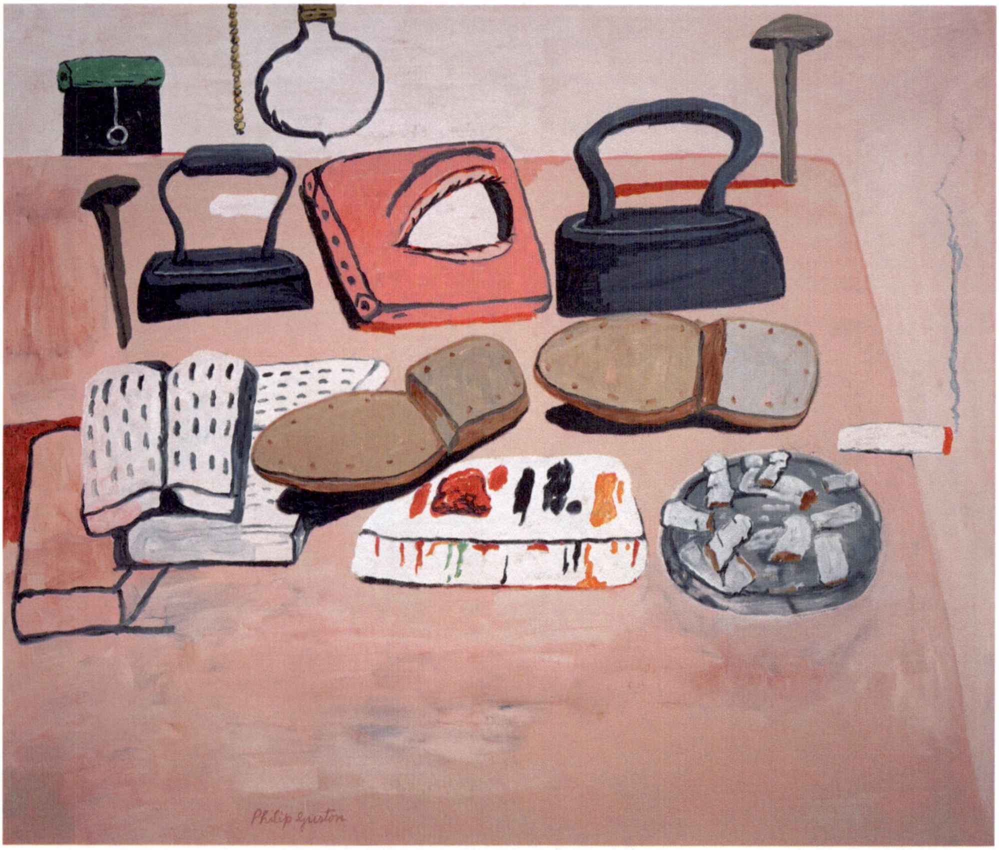

Plate 3 *Painter's Table*, 1973, Philip Guston, oil on canvas, 196.2 × 228.6 cm ($77\frac{1}{4} \times 90$ inches) framed: 197.8 × 231.2 × 5 cm ($77\frac{7}{8} \times 91 \times 1\frac{15}{16}$ inches). Gift (partial and promised) of Ambassador and Mrs. Donald Blinken in memory of Maurice H. Blinken and in honour of the 50th anniversary of the National Gallery of Art. 1991.69.1. National Gallery of Art, Washington.

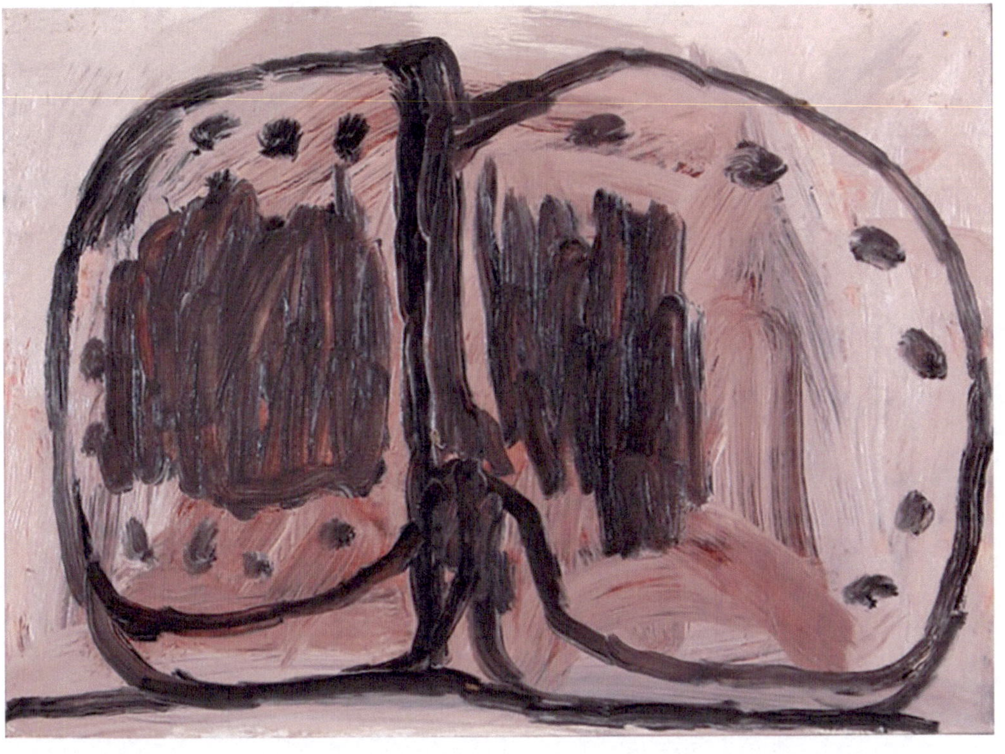

Plate 4 Untitled, 1970, Philip Guston, oil on panel, 30.5 × 40.6 cm (12 × 16 inches).

Image courtesy of The Estate of Philip Guston. © The Estate of Philip Guston.

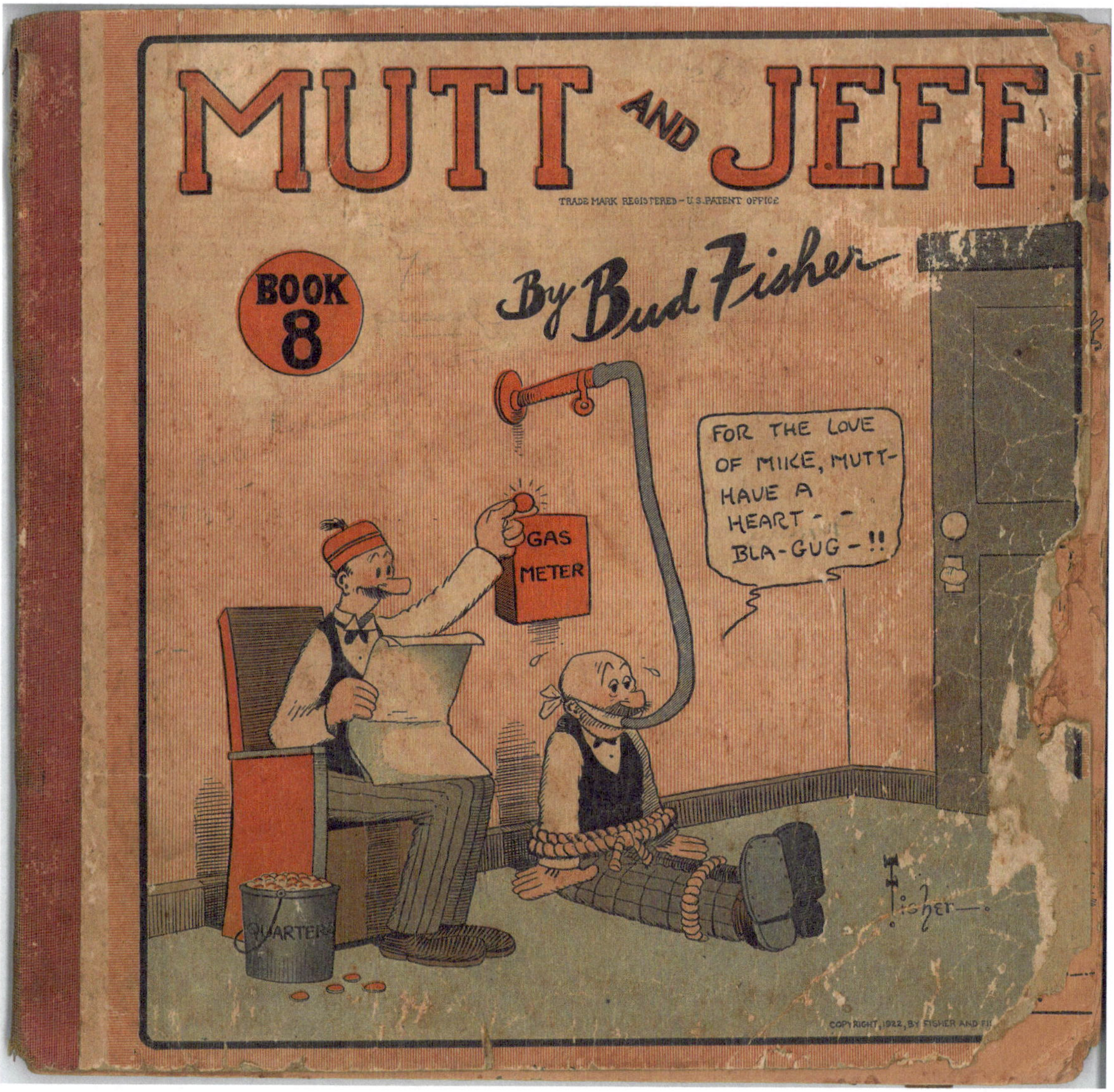

Plate 5 Mutt and Jeff, Book 8, 1922, Bud Fisher.

Image credit: The author.

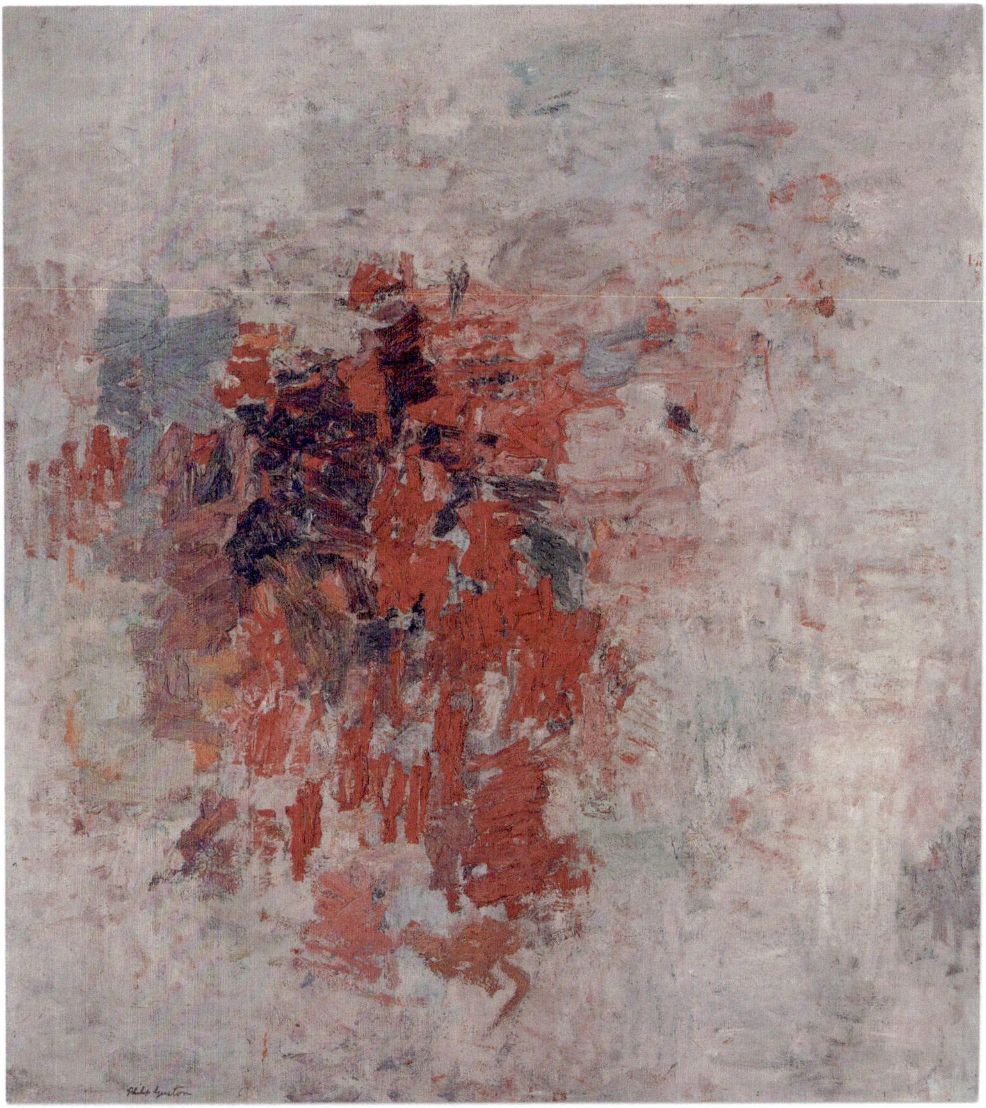

Plate 6 *Beggar's Joys*, 1954–5, Philip Guston, oil on canvas, 182.9 × 172.7 cm (72 × 68 inches).

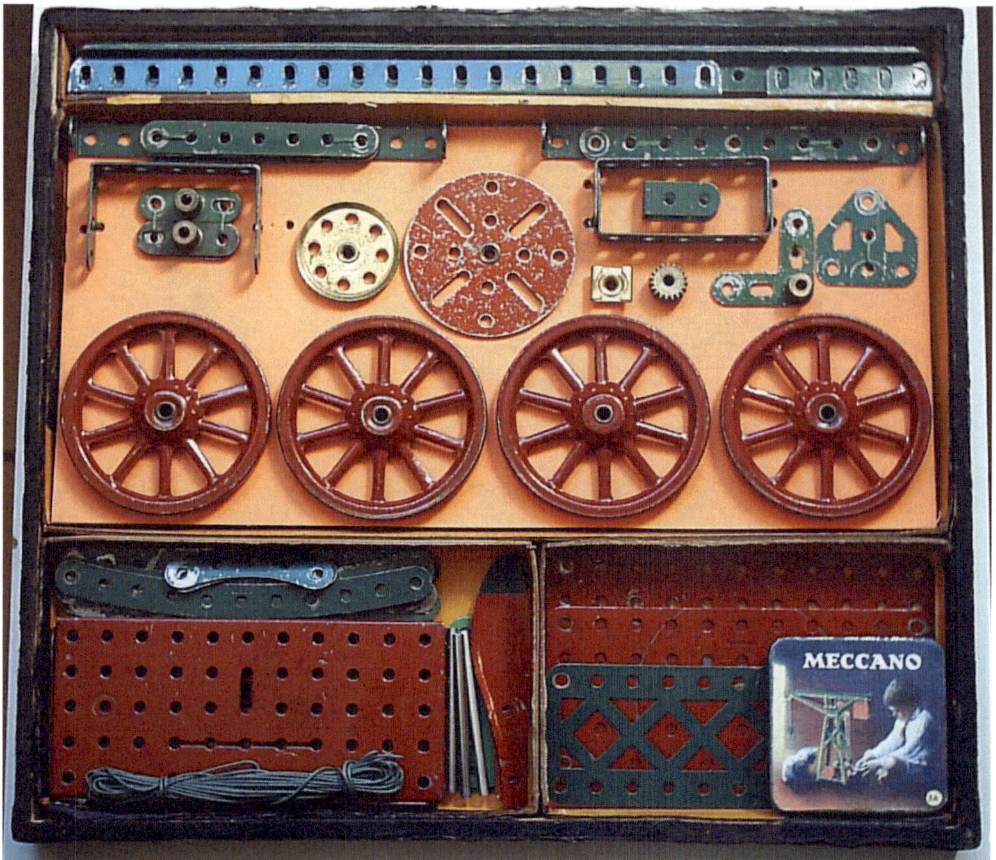

Plate 7 Meccano set, c. 1920.

Image courtesy of Peter Sullivan.

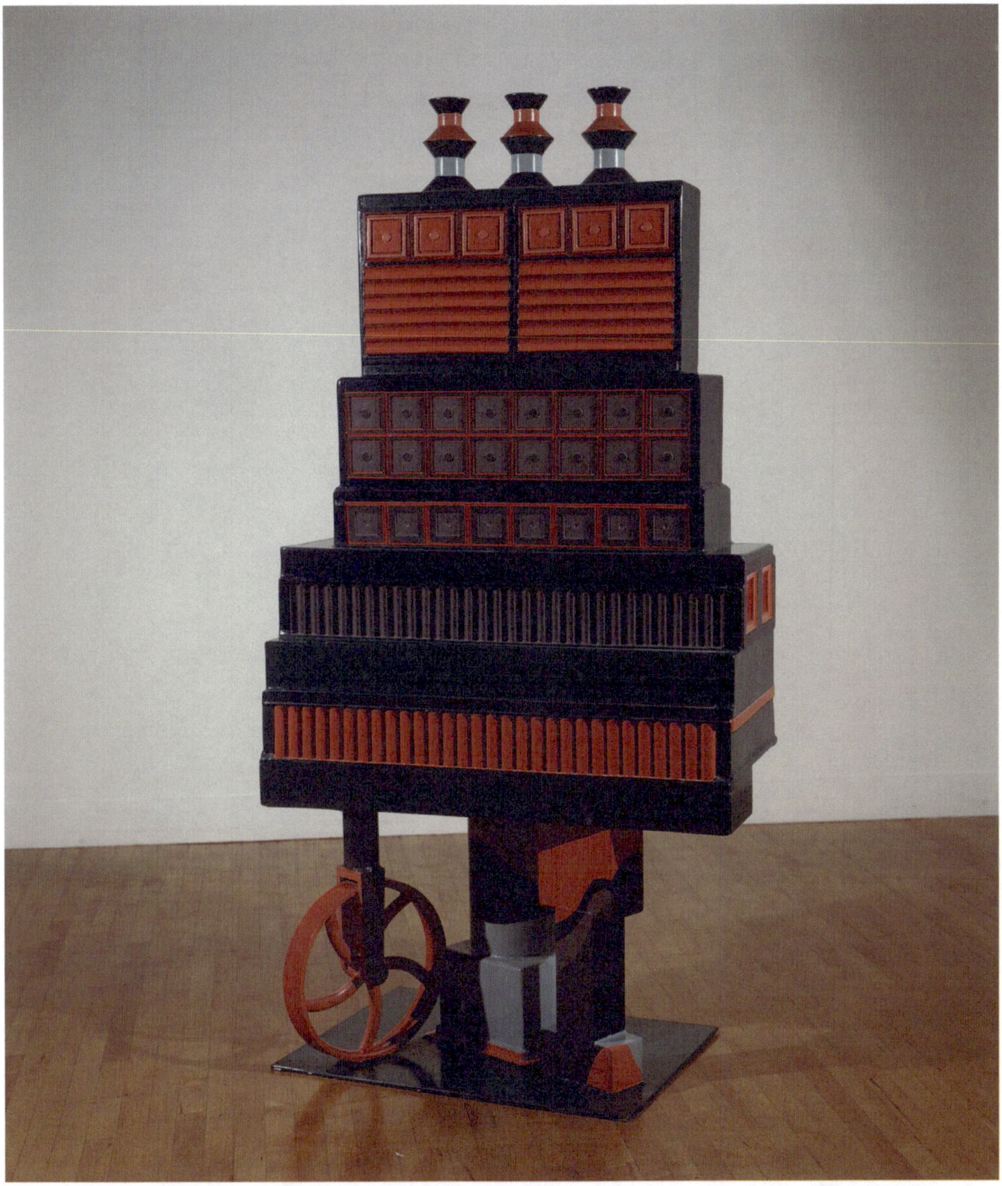

Plate 8 The City of the Circle and the Square, 1963/6, Eduardo Paolozzi, painted aluminium, 210.8 × 102.2 × 66.7 cm, Tate Gallery, London.

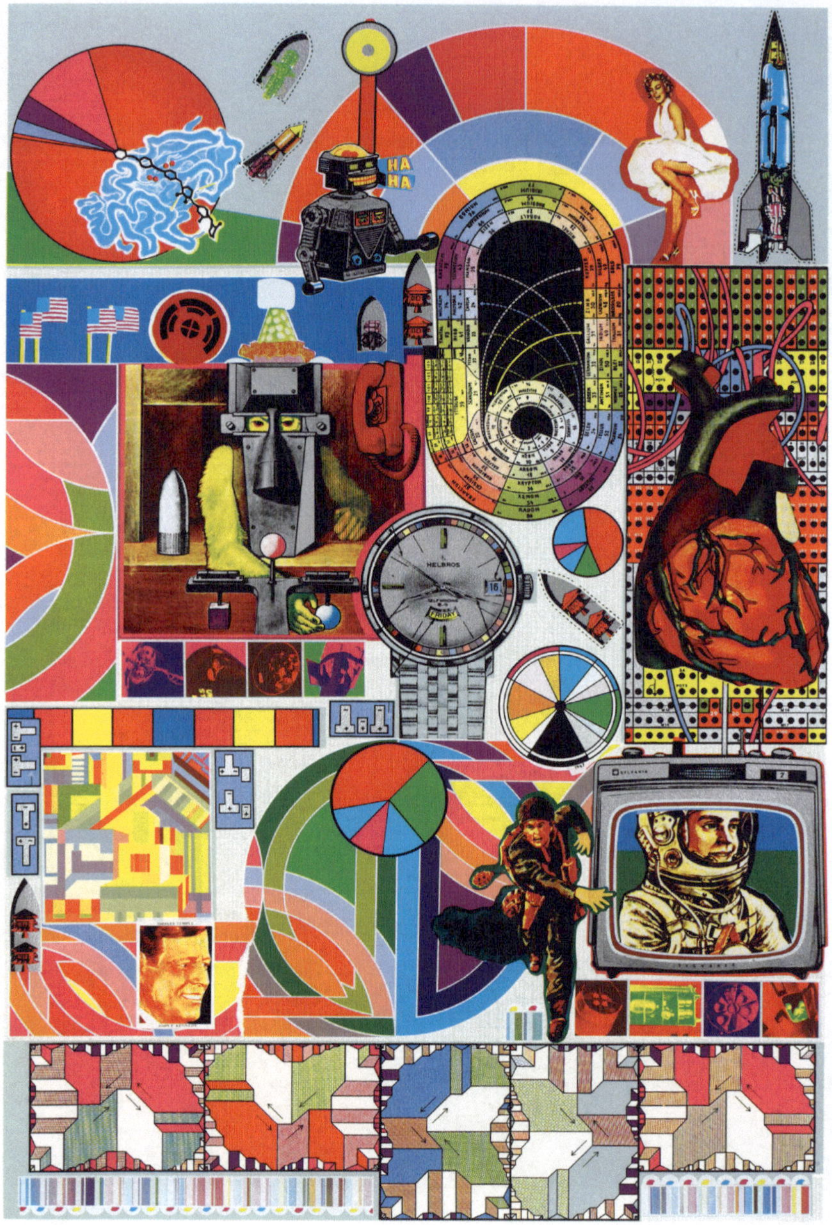

Plate 9 B.A.S.H., 1971, Eduardo Paolozzi, screenprint, 85 × 70 cm.

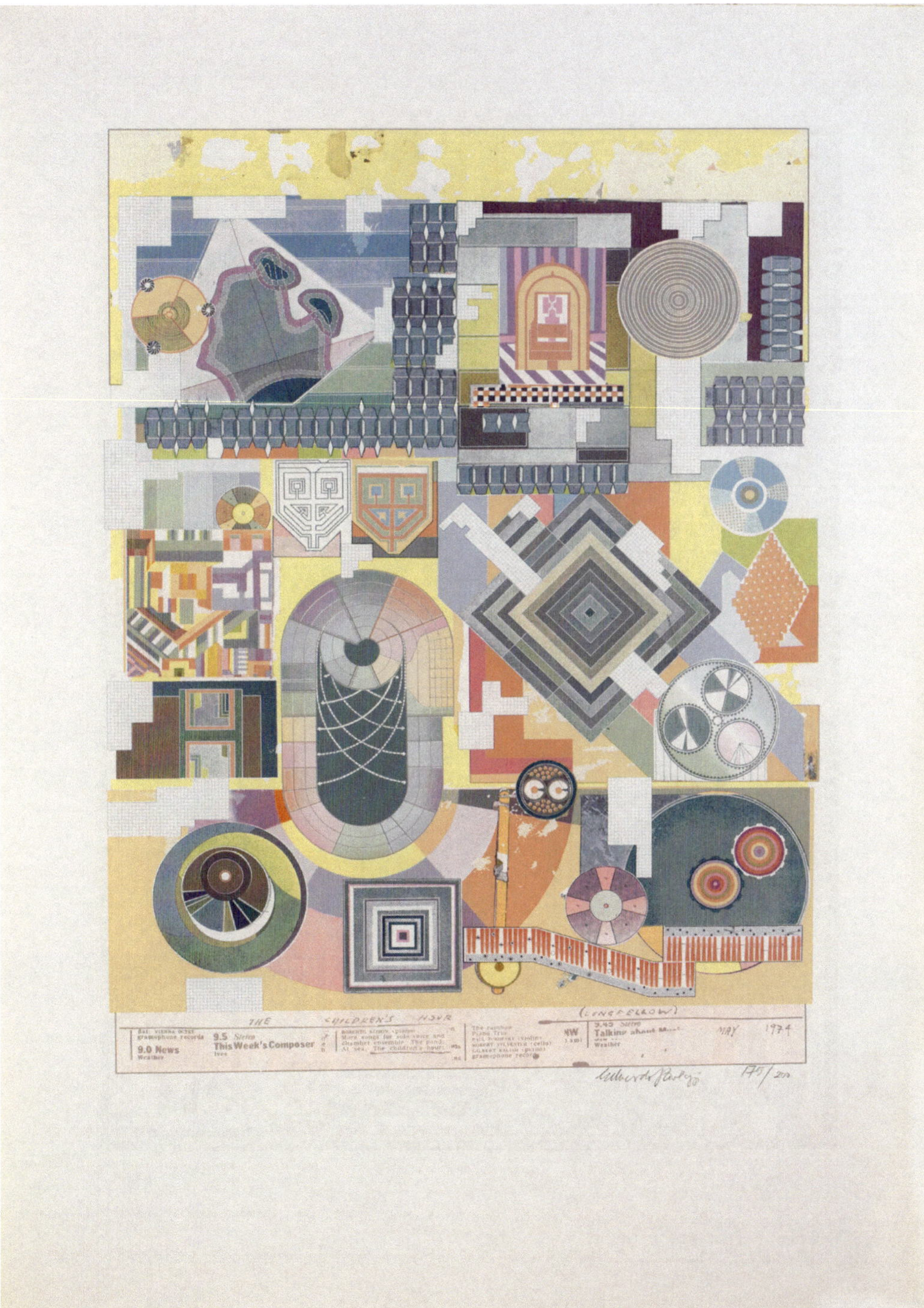

Plate 10 The Children's Hour, 1974–6, Eduardo Paolozzi, screenprint, 99 × 69 cm.

Image courtesy of Sims Reed Gallery. © Trustees of the Paolozzi Foundation, licensed by DACS 2018.

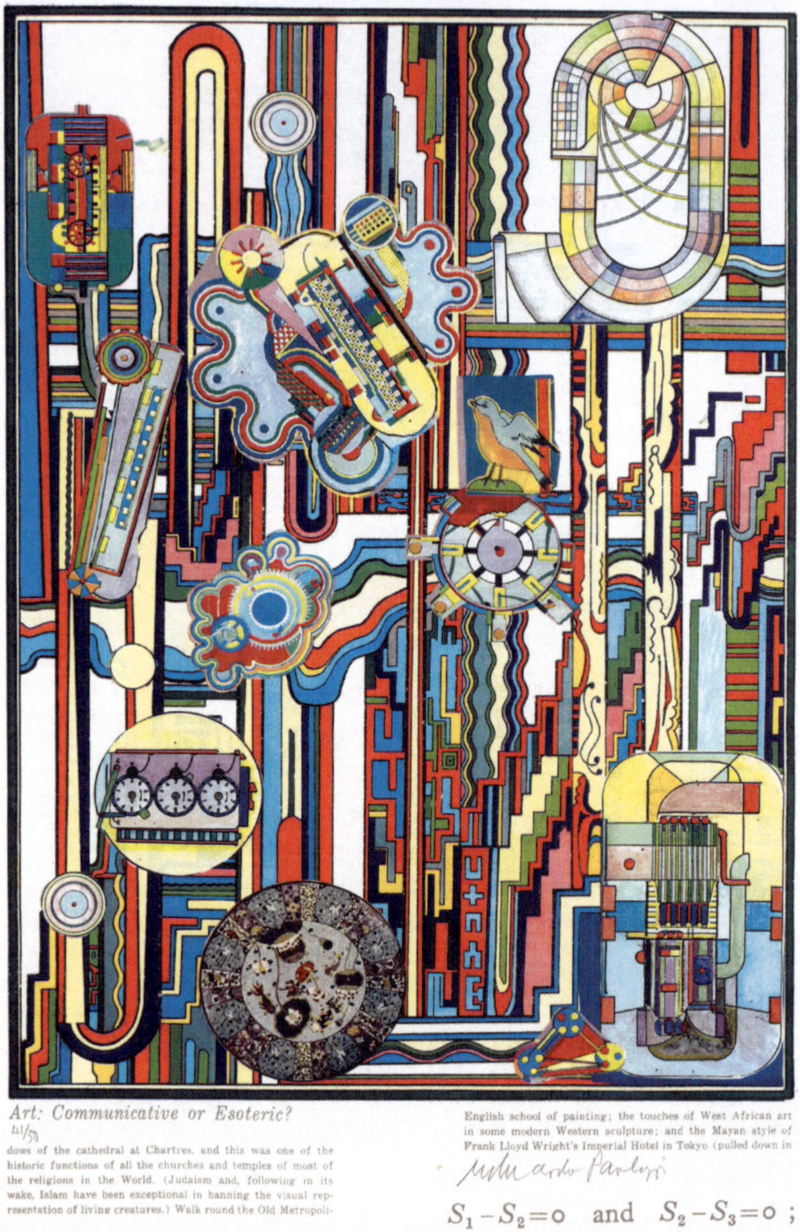

Plate 11 *Turing* 7, 2000, Eduardo Paolozzi, screenprint, 76 × 56 cm.

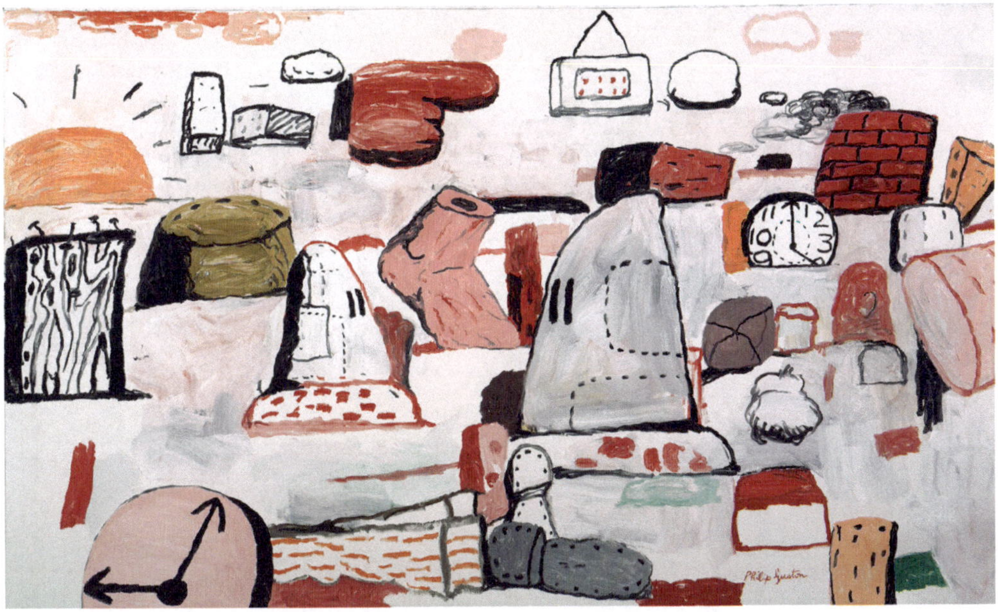

Plate 12 *Flatlands*, 1970, Philip Guston, oil on canvas, 177.8 × 290.83 cm (70 × 114 ½ inches), San Francisco Museum of Modern Art, fractional and promised gift of an anonymous donor.

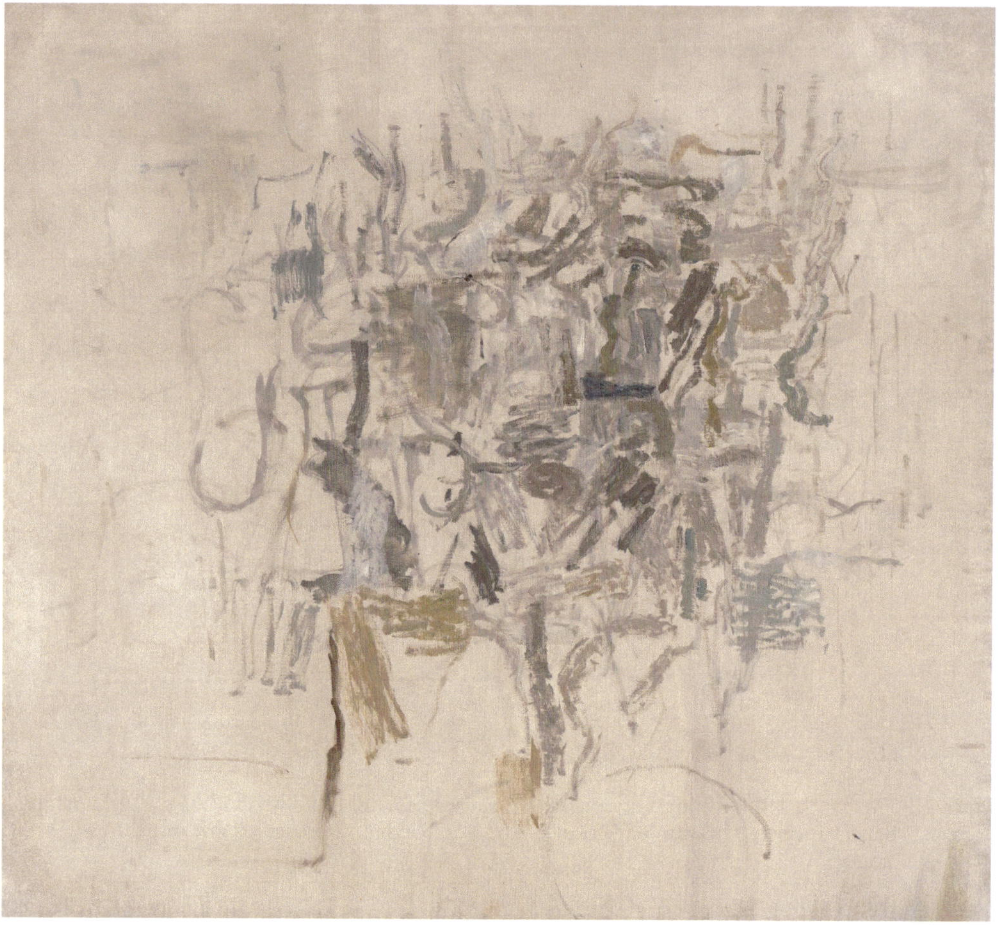

Plate 13 *White Painting, I*, 1951, Philip Guston, oil on canvas, 147 × 157.16 cm (57 7/8 × 61 7/8 inches). San Francisco Museum of Modern Art, T.B. Walker Foundation Fund purchase.

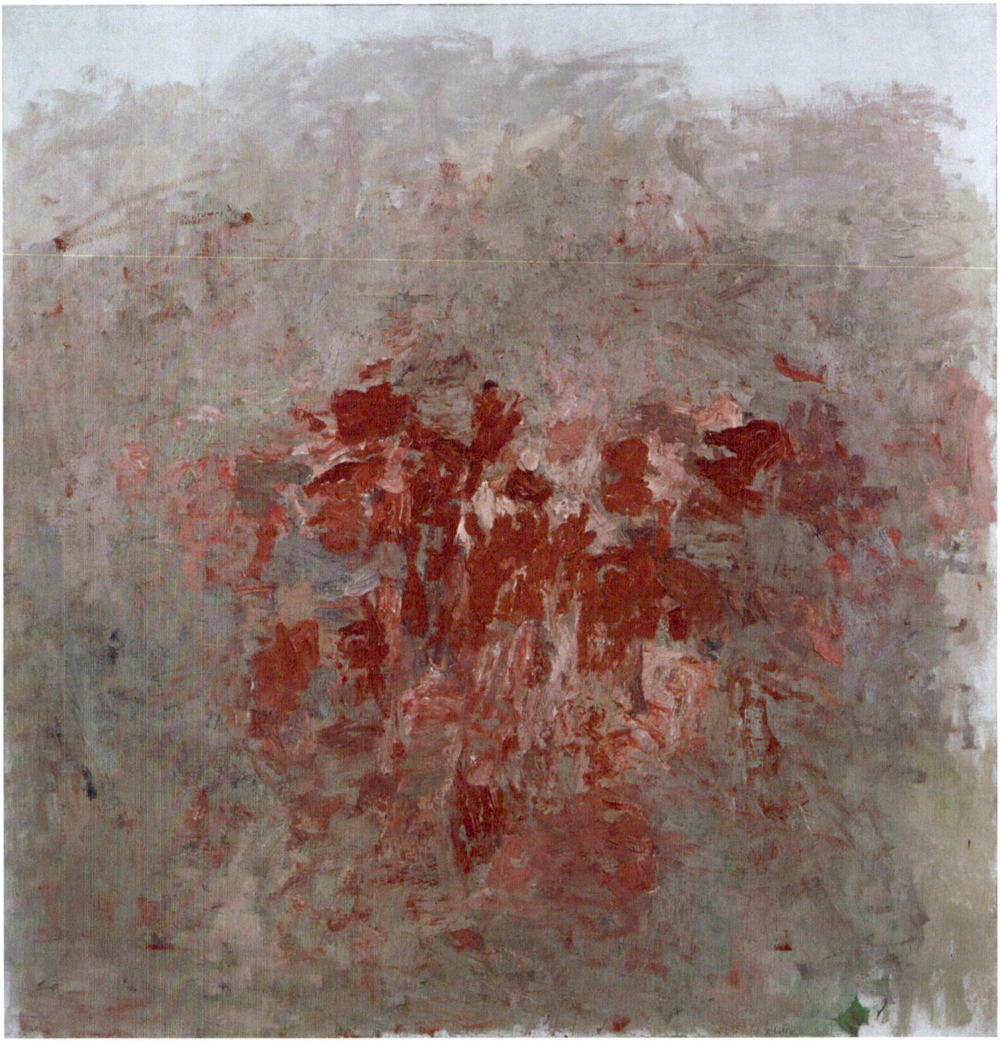

Plate 14 *Untitled*, 1955–6, Philip Guston, oil on canvas, 192.7 × 182.9 cm (75 7/8 × 72 inches). Collection of Lyn and Jerry Grinstein.

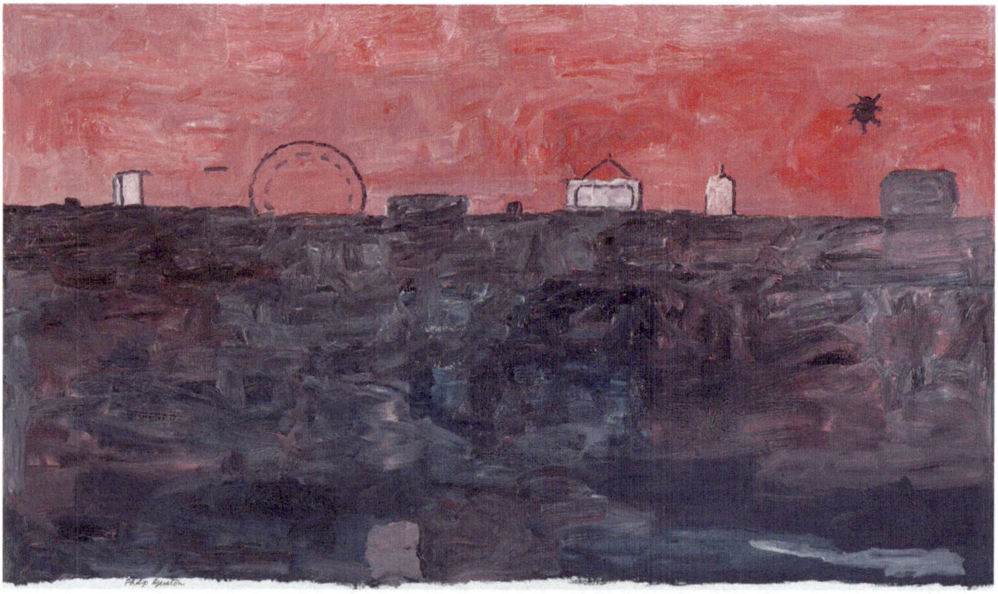

Plate 15 *The Deluge*, 1969, Philip Guston, oil on canvas, 195.6 × 325.1 cm (77 × 128 inches). Museum of Fine Arts, Boston. Bequest of Musa Guston 1992.509.

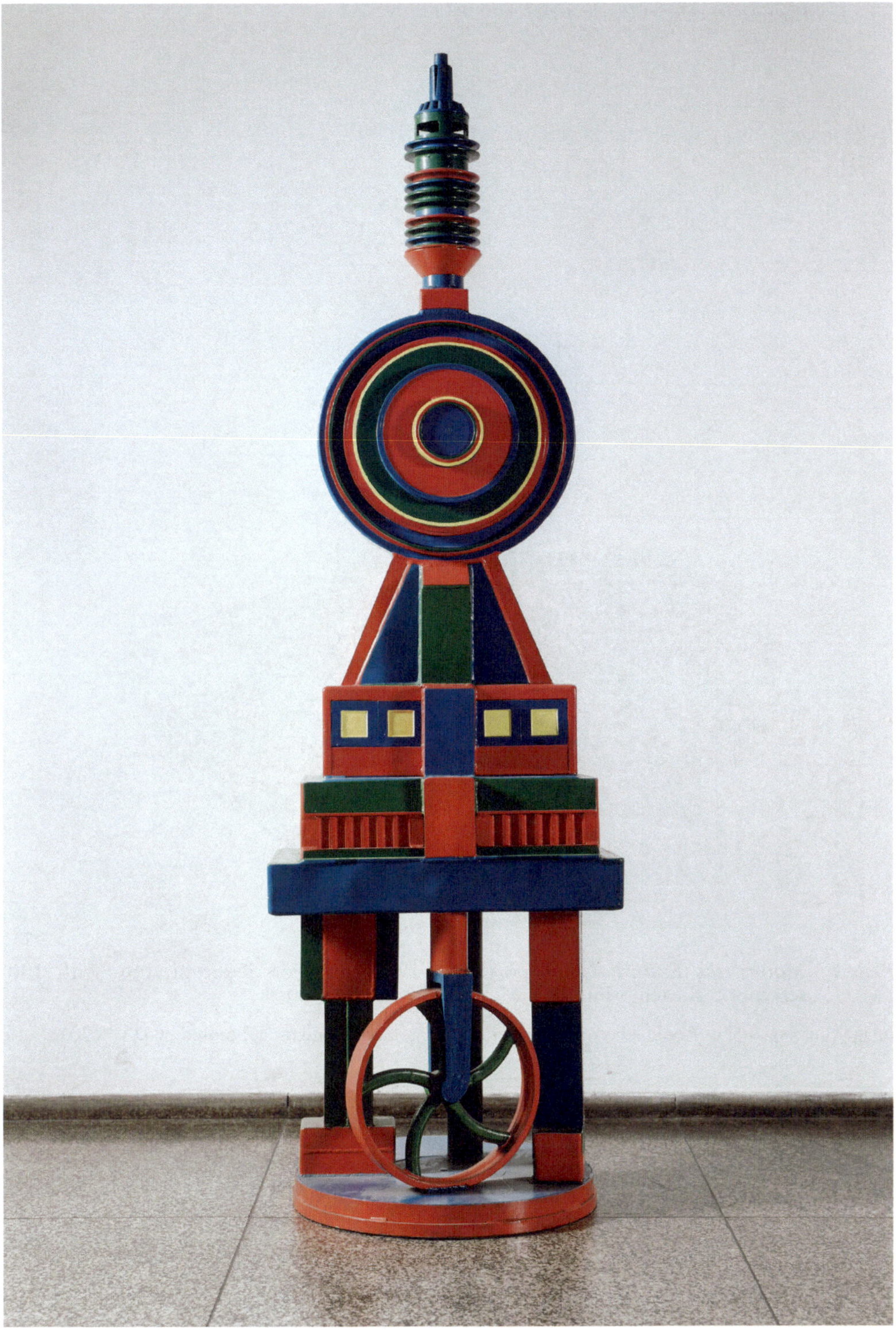

Plate 16 *The Last of the Idols*, 1963, Eduardo Paolozzi, aluminium, height 243.8 cm (96 ¼ inches), Ludwig Museum, Cologne.

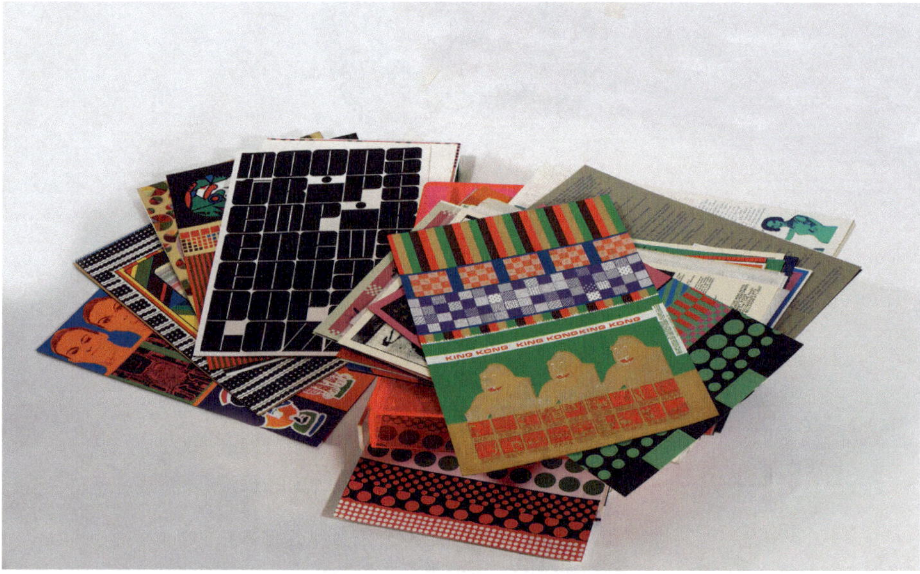

Plate 17 Moonstrips Empire News portfolio, 1967, Eduardo Paolozzi, box with 100 screenprints, each print: 38 × 25.5 cm (15 × 10 inches).

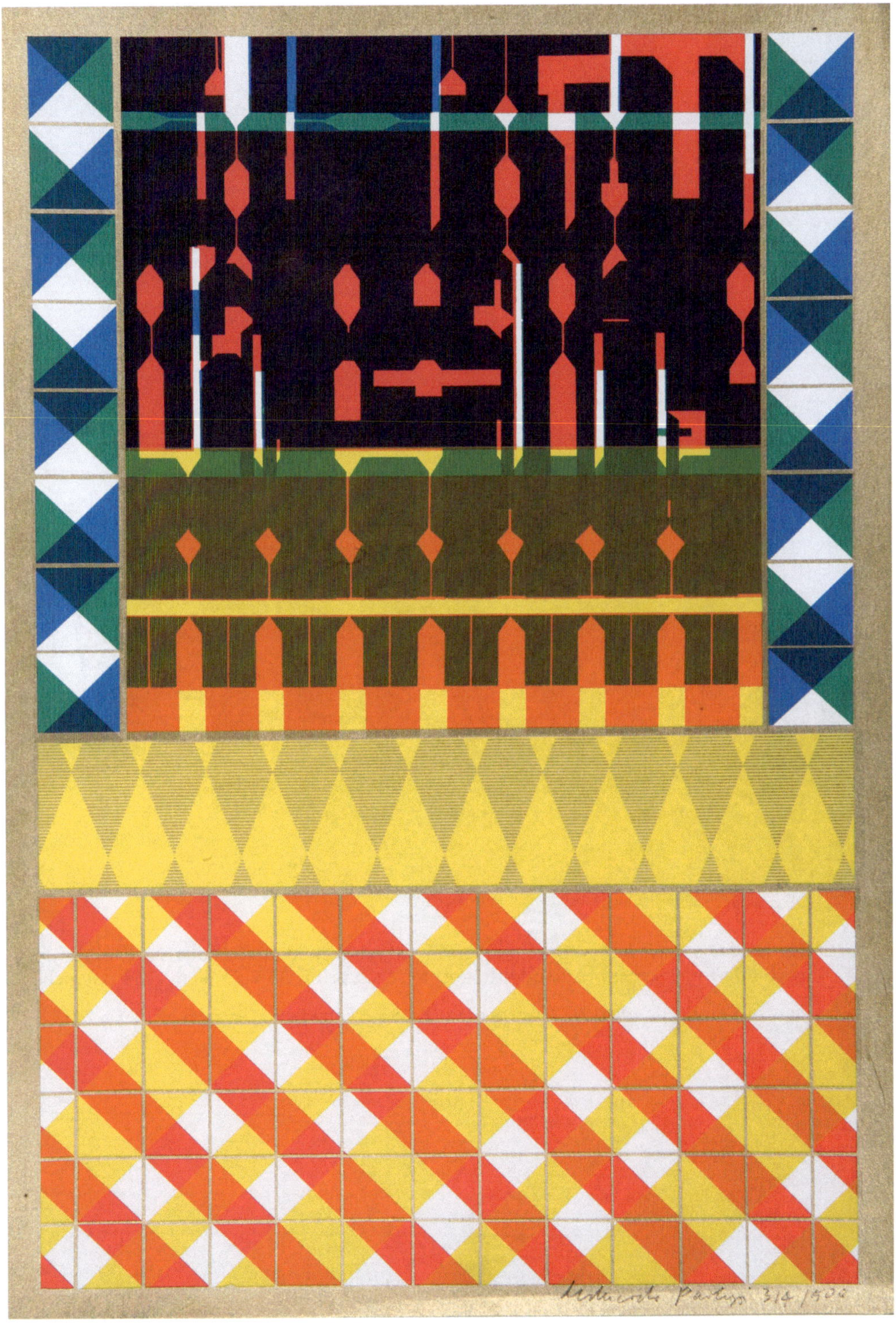

Plate 18 *Cover for a Journal* from *Moonstrips Empire News* portfolio, 1967, 38 × 25.5 cm (15 × 10 inches).

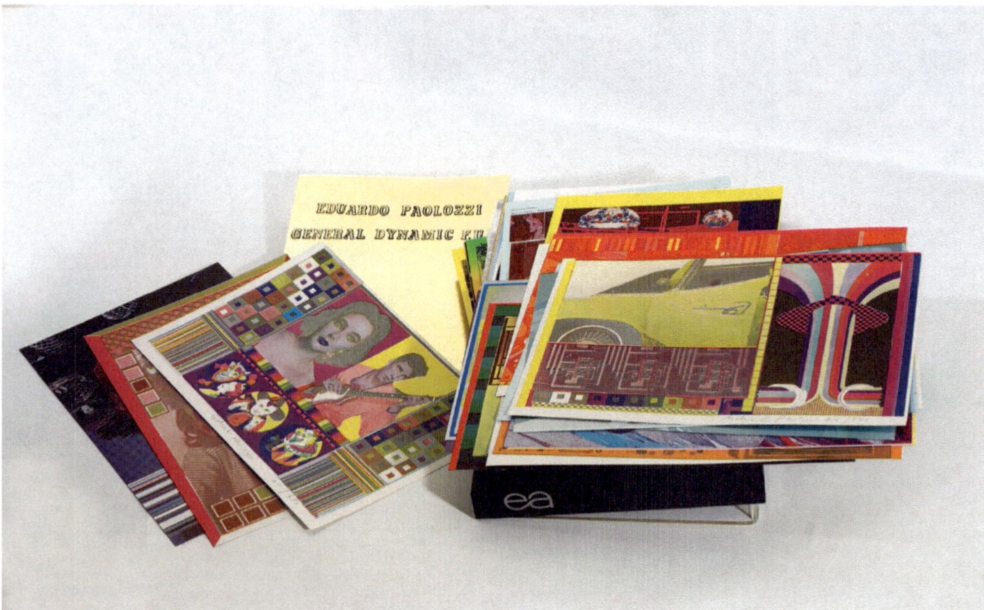

Plate 19 *General Dynamic F.U.N.* portfolio, 1965–70, published 1970, Eduardo Paolozzi, box with 50 prints, screenprint and lithography, each print: 38 × 25.4 cm (15 × 10 inches).

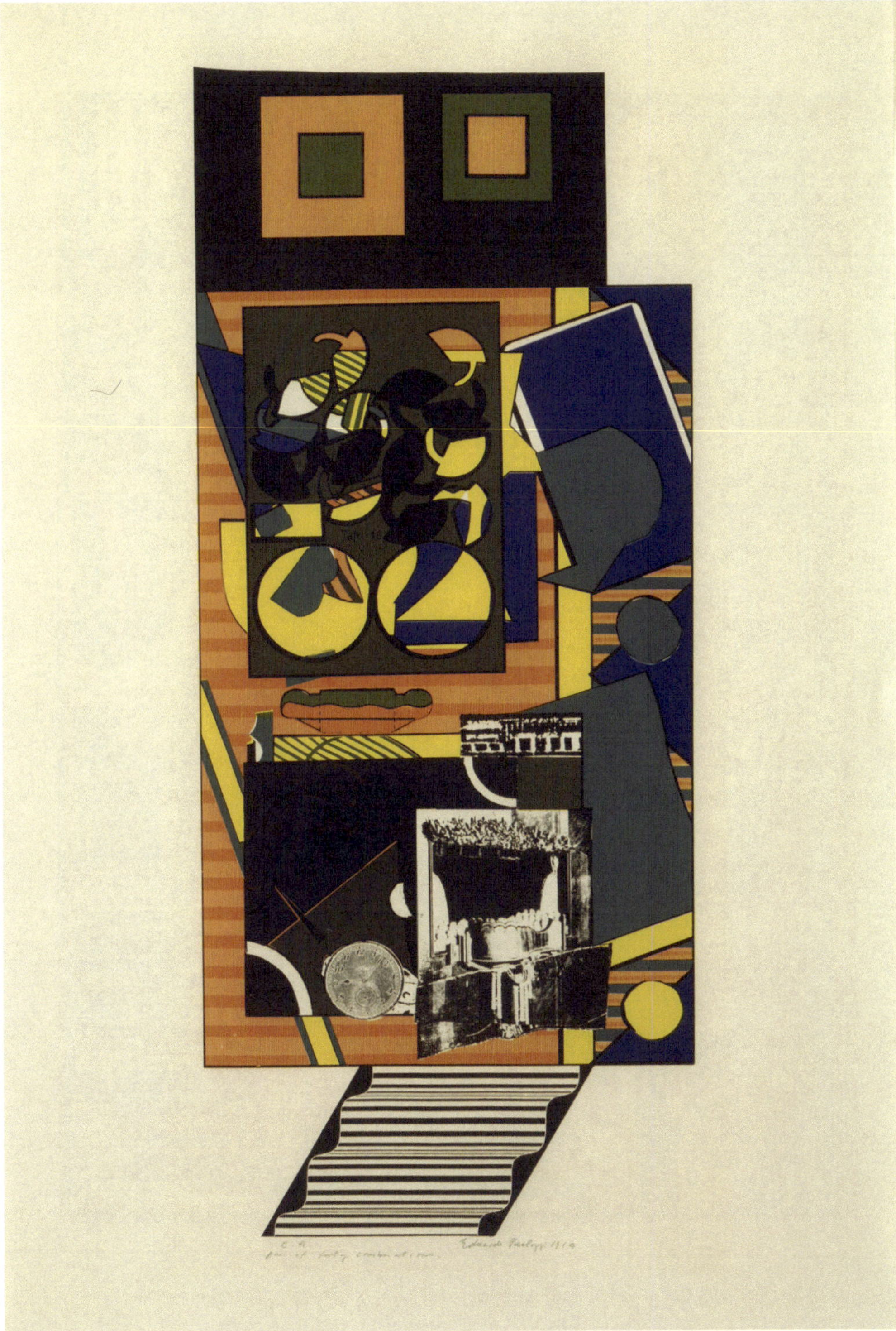

Plate 20 Tafel 16, 1964, Eduardo Paolozzi, screenprint, 52.5 × 89 cm (20.6 × 35 inches).

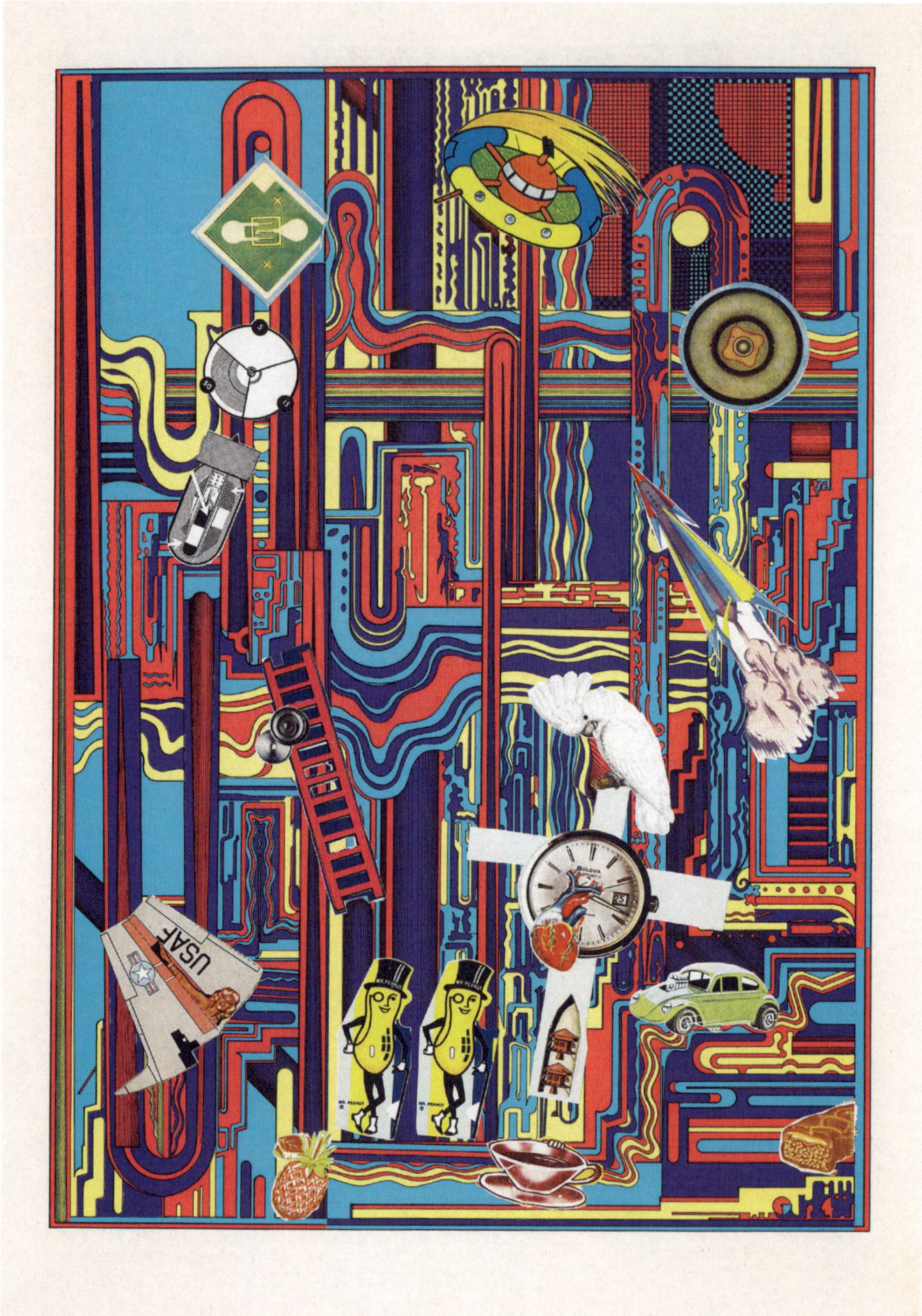

Plate 21 *Mr Peanut*, 1970, Eduardo Paolozzi, screenprint, 70 × 48.5 cm (27 ½ × 19 inches). National Galleries of Scotland. Scottish National Gallery of Modern Art Archive.

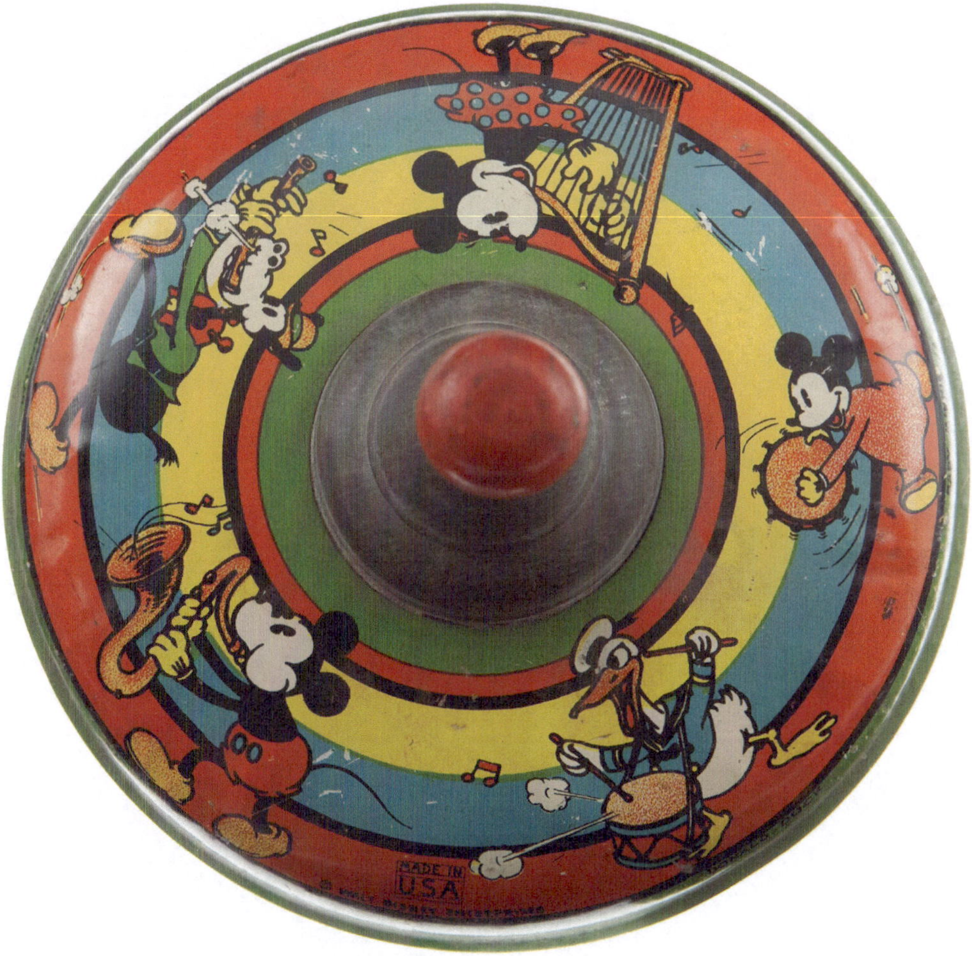

Plate 22 Spinning top toy, 1930s, Fritz Bueschel.

Image courtesy of Heritage Auctions, HA.com.

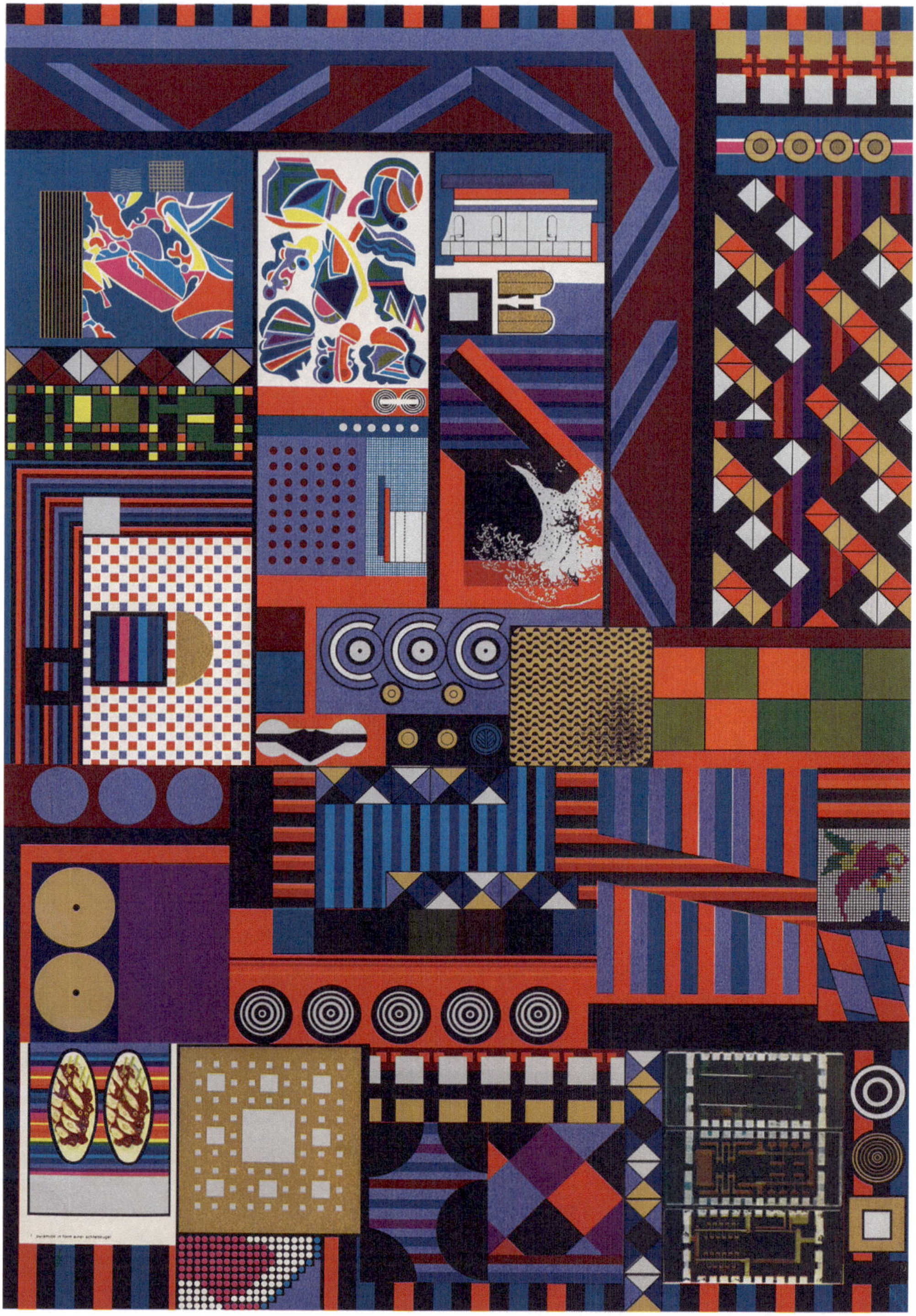

Plate 23 *7 Pyramide in form einer achtel skugel*, 1967, Eduardo Paolozzi, screenprint on paper, 89 × 61 cm (36 × 24 inches).

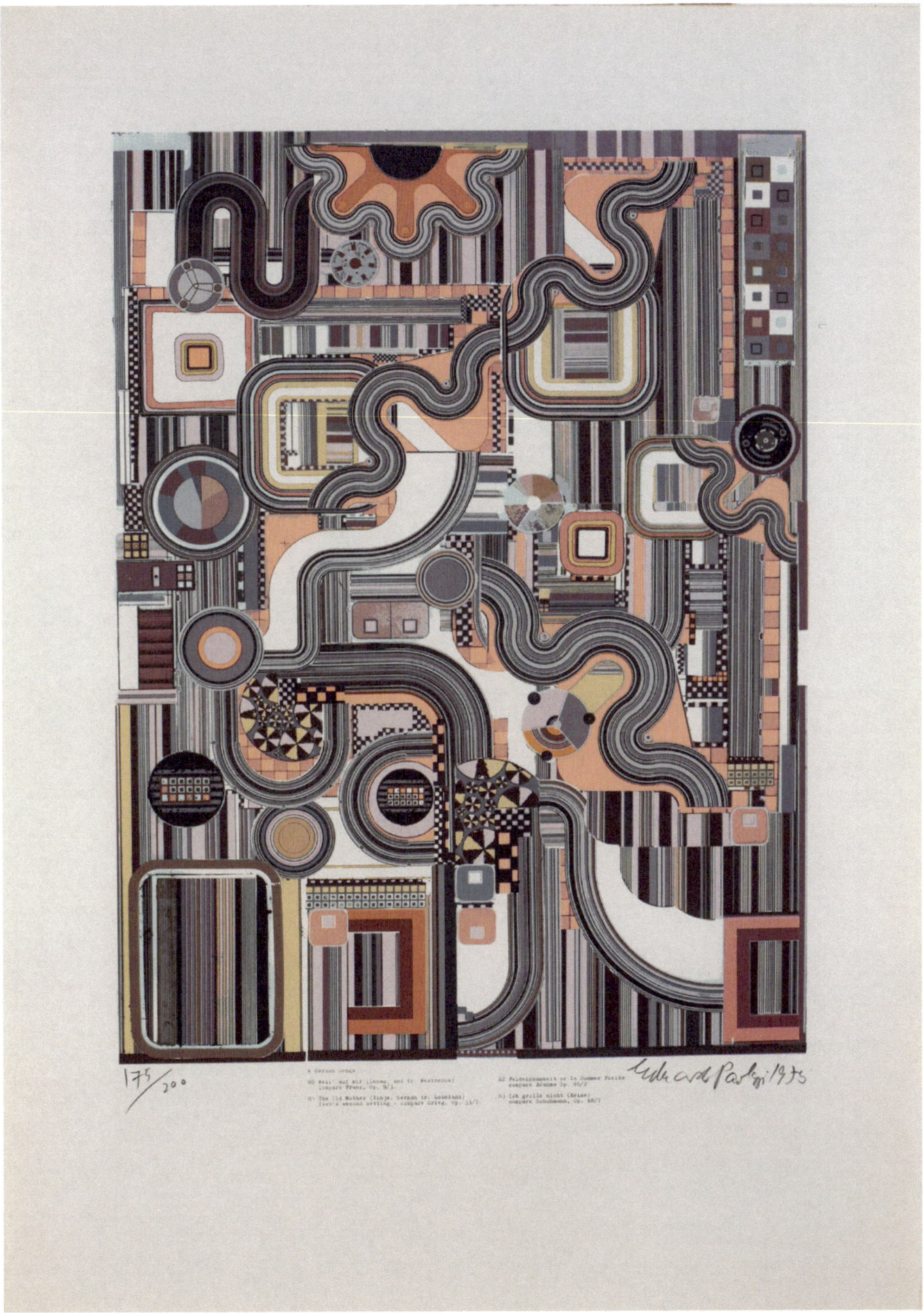

Plate 24 *Four German Songs, Calcium Light Night* portfolio, 1974–6, Eduardo Paolozzi, screenprint, 99 × 69 cm (39 × 27 ¼ inches).

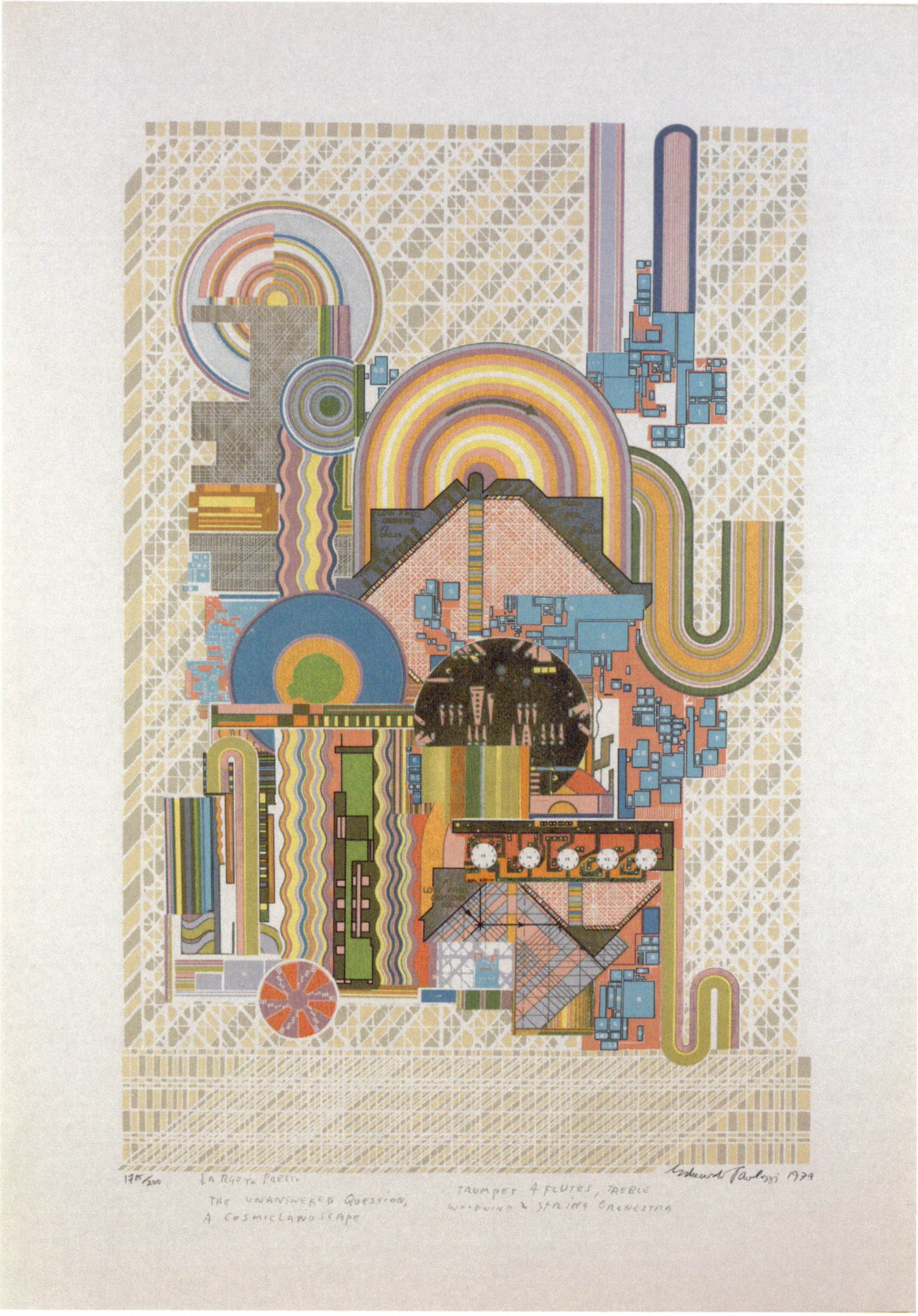

Plate 25 Largo to Presto, Calcium Light Night portfolio, 1974–6, Eduardo Paolozzi, screenprint, 99 × 69 cm (39 × 27 ¼ inches).

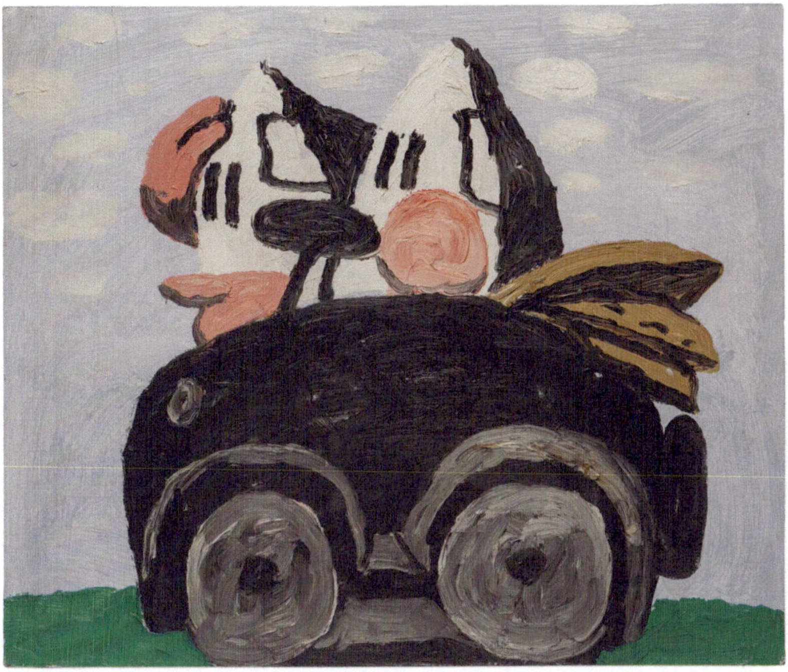

Plate 26 *Untitled (Hoods in Car)*, 1970, Philip Guston, oil on panel, 30.5 × 35.6 cm (12 × 14 inches).

Image courtesy of The Estate of Philip Guston. © The Estate of Philip Guston.

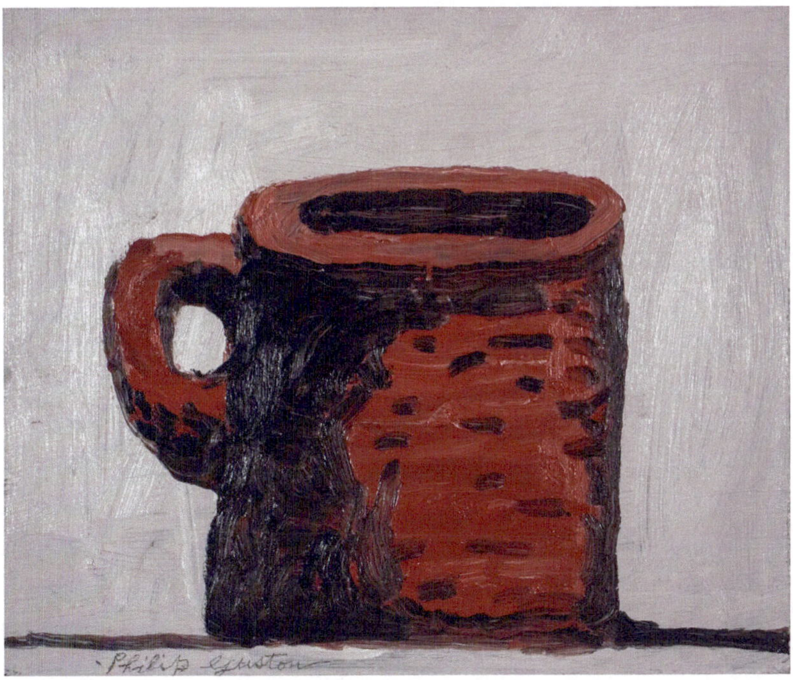

Plate 27 *Cup*, 1972, Philip Guston, oil on panel, 30.5 × 35.6 cm (12 × 14 inches).

Image courtesy of The Estate of Philip Guston. © The Estate of Philip Guston.

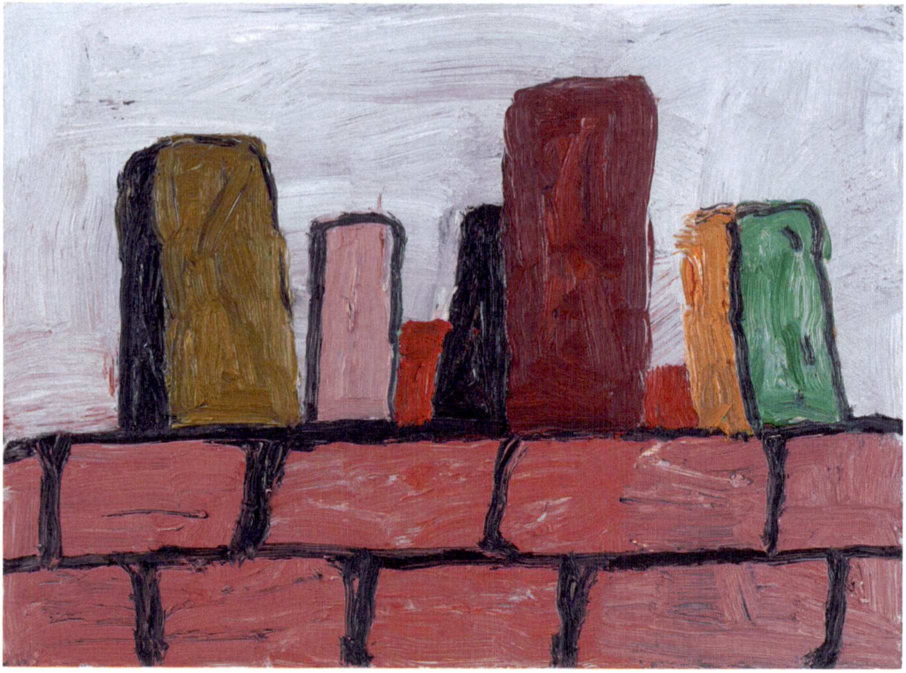

Plate 28 Untitled (Wall), 1968, Philip Guston, oil on panel, 22.9 × 30.5 cm (9 × 12 inches). Image courtesy of The Estate of Philip Guston. © The Estate of Philip Guston.

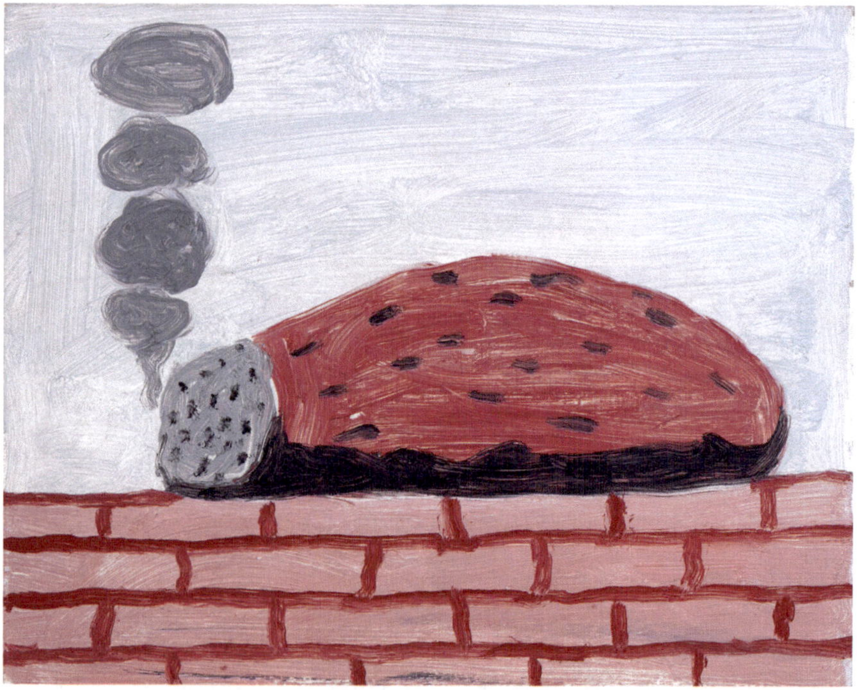

Plate 29 Untitled (Cigar), 1968–73, Philip Guston, oil on panel, 22.9 × 27.9 cm (9 × 11 inches). Image courtesy of The Estate of Philip Guston. © The Estate of Philip Guston.

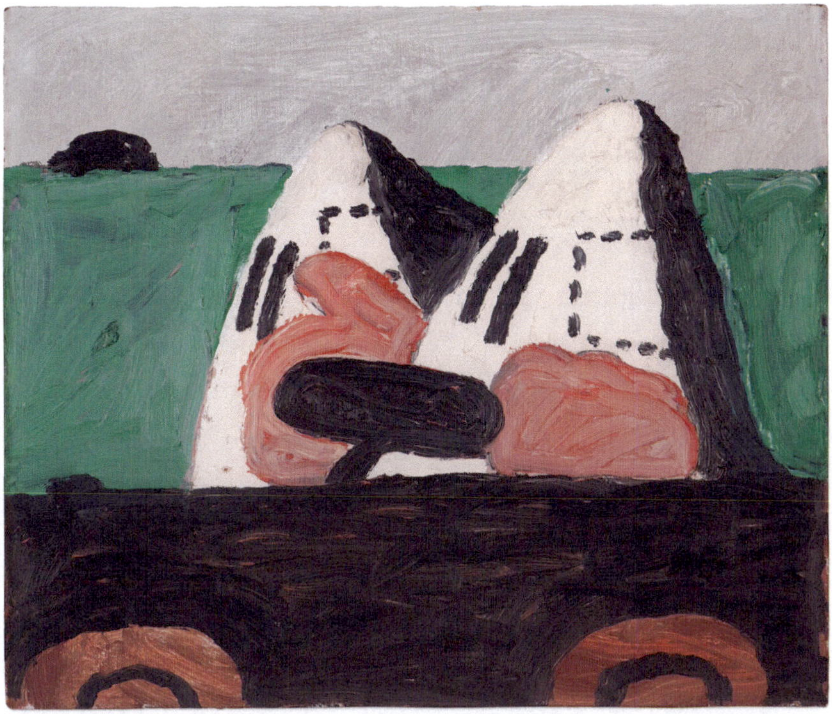

Plate 30 Untitled (Two Hooded Figures in a Car), 1971, 30.5 × 35.6 cm (12 × 14 inches).

Image courtesy of The Estate of Philip Guston.

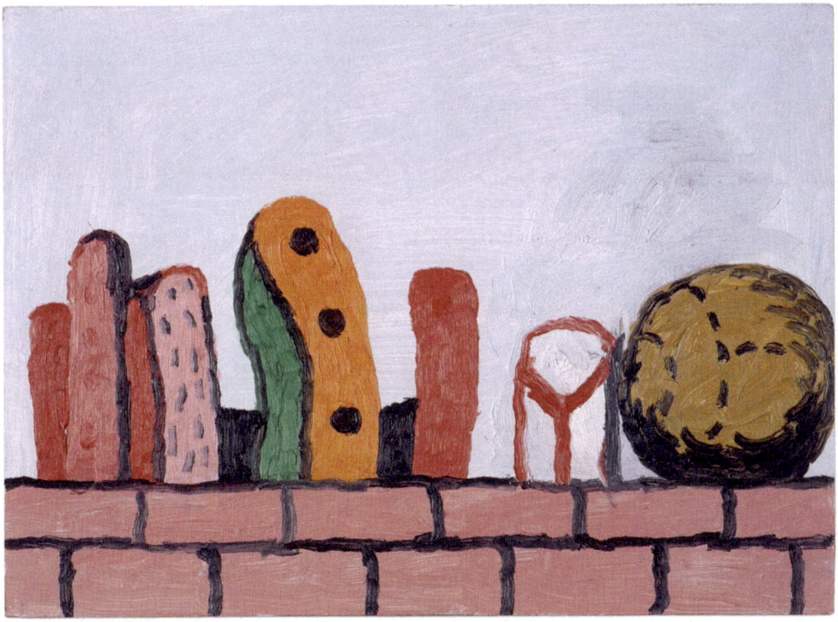

Plate 31 Untitled (Wall), 1970, Philip Guston, oil on panel, 30.5 × 40.6 cm (12 × 16 inches).

Image courtesy of The Estate of Philip Guston.

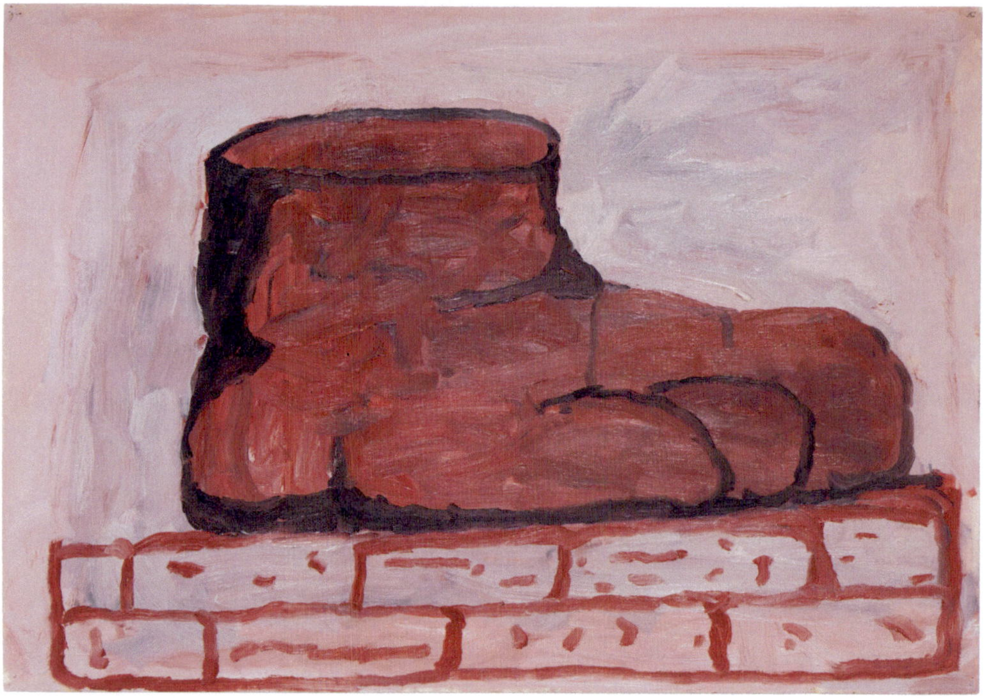

Plate 32 Untitled (Foot on Wall—Roma), 1971, Philip Guston, oil on paper, 48.9 × 70.5 cm (19 × 28 inches).

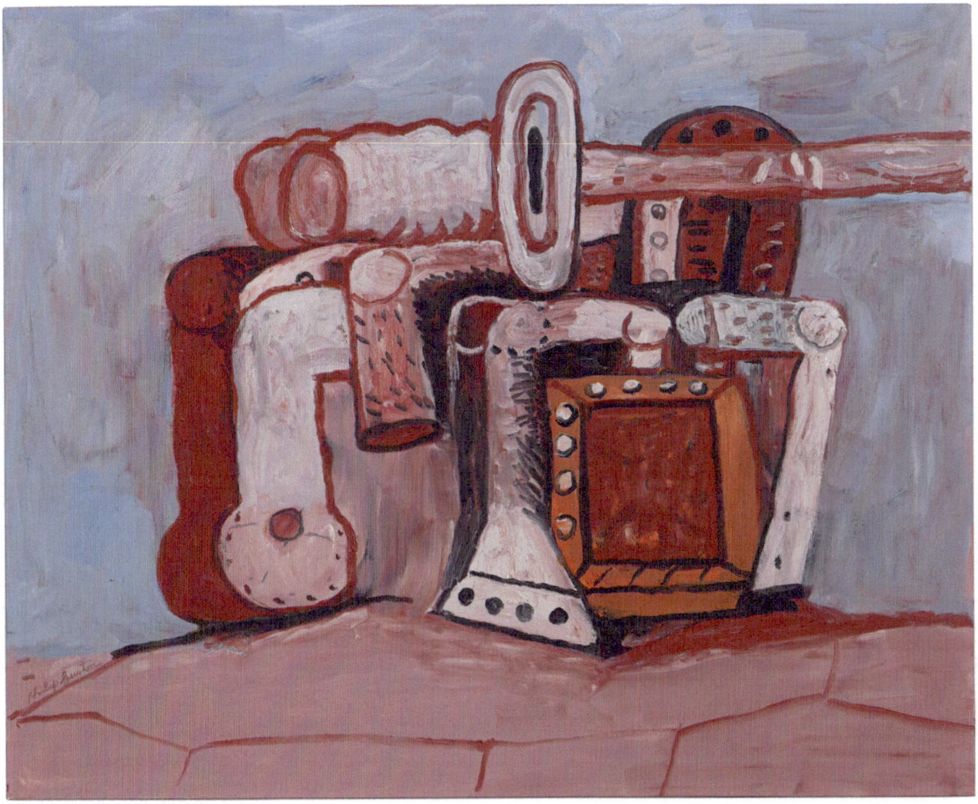

Plate 33 *Forms on Rock Ledge*, 1979, Philip Guston, oil on canvas, 152.4 × 182.9 cm (60 × 72 inches).

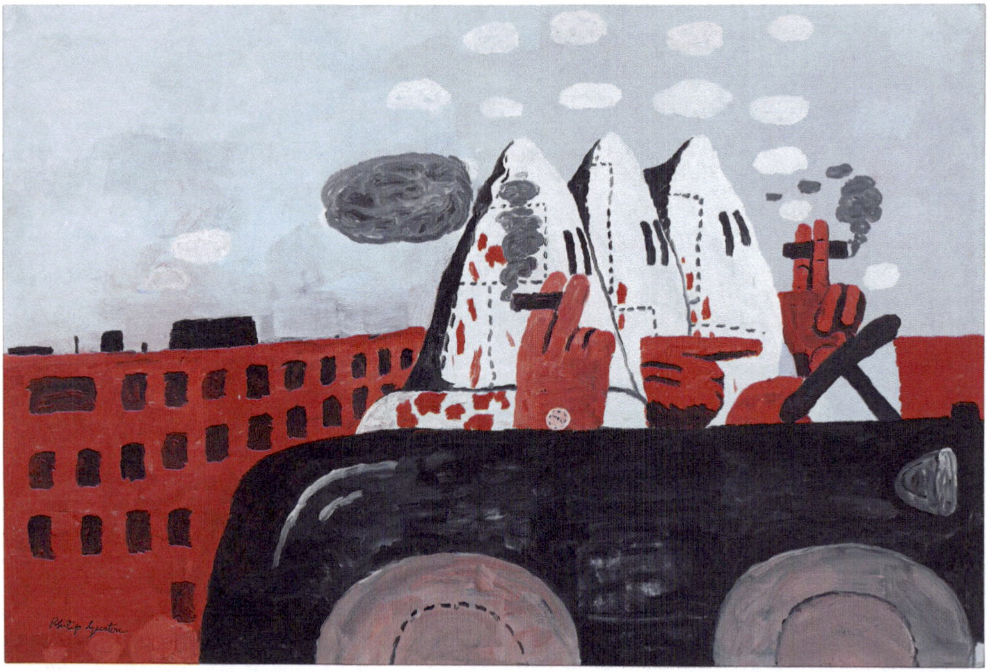

Plate 34 Riding Around, 1969, Philip Guston, oil on canvas, 137 × 201 cm (54 × 79 inches).
Image courtesy of The Estate of Philip Guston. © The Estate of Philip Guston.

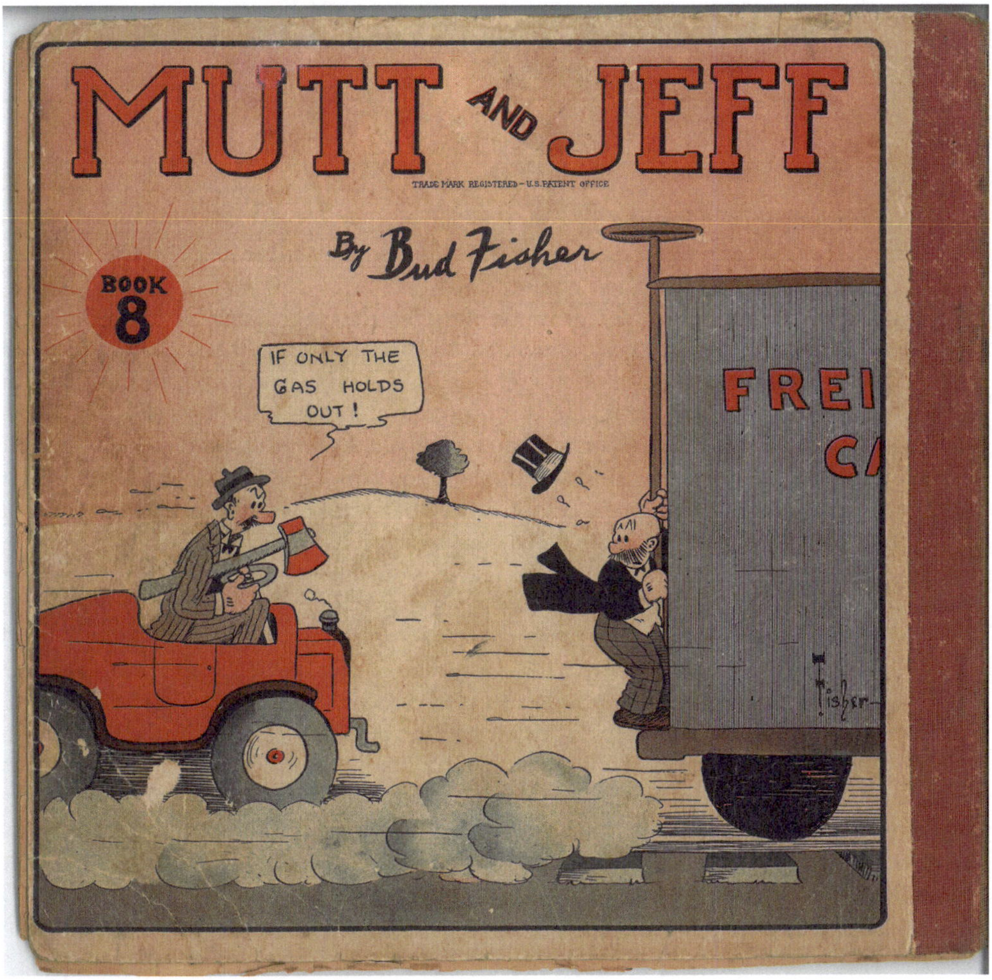

Plate 35 Mutt and Jeff, Book 8, 1922, Bud Fisher.

Image credit: The author.

4 Eduardo Paolozzi's Playgrounds

Contradictions in Art and Play

"Loose Parts": Contradictions at Play

In conversation with Philip Oakes at the Royal College of Art in 1985, Eduardo Paolozzi discussed the studio methods behind his public sculpture:

> I work with a model maker now. We start by making the thing in wood. It's to scale and you can move things around. I've tried to apply these things to what I call social sculptures—suitable for playgrounds—I started with Conran. He commissioned a sculpture, provided an area and gave me an absolutely open briefing . . . It was for children to clamber over. I got the idea first when I saw kids forbidden to climb over sculpture at the open-air exhibition held by the LCC at Battersea. A child sees a piece of sculpture and simply wants to climb on top of it. Why not? My pieces are quite sturdy enough.[1]

In this chapter, I will explore how Paolozzi's discussion with Oakes reveals a tension or contradiction that lies at the centre of Paolozzi's playground sculptures. In the previous two chapters, we have seen how Paolozzi's own studio methods can be understood as having been predicated on play processes through interaction with a collection of forms that allowed the artist to "move things around." These processes share significant similarities with the assertions made in the radical and progressive literature on playground provision contemporaneous with Paolozzi's own playground sculptures. In 1972, drawing on research on adventure playground environments, Simon Nicholson published "The Theory of Loose Parts, an Important Principle for Design Methodology." Nicholson described his Theory of Loose Parts as follows: "In any environment, both the degree of inventiveness and creativity, and the possibility of discovery, are directly proportional to the number and kind of variables in it."[2] For Nicholson, "most environments that do not work such as schools, playgrounds . . . do not do so because they do not meet the 'loose parts' requirement; instead, they are clean, static and impossible to play around with."[3] While Paolozzi's own sculpture, printmaking and playground models were formulated through a studio environment that provided an ever growing and changing collection of variables and loose parts (or "loose characters," to use Paolozzi's term), his finalised playgrounds were almost entirely "static." The 1973 Terence Conran commission, discussed by Paolozzi in his interview with Oakes, brought together a collection of six aluminium sculptures to create a play space at Habitat's Wallingford store (Figure 4.1). However, the possibilities for play afforded by the sculptures limited children's interaction to objects they

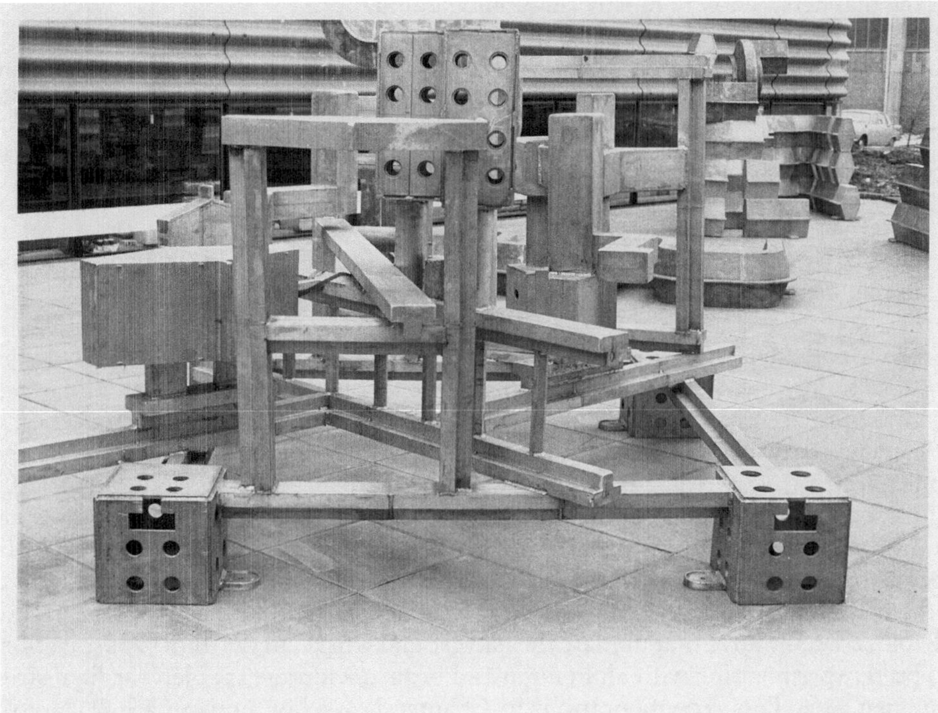

Figure 4.1 *Wallingford Playground*, 1973. Eduardo Paolozzi, cast and welded aluminium, site: Wallingford Offices, Hithercroft Road, Wallingford, Oxfordshire. National Galleries of Scotland. Scottish National Gallery of Modern Art Archive.

could "clamber over." We see this repeated in *Homage to Gaudi* (1973), Paolozzi's cast concrete playground for Santa Cruz, Tenerife, and later public works such as the playground for the Central School in Köln-Pesch (1982) (Figure 4.4). Correspondence from Paolozzi's assistant Marlee Robinson regarding the Pesch playground reveals that Paolozzi was continuing to play with the configuration of the playground sculptures almost up to the final installation. Safety engineers were even involved in deciding the final structure, with meetings to discuss the arrangement of the collection of sculptural elements. However, this open, collaborative process, which employed a collection of "loose parts," is then seemingly undermined by its finalisation in an immoveable structure that is offered as a play space for children.

Writing four years before Nicholson, in her publication *Planning for Play*, Lady Allen of Hurtwood, the chief proponent of the adventure playground movement in post-war England, asked: "Why are so many of the new playgrounds stagnant?"[4] For Lady Allen,

> children of all ages, all over the world, are happiest when they can move things around to their own liking. They have an irresistible urge to build houses and

> dens, dig holes. . . . These are all delightfully messy occupations and they make the planners, who are mostly tidy-minded, unhappy.[5]

Paolozzi's playgrounds were born out of his own messy, cluttered studio environment, and yet the sculptures do not allow for what Lady Allen describes as the "messiness" of children's play. For Nicholson, this is the common pitfall of most design:

> What happens is that adults—in the form of professional artists, architects . . . have had all the fun playing with their own materials, concepts and planning alternatives, and then builders have had all the fun building the environments out of real materials; and thus all the fun and creativity have been stolen.[6]

However, one could question whether this limitation was one of Paolozzi's design, or a constraint that was imposed on his work through the requirements of working in the public sphere. In fact, Lady Allen provides one answer to the question of the stagnancy of the new playgrounds; according to Lady Allen, "there is another conflict which is very real. Because local authorities fear accidents (and litigation)."[7] Significantly, the contradiction at the centre of Paolozzi's playground sculptures had not been present in a number of earlier works. The lack of continuity between the play process that generated the sculptures and the possibilities for interactive play offered by the final immoveable structures is a disjuncture that had not been present in three of Paolozzi's sculptures that predate the playground works. In the mid-1960s, Paolozzi had been experimenting with aluminium and bronze sculpture that left the final structure open to endless reconfiguration. In Chapter 2, we saw how, in 1962, Paolozzi began using a collection of mass-produced prefabricated aluminium units that were combined to create a series of configurations. In early pieces such as *Towards a New Laocoon* (1963), *The City of Circle and the Square* (1963/6) and *Mechanik's Bench* (1963), Paolozzi played with repetition and recombination through the use of mass-produced elements that recur across the works in differing configurations. But, by the mid to late-1960s, Paolozzi's fascination with recombination and the unresolved had been pushed further to engage with moveable, changeable structures. *Rio* (1965–6), *Hamlet in a Japanese Manner* (1966) and *Domino* (1967–8) are works comprised of a collection of moveable elements that can be reconfigured to create new combinations and structures.

Domino (Figure 4.2) consists of nine moveable aluminium units. The title clearly invites associations with game pieces. In place of the finality of a welded structure present in earlier aluminium works, the units in *Domino* remain as an assertively unresolved collection of distinct elements. Resembling a collection of enlarged toy building blocks, the units can be animated through a process of stacking and reshuffling. However, due to practical concerns both for audience and artwork, *Domino* is currently displayed at the Scottish National Gallery of Modern Art with the units secured in place, limiting the changeable "life" of the work.

The moveable sculptures, then, point to a possibility as to the presence of the contradiction at the centre of the later immoveable playground sculpture. This contradiction emerges from the choice of materials, health and safety concerns and the need for durability or longevity. However, it is possible durability was not simply a requirement imposed on Paolozzi's public sculpture by the sculptures' commissioning bodies. Paolozzi displayed an ongoing concern with the longevity of his work. In an interview

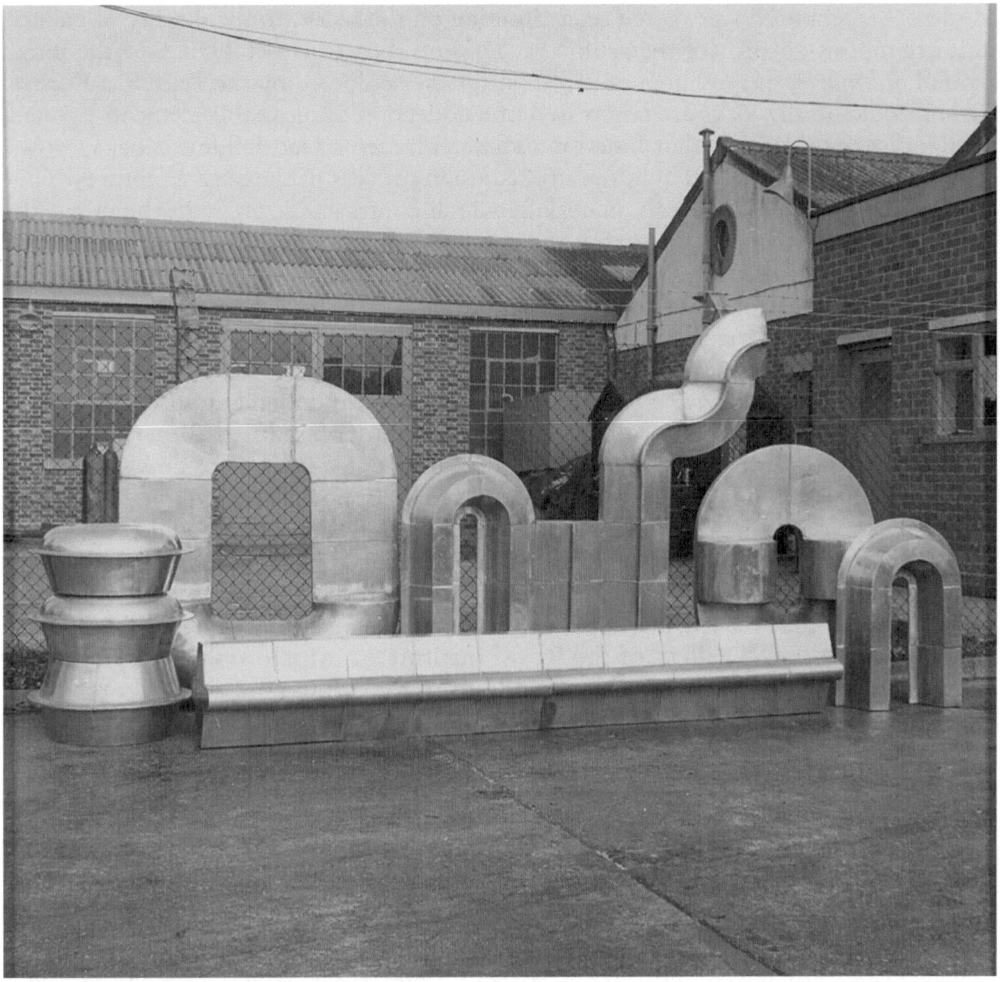

Figure 4.2 *Domino*, 1967–8, Eduardo Paolozzi, polished welded aluminium (9 elements). Collection of Scottish National Gallery of Modern Art. Scottish National Gallery of Modern Art Archive.

with Edouard Roditi in 1960, Paolozzi described his disappointment at the deterioration of many Dadaist and Surrealist works: "They soon fade or rust, and they tend to disintegrate like cheap artificial flowers left out in the wind or the rain on a grave in a French cemetery."[8] Paolozzi then went on to explain his choice of more durable materials: "I am anxious that my works should have a permanent quality and not be subject to unnecessary change, except in so far as they may acquire with time the normal patina of a matured bronze."[9] The desire for a "permanent quality" and the need to avoid "unnecessary change" clearly created a rupture between the artist's working processes and the final works, severing a connection to the shifting mass of changeable elements that characterised the artist's studio methods.

When *Domino* was first installed in the grounds of the Scottish National Gallery of Modern Art, children were often seen climbing on the work, to the dismay of gallery staff attempting to protect the sculpture. *Domino* bears a resemblance to the playground *Submarine* (1969) created a year after the sculpture by the French collective Group Ludic. Both works are comprised of a collection of moveable elements formed from industrial materials that function like an enlarged set of building blocks. However, Group Ludic involved children in the design process of the play sculptures. This is reflected in the child-friendly materials, which contrast sharply with the unwieldy aluminium used to create *Domino* and Paolozzi's subsequent playground sculptures. Significantly, none of the original Group Ludic playgrounds are still in existence. By contrast, although *Domino* remains intact, both the artist and the museum's desire to protect and preserve the artwork has masked the initial generative spirit of the work and the studio processes that lay behind it.

In examining the history of *Domino*, one can begin to understand how Paolozzi's choice of materials have either inhibited or facilitated possibilities for play. By making comparisons with Group Ludic's playgrounds, one can explore how Paolozzi's choice of materials have affected interactivity, but importantly, *Domino* also provides a way to question how the materials have affected the extent to which the viewing audience is able to access the artist's improvisatory methods and play processes through the final artwork. In 2015, the architecture collective Assemble created an installation that placed materials at the centre of a re-imagining of the brutalist playground. In the gallery of the Royal Institute of British Architects, Assemble recreated sections of brutalist playgrounds from the 1960s, designed by architects including Ernö Goldfinger, Philip Powell and Hidalgo Moya. However, instead of using concrete—the material that has come to define perceptions of the brutalist playground—Assemble used reconstituted foam in shades of pastel pink, turquoise and grey. Assemble have pointed to the humour in the work; for Joe Halligan (a member of the collective), "it's a sort of in-joke, that in order for these postwar structures to meet current safety standards, everything has to be squidgy."[10] But the change in material also introduced the aspect of play that was key to Nicholson and Lady Allen's assessment of adequate playground provision, namely moveable elements or "loose parts." Powell and Moya's immoveable, concrete mountain built from hexagonal columns for the playground of the Churchill Gardens estate, in Pimlico, London, was re-designed by Assemble as a collection of moveable foam building blocks. Powell and Moya's structure was transformed from a sculpture to "clamber over" (to use Paolozzi's phrase) into a collection of elements visitors could rearrange and restructure.

Halligan echoes Nicholson in his assessment of Goldfinger's playground design for the Balfron Tower in East London. For Halligan, "it's the stuff Goldfinger couldn't do on the tower, so he let his mind go wild in the playground. I don't know how much he actually thought about how good it would be to play on—which is the beauty of it really."[11] Once again, it is the architect that is seen to have the freedom to play in the playground, while the resulting design is perceived to inhibit children's capacity to affect their environment creatively. In the translation from model to realised playground, the potential for play has been restricted. Through a shift in material, Assemble's brutalist playground produced expanded possibilities for play to bring a closer connection to the imaginative freedom expressed in the model.

The Model

Paolozzi produced his first design for a playground as early as 1950–1. This was a commission from the architects Maxwell Fry and Jane Drew for a block of flats in Whitefoot Lane, Bromley, London (Figure 4.3). Although the project was never realised, from Paolozzi's model it is hard to imagine the playground offering a substantial range of play potential for children. Comprised of a collection of variously shaped blocks that resemble a cityscape, the playground would have provided a static, concrete environment in which children's play would largely have been limited to games of hide and seek, climb and crawl. In its unrealised state, Paolozzi's model suggests a connection to William Turnbull's *Playground (Game)* (1949). A friend of Paolozzi from their student days at the Slade School of Fine Art, Turnbull, created the piece in 1948, when he and Paolozzi were living in Paris. Judith Collins has suggested that it is during this time that Paolozzi and Turnbull would have become aware of Alberto Giacometti's works, which resemble board games and playgrounds, including *No More Play* (1931–2) and *Project for a Square* (1931–2).

Paolozzi's first playground model also bears a marked resemblance to a set of toy building blocks. The sets of building blocks, now held in the Krazy Kat Arkive at

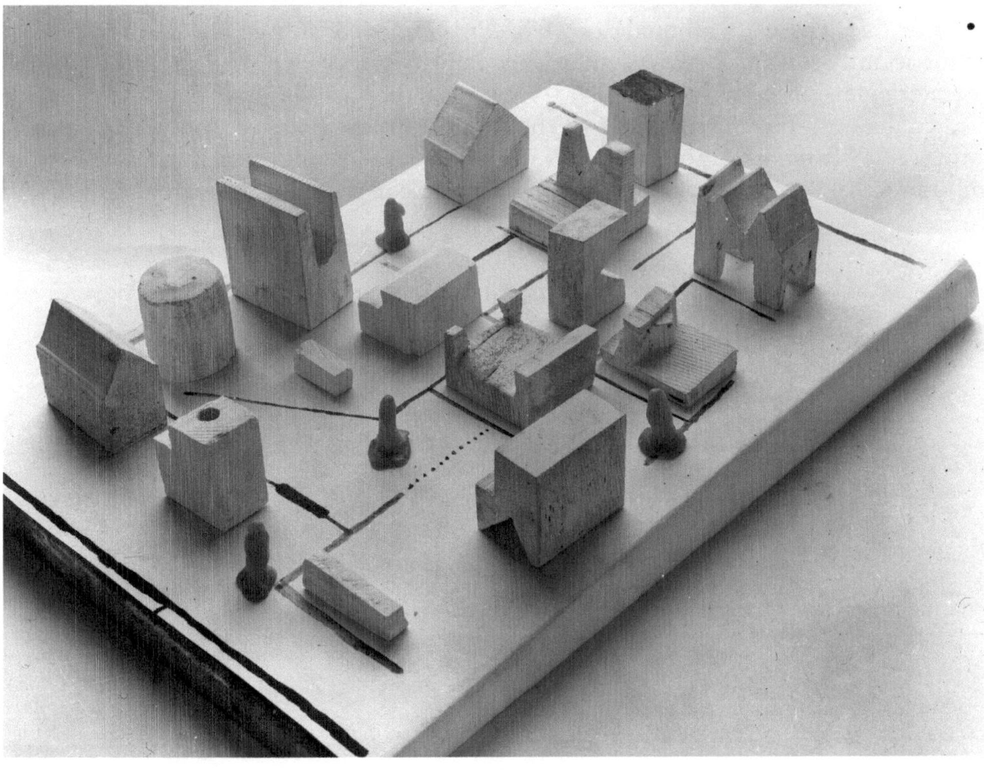

Figure 4.3 Photograph of *Study for a playground for a block of flats, Whitefoot Lane, London, c.1950–1*, Eduardo Paolozzi, plaster, wood, cardboard and wax for poured concrete, approx. 22.8 × 96.5 × 76 cm (9 × 38 × 30 inches).

Photographer: Nigel Henderson. Image credit: © Tate, London 2017.

the Victoria and Albert Museum, evidence how Paolozzi's interest in the toy continued into adult life. I would suggest that through this connection to the toy, one can consider how Paolozzi's playgrounds come closest to a connection to play, as it was understood by Nicholson and Lady Allen, when they remain in an unrealised state as models. The schism between playground sculpture and model is perhaps most clearly pronounced in Paolozzi's *Pesch Playground* (1982) (Figures 4.4 and 4.5), created thirty years after the artist's first unrealised playground design. Assembled from a collection of Paolozzi's aluminium elements that had remained unused from his work in the 1970s, together with some newly made components, the finalised sculpture seems to fall within Lady Allen's category of the "over-elaborate, over-clever . . . play sculpture . . . fixed in unalterable form."[12] Lady Allen was uncompromising in her condemnation of highly designed play sculptures, stating that "children quickly tire of the inflexible ironmongery."[13] By stark contrast, in Paolozzi's wooden model for the playground, Lady Allen and Nicholson's definitions of the dynamics of play are made manifest. The individual wooden elements present a collection of flexible, moveable parts, or building blocks. One thinks of the artist's hand through the haptic and rhythmic qualities of the work. Each wooden piece could be easily handled and toyed with. This allows us to think of the structure as mobile, improvisatory and responsive, reconnecting us with Winnicott's description of the vitality of the toy. In its unrealised state as model, the structure is provisional, just one possibility among innumerable. These are all qualities we become removed from in the final sculpture.

Importantly, within the Pesch model, the improvisatory elements play off a defined geometric structure. Two rectangular frames form the base, while an asymmetric, jumbled configuration is mirrored across the frames. So, the structure, however improvisatory, is far from arbitrary. Paolozzi's use of a counterpoint to the frame evokes the importance of the grid for the artist's friends and collaborators, the architects Alison

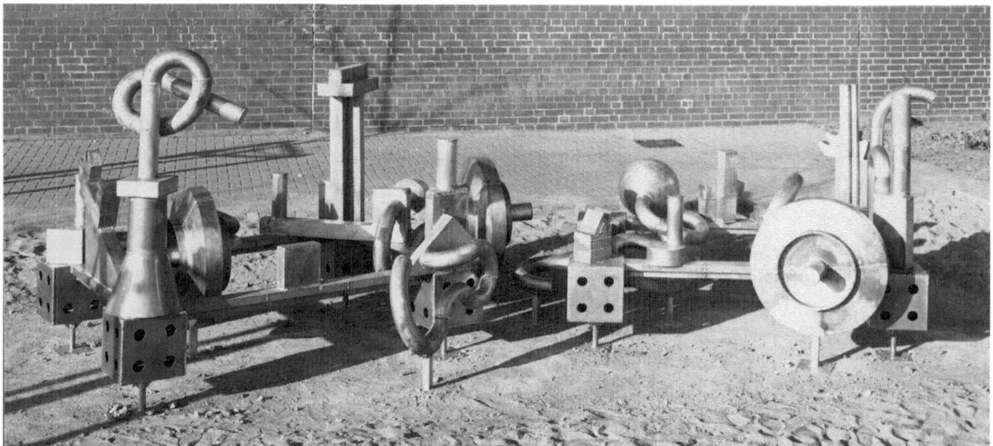

Figure 4.4 *Pesch Playground*, 1982, Eduardo Paolozzi, aluminium sections, site: Schulzentrum Köln-Pesch, Schulstrasse, Cologne, commissioned by the City of Cologne. National Galleries of Scotland. Scottish National Gallery of Modern Art Archive.

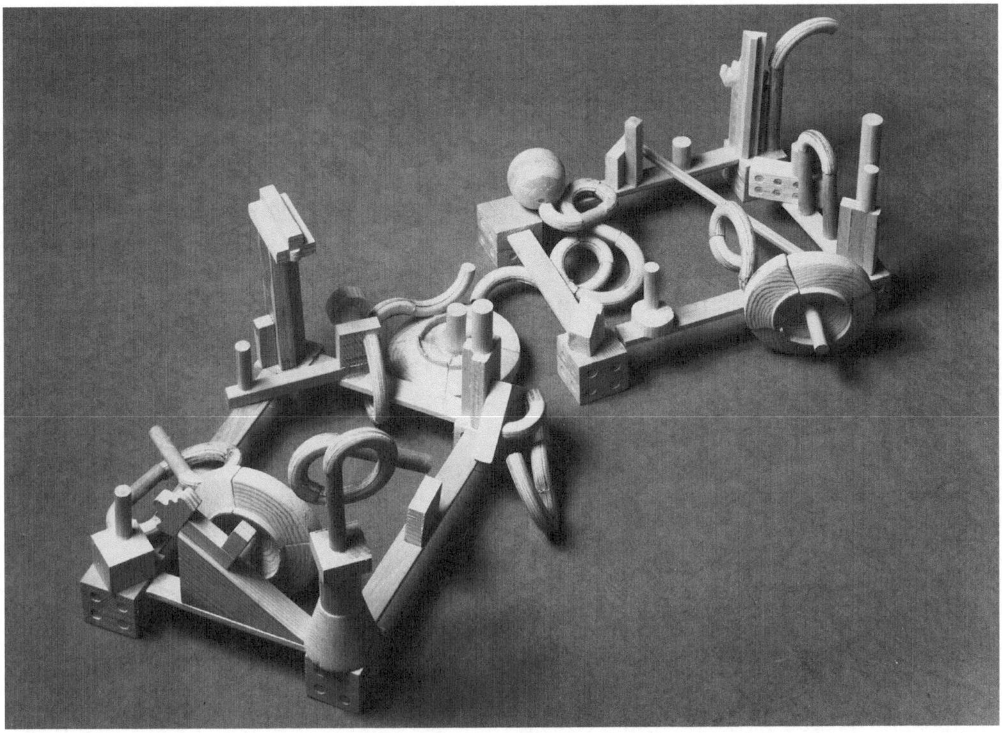

Figure 4.5 Model for "Pesch Playground" (Schulzentrum Köln-Pesch, Schulstrasse, Cologne), 1982, Eduardo Paolozzi, wood. National Galleries of Scotland. Scottish National Gallery of Modern Art Archive.

and Peter Smithson. The Smithsons employed "random aesthetics"[14] in reaction to Le Corbusier's emphasis on an ordering system based on the grid. For the Congrès Internationaux d'Architecture Moderne (CIAM) (1928–59)—among whom Le Corbusier was a leading member—the city could be understood in terms of four basic functions: living, working, moving and relaxing. CIAM proposed that the design of a modern city should clearly delineate these four functions into distinct areas. The Smithsons were among younger members of CIAM that shared concerns about the functionalist model, arguing that it failed to take account of the complex network of social relations that take place within the built environment. In 1953, at the ninth CIAM conference in Aix-en-Provence, the Smithsons presented their Urban Re-Identification Grille, a display grid that demonstrated how Nigel Henderson's photographs of children playing in the streets of the East End of London had led directly to the Smithsons' development of aformalism, or a "random aesthetic." Through Henderson's photographs and the Smithsons' subsequent diagrams, the city is presented as a site of intricate social connections, a concept they would name "cluster city." Children's street play is seen to disrupt the functionalist geometric categorisation of place. Through play, children are understood to creatively reinvent their environment according to need.

In Paolozzi's model for a children's playground in Pesch, we encounter a cluster formation that disrupts the model's geometric foundations. But the model also, once again, reveals a contradiction. One could understand this contradiction through the Smithsons' use of the term "aesthetic": the model provides the "random" as an aesthetic that is designed, as opposed to the pattern emerging as a structure that is found and remade endlessly through use. In other terms, one again confronts the restrictions imposed by the designer, albeit with a renewed aesthetic. This returns us to Lady Allen's plea to lessen the role of the designer to expand the play potential of a given environment.

In the years following the ninth CIAM conference, the Smithsons grouped together with the younger generation of architects reacting against CIAM functionalism to form the international architecture group Team 10. Among its members was one of the most influential post-war playground designers, the Dutch architect Aldo van Eyck. The architect designed over 700 playgrounds, many of which were built on bombsites and waste ground, in parallel with the spaces provided for junk playgrounds in post-war Britain. In both cases, playgrounds were considered a site of future building; through the provision of a space for creative play, it was hoped that society could construct good citizenship. However, while the junk playground's anti-aesthetic risked complaints from local residents, van Eyck declared that "the public playground has to be attractive as a meeting place for everyone, including adults, if its existence is justified. It also has to be acceptable to the city even without the movement of the child."[15] Van Eyck's playgrounds were comprised of fixed metal frames, geometric concrete structures and sandpits that provided a moveable play material. Despite the repetition of these basic elements, van Eyck never repeated the same configuration; every playground layout was unique. The climbing frames could also be assembled in a range of combinations. The metal structures were constructed from a collection of tubular steel, designed by van Eyck; this catalogue of forms allowed the architect to create climbing frames specifically for a given site. After the ban on aluminium was lifted in 1954, the steel structures were replaced with aluminium. The specificity of playground to site has led Liane Lefaivre to describe van Eyck's playgrounds as "the first site-specific sculptures of the postwar period."[16] In *Aldo van Eyck, the Playgrounds and the City*, Lefaivre declares her discussion of van Eyck will not engage with "the top-down compositional component of the playground, imposing from the outside."[17] For Lefaivre, the important points of emphasis are van Eyck's contributions to place-making and locality, with the playgrounds considered as site-specific works of art.

Lefaivre's essay provides a productive shift in perspective with which to return to Paolozzi's playground designs and their connections to van Eyck (who would have been known to Paolozzi through the Smithsons). In correspondence regarding the Pesch playground (1982), Paolozzi's assistant Marlee Robinson consistently describes the work as *sculpture for* the playground. This is a work of art built specifically for a playground setting. This returns us to Paolozzi's statement that opened the chapter, in which he declared that "a child sees a piece of sculpture and simply wants to climb on top of it. Why not?" In Paolozzi's statement, one hears echoes of the voice of Herbert Read, who himself had been a significant source for van Eyck. In Read's 1943 publication, *Education Through Art*, he declared that "art should be the basis of education."[18] Written during the Second World War, the book argues that an aesthetic education is fundamental to the means by which one can build a peaceful society. For Read, art allowed children to create harmonious relationships with the external world. With the construction of an "integrated personality,"[19] seen as a key role of education, Read is critical of educational systems that separate learning into distinct categories. Similarly, Read states that "the best works of art"[20] appeal to more than one sense at a time. With this in mind, Paolozzi's sculptures for the playground can be seen as educational art for children. While the works may not offer the expansive possibilities for play advocated by Lady Allen and the adventure playground movement, the sculptures can be said to facilitate a particular form of looking, one that integrates the senses through touch and movement, providing an experience that combines the elements of what Read defined as a visual, plastic and kinetic education.

When creating the Wallingford playground in 1973–4, Paolozzi recycled two aluminium sculptures made in 1966: *Trishula* and *Es-Es*. Originally painted with vibrant red and blue gloss, *Es-Es* was first exhibited in 1967 in Paolozzi's two-person exhibition with Anthony Caro at the Kröller-Müller, Otterlo, the Netherlands. Later that year, the work was exhibited in the Economist Plaza designed by the Smithsons. When Paolozzi revisited the sculpture for Wallingford, he removed the paintwork. Now renamed *Suwasa*, the sculpture joined *Trishula* and four more aluminium works designed specifically for the playground: *Kalasan*, *Yantra*, *Manuk* and *Utpala*. By stripping away the primary colours to leave unifying bare metal surfaces, it is almost as if the artist declared that the works should not be mistaken for toys. Despite the fact that the sculptures are designed to be climbed on, without the shiny paintwork, the sculptures seem to assert themselves as "art." In Chapter 2, I explored how the toy-like colours of Paolozzi's painted sculptures of the 1960s state a connection between childhood toys and adult creativity. In a reversal of this equation, the raw aluminium surfaces of Paolozzi's playground sculptures indicate their presence as art for children. Through their appeal to a combination of sight, touch and movement, Paolozzi's playground sculptures are artworks placed in physical time. The works exist within process, with the sculptures continually restructured through the physical experience of climbing and looking.

In the previous chapter, I explored material connections between Paolozzi's sculptures of the late 1950s and the materials and processes of the junk playground. In this chapter, we have seen how Paolozzi's aluminium sculptures of the 1960s and 1970s provide material connections with van Eyck's playground structures. Both architect and artist used a catalogue of aluminium components that could be endlessly recombined. These shared construction methods suggest an evolution of Paolozzi's aims, stated in a lecture at the Institute of Contemporary Arts, London, in 1958, when he declared "what I have in mind. . . . Sites for imaginary ball games. . . . Non-mechanical toys. . . . A historical playground for fantastic people."[21] These statements led Michael Middleton to describe Paolozzi's work, with that of Turnbull, as "playgrounds for the mind."[22] Paolozzi's painted sculptures, such as *The Last of the Idols* (1963) (Figure 4.6) and *The City of the Circle and the Square* (1963/6) (Figure 2.4), invite a play of fantasy in an imaginary landscape. Their geometric forms and bold colours trigger haptic associations with play that appeal to a combination of the senses. The work repeatedly calls for a kinaesthetic reading: the anchored wheel that recurs through the sculptures of the period implies movement, while the circular central pieces of *Last of the Idols*, *Wittgenstein at Cassino* (1963) and *Diana as an Engine I* (1963–6) are strongly reminiscent of the spinning tops of the 1930s. It is with this confusion between playground and sculpture that I want to turn to the next chapter. In thinking of the work of both Guston and Paolozzi as "playgrounds for the mind," one

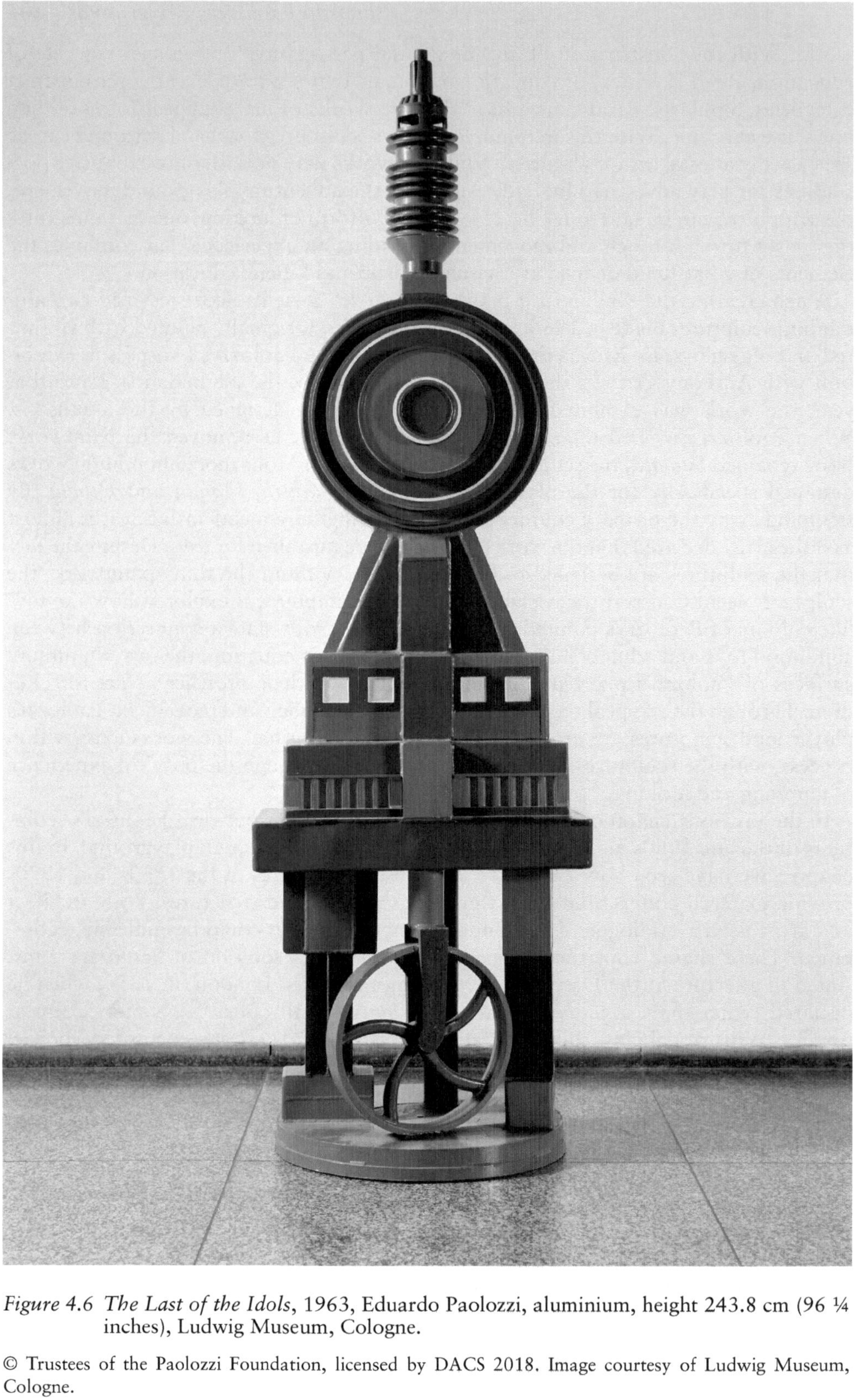

Figure 4.6 *The Last of the Idols*, 1963, Eduardo Paolozzi, aluminium, height 243.8 cm (96 ¼ inches), Ludwig Museum, Cologne.

can invite the viewer to play an interactive role, one that appeals to an integration of the senses to place the work continually within process as it becomes restructured through the multi-sensory act of looking.

Notes

1. From a file marked "Magic Kingdoms," in the as yet uncatalogued Paolozzi collection in the Tate Archives, London.
2. Simon Nicholson, "The Theory of Loose Parts, an Important Principle for Design Methodology," *Studies in Design Education Craft & Technology*, Vol. 4, No. 2 (Spring 1972), accessed June 11, 2018, https://ojs.lboro.ac.uk/SDEC/article/view/1204
3. Ibid.
4. Lady Allen of Hurtwood, *Planning for Play* (London: Thames and Hudson, Ltd., 1968), 15.
5. Ibid.
6. Nicholson, "The Theory of Loose Parts."
7. Lady Allen, *Planning for Play*, 16.
8. Eduardo Paolozzi, "Dialogues on Art, 1960," *Writings and Interviews*, ed. Spencer (Oxford, NY: Oxford University Press, 2001), 89.
9. Ibid., 90.
10. Joe Halligan as quoted in Oliver Wainwright, "Brutalist Playgrounds: 1960s Concrete Jungle Gyms Remade in Pastel Foam," *The Guardian*, June 9, 2015.
11. Ibid.
12. Lady Allen, *Planning for Play*, 18.
13. Ibid., 55.
14. Roy Kozlovsky, *The Architectures of Childhood: Children, Modern Architecture and Reconstruction in Postwar England* (Farnham: Ashgate, 2013), 235.
15. Aldo van Eyck as quoted in Kozlovsky, *The Architectures of Childhood*, 237.
16. Liane Lefaivre, "Space, Place and Play," in *Aldo van Eyck, the Playgrounds and the City*, ed. Liane Lefaivre and Ingeborg de Roode (Amsterdam: Stedelijk Museum Amsterdam, 2002), 36.
17. Ibid., 28.
18. Herbert Read, *Education Through Art* (London: Faber and Faber, 1961), 1.
19. Ibid., 7.
20. Ibid., 16.
21. Eduardo Paolozzi, "Notes from a Lecture at the Institute of Contemporary Arts, 1958," in *Writings and Interviews*, ed. Spencer, 83.
22. Middleton Michael, *Art in Progress, Eduardo Paolozzi* (London: Methuen, 1963), 36.

5 Shuffle/Spin/Stack

Emergent Narrative

In this chapter, I examine how Guston and Paolozzi's repeated use of a kit of forms provides the viewer with an interactive role. The chapter suggests that an understanding of Guston and Paolozzi's studio methods allows the audience to step beyond the finality of the art object to play with the narrative life of forms. I explore methods by which both artists' use of unresolved narrative places form within change. Functioning without a drive towards finality, emergent narrative will be seen to provide characters with independence from a plotline. In offering the audience an active role in the construction of narrative, artworks are seen to exist in a mutating present. If one were thinking of emergent narrative in terms of form, one might imagine a spinning top, an endlessly shuffled pack of cards or a continuous process of sedimentation and disintegration.

Split—Shuffle

During a lecture to students at the Glasgow School of Art in 1997, Paolozzi discovered that his sequence of slides had been accidentally scrambled. He had two slide projectors set up to project four images simultaneously. The sequence of slides had been prepared for a talk in which Paolozzi would describe connections between the images. However, Paolozzi watched with dismay as his careful planning was sent into disarray by the misfiring projectors. The artist Fiona Mathison was in the audience and recalls that Paolozzi was initially furious. He began his talk by struggling against the mishap. As the slides went by, he tried to stick to his planned talk by describing the slides that should have appeared. But then Mathison noticed Paolozzi's fury turn to delight as he began to discover connections and meaning emerge through the shuffled sequence. The planned talk was discarded and Paolozzi continued the lecture by weaving connections in the moment, improvising the talk as the slides appeared.[1]

Mathison's recollection of the Paolozzi lecture provides an important window onto the artist's relationship with material and process. We are able to see that Paolozzi might have begun a work with a plan, but that this could be discarded when the material started going its own way and, importantly, that Paolozzi was not only prepared to respond, but that perhaps after initial frustration he could revel in the emergent and the unforeseen. While the scrambled sequence in the lecture that went "wrong" appeared through sheer accident, a shuffling process was far from new to Paolozzi's work. In this section, I want to look at the ways in which Paolozzi deliberately employed such a process to allow for the emergence of unscripted narrative. I will show how focus on a shuffling process allows us to explore the means by which Paolozzi extended his own studio processes to the viewer to allow the audience to become a player within a game of improvised narrative.

In Paolozzi's 1967 print suite *Moonstrips Empire News*, the action of the shuffle is used to open the work to audience interaction (Figure 5.1). In an introductory text, written by Christopher Finch, the print suite invites the audience to physically engage with the work to alter the sequence of its one hundred sheets. Through interaction, Paolozzi enables the work to gain a life independent from the dictates of an author, to allow each reading to become unique to the viewer. Paolozzi created the print suite using his vast collection of printed ephemera. The collaged text and imagery were culled from a dizzying array of source material, including pulp novels, science journals, magazine adverts, instruction manuals and newspaper articles.

In the print suite, the majority of the text is printed almost impossibly closely. The font size is, for the most part, so small it obstructs attempts to focus and follow the text in a traditional linear manner from left to right (Figure 5.2). I have found that one initially struggles against these obstacles as one searches for unifying themes or a narrative thread. There is a frustration experienced through the texts' lack of intelligibility. However, after a time one allows this difficulty to suggest an alternative reading, to see that the obstacles provided by grammar, font and format are not necessarily hurdles to be overcome through sheer force of effort and persistence but rather may exist to formulate a different approach to text, narrative and meaning. The eyes, when set free from the constraints of convention, flicker across the text, jump paragraphs and scramble sequences to forge new connections.

As with the sheets of highly coloured geometric patterns that also comprise the *Moonstrips* suite (Figure 5.3), the text produces readings in which forms and associations interweave. Words, statements and imagery begin to break and reconnect, spanning columns and sheets to trigger fresh and innumerable associations

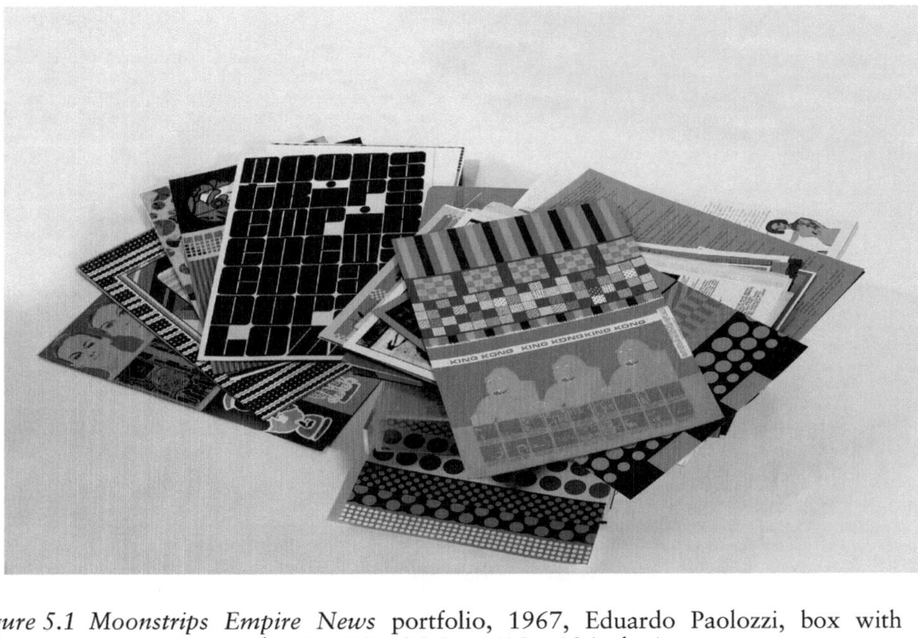

Figure 5.1 *Moonstrips Empire News* portfolio, 1967, Eduardo Paolozzi, box with 100 screenprints, each print: 38 × 25.5 cm (15 × 10 inches).

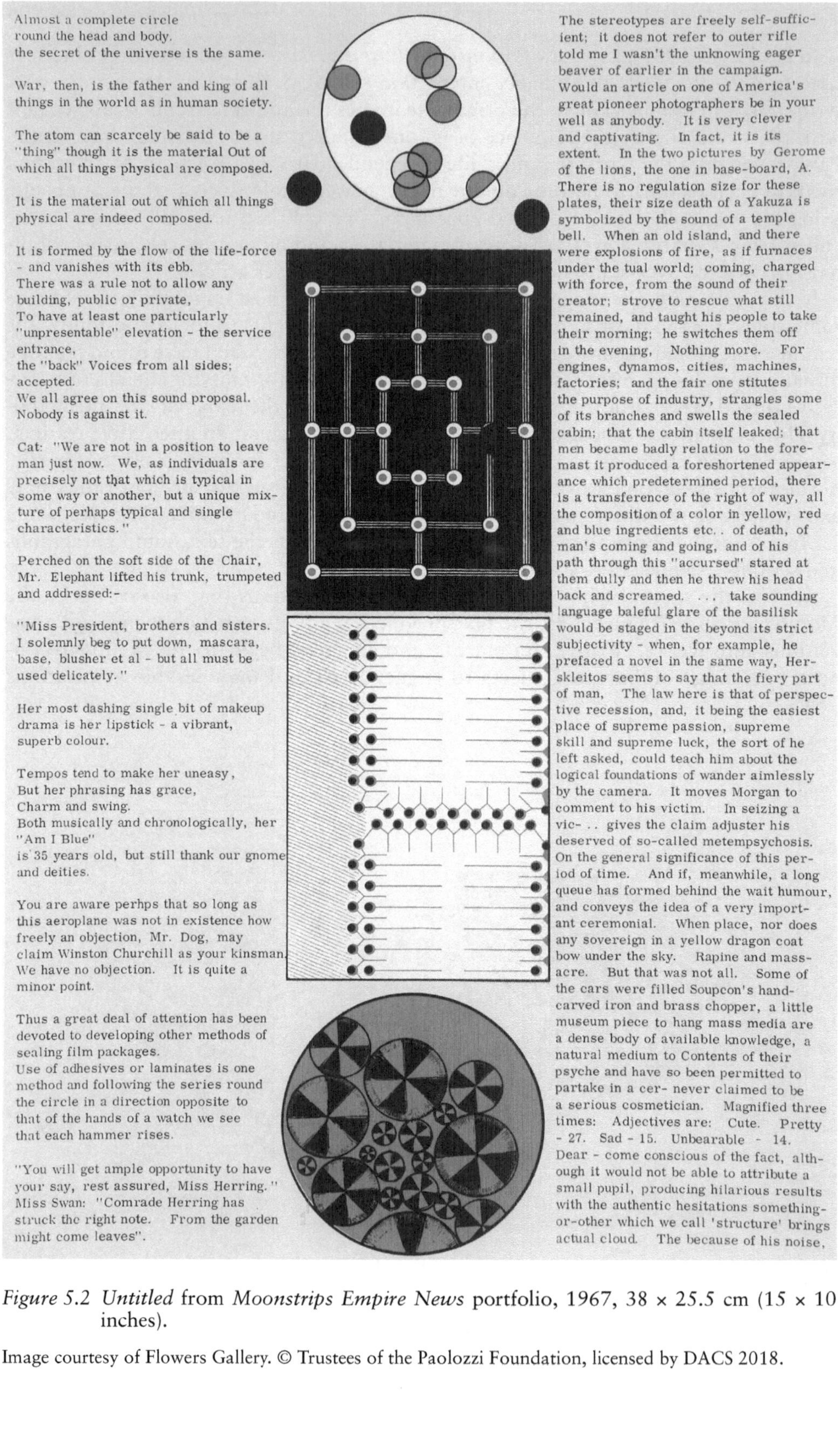

Almost a complete circle
round the head and body.
the secret of the universe is the same.

War, then, is the father and king of all
things in the world as in human society.

The atom can scarcely be said to be a
"thing" though it is the material Out of
which all things physical are composed.

It is the material out of which all things
physical are indeed composed.

It is formed by the flow of the life-force
- and vanishes with its ebb.
There was a rule not to allow any
building, public or private,
To have at least one particularly
"unpresentable" elevation - the service
entrance,
the "back" Voices from all sides;
accepted.
We all agree on this sound proposal.
Nobody is against it.

Cat: "We are not in a position to leave
man just now. We, as individuals are
precisely not that which is typical in
some way or another, but a unique mix-
ture of perhaps typical and single
characteristics."

Perched on the soft side of the Chair,
Mr. Elephant lifted his trunk, trumpeted
and addressed:-

"Miss President, brothers and sisters.
I solemnly beg to put down, mascara,
base, blusher et al - but all must be
used delicately."

Her most dashing single bit of makeup
drama is her lipstick - a vibrant,
superb colour.

Tempos tend to make her uneasy,
But her phrasing has grace,
Charm and swing.
Both musically and chronologically, her
"Am I Blue"
is 35 years old, but still thank our gnome
and deities.

You are aware perhps that so long as
this aeroplane was not in existence how
freely an objection, Mr. Dog, may
claim Winston Churchill as your kinsman.
We have no objection. It is quite a
minor point.

Thus a great deal of attention has been
devoted to developing other methods of
sealing film packages.
Use of adhesives or laminates is one
method and following the series round
the circle in a direction opposite to
that of the hands of a watch we see
that each hammer rises.

"You will get ample opportunity to have
your say, rest assured, Miss Herring."
Miss Swan: "Comrade Herring has
struck the right note. From the garden
might come leaves".

The stereotypes are freely self-suffic-
ient; it does not refer to outer rifle
told me I wasn't the unknowing eager
beaver of earlier in the campaign.
Would an article on one of America's
great pioneer photographers be in your
well as anybody. It is very clever
and captivating. In fact, it is its
extent. In the two pictures by Gerome
of the lions, the one in base-board, A.
There is no regulation size for these
plates, their size death of a Yakuza is
symbolized by the sound of a temple
bell. When an old island, and there
were explosions of fire, as if furnaces
under the tual world; coming, charged
with force, from the sound of their
creator; strove to rescue what still
remained, and taught his people to take
their morning; he switches them off
in the evening, Nothing more. For
engines, dynamos, cities, machines,
factories; and the fair one stitutes
the purpose of industry, strangles some
of its branches and swells the sealed
cabin; that the cabin itself leaked; that
men became badly relation to the fore-
mast it produced a foreshortened appear-
ance which predetermined period, there
is a transference of the right of way, all
the composition of a color in yellow, red
and blue ingredients etc.. of death, of
man's coming and going, and of his
path through this "accursed" stared at
them dully and then he threw his head
back and screamed. ... take sounding
language baleful glare of the basilisk
would be staged in the beyond its strict
subjectivity - when, for example, he
prefaced a novel in the same way, Her-
skleitos seems to say that the fiery part
of man, The law here is that of perspec-
tive recession, and, it being the easiest
place of supreme passion, supreme
skill and supreme luck, the sort of he
left asked, could teach him about the
logical foundations of wander aimlessly
by the camera. It moves Morgan to
comment to his victim. In seizing a
vic- .. gives the claim adjuster his
deserved of so-called metempsychosis.
On the general significance of this per-
iod of time. And if, meanwhile, a long
queue has formed behind the wait humour,
and conveys the idea of a very import-
ant ceremonial. When place, nor does
any sovereign in a yellow dragon coat
bow under the sky. Rapine and mass-
acre. But that was not all. Some of
the cars were filled Soupcon's hand-
carved iron and brass chopper, a little
museum piece to hang mass media are
a dense body of available knowledge, a
natural medium to Contents of their
psyche and have so been permitted to
partake in a cer- never claimed to be
a serious cosmetician. Magnified three
times: Adjectives are: Cute. Pretty
- 27. Sad - 15. Unbearable - 14.
Dear - come conscious of the fact, alth-
ough it would not be able to attribute a
small pupil, producing hilarious results
with the authentic hesitations something-
or-other which we call 'structure' brings
actual cloud. The because of his noise,

Figure 5.2 Untitled from *Moonstrips Empire News* portfolio, 1967, 38 × 25.5 cm (15 × 10 inches).

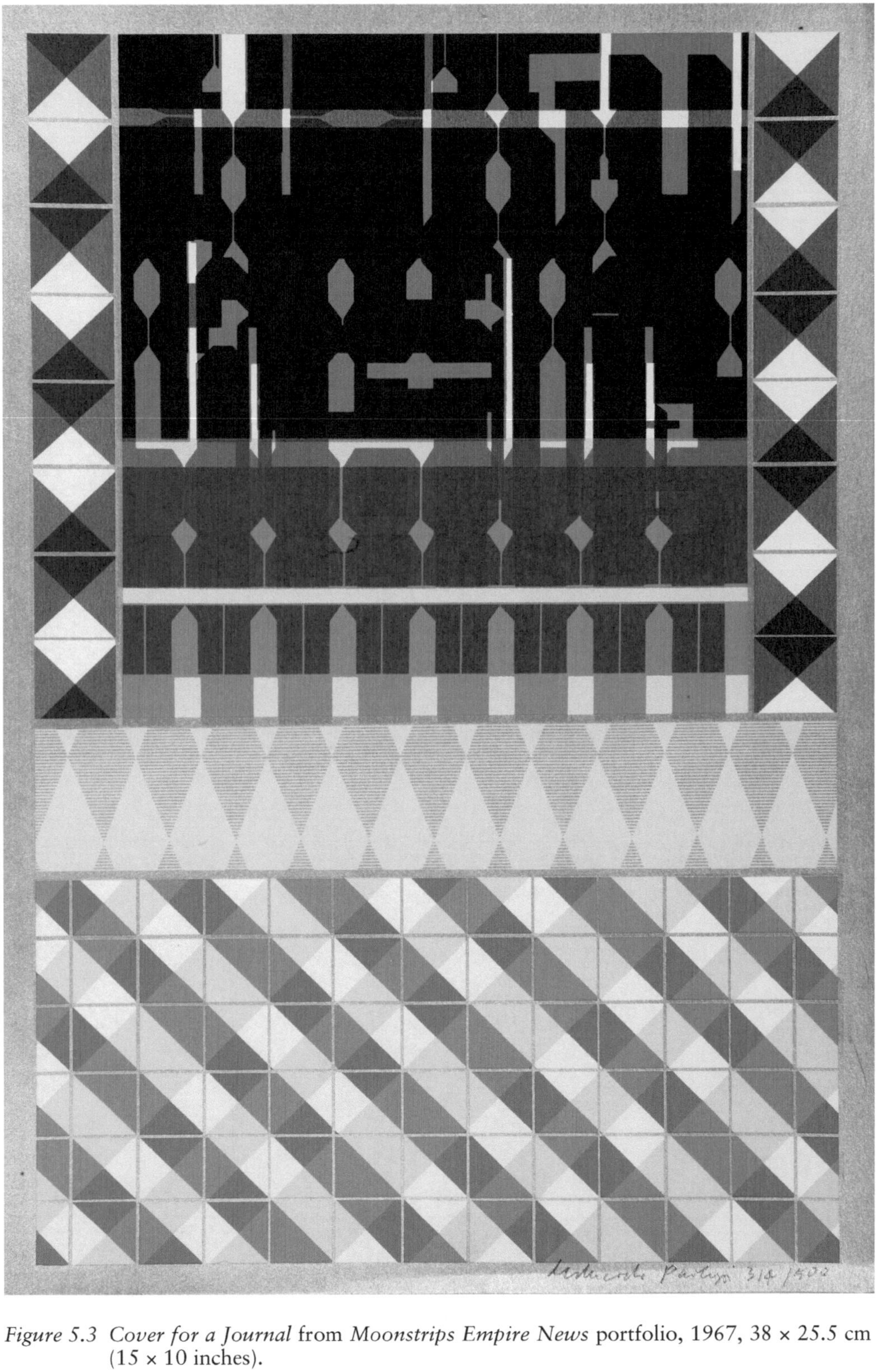

Figure 5.3 *Cover for a Journal* from *Moonstrips Empire News* portfolio, 1967, 38 × 25.5 cm (15 × 10 inches).

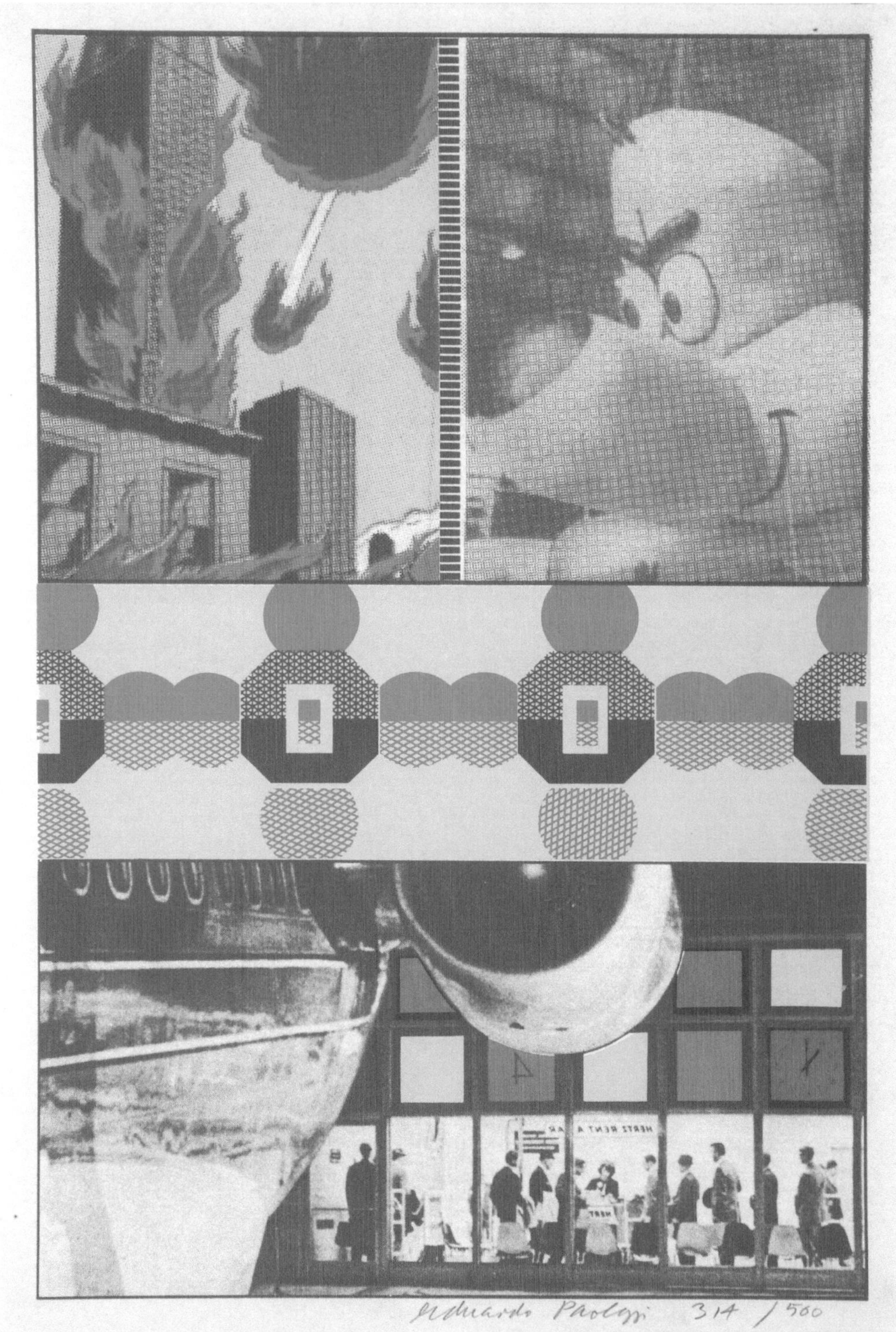

Figure 5.4 *Ernie and T.T. at St Louis Airport* from *Moonstrips Empire News* portfolio, 1967, 38 × 25.5 cm (15 × 10 inches).

(Figure 5.4). The movement from element to element is no longer a step, but a jump; the fracture need not necessarily be seen as a break to be resealed, but perhaps a gap in which each word-unit has become free to interrelate multi-directionally. Through this interaction, text and image become insufficient descriptions for the prints. The sheets become game elements as one begins to push back and respond to the material. Effectively, the print suite becomes a tool for play, a tool to generate narrative and meaning.

There is a marked similarity between the play potential offered by Paolozzi's print suite and the improvisation games invented for actors by the theatre director and playwright Keith Johnstone. In *Impro: Improvisation and the Theatre*, Johnstone provides exercises to enable actors to generate improvised narratives.[2] The games had evolved from Johnstone's own struggles with writer's block and were devised to allow narrative content and meaning to emerge. Johnstone provides actors with games of association, asking them to spontaneously connect disconnected words or images, or respond to a series of question prompts regarding character and place. Johnstone defines narrative building as the creation of links between elements and the reincorporation of past events. For Johnstone, once an actor grasps these principles, they are able to improvise narrative by creating links between disconnected material.

Johnstone provides us with a productive focus with which to return to the *Moonstrips* print suite. Following Johnstone, we can see the prints as an improvisation game which prompts the viewer to create narrative through the creation of links between the collaged elements. One can think of the difficulty in reading the text in a linear manner as forcing us to become active participants; we become improvisers that join Paolozzi in a game of meaning as we create links between the "jumps" our eyes are forced to make by the obstacles in the text. Johnstone's emphasis on reincorporation is also immensely useful. However, while for Johnstone the reincorporation, or recapitulation, of a past scene gives the audience a sense of satisfaction and is often taken as a signal that an actor/improviser has completed a story, with the print suite there is no finalisation to the narrative. *Moonstrips* becomes an unending game of reincorporation as the prints resurface as they are shuffled by the viewer/player. Effectively, we become caught in a cycle of breaks and links as the prints are reshuffled and different narratives form.

Johnstone's improvisation games and the *Moonstrips* print suite both recall the parlour games employed by the Dadaists and Surrealists. The games were employed to free work from the limits of rational control by employing chance and incongruity. Paolozzi's collaged text has as its precedent the poetry cut-ups produced by Dadaists in the 1920s (Figure 5.5). These poems were created by cutting up existing texts and then scrambling the order of the words and phrases. A chief proponent of this method was the poet Tristan Tzara, who Paolozzi met while living in Paris from 1947 to 1949. William Burroughs famously later promoted the technique in the 1950s and 1960s. Paolozzi discussed Surrealist techniques in a conversation with the writer J.G. Ballard in 1971. Ballard had written the introduction to the second part of the *Moonstrips Empire News* print suite, *General Dynamic F.U.N.* (1970) (Figure 5.6). During the discussion, Ballard stated that as a writer he had no use for the Surrealist technique of automatic writing. If Surrealist games were intended to release the unconscious to create a waking dream state, it seemed to Ballard that we lived in an age where this exercise was now redundant. For Ballard, the world of dream and fantasy could now

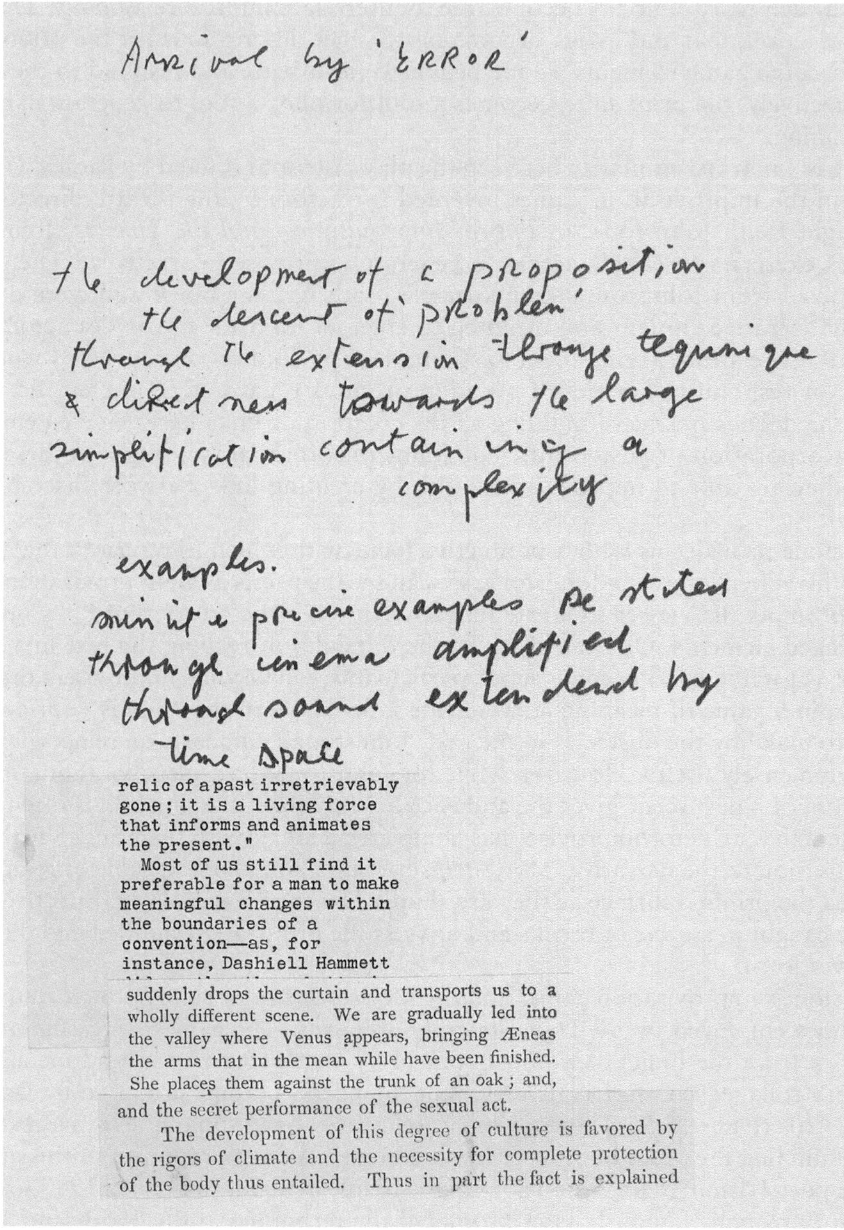

Arrival by 'ERROR'

the development of a proposition
the descent of 'problem'
through the extension through technique
& directness towards the large
simplification containing a
complexity

examples.
minute precise examples be stated
through cinema amplified
through sound extended by
time space

relic of a past irretrievably
gone; it is a living force
that informs and animates
the present."
Most of us still find it
preferable for a man to make
meaningful changes within
the boundaries of a
convention—as, for
instance, Dashiell Hammett

suddenly drops the curtain and transports us to a
wholly different scene. We are gradually led into
the valley where Venus appears, bringing Æneas
the arms that in the mean while have been finished.
She places them against the trunk of an oak; and,

and the secret performance of the sexual act.
The development of this degree of culture is favored by
the rigors of climate and the necessity for complete protection
of the body thus entailed. Thus in part the fact is explained

Figure 5.5 Cut-ups for *Moonstrips Empire News* portfolio (preparatory work), c. 1967, Eduardo Paolozzi, ink and collage on paper. National Galleries of Scotland. Scottish National Gallery of Modern Art Archive.

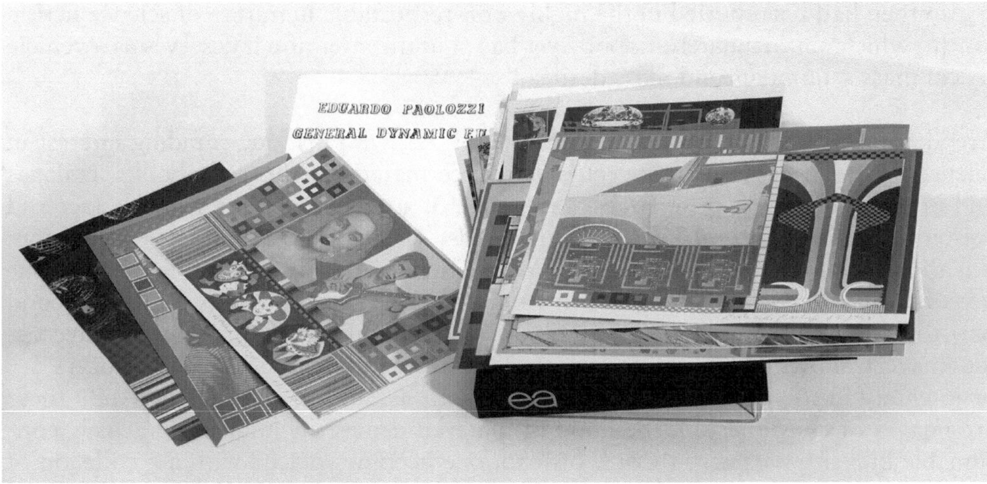

Figure 5.6 *General Dynamic F.U.N.* portfolio, 1965–70, published 1970, Eduardo Paolozzi, box with 50 prints, screenprint and lithography, each print: 38 × 25.4 cm (15 × 10 inches).

Image courtesy of Sims Reed Gallery. © Trustees of the Paolozzi Foundation, licensed by DACS 2018.

be primarily experienced by looking not inward but outward, towards the stuff of day-to-day life:

> Surrealism took one of its main inspirations from psychoanalysis, accepted the distinction between the inner world of the mind and the outer world of reality . . . the whole idea of the unconscious as a narrative stage. Surrealism moulds the two worlds together, remakes the external world of reality in terms of the internal world of fantasy and fiction . . . today . . . this position has been reversed. It's the external world which is now the . . . paramount realm of fantasy. . . . The fiction is all out there.[3]

Ballard went on to explain that the reason he admired the work of Paolozzi was that "he's accommodated himself to this change . . . [where he was once] overlaying an external reality . . . with his own fantasies. . . . He is now analysing external fictions."[4] Although Paolozzi asserted during the conversation that he liked to see his own work as "an extension of radical Surrealism," he was in agreement with Ballard that the external world provided a landscape more bewildering than any dream: "I'm also thinking about the way in which reality surpasses the fictions of even the wildest imagination. Like a machine for milking a rat. Incredible, yet it actually exists."[5] The *Moonstrips Empire News* print suite was created ten years after the first successful launch of a satellite into space, an event that triggered the Space Race. In 1958 (the following year), Hannah Arendt wrote in the Prologue of *The Human Condition* that the space programme marked a point at which science was merging with the realm of mass fantasy:

> Here, as in other respects, science has realized and affirmed what men anticipated in dreams that were neither wild nor idle. What is new is only that one of this

> country's most respectable newspapers finally brought to its front page what up to then had been buried in the highly non-respectable literature of science fiction (to which, unfortunately, nobody yet has paid the attention it deserves as a vehicle of mass sentiments and mass desires).[6]

Arendt's analysis would have appealed to Paolozzi, with his long-standing interest in science fiction, a presence that recurs as source material in his scrapbooks, collages and prints. Indeed, the print suites' vast range of source material scrambles fact and fiction through the use of instruction manuals, science journals and science fiction; it is thus no longer possible to identify where the borders of fact and fiction lie. The texts become blended in a play of, in Arendt's terms, "mass desires." In the second part to *Moonstrips*, *General Dynamic F.U.N.*, the dominating presence of advertising imagery allows us to analyse how these fantasies are commodified. Paolozzi's use of intensely lurid colours renders the images an assault on the senses. While these are images of consumerism, the flood of material denies the audience an easily consumable bite-size narrative thread. Instead, one becomes placed within a collision of material, creating an uncomfortable, disorientating experience for the viewer/player. Despite their tactile engagement with the print suites, the viewer never feels they have grasped the material. While Paolozzi hands over control of the sequence of prints to the viewer/player, within the work control becomes a very tenuous state. As the juxtapositions of image and text shift and mutate, the material appears to wrestle back control from the viewer, to slip away from the knowable. With no means to establish the position of a narrator, we become a player caught in a collision of states. The print suites plunge us into the flux of daily life to succumb to the fractured quality of an age infused by the media. But this uncertain quality also reveals something of the nature of improvised narrative and game playing. Just as Gadamer had declared that the game plays the player, Johnstone stated that the improviser learns "how to abandon control while at the same time they exercise control."[7] Paolozzi's print suite forces us to negotiate this contradiction; taken as an improvisation game, our interaction is one of a collection of responses that appear unable to control the total structure.

Through the print suite, perhaps more than any other Paolozzi work, we come in contact with the way in which the artist engaged with material in his studio. By placing us within the uncertainty of the messy mass of material, Paolozzi asks us to actively join the artist in engaging in an analysis of the material of shared fantasy consumed through the mass media.

Effectively, in inviting the viewer to shuffle the prints, Paolozzi extended his own studio methods to the audience. Mathison recalls that, in his studio, Paolozzi would surround himself with banks of imagery that were continuously being cut and reshuffled (Figure 5.7). Around the studio, chairs would be placed next to groups of images associated with a particular project. Paolozzi would move from chair to chair, sorting and shuffling the images—actions through which the work would grow and form. But it seems that the pleasure in this process could lead to a frustration in having to finalise an image.

Robin Spencer tells us that Paolozzi hated sticking things down and would resist fixation to the very last.[8] Spencer recalled witnessing Paolozzi put together his very last print, that was created for the Turing Collection. Spencer watched as Paolozzi kept shuffling the collage elements that formed the basis of his screenprints. Paolozzi's indecisiveness eventually led him to turn to Spencer and ask him to have a go. As

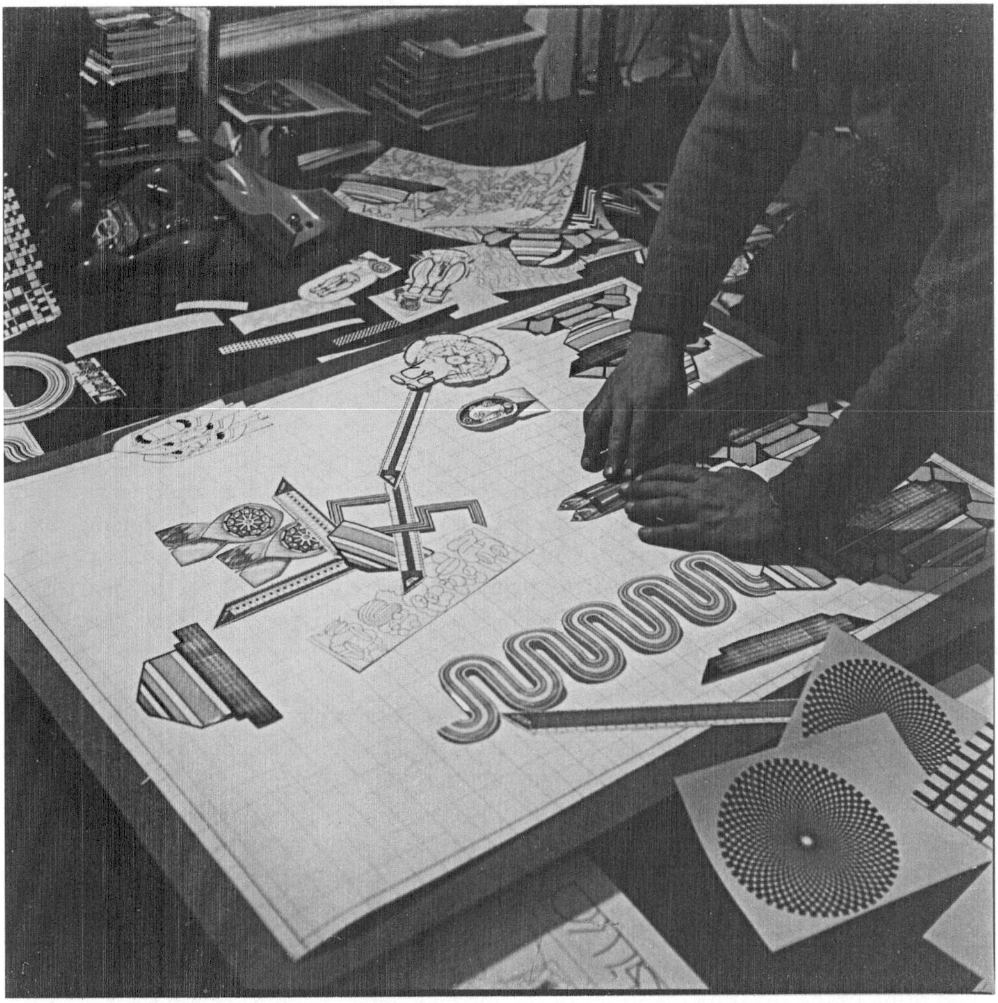

Figure 5.7 Paolozzi's studio floor, with the artist and screenprint elements, 1970s (circa). National Galleries of Scotland. Scottish National Gallery of Modern Art Archive.

Spencer began shuffling the pieces, Paolozzi suddenly demanded he stop at one configuration, and the pieces were fixed. According to Spencer, the incident seemed to suggest that, at times, Paolozzi needed the distance provided by others to help him reach the decisive moment.

In the *Moonstrips Empire News* print suite, Paolozzi is saved from the somewhat painful decisive moment. There is no finalisation to his shuffling game, as the process continues in the hands of the audience. J.G. Ballard's daughter, Fay Ballard, has recalled playing with the print suite as a child; she would spread the sheets out across the floor of her father's study in order to play with the collection.[9] However, the hands-on role for viewers of the print suites has provided real problems for museums and galleries when it comes to display. While Fay Ballard's recollections seem to bring the spirit of the work to life, the gallery's obligation to preserve has meant that the print suite is often encountered in a manner that seems to contradict and undermine its very logic. While the very life of the work exists in the actions and reactions that the prints engender, the interactive logic is often lost to the permanence of frames and wall mounts.

When not neatly framed in a line on the wall but engaged with as a collection of shuffled cards, the experience of playing with the prints is akin to finding oneself at the centre of a metropolis, caught in a dense overlap of information spillage. As time unfolds through the action of the shuffle, one becomes submerged in a landscape of lurid colours, chance encounters and half grasped text "noise." The collaged text appears simultaneously as word and graphic, like the flickering presence of street signs and billboards as one weaves through a city. It is almost as if Kurt Schwitters' collages of the 1920s and 1930s that Paolozzi so admired, bursting with bus tickets and yellowing remnants of printed ephemera, had been updated for a louder time: an interactive, electronic age, glowing with neon and humming with muzak.

The scholar Lev Manovich sees the notion of time as "spatial wandering" as a defining characteristic of computer media. Random access and interactivity—the key factors at play in the *Moonstrips* print suite—are seen to lie at the heart of a spatialisation of time. In *The Language of New Media*, Manovich asserts that, with computer media,

> time became a . . . landscape, something to look at or navigate through. If there is a new rhetoric or aesthetic possible here, it may have less to do with the ordering of time by a writer . . . and more with spatial wandering.[10]

But as with the *Moonstrips Empire News* print suite, this mutable, potentially infinite form would not be possible were it not for the simple feature of modularity. Manovich highlights that "media elements maintain their separate identities and can be assembled into numerous sequences. . . . In addition, because the elements themselves are broken into discrete samples . . . they can be created on the fly."[11] We could think of the separate identities of the media elements, which retain their identity through reordering, as directly comparable to the individual sheets and text elements within Paolozzi's print suite. While the part exists as a complete entity, the total structure becomes fluid and emergent, allowing each user to improvise an individual path through the material.

Manovich sees new media as potentially reawakening the ancient neglected form of spatial narrative, in which each part of a drama may appear together simultaneously. With the use of spatial montage, Manovich highlights that "the logic of replacement, characteristic of cinema, gives way to the logic of addition and coexistence. Time becomes spatialized, distributed over the surface of the screen."[12] With time understood in spatial terms, the past is no longer progressed beyond but is active and alive, embedded within the present. The *Moonstrips* print suite and new media's use of spatial montage provide us with a model in which the new is formed through an endlessly reshuffled past. Despite the technological gulf between Paolozzi's tangible paper-based print suite and the electronic domain occupied by interactive computer programmes, it appears they both may share a common logic.

With its logic of endless permutation, simultaneity and user specificity, the Paolozzi print suite seems to have generated a mechanism that broke with the determinism characteristic of industrial mechanisation to predict the interactive age of the computer. Here, Paolozzi may be indebted to two Marshall McLuhan's publications: *The Mechanical Bride* (first published in 1951) and *The Gutenberg Galaxy: The Making of Typographic Man* (1962), particularly as McLuhan had been discussed at Independent Group meetings. The mutable, non-linear structure of Paolozzi's print suite follows McLuhan's invitation in the preface to *The Mechanical Bride*, in which the author encourages the reader to engage with the text in any sequence. *The Gutenberg Galaxy* focuses on the history and effects of the printing press and the mass media. The text charts the development of "the tool" as an extension of the body through the creation of closed systems. But, for McLuhan, technological progress came at the expense of a loss of an integration of the senses. In an age of rapidly developing electronic technology, McLuhan called for a departure from the closed systems that he saw as dominating culture from the birth of the printing press in favour of a return to a condition of simultaneity.

> Now, in the electric ages, the very instantaneous nature of co-existence among our technological instruments has created a crisis quite new in human history. . . . Our technologies, like our private senses, now demand an interplay and ratio that makes rational co-existence possible.[13]

With a separation of the senses, McLuhan asserts that print culture brought to narration an "inner direction" or stable, fixed perspective, where once there had been the variation of the "audile–tactile" culture of the manuscript. Despite having been generated through the print medium, the texts in the *Moonstrips* print suite are defined by multiplicity and instability, seeming to undermine the very nature of the technology that brought them into being. Cut and collaged from a plethora of sources, Paolozzi's texts deny the reader the guidance of a single narrator. Through a jigsaw puzzle of cut and paste narratives, one is thrown into the midst of a crowd of authors that ceaselessly interrupt any notion of lineal flow. We have the sense of a renunciation of notions of fatalism and narrative coherence, to place one in an immersive here and now. In 1971, Paolozzi created the screenprint *B.A.S.H.* (Figure 2.8) and would compare the process behind the work to television channel hopping; the description serves well as an explanation of the process that informed the earlier two interactive print suites:

> All the things on that piece of paper have been moved around and anchored into position. They're a scattering of what you would see just sitting down to a television evening turning the knob from one channel to another. Bash is also kind of politically active. I've grown up in a bomb culture . . . and it rather looks as if one is going to spend the rest of one's life opening newspapers and seeing the most terrible things. . . . I want to show that I'm not an escapist.[14]

The analogy Paolozzi draws between his prints and channel surfing can readily be updated to the experience of scanning websites, or scrolling through social media; again, one encounters a landscape of *competing* narratives. But if the material within Paolozzi's prints declares that the artist is "not an escapist," it is also concerned with the ways in which the mass media flattens experience. In prints such as *B.A.S.H.*, real life atrocities and weapons of war sit beside Hollywood icons and science-fiction robots; all reach an equivalence as images of consumption placed in a theatre of lurid entertainment. With the individual elements removed from context, we become emotionally detached from any sense of cause and effect. As interactive viewers, Paolozzi forces us to acknowledge how we become complicit in this terrible absurdity; as players, we begin to treat all images as "play" material.

Despite the troubling possible outcomes, for Paolozzi, material drift also becomes, more widely, a metaphor for creativity. In effect, the *Moonstrips* print suite can be seen as a microcosm, providing a model of the artist's relationship with material and process. The prints present an unending fascination with the means by which images are translated and mistranslated, disassembled and recombined to collide with new contexts. Paolozzi's first print suite was created in 1964, three years prior to *Moonstrips*. *As Is When* was based on the life and work of the philosopher Ludwig Wittgenstein. Paolozzi, then, would undoubtedly have been aware of the fact that Wittgenstein compared language to a game. For David Egan, Wittgenstein's concept can be understood in terms of the variation in language use: "Wittgenstein acknowledges the fluidity of language: 'If we look at the actual use of a word, what we see is something constantly fluctuating.'"[15] Here then, there seems to be an inconsistency thrown up between Wittgenstein's use of the term "game" and that put forward in Chapter 2, in which, through Huizinga, the game was seen to be defined in terms of "contest." Egan offers some clarification by suggesting that with Wittgenstein, "the boundary between games and non-game play [is taken] to be more fluid than it might appear. . . . Wittgenstein's analogy works at a deeper level: discussion is possible because, like a game, language is something we play."[16] We can understand Paolozzi's engagement with Wittgenstein's concept of language use through the artist's employment of reproduction techniques, described by the artist in 1958 as a "Dictionary of Design Elements" and an "Alphabet of Elements."[17] Here, we find Paolozzi playing a game of meaning that is infinitely evolving as material drifts away from its source, as he explained in an essay in 1982:

> Advertising imagery I have used in both graphics and sculpture over the years is transformed from its original context and form. It may be redrawn, traced, fractured or cut into strips. One process alters the next. With the introduction of colour Xerox and instant enlarging machines, those image-metaphors formerly glued to a fixed, frozen picture can now permutate into a million possibilities, heightening the drama, deepening the meaning. . . . It suggests that perspective and history can be torn apart and reassembled.[18]

In Paolozzi's statement, the "frozen picture" of the past clearly connects to Paolozzi's sense of the "act of betrayal" the artist experienced in finalising a work.[19] In Chapter 2, we saw how Paolozzi described the process of sticking down the elements of a collage as one in which "the loose characters . . . [were condemned] to a life of frozen violence."[20] For Paolozzi, reproduction techniques such as screenprinting and photocopying allowed the characters to live again, to find new dramas, new meanings in an unending narrative. Egan's interpretation of Wittgenstein's game analogy for language use can be connected to Paolozzi's collage and "kit" methods, through which material drifts from prescribed, predetermined definitions to adapt and respond to a present context in which meaning becomes an emergent force. But here we see that the process of infinite recombination could also be understood as a rejection of the privileging of one perspective over others, dispelling a hierarchical relationship to structure in order to democratise material. Indeed, Paolozzi's fascination with the processes by which images shift through translation led him to declare that if given a choice between the Mona Lisa and a carpet bearing an image of the painting, he would rather have the carpet.[21] What is important in Paolozzi's example is that he chooses one of the most venerated works of Western art and enjoys how it becomes absorbed within popular culture. There is a levelling of the distinction between high and low culture that was so important to the work of the Independent Group, famously later defined by Independent Group member, art critic and curator Lawrence Alloway as "the long front of culture," in his 1959 essay of the same title. It is this equalising trajectory that is crucial to this form of material drift.[22] Importantly, in Paolozzi's statement there are also implications for how one perceives one's relationship with one's own history, one's own narrative. If, according to Paolozzi, this process of endless recombination suggests that "history can be torn apart and reassembled," one can consider the continuing presence of play as rendering one's own childhood active and alive. Paolozzi's childhood obsessions with collecting, scrapbooking, reproduction and mass culture are all present within *Moonstrips Empire News*. Through the print suite, they allow us a tangible connection with the processes by which childhood play becomes part of an endlessly shifting landscape that finds new resonance as it collides with the present.

Resting, Remaining, Spinning

Paolozzi's screenprint *Tafel 16* (1964) (Figure 5.8) presents us with a cacophony of form. A dense knot of curves meets the hard geometry of the square, while an interplay of stripes appears to tremble and vibrate. Rhythmic interweaving line interspersed with jarring angular form prevent the eye from settling on one area. Instead, one's eyes are forced to jump, skip and dart, jolting the viewer into an ever changing, simultaneous present. The print allows connections to be formed by the beholder, seeming only then to rupture, scatter and reconfigure. As we saw previously in the *Moonstrips Empire News* print suite, a tussle between interruption and construction seems to be central to the workings of *Tafel 16*. Once again, the print invites the viewer to become a participant, playing a game of connection and recapitulation with the artist's kit of forms. However, in contrast to *Moonstrips*, here the shuffling process appears among the elements on a single print; the animation of the image occurs through the viewer's visual interaction, condensing the experience of *Moonstrips* into a single image.

In this section, I will explore how Paolozzi's prints provide the viewer/player with the means to construct a narrative form that rests in the present. For Fink, "play is conspicuously set apart from the whole futural character of life. . . . It does not happen for the sake of the 'final purpose' . . . playing has the character of a pacified 'present' and self-contained sense."[23] While, as an apparently finalised artwork, a Paolozzi print such as *Tafel 16* seems to present a "final purpose" in contradiction of play, I will explore how the print, in continuity with the *Moonstrips* print suite, provides a structure that is an answer to the artist's frustration with the "frozen picture." I will examine how Paolozzi offers the viewer works that seem to thwart finality, to place an image within a continuing process, giving form to Fink's emphasis on the presentness of play.

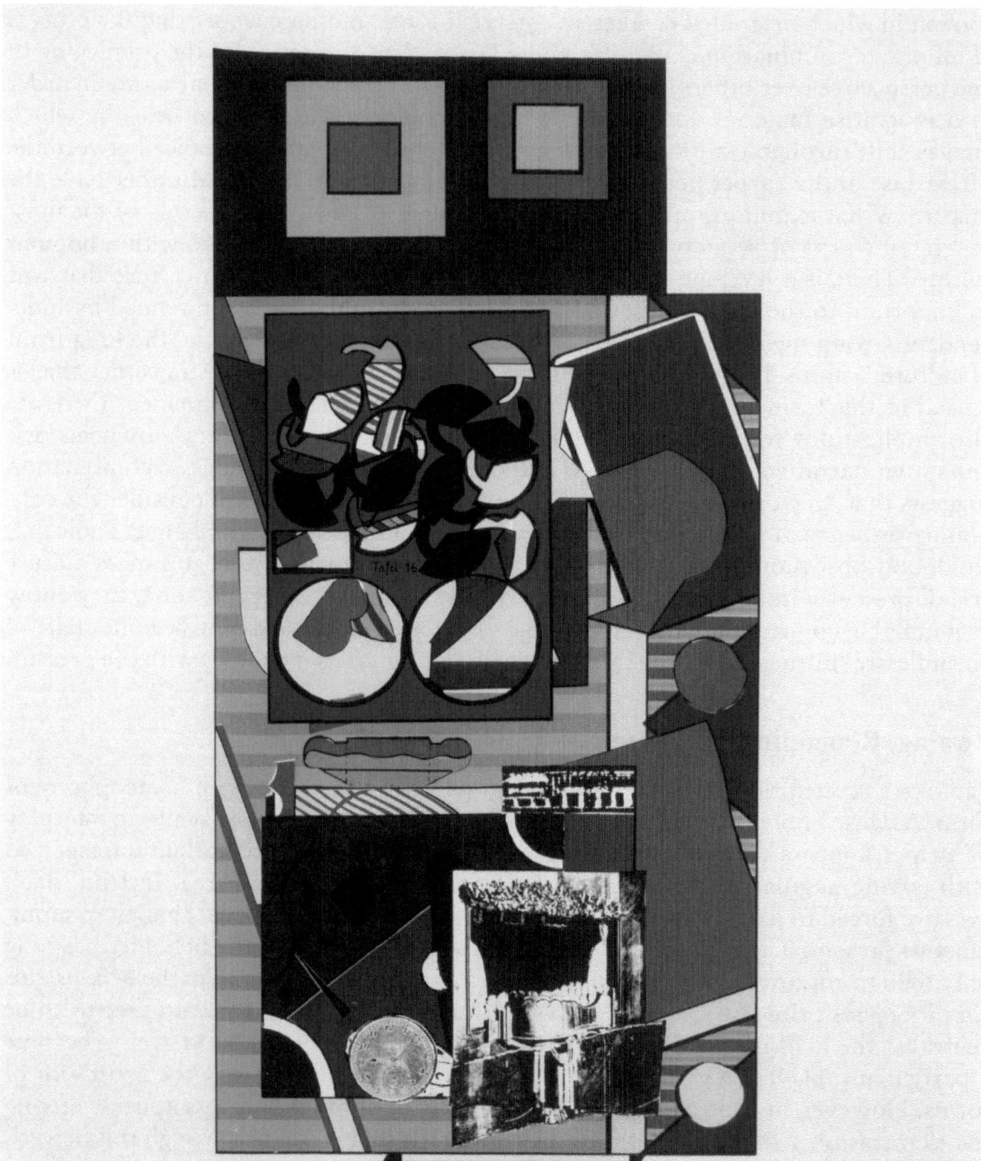

Figure 5.8 Tafel 16, 1964, Eduardo Paolozzi, screenprint, 52.5 × 89 cm (20.6 × 35 inches).

Image courtesy of the British Council Collection. © Trustees of the Paolozzi Foundation, licensed by DACS 2018.

Tafel 16 appears to be caught in a condition in which connections are continually in the process of being forged and severed. In effect, a pattern of eye movement begins to emerge through the process of looking at the print. The stair formation at the base leads the eye inwards to a tight knot of forms that seems to twist and writhe, while the squares at the top of the image seem to force the eye out to begin the circuit again, as a mutating loop. The relationship between the squares above and the square(ish) photographic image below seems to push and pull attention to and from the knotted forms. Repetition and change thus become inextricably entwined in the physical encounter with the work as one is placed in a maze of looped readings that build duration into the experience of the print.

Presented with a work such as *Tafel 16*, one might wonder about the need for the term narrative at all. I would suggest that by framing Paolozzi's screenprints as narratives, it becomes clear these works do not operate in the realm of the abstract. The prints can be seen to disrupt or play with references to the abstract. Narrative allows us to place Paolozzi's collaged material within duration, to allow the audience to continue to bring life to form through an evolving accumulation of connections. By turning to a theory of narratology, this chapter will be able to elaborate more fully on just what this term might offer a reading of Paolozzi's print-work.

Mieke Bal's text *Narratology: Introduction to the Theory of Narrative* (1985) provides a detailed outline of the key components of narrative. Bal highlights that at the centre of a narrative is a connected series of events known as the fabula, which are caused and experienced by protagonists. Perhaps Bal states the obvious when she declares that an event "always takes up time in reality"[24] and that "events always occur somewhere,"[25] but this fact is nevertheless helpful as it emphasises that the term narrative would allow the elements within a Paolozzi print such as *Tafel 16* to be seen as a related collection of events, and these events would generate time and a sense of place. This activates the work. It brings out the physicality of looking and the sense of movement that seems to emanate from the images as our eyes are forced to circulate the print. Rather than a static collection of forms, the print can become a site in which events occur and forms collide.

However, there are crucial differences between the particular narrative form I want to put forward in this chapter and the theories discussed by Bal in *Narratology*. Firstly, they diverge when it comes to sequential ordering. Bal highlights that the fabula "starts from a teleological relation between the elements of the story: the actors have an intention: they aspire towards an aim."[26] By contrast, I want to present a non-teleological narrative form in relation to Paolozzi's work. Following Fink's definition of play as set apart from the "futural character of life," I am examining an approach to narrative that is continually within process. With a print such as *Tafel 16*, there is no remote or invisible goal; all elements of the narrative appear simultaneously. Without a distant aim, the viewer/player's experience of form is seen to rest within a shifting present.

Bal's discussion of the scene could be helpful here. Bal describes a scene as "often a central moment from which the narrative can proceed in any direction. In such cases, the scene is actually anti-linear."[27] Looking once again at *Tafel 16*, we can see Paolozzi as presenting a collection of anti-linear scenes, scenes that spin and shuffle, but scenes for which there is, as yet, no narrative. The narrative component can be understood as structured by the viewer through the act of looking. This interactive narrative emerges through an evolving process, in which events unfold in the present through the interaction of form. The audience, once given the position of narrative agents, becomes placed within an unfolding drama.

In a later publication, *Louise Bourgeois' Spider: The Architecture of Art-Writing* (2001), Bal contrasts story *telling* with narratives of presentness. Bal outlines that, in visual art,

> the most common narrative modes can be characterized by their positioning as anterior stories. In the sharpest formulation, a visual work is thus considered an illustration of the narrative that precedes it and to which it is subordinated.[28]

In considering the powerful physical act of viewing that Louise Bourgeois' Spider elicits, Bal calls for a temporal shift in the way one discusses narrative in relation to the installation. For Bal, the work invites and yet resists narrative in its push and pull between its fragments of the past and the presentness of viewing. Bal asks us to see the work as fighting a battle with anterior narrative to activate the work in the present through the act of viewing. For Bal, "this work does not tell a story but builds one."[29] In addition to narrative building, Bal provides us with the term "performative narrative."[30] In both cases, we are given the means to articulate a form of narrative in which the viewer's creative interaction becomes central. Additionally, with narrative constructed in the physical engagement with a work, we can see form as set free from a servile function. Form now generates narrative, rather than serving it.

However, although Bal offers an emphasis on presentness, physicality and reordering through viewing, there is a point where the narrative process she sets out for Bourgeois' Spider diverges from the form of emergent narrative this chapter explores through the work of Paolozzi and Guston. Significantly, the difference hinges on the use of the fragment. For Bal, "the predominant element in spider is fragmentation incarnated: the fragments of tapestry that are hung, stretched. . . . The cloth fragments are shards of the past."[31] Bal elaborates that these relics of the past speak of "the whole they once were and can become again . . . through restoration."[32] For Bal, Spider builds narrative through fragmentation and absence, and through the gaps that ask for and yet resist wholeness.

By contrast, if one continues to read the Paolozzi prints through the analogy of the kit, the picture elements are not fragments that ask to be restored to a whole but, to use Paolozzi's words, "bits complete in themselves" that can be endlessly reconfigured.[33] Therefore, while for Bal Bourgeois' installation draws the viewer into a process of reconstruction, with Paolozzi's prints the viewer is able to create narrative through the interaction of picture elements that behave like game elements. So, although both artists' narratives can be read as unresolved, the term points to something distinct in each case. In Bal's reading of Bourgeois' Spider, broken elements of the past remain disjointed, unable to become whole again. In contrast, in this chapter I will continue to explore methods by which a Paolozzi print, such as *Tafel 16*, employs the unresolved as a means to place a kit of forms within an ongoing process to perpetuate an ever-changing present. Once again, Fink's emphasis on the presentness of play becomes pertinent. For Fink,

> precisely what is purely self-sufficient about play, the self-enclosed, circular sense of the activity of play, lets a possibility of human sojourn within time appear, one that does not have the character of tearing away and driving forward but rather

allows one to tarry. . . . Because it is the child who predominantly plays, this feature of time is peculiar to the child most of all.[34]

With Paolozzi's prints, it is possible to give form to Fink's assertion that the "circular" nature of a play activity allows a player to rest in the present. I have placed the Paolozzi print *Mr Peanut* (1970) (Figure 5.9) next to an image of a toy spinning top that would have been in circulation during Paolozzi's childhood (Figure 5.10). The print appears to offer us a sense of the tops caught in perpetual motion. As with *Tafel 16*, this sense of motion seems to be generated by the work's ability to force the eye to circulate the image. The spin or mutating loop is obviously motion that offers us an independence from a goal. While resting on the spot, the spinning top moves, but effectively goes nowhere. The past is not progressed beyond but is enfolded within the present. It is this that emerges as a key characteristic of Paolozzi's use of emergent narrative; the movement is produced by structures that actively thwart progression.

Unlike a classic example of sequential motion as presented by a series of Eadweard Muybridge stills, *Mr Peanut* offers us a total structure on a single frame. The outer limit is set, the image is complete, and yet through the movement of the eye across the plane the print appears in motion. As Fink describes of a play activity, the motion is not "of tearing away and driving forward but rather allows one to tarry." Fink was a student of Martin Heidegger, and in Fink's declaration one hears echoes of Heidegger's notion of dwelling. In his essay *Building, Dwelling, Thinking* (1951), Heidegger discusses a limit or "boundary" in relation to a notion of Being. For Heidegger, "a boundary is not that at which something stops but . . . that from which something begins its essential unfolding."[35] Dwelling was, for Heidegger, crucial to a notion of Being; to remain, to rest, in place of a strain towards an abstract, invisible goal. The boundary could then be seen as a device that interrupts progression and a drive towards a destiny—not to confine but to allow a work to unfold within the present. But, crucially for Heidegger, the rest is not one of stasis. In an earlier text, *The Origin of the Work of Art* (written between 1935 and 1937 and reworked for publication in 1950), Heidegger asserts that "only what is in motion can rest."[36] In discussing a work of art's ability to set up a world and make manifest the form of being, Heidegger discusses a very particular type of motion. This is, in Heidegger's words, an "inner concentration of motion, hence supreme agitation . . . the repose of the work that rests in itself is of this sort."[37] The motion evoked by Heidegger is one in which form and material are allowed to come to the fore. Returning to Paolozzi's print, *Mr Peanut*, it appears almost as though the movement that emerges is that of the body at rest. This is the pulsing, circular movement basic to life, like that of respiration or blood circulation. It is as if the print is breathing rather than running. Although physically static, the work appears to pulse and writhe through connections formed in the present moment, through the movement of the eye. The viewer thus becomes an active participant within the work, generating a sense of movement from within.

The circular movement at play in the prints also evokes the circularity characteristic of innumerable board games, including, for example, Monopoly and Sorry. Associations with board game layouts come to the fore in the Paolozzi print *7 Pyramide in form einer achtel skugel* (Figure 5.11), part of the *Universal Electronic Vacuum* print suite (1967). As with numerous Paolozzi prints, the originally collaged material has been set out in a loose grid-like formation that in itself evokes the landscape of the board game. Furthermore, the grid pattern is pushed and pulled with the interruption

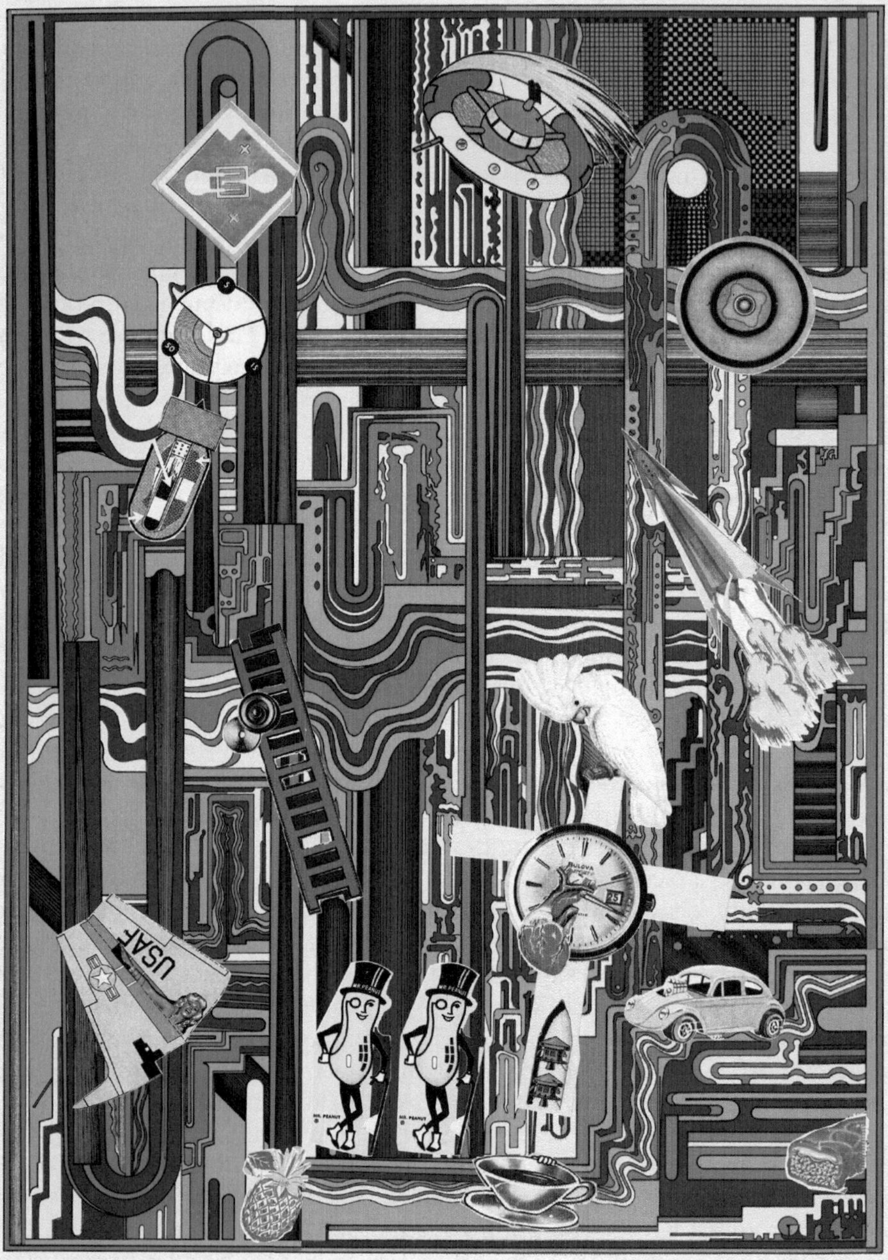

Figure 5.9 Mr Peanut, 1970, Eduardo Paolozzi, screenprint, 70 × 48.5 cm (27 ½ × 19 inches). National Galleries of Scotland. Scottish National Gallery of Modern Art Archive.

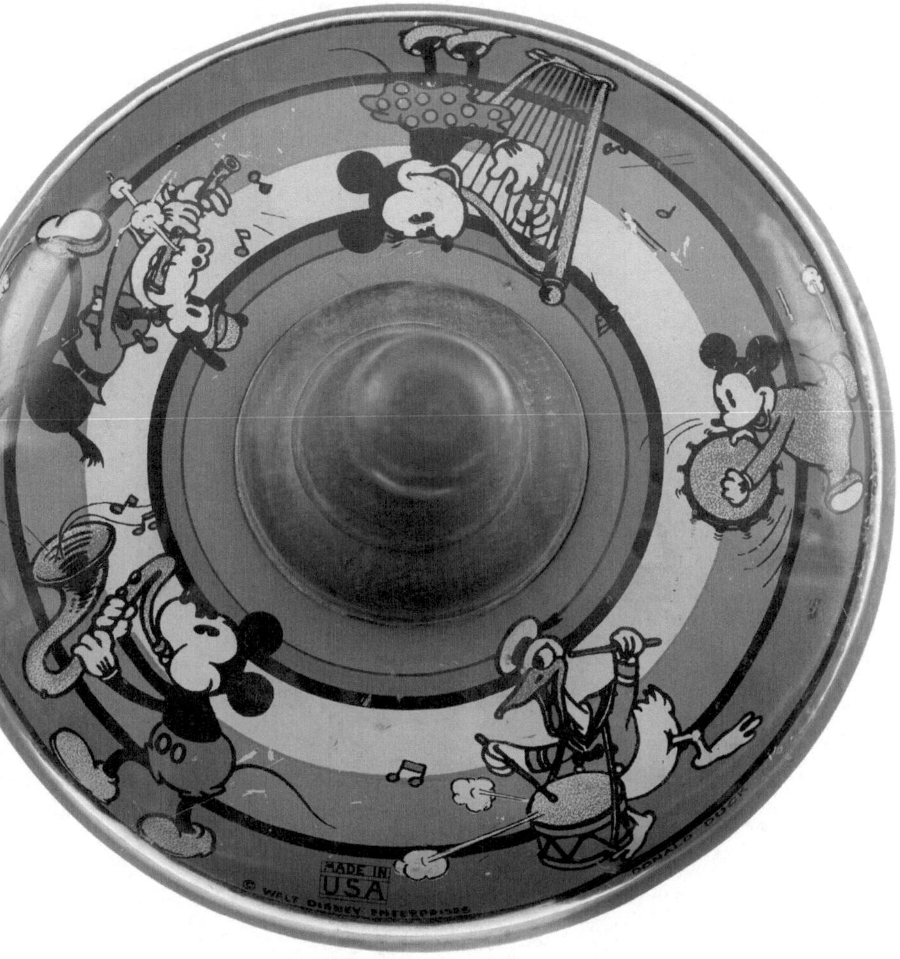

Figure 5.10 Spinning top toy, 1930s, Fritz Bueschel.

Image courtesy of Heritage Auctions, HA.com.

of sliding forms that appear to denote a direction of travel, as in a game of Snakes and Ladders. There are even elements that begin to read as counters making their way around the "game's" landscape. Once again, the print's pattern forces the eye to circulate the image, generating the sense that the "counters" are in play. Indeed, the print even includes an image of a circuit board on the bottom right-hand corner, as if to suggest something approaching a self-similar, circular repeating pattern. But games have goals, seeming to contradict the notion of rest and presentness put forward previously. However, here once again, Benjamin and Huizinga's emphasis on play and repetition becomes pertinent. With repetition considered central to an understanding of play, the goal or end-point is merely the place to begin the game again. And as the game repeats, the action unfolds through different paths. Additionally, as we saw

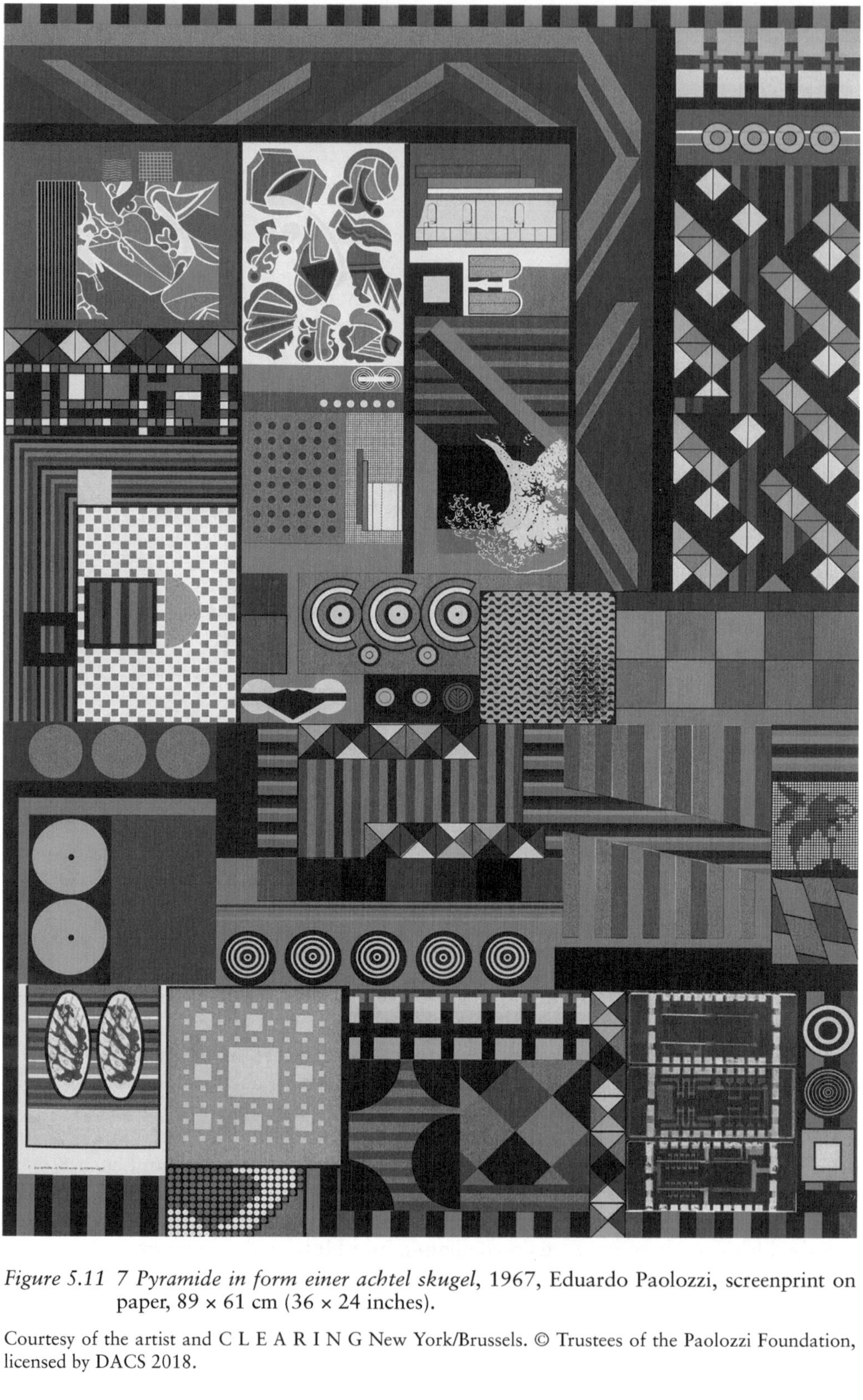

Figure 5.11 *7 Pyramide in form einer achtel skugel*, 1967, Eduardo Paolozzi, screenprint on paper, 89 × 61 cm (36 × 24 inches).

in Chapter 3 with Guston's paintings, such as *White Painting I* (1951) and *Untitled* (1955–6), Paolozzi's prints appear forever caught within the scrummage of the game, never reaching conclusion.

Paolozzi's screenprints are striking in their rejection of linear perspective. As with the artwork of board games, this frees the viewer/players from a fixed viewpoint. The viewer/players, then, are no longer characterised as clearly demarcated spectators, but are once again offered a means by which to achieve a condition of mobility and immersion, as players in the game. The two-dimensionality also brings with it the tactility of games boards and counters. However, this may also be another element of Paolozzi's print work that is heavily informed by McLuhan's *The Gutenberg Galaxy*. While, for McLuhan, the movement recorded by Muybridge places an object in a static pictorial form, the two-dimensional produces a condition of dynamic simultaneity. According to McLuhan, "the 'two-dimensional' mosaic or painting is the mode in which there is muting of the visual as such, in that there may be maximal interplay among all of the senses."[38] In 1976, Paolozzi published *Calcium Light Night*, a print suite dedicated to Charles Ives that takes its title from a piece of music by the composer. The print suite actively calls for an "interplay among all of the senses," reflected across the titles of the individual prints, which include *Allegro Moderato Fireman's Parade* (1974), *Four German Songs* (1974) (Figure 5.12) and *Largo to Presto* (1974) (Figure 5.13). And once again, the two-dimensionality of the prints emphasises the tactile with the optical. Significantly, Ives created soundscapes that collage together a vast array of musical forms from marching bands to popular songs and string orchestras. Ives' musical collage embraced interruption and dissonance to create an immersive sound world. We see the use of both interruption and dissonance embedded in a Paolozzi print such as *Four German Songs*. As with most of Paolozzi's prints, the work began as a collage. The print offers us a structure in which the eye and mind are unable to resolve the relationships between the forms and, consequently, the work refuses to settle. Flowing, twisting lines lead the eye not to resolution but disruption. The eye is forced to jump and thus frustrate notions of completion.

Importantly, the print suite is just one example of numerous works in which Paolozzi used elements from the print *Stille Nacht* (1927) by Hugo Meier-Thur. The print is a visual interpretation of organ music. Elements from Meier-Thur's work occur in the Paolozzi print *Mr Peanut* (1970), discussed earlier in this chapter. And they recur across the *Calcium Light Night* portfolio. So, while an individual print such as *Mr Peanut* or *Four German Songs* seems to suspend finality to force the eye to circulate the print, this connection to an unfolding process becomes amplified when the constituent elements are seen as part of a process of reconfiguration that resurfaces in screenprints, etchings and reliefs. The elements of the prints thus become akin to a musical motif that is repeated and altered across a composition. Time is then built into the reading of the works, achieved through the presence of form that is both connected and yet in a state of dispersal. However, with Paolozzi's structures there is no designated before and after. Free from linear time and a notion of progression, Paolozzi's works are placed in a present that appears capable of a continuous unfolding.

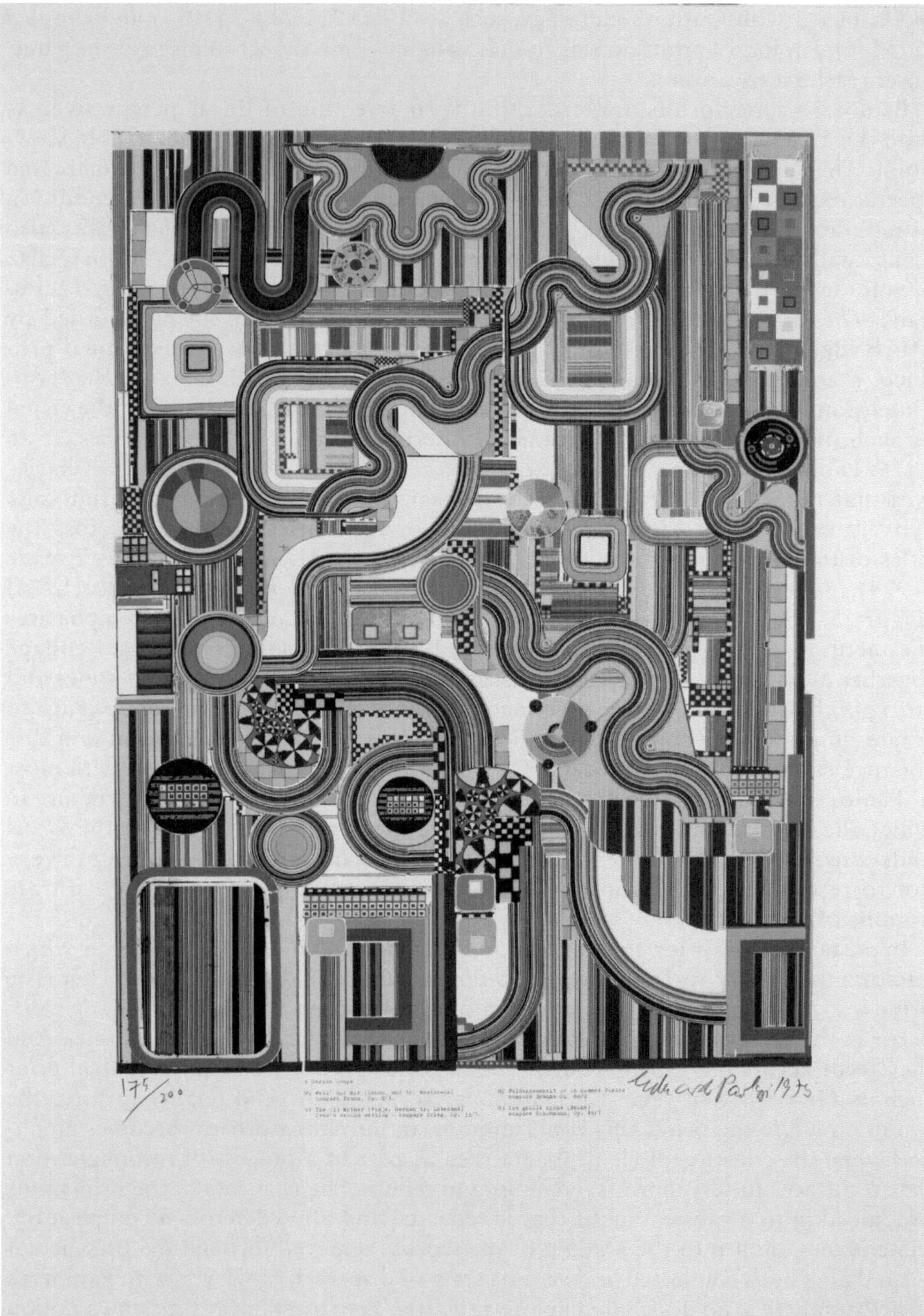

Figure 5.12 Four German Songs, Calcium Light Night portfolio, 1974–6, Eduardo Paolozzi, screenprint, 99 × 69 cm (39 × 27 ¼ inches).

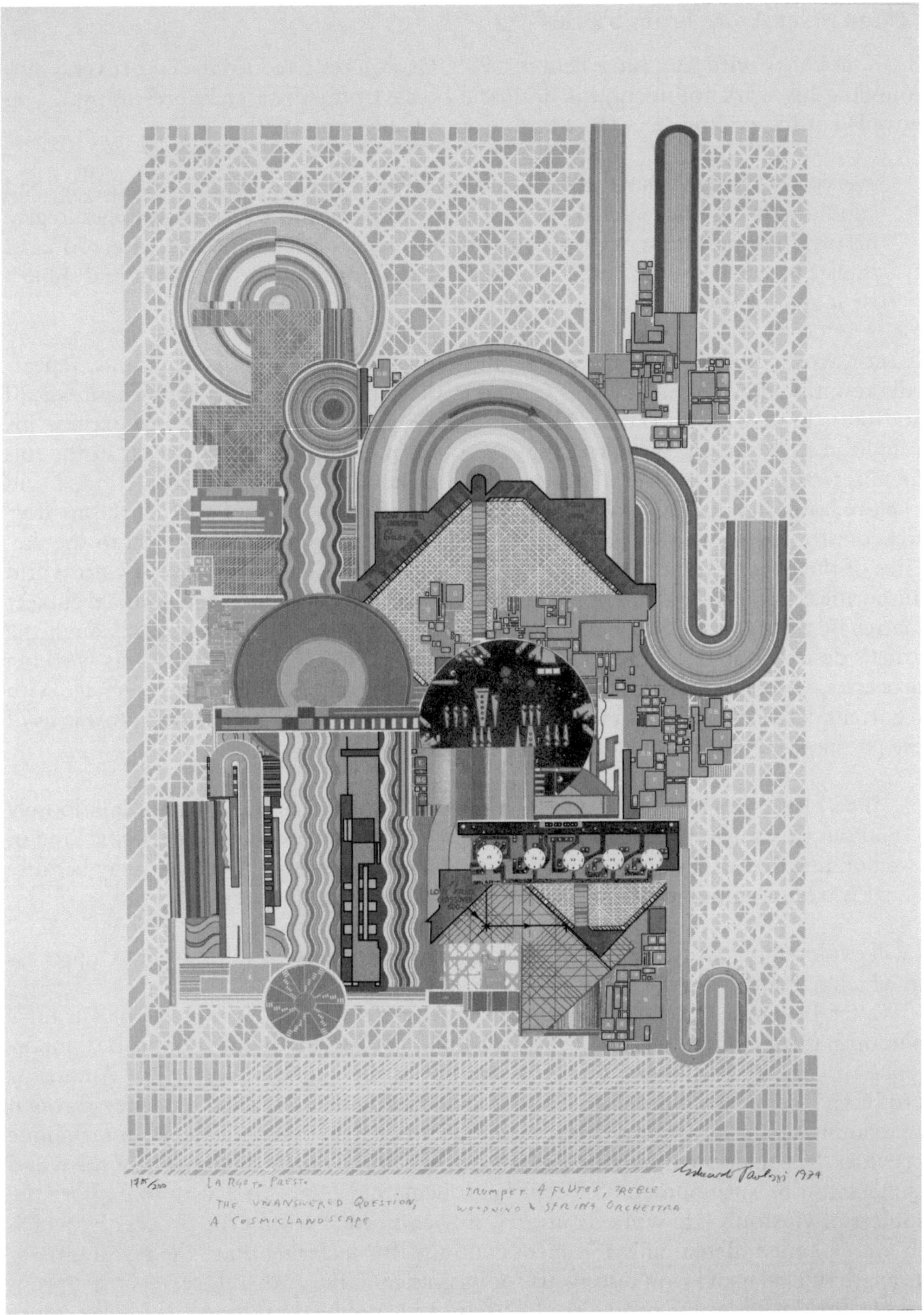

Figure 5.13 *Largo to Presto, Calcium Light Night* portfolio, 1974–6, Eduardo Paolozzi, screenprint, 99 × 69 cm (39 × 27 ¼ inches).

"I Can't Get Away From Stories"

In an interview with Jan Butterfield in 1979, Guston reflected on the controversy surrounding his work following his dramatic break from Abstract Expressionism, first unveiled at his exhibition at the Marlborough Gallery in 1970:

> everybody thought those paintings were about the hooded figures and the bad condition in America and so on. And that was part of it. Every artist hopes to give his own interpretation of the world. But they were about something else, too. . . . I think I like de Kooning best . . . he said, "You know, Philip, what your real subject is? It is freedom!" And I said, "That's right, Bill. You've got it!"[39]

Guston would joyfully repeat de Kooning's response on countless occasions, repeatedly restating that "freedom" was central to the subject of the paintings (Figures 2.20 and 6.3). In another interview, Guston even extended the anecdote, to express his delight in de Kooning characterising the conformity expected of an artist in the following terms: "as if we're all on the same baseball team."[40] In this section, I will explore how Guston's late paintings present the artist as a player seeking the creative freedom to invent his own games and break his own rules, in opposition to the dictates of the passing trends in the art world or the judgements laid down by art world authorities. Guston's statement provides a means to explore how the political subject matter of the paintings does not precede the work but rather *emerges* through the artist's desire to be free to follow the driving obsessions at the centre of his working processes. Guston's late work therefore also provides the opportunity to engage with recurrent definitions of play in terms of freedom. Sutton-Smith helpfully informs us of the paradoxical nature of play as a free activity:

> [Play] frees you from one self by binding you to another. One cannot talk loosely about play meaning freedom without also taking into account the specific kind of bonding that then reigns over the player's being. To say something is play because it is free or voluntary seems to be an insufficient explanation.[41]

I will explore how Guston's freedom becomes concerned with submitting to a process in which narrative emerges.

Walter Benjamin provides a means of reaching the political subjects of Guston's paintings through material and process. Benjamin's writing became of central importance to Guston in the last decade of his life. In Benjamin's essay "The Author as Producer," Benjamin connects a literary tendency with a political tendency through an examination of what he terms "technique." For Benjamin, a concept of technique provides "the dialectical starting-point from which the sterile dichotomy of form and content can be surmounted."[42] From here, Benjamin offers us a way to explore the subject of Guston's late work as inextricably embedded within the process by which they are painted. Benjamin's argument continues by declaring that "the revolutionary strength of Dadaism lay in testing art for its authenticity . . . therefore, technical progress is, for the author as producer, the basis of his political progress."[43] I will explore how Guston's late work appears to take these words as a clarion call. Furthermore, and perhaps most central to the focus of this book, Benjamin states that, with the concept of technique, the author

> will never be concerned with products alone, but always, at the same time, with the means of production. In other words, his products must possess an organizing function besides and before their character as finished works. And their organizational usefulness must on no account be confined to a propagandistic use.[44]

Time and again, Guston refuses to discuss the meaning of his work, declaring it "impossible"[45] or, perhaps more significantly, describing the "hood" imagery specifically as "too simple" to require explanation.[46] It is by focusing on Guston's process, or in Benjamin's terms "the means of production," rather than the meaning of a singular finished painting, that both artist and viewer are offered a collision of complex meanings and political implications through which narratives continue to emerge. However, in the final chapter on the absurd, I will take a closer look at the processes and symbolism enfolded within the hood imagery.

Guston's lectures offer generous insights into the thinking behind his working processes. During a lecture at Yale Summer School of Music and Art in 1973, the artist repeatedly insisted he was "not writing political tracts."[47] Guston elaborates by stating, "I think it went through my mind that I was just using symbols. But, to be truthful, I was having such a good time painting that it was releasing."[48] It is this joy in the freedom of a process that allowed for release that Guston wanted to share with the students above all. This is the freedom to follow one's creative imagination wherever it leads, without being policed, either by one's own inner demons or by power structures in the wider world. Indeed, Guston's break back into figuration in 1968 can be seen as a release of all that had been suppressed in his painting over the course of his professional career. What came flooding through was a landscape of childhood loves and fears. We find the artist's lifelong love of cartooning, satire, literature and movies, together with references to his childhood cupboard-studio. The hooded figures themselves are a re-confrontation with the Ku Klux Klan that had terrified Guston in his youth, now rendered as images of pitiful, dumb depravity. This torrent of imagery, narrative and history all flowed from the artist's love of animate line, which was once again allowed to transform into anything: a shoe, a book, a hand. . . . Tired of "purity," Guston's line now met a desire to engage with the messiness of the world. Here, once again, one can recall Guston's much quoted statement on his reaction to the violence of the times:

> When the 1960s came along I was feeling split, schizophrenic. The war, what was happening in America, the brutality of the world. What kind of man am I . . . going into a frustrated fury about everything—and then going into my studio *to adjust a red to a blue*. . . . I wanted to be complete again, as I was when I was a kid. . . . I wanted to be whole between what I thought and what I felt.[49]

In this context, one can see Guston's own desire for creative freedom colliding with the artist's rage at government brutality meted out in the name of law and order and democracy. The hooded figures become a symbol for the suppression of intellectual freedom, difference and dissent. It is this, most of all, that Guston wanted to convey to his students.

During his 1973 lecture at Yale, Guston went on to state that he had frequently used drawing to plan the hood paintings quite carefully in advance. This in itself is significant. By using preparatory drawings, Guston was breaking a central tenet of Action Painting. Throughout the 1950s and 1960s, Guston had agreed to the premise that a painting should be found on the canvas through the act of painting. As Rosenberg had articulated, "to work from sketches arouses the suspicion that the artist still regards the canvas as a place where the mind records its contents."[50] However, importantly, once Guston had transgressed, and revelled in that transgression, he began to return to a process in which the painting was discovered on the canvas. It was as if Guston could now claim this process, this game, on his own terms, knowing he was free to break the rules.

However, if Guston's return to figuration was an act of release, it seems as if the images were only ever hidden just beneath the surface. Indeed, there is a remarkable consistency in Guston's writings and lectures that continues through the apparently dramatic break from abstraction. As I have been exploring throughout the chapters, the desire to treat paint as a living substance was central throughout. For Guston, this focus brought the seemingly unavoidable presence of narrative, as the artist revealed in 1968:

> Ten years ago I wanted to get away from my past. . . . Forms were threatening each other or kissing or moving into each other or coming together or leaving each other. I mean, it seemed like fairy tales. You know, stories. And I wanted to get away from that. Well, now that I'm working in this terribly reduced way, they're still stories, I can't get away from stories, whether they're heads or lines.[51]

Guston made no attempt to conceal these discoveries, for even during the artist's apparently abstract work, the paintings acquired titles that overtly pointed to the emergence of narrative; these include *Fable I* (1956–7), *The Return* (1956–8), *Traveler I* (1959) and *Voyage* (1956). The process Guston articulated in 1968 as storytelling described the emergence of responsive relationships between elements perceived as living forms or personas. Recalling Bal's discussion of the "scene" applied to Paolozzi's print *Tafel 16*, we can think of a Guston work such as *Fable I* as the accumulation of improvised anti-linear scenes formed through connections that are free from a prescribed plotline. It is this notion of the scene that I want to bring to Guston's small panel paintings, first created in 1968 (Figure 5.14).

As we saw in Chapter 2, Guston returned to figurative painting by first creating hundreds of images of simple objects: boots, books, cigars, cups, lightbulbs, bricks, paintings of paintings. . . . Buildings also began to appear, together with hooded figures. One can consider these panel paintings variously as actors without a play, sets without a film and scenes without a narrative. The vast cast of actors gradually became primed and ready to respond to Guston's emotional and intellectual life as it unfolded day to day. Narratives *emerged* through the juxtaposition and accumulation of scenes and actors, finally coming together on Guston's canvases in 1969. As with Paolozzi's kits of forms generated through a mass of collected material, Guston's narrative kit was assembled without a singular purpose or aim. It was the *completeness* of the elements as a collection of individuals that allowed them to exist outside a

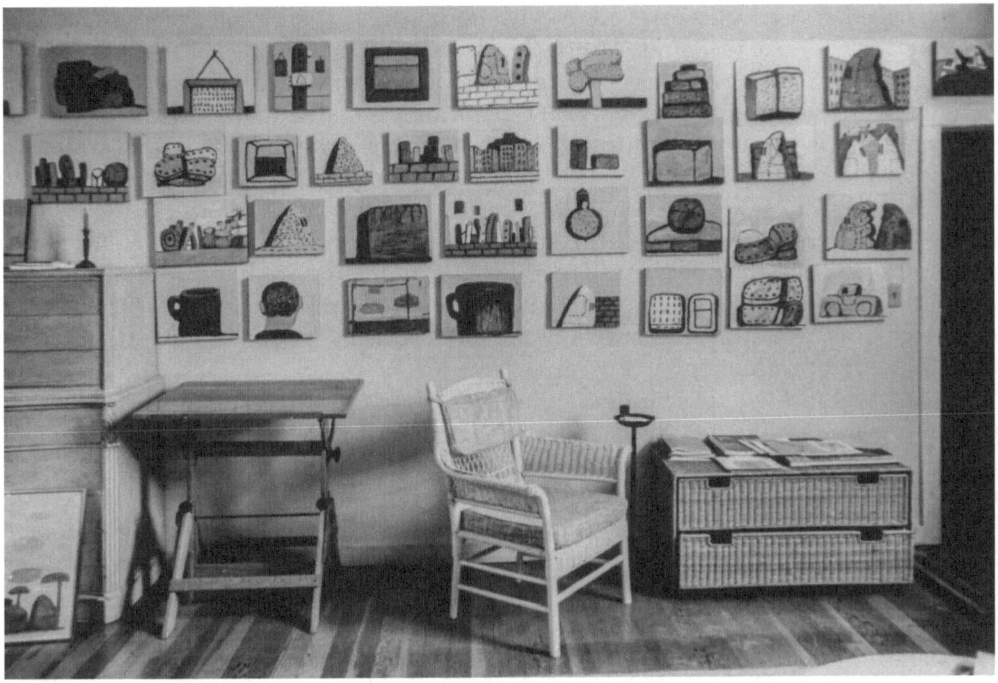

Figure 5.14 Wall hung with Philip Guston's small panel paintings, the artist's Woodstock studio, 1975.

Photographer: Denise Hare. Image courtesy of The Estate of Philip Guston.

sequence. The "actors" could then continue to adapt and respond to unfolding dramas. Guston's large canvases emerge out of these building blocks of narrative.

In a striking parallel with Paolozzi's studio processes, Guston wrote to his friend, the poet Bill Berkson, of the use of a shuffling process. In 1976, he described to Berkson how he had shuffled paintings around for hours and delighted in the meanings that emerged. The action of the shuffle became a means for Guston to renew his relationship to the work. As he played with sequences, imagery gained an existence beyond the prescriptive intent of the artist. Once again, one can see the shuffle as a means to create new connections within which narratives can flourish. Through a mutable scattered structure, the images achieve a multifarious, evolving existence. So, although the individual images remained unchanged, the new juxtapositions created contexts in which the works became unfamiliar. As Guston wrote to Berkson:

> Yes—I too puzzle over "meanings"—I mean the linkage of images when they are together in a certain way and then how all changes, when in another combination on the wall. Last month, trying to select 9 or 10 paintings from about 40 for [the] McKee show, I shifted pictures around for days and nights, reeling from the diverse possible meanings the pictures possess when in different image relationships.[52]

Effectively, Guston's paintings began to behave in a manner akin to Paolozzi's *Moonstrips Empire News* print suite; with both artists, a shuffling process becomes a method to generate meaning. Although all of Guston's paintings of the last decade of his life are related as images summoned from the same parallel world, with no designated sequence, each of Guston's paintings is individually complete in the present. Even in the hood paintings, where meaning is more overt, there is nevertheless no developmental arc. Rupturing a sequence, then, does not simply destroy an existing order but rather becomes a means to offer the work an evolving existence. This alters the artist's relationship to the work, and to meaning itself. With a multitude of possible meanings emerging through an unfolding process, there is no point of separation between form and content. In Benjamin's terms, "the sterile dichotomy of form and content can be surmounted" by placing the paintings continually within production.

In Michael Blackwood's film *Philip Guston: A Life Lived*, we see Guston playing a game of interpretation with his friend, the poet Clark Coolidge. In the artist's studio, in front of a wall covered in small panel paintings, Guston and Coolidge speculate together on the identity of the forms. Guston gestures to one of his paintings to ask whether it is "a rock, or a root."[53] And when looking at a small painting of a hooded figure that appears to be clearly covered in blood, Guston asks whether perhaps the character has spilt some jam on himself. Nothing seems stable. Images do not cling to a fixed object identity, while the relationship between tragedy and comedy slips and slides. Indeed, in Guston's lectures, the artist talks repeatedly of wanting to create works that "baffle" him.[54] Here, with the shuffled sequences of the panels, there are the tools to allow meanings to drift and narratives to emerge. In this potentially endless shuffling game, the paintings are placed in a process that recalls Gadamer's characterisation of the movement of play. Drawing on Huizinga's assertions as to the centrality of repetition, Gadamer contends that play can be defined as

> to-and-fro movement that is not tied to any goal that would bring it to an end; rather, it renews itself in constant repetition. The movement backward and forward is obviously so central to the definition of play that it makes no difference who or what performs this movement.[55]

Following Gadamer, we, as viewers, can take the "to-and-fro movement" of Guston's shuffling game to a reading of the artist's late paintings. We can join Coolidge and Guston as participants and begin to play Guston's game of interpretation. Not to reach a singular meaning hidden within the paintings, nor to discover the original intention of the artist, but rather to follow Guston's *process* and use the paintings to continue to generate narrative games. Indeed, Gadamer defines the work of art as play, hereby offering the audience an active role by placing the viewer in the place of "the player."[56] For Gadamer, then, a picture cannot be separated from its presentation. It has its own being that embraces surrounding space, drawing in the contingent to become an unfolding presentation. Gadamer sees the audience as completing a work through a game of recognition and understanding.[57] However, with Guston's late paintings we can productively bring together Gadamer's proposition regarding the picture, with his analysis of the performing arts, to see Guston's paintings as providing an experience that can be *performed*. While for Gadamer, the play of interaction between viewer and picture is always tied to the presentation of the original, with the performing arts, repetition and change are embedded in the presentation of the work:

> The performing arts have this special quality: that the works they deal with are explicitly left open to such re-creation and thus visibly hold the identity and continuity of the work of art open towards its future.[58]

However, with Guston's shuffling process, we are no longer tied to the sense of an unchanging original. Rather, we can see the paintings as providing an experience that is performed through changing presentation. One can bring a notion of the anti-linear scene to Guston's panel paintings of 1968, and beyond them the paintings created during the last decade of the artist's life. With this approach, each time the paintings (or scenes) are hung in new juxtapositions new narratives emerge. As we walk through an exhibition of the artist's paintings, we, as viewers/players, can understand ourselves as participating in the changing, evolving life of the work. Guston would talk of imagining a life's work "as one picture," and an individual painting as a "pause."[59] With the viewer as player, the audience can, in a sense, take the paintings off pause, to animate the work in unending dramas. Gadamer described the performance of a work as essential to the work itself, as it "completes" what the work is.[60] However, with Guston's late painting, and Paolozzi's *Moonstrips Empire News print suite*, the viewer/player is not so much completing the works as placing them within production, restructuring the works through a continually shuffled collection of connections.

However, importantly, Guston's paintings do not *lead* anywhere. In Fink's terms, they are not tied to the "futural character of life." If one turns to a collection of Guston's small panel paintings created between 1969 and 1973, one finds that, unlike the progression one might discover in the linear sequence of a comic strip, the proximity of one panel to another does not further an over-arching understanding that would resolve the connections between the elements. There are significant gaps between the images. It is in these gaps that we become active participants through the connections we construct. But, as with Paolozzi's *Moonstrips* print suite, these links never settle into solidity. It is rather that the elements can continue to play off one another, to resist and react to one another, to reach, not resolution, but a condition of agitated presentness.

In the panel paintings, the hooded figures may first appear to be the central protagonists (Figure 5.15), but one soon recognises that with each panel the same size, whether it is dedicated to a form such as a cup (Figure 5.16), a brick or a hood, these elements are not mere background props. The objects/images achieve equal status. We can regard every form as carrying its own narrative. For it is not only the hooded figures that provide a conspiratorial human presence; everything seems to be "up to something." There are collections of junk that appear to be intensely engaged in discussion while half concealed behind walls (Figure 5.17). Several panels feature cigars that seem to have gained their own life as mollusc-like creatures (Figure 5.18), the smoke issuing from them in an ominously thoughtful manner, as if plotting their next move. Even the words on the pages of stone tablet-like books seem to be earnestly engaged in discussion (Figures 2.14 and 2.15). Everything seems to be formed of a buzzing multitude. The paintings absorb the viewer in a collision of multiple, overlapping narratives; unable to find a path through, we are thrown into a landscape of the here and now.

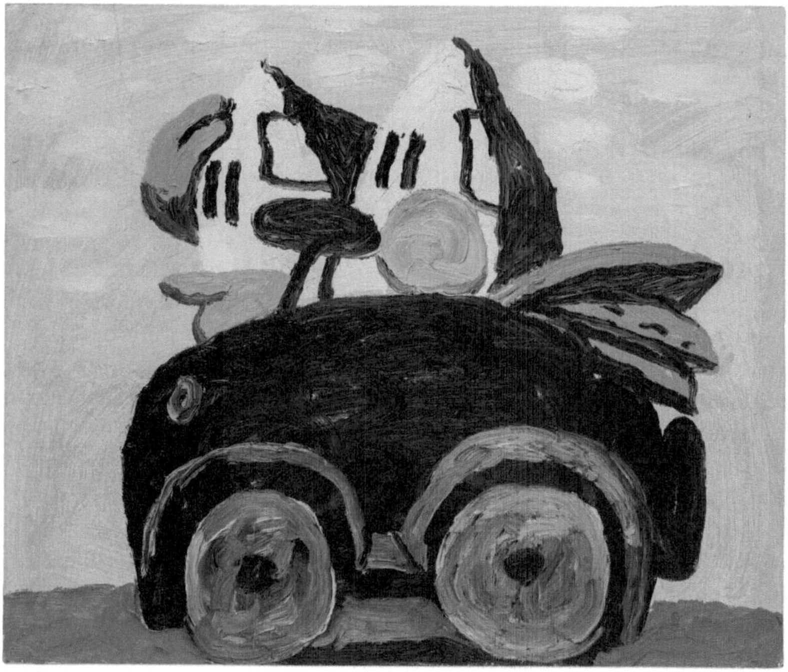

Figure 5.15 *Untitled (Hoods in Car)*, 1970, Philip Guston, oil on panel, 30.5 × 35.6 cm (12 × 14 inches).

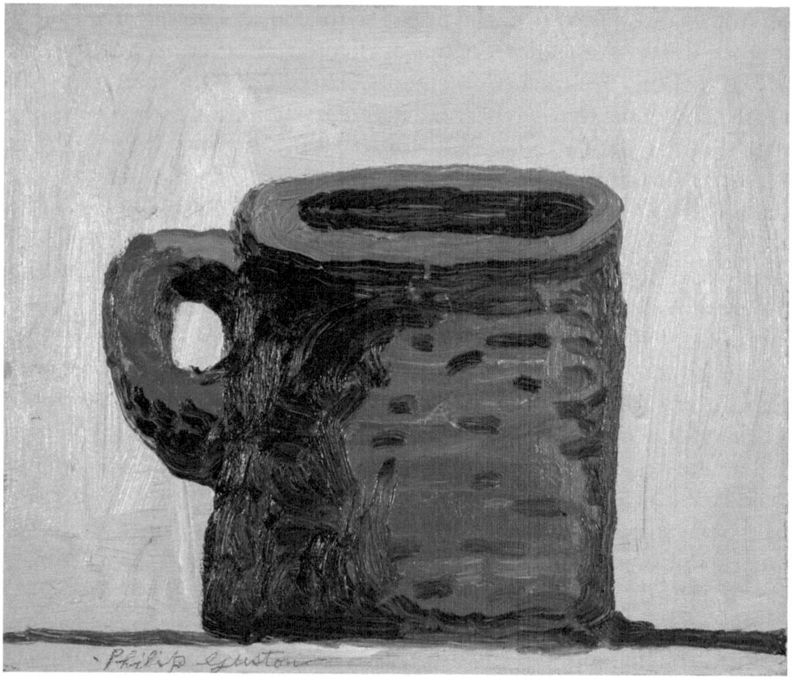

Figure 5.16 *Cup*, 1972, Philip Guston, oil on panel, 30.5 × 35.6 cm (12 × 14 inches).

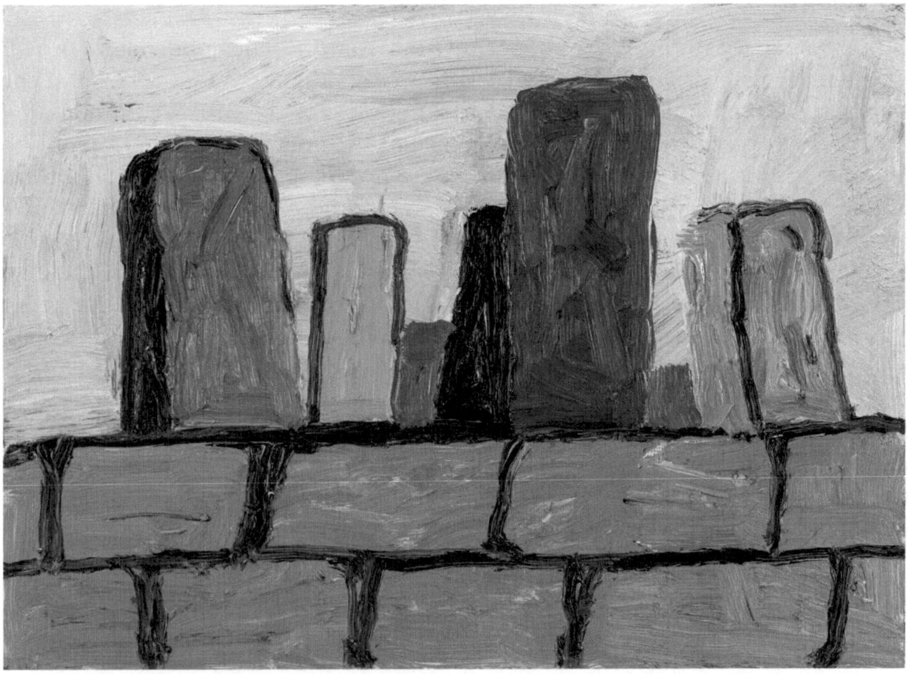

Figure 5.17 Untitled (Wall), 1968, Philip Guston, oil on panel, 22.9 × 30.5 cm (9 × 12 inches).

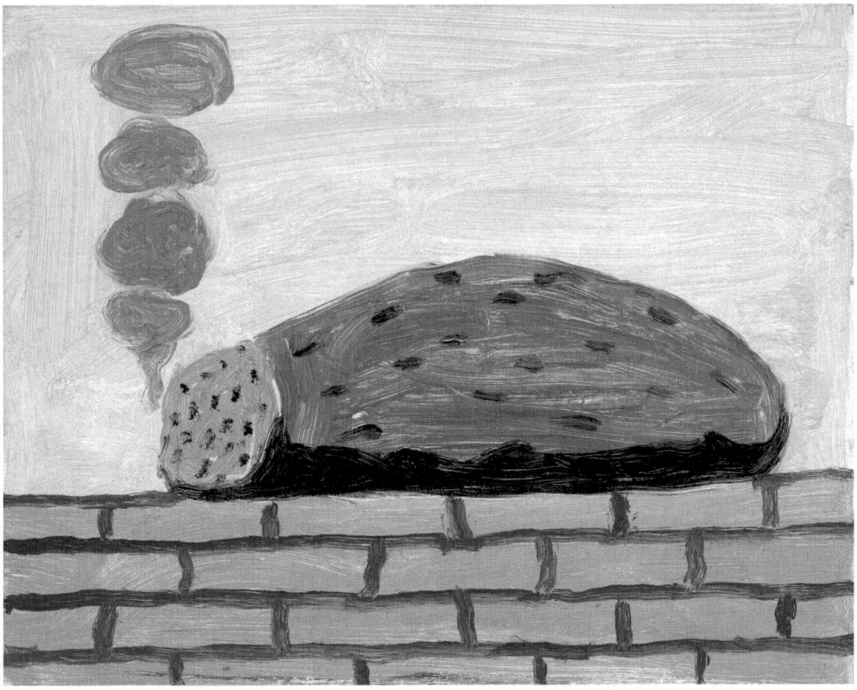

Figure 5.18 Untitled (Cigar), 1968–73, Philip Guston, oil on panel, 22.9 × 27.9 cm (9 × 11 inches).

Within the panel paintings, scenes repeat with variation. The hooded figures recur in front of buildings or driving Mutt and Jeff-like cars (Figures 5.15 and 5.19). Lengths of lumber appear repeatedly behind walls (Figures 5.17 and 5.20). We cannot help but connect these images. Therefore, any sequence of the images, taken in random order, makes sense, particularly when the paintings are not hung in a single line, but brought together as a block of images, as Guston had in his studio (Figure 5.14).[61] In this way, one does not read the work from left to right looking for linear progression; rather, one engages with the work through the connections one builds between the images. We gain an unsettling response to the work, animating the pictures in the here and now through our eye movement. The result is almost cinematic. We appear to be presented with cutaway scenes, and even the close-up. There are repeat images of hoods in cars from different view-points, as if the camera has zoomed in and zoomed out. As we connect the repeat images, we experience an uncanny sense of movement, as if the hooded figures are in motion. But once again, the movement does not lead anywhere; the images together present an emphatic sense of the now. The work builds duration through its obduracy. In the work's refusal to progress, time accumulates.

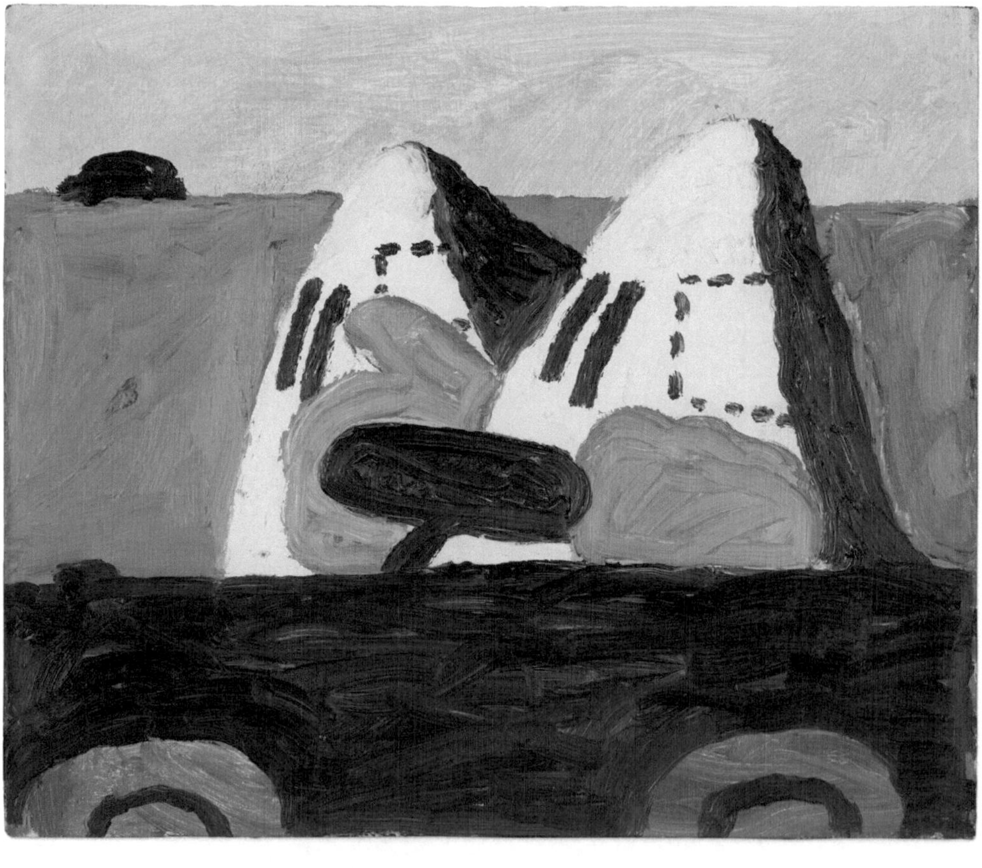

Figure 5.19 Untitled (Two Hooded Figures in a Car), 1971, 30.5 × 35.6 cm (12 × 14 inches).

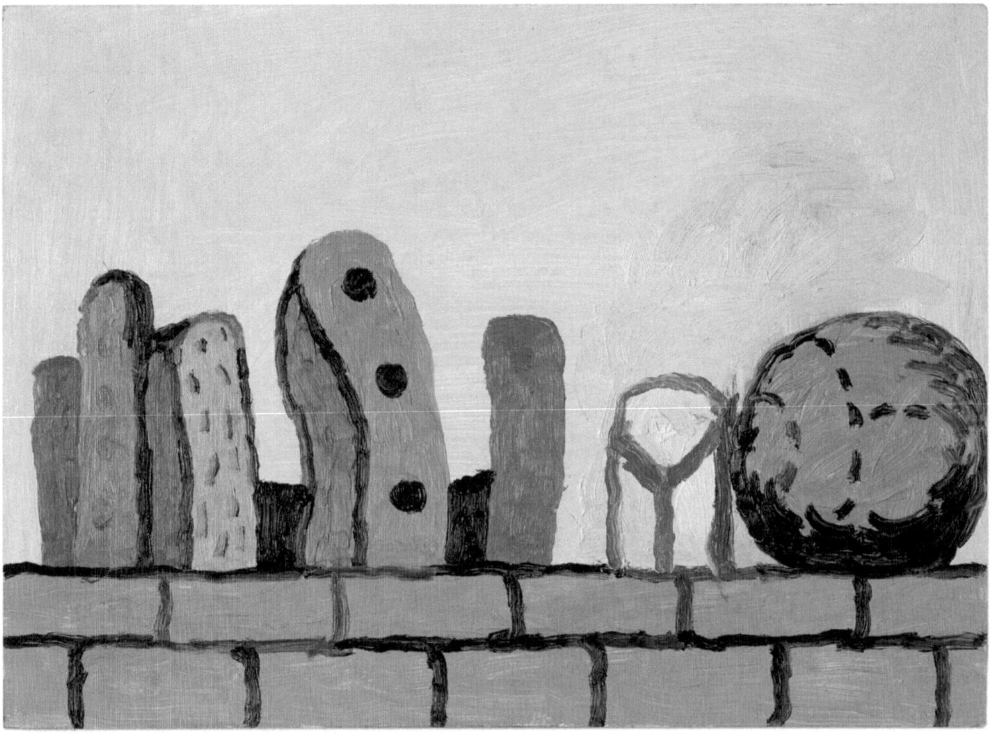

Figure 5.20 Untitled (Wall), 1970, Philip Guston, oil on panel, 30.5 × 40.6 cm (12 × 16 inches).
Image courtesy of The Estate of Philip Guston. © The Estate of Philip Guston.

It was during the time Guston created these panel paintings that the artist spoke of feeling as if he were a movie director. But with Guston's paintings understood as collections of anti-linear scenes, the artist's "movie" never receives the final cut. Instead, the work achieves an infinite unfolding by remaining open to a multitude of unforeseen possibilities. We see Guston present an avowedly anti-linear approach to narrative in his 1978 painting *Story* (Figure 5.21). The painting condenses the scattered structure of the panel paintings into a single image. However, this is a single image that refuses singularity. The collection of discontinuous elements presents gaps, within which we can continue to improvise narrative.

Battle Scars

During the last ten years of his life, Guston created a world of objects populated by the battered, the bruised, the patched, the weathered and the care-worn. Here, among Guston's repertoire of forms gathered from the mundane, life accumulates. For Ross Feld, it was as if "he had found a way to paint images that almost brimmed with transience and time."[62] The patched kettles (Figure 5.22) and dog-eared shoes that feature in Guston's wastelands wear their past to exert a presence infused with history. In this section, I will further examine how Guston employed a narrative form that does not serve sequential time; Guston's paintings are able to compress duration into a single

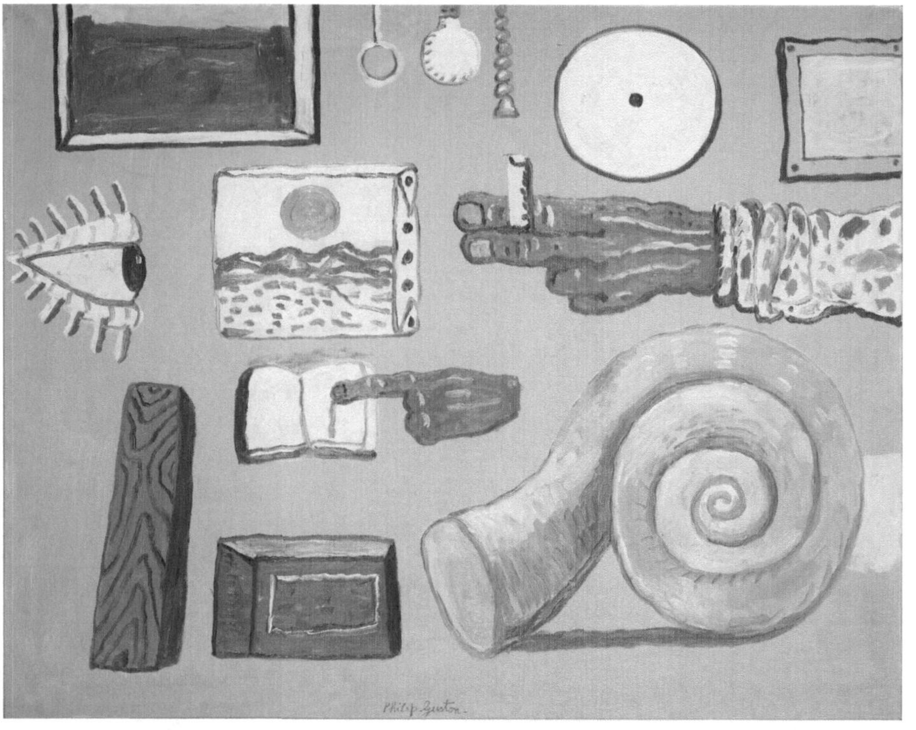

Figure 5.21 *Story*, 1978, Philip Guston, oil on canvas, 121.9 × 152.4 cm (48 × 60 inches).

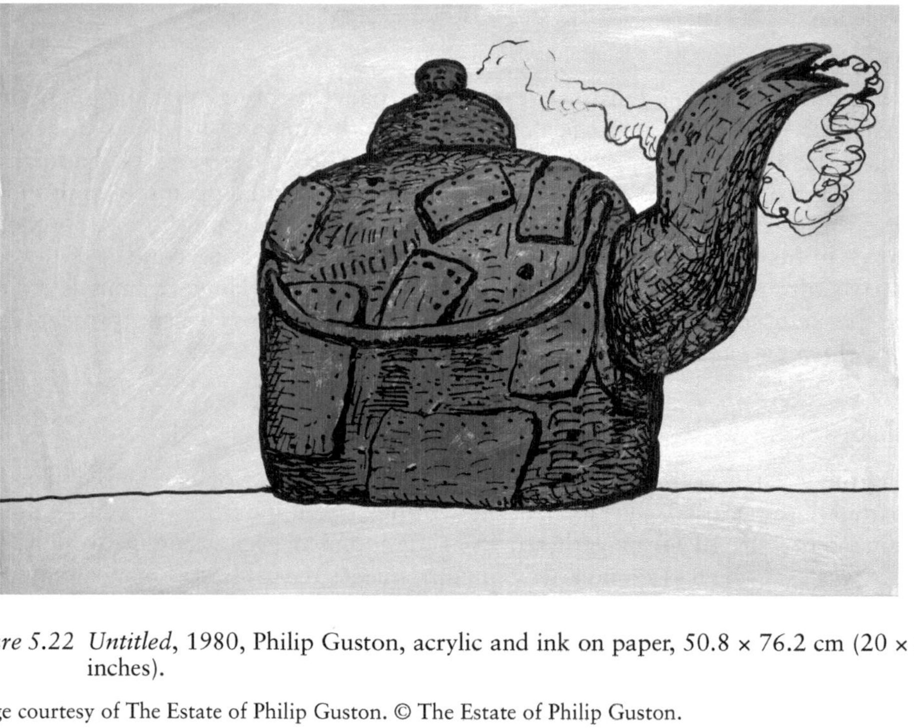

Figure 5.22 *Untitled*, 1980, Philip Guston, acrylic and ink on paper, 50.8 × 76.2 cm (20 × 30 inches).

image that promises change. In Guston's world, time is represented not as a series of events to be encountered and overcome, but rather as a "living" history embedded within form, present through the traces of events that accumulate and condense over scarred surfaces. Notably, even the painters depicted in *Painter's Head* (1975) and *In the Studio* (1975) wear scars that are strangely reminiscent of Guston's paintings of the 1950s, such as *Beggar's Joys* (1954–5) (Figure 1.11) and *Untitled* (1955–6) (Figure 3.4): a self-mocking acknowledgement, perhaps of the artist's own battles, and a recognition that the work of the past is not past but is still actively enfolded within ongoing creative concerns. It is as if these bruised and care-worn personas in Guston's late painting give form to the words of the artist's friend, the poet Stanley Kunitz: "We learn as the thread plays out that we belong less to what flatters us than to what scars."[63]

Here one recalls that among some scraps of paper Guston's daughter discovered in the artist's studio after he died was a note that read, "Thickness of things. Shoes. Rusted iron. Mended rags. Seams. Dried blood stains."[64] It is for Guston in the "thickness of things" that life forms. As the effects of past events pile up, the aged object expands to intertwine life and time within the concrete. Wear and tear, function as a means by which objects are given their own individual history: a history that is contained within form itself, rather than played out through sequential narrative. The anthropomorphic character of Guston's heavy, care-worn shoes house a life. Within them, time is presented as a process of sedimentation and disintegration, with duration accessible to the viewer in the present tense. Guston's 1977 painting *Pyramid and Shoe* pushes a depiction of the intertwined lives of objects and humans to its furthest point. A gargantuan boot, its sole thick with sediment, has come to rest beside a pyramid. Together, they suggest that all human life, however regal or humble, eventually reaches an equivalence in the material realm as accreted matter.

However, the concern with duration was not new to Guston's work. In 1960, Guston spoke of his desire for an image that embodied time and experience: "I would like to think a picture is finished when it feels not new but old. As if the forms had lived a long time in you."[65] In the 1950s, duration is embedded in Guston's painting through a process of layering and scraping. Time is built into the work through the visible accumulation of action. Once again, time is presented as a process of stacking and etching, but here it is made manifest in material form, as opposed to the images of patches and dents that appear across the objects of the 1970s. The narrative, then, is one of the tangible history of the painting as it emerged and formed on the canvas.

In Guston's late figurative work, the engagement with narrative processes is made overt, whether it is through the use of individual panels that can be shuffled, or, as we saw in Chapter 3, the painting process is given symbolic representation in the battle paintings and deluge works. However, although the late paintings give representation to the inscription of time, there was also a marked continuity with the processes at play in Guston's abstract work. Processes of layering and erasure were employed to actualise the sedimentation of time. Indeed, it often seems as if Guston needed to begin a painting over an old work. The ground of the painting, then, provides the forms with a past. There are even many works on paper that present a considerable amount of overpainting, such as *Untitled (Foot on Wall—Roma)* (1971) (Figure 5.23). Underneath the line painting of a lumpen, boot-like foot, it is possible to discern another painting that was begun in black and cadmium red, and then rapidly painted over with pink and dirty white. The greyish pink "dirt" can be read in David Trotter's terms as mess—open to contingency, pronouncing the work's history.

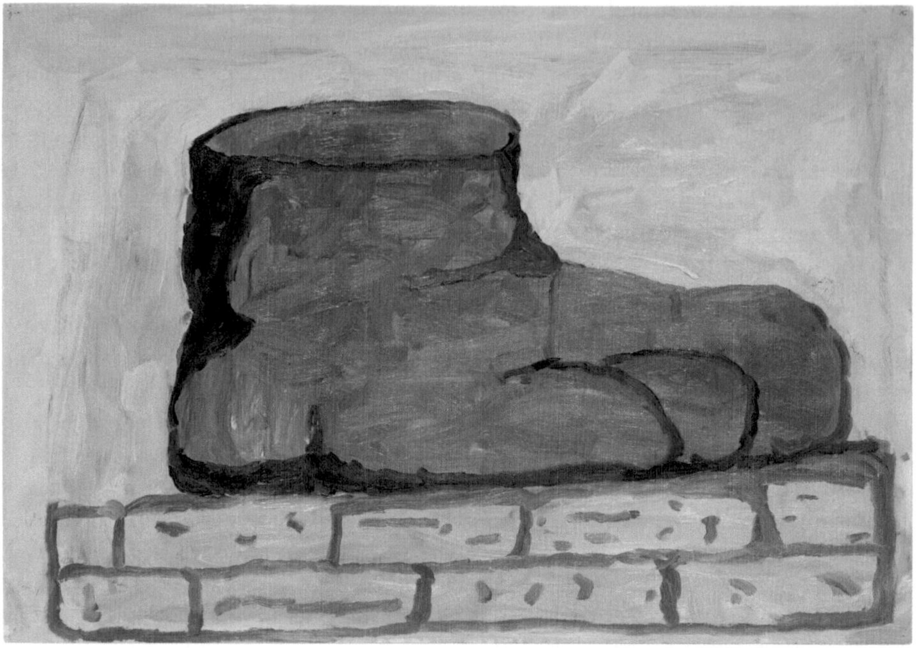

Figure 5.23 *Untitled (Foot on Wall—Roma)*, 1971, Philip Guston, oil on paper, 48.9 × 70.5 cm (19 × 28 inches).

There is an urgency to the brush marks as they push back one image to make way for another. However, the overpainting does not act negatively; it transforms into a layer of past events that add weight, history and pathos to the image. Indeed, the foot becomes less an image and more a sculpture through the accretion of matter. Despite the limited amount of descriptive detail, the image is weighted in the world of gravity and experience. The thick, heavy red line that sits as the top layer of sediment creates a form that appears pulled down under the strain of physical forces.

In acknowledging Guston's asserted use of overpainting, we can apply Guston's shuffling process (explored in the previous section) to a reading of a single image. Within a work such as *Untitled (Foot on Wall—Roma)* (1971), it is almost as if Guston's shuffling process is taking place on the paper and leaving traces. By acknowledging the erasures and overpainting within Guston's late work as active presences, we can think of the elements as having moved around the canvas, acquiring a history before we encounter them in their present state. In fact, in 1965, sometime before Guston's panel paintings, when the artist's work was still abstract, Guston described how his painting was concerned with creating an "unsettled" image. Guston describes a process that seems to enfold the shuffling process of the later works into a single image, to allow one to feel as if the forms were living out a life within the canvas:

> It must of necessity be an image which is unsettled . . . [it] must feel as if it's been in many places all over this canvas, and indeed there's no place for it to

> settle—except momentarily. . . . The image must feel as if it's lived. A picture is finished when it's in this unsettled, hovering state . . . because it's lived a long time everywhere else, lived in me, lived in previous paintings of mine, and now in this picture it's in a new and very particular situation.[66]

In the painting, *Position I* (1965), we encounter a dense black form in a tumultuous sea of grey brush marks. Taken together with Guston's statement, we gain the sense of the form having been kicked around the canvas like a ball before returning to its first position. This is the "to-and-fro movement" Gadamer describes as characteristic of play. And although the painting is complete, seeming to contradict the goalless, endless process defined by Gadamer, for Guston the aim is almost the impossible—to create a work that is poised on the verge of change. However, if we consider the painting not in isolation, but as part of a wider non-sequential series, we acquire the sense of the form hovering before its next move, reaching the tipping point before it recurs in works such as *Arrival* (1965) and *Air II* (1965).

The "unsettled" image remained one of Guston's central concerns, continuing through the artist's return to figurative painting. There appears to be an endless fascination with attempting the improbable—finding a single image that promises change. This desired image is not a frozen scene isolated from a linear sequence, but one that carries an accumulation of time and events to give the sense that the painting is just pausing before its life continues. As late as 1979, the year before Guston's death, the artist was still articulating a need for a still image that defied its stillness: "It is a very anxious fix. And that fix should promise other conditions of the same attitude. It is a continuous thing."[67] For Guston, the work of Piero della Francesca presented a tireless model: "I think Piero is the highest type of order. . . . And by that I mean never really fixed . . . it always gives you the potentialities of its moving into another kind of order."[68]

For many years, postcards of Piero's paintings the *Baptism of Christ* (c. 1445–50) and the *Flagellation of Christ* (1455–60) hung on Guston's kitchen wall. The whip from the *Flagellation* occurs repeatedly in Guston's late painting, featuring in works that include *The Door* (1976) (Figure 3.9), *Green Rug* (1976), *Night Room* (1976) (Figure 5.24) and *Room* (1977). These last three works exist among numerous Guston paintings in which a whip appears to force a tangled knot of legs to dance (or march) for eternity against a blackened abyss. Despite this hellish theme, I think it is possible to connect these works to Guston's desire for an "unsettled" image. The whip presents a force that compels forms into action. Here, Craig Burnett's analysis of Guston's regard for Piero della Francesca is helpful in what it reveals about Guston's engagement with narrative themes. During a lecture given to students at the New York Studio School in 1971, Guston conveyed to the students his love of Piero's *Tortura dell'Ebreo* (*The Torture of the Jew*, c. 1455). Guston described how he was tirelessly thrilled and entranced by "the overlapping of the forms resolved in this particular suspension."[69] However, Burnett notes that when a student asked Guston about the "story" contained in the painting, Guston confessed he did not know, explaining that he had a "bad memory for iconography."[70] For Burnett, this is both perplexing and significant: "What are we to make of Guston's claim that he turned to figuration because he wanted to 'tell stories' when he wasn't even interested in the stories being told by his favourite painter?"[71] This becomes even more difficult to comprehend when one considers the narrative theme in relation to Guston's own

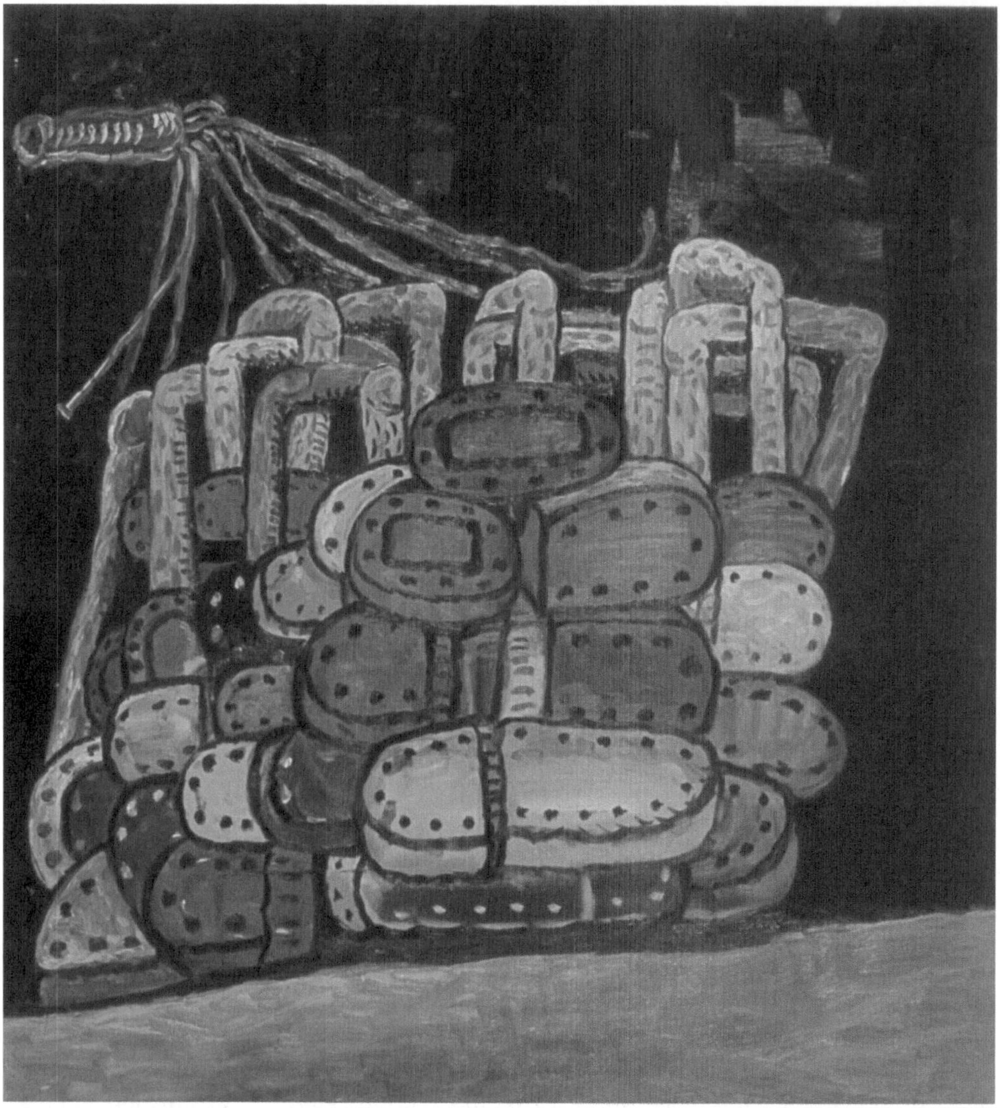

Figure 5.24 *Night Room*, 1976, Philip Guston, oil on canvas, 203.2 × 175.3 (80 × 69 inches).

Jewish identity. For Burnett, the story that fascinated Guston was the "disposition of forms."[72] Burnett uses Guston's reading of the work of Piero as a way into the artist's own approach to narrative. In his analysis of Guston's painting *The Studio* (1969), Burnett argues that it is Guston's painting process, together with the formal qualities of the painting, that provides a story of complexity that overrides anything that could be reduced to a narrative theme; for Burnett it is the "picture as a picture" that "perpetually renews itself."[73]

Burnett's contention that Guston's failure to recall the story contained in *Tortura dell'Ebreo* revealed something far more profound than a memory slip finds firm foundation in Guston's own writing on Piero. In Guston's short essay "Piero della Francesca: The Impossibility of Painting" (1965), one finds that Guston made no attempt to engage with the themes within Piero's paintings. Guston's focus is the location and rhythm of the forms that seem to promise movement. Guston effectively dismantled the prescribed Christian themes to play with the structures and meanings of Piero's paintings. Specifically, in "failing" to remember the story depicted in Piero's *Tortura dell'Ebreo*, Guston rejected a theme of persecution with profound personal significance to create something joyous.

It appears that for Guston, narrative is enjoyed as a presence that *emerges* from setting a work in motion through the disruption of meaning. We can take Guston's reading of Piero to Guston's own work, not to trace it back to the meaning of its origin, but rather to place the work within a narrative process to keep the work in a state of animation. Specifically, one can return to the artist's repeated use of whip imagery borrowed from *The Flagellation*. This image can be seen in Guston's terms as a "disturbance" that continually unsettles the painting.[74] The whip resembles at times a frayed paintbrush, and at others a paintbrush whip, as in *The Desert* (1974). Here, I will resist making a rather crass point about the whip imagery symbolising the pain and pleasure of creativity. I think one can see the paintbrush–whip conflation in rather more complex ambiguous terms, as a force that sets things in motion. In *The Desert*, a figure brandishes a cat-o'-nine-tails to the left of a pile of shoes. Figure and shoes are both framed by a low-hanging light bulb to the right and a blind cord to the left. The composition forcefully recalls the words of a previously quoted note written by the artist, found in his studio: "A pile of junk between two telephone poles. The itch to kick it, disperse it."[75] Again, we encounter the opposing forces of piling and dissolution, placing the work in a cycle of building and destruction. The work is held in a state of tension between the two poles, both formally and metaphorically. Indeed, in the 1972 painting *The Road*, a pile of shoes is painted between two telephone poles; to the left of the pile, instead of a whip, we encounter a pot of paintbrushes, as if at the ready to push the pile of forms off into new configurations. One can connect these non-progressive cycles of reconfiguration to the circular movement at work in Paolozzi's prints that appear to be spinning on the spot. Again, one encounters Fink's assertion as to the "circular sense of the activity of play" that has no ultimate goal or end. Guston's knotted legs and shoes that appear repeatedly in works including the *Rug* series (1976), *Monument* (1976) and *Night Room* (1976) (Figure 5.24) all give form to this circular non-progressive movement. These are feet that are stamping and charging but going nowhere. And again, as with Paolozzi's prints, the very form of the painting produces such a reading, leading our eyes in a looped pattern, through the maze of long, knotted legs and then pushed out by the circular forms of the shoes to start the loop again.

The knotted legs, running while rooted, can exist as a metaphor for the artist's tireless return to a limited collection of mundane objects. Like the spinning top, the knotted legs can become a symbol for play. Through their limited and repetitive movement, meaning builds. This returns us to an acknowledgement of play's contradictory relationship with freedom, with which I began this chapter's discussion on Guston's narrative processes. It seems that Guston's freedom in his late work paradoxically came from the creation of limits. Monica Vilhauer explains how this contradiction between freedom and limitation sits at the centre of an understanding of play:

> Human play . . . involves the intention, willingness or choice to constrain one's own freedom to the rules of a game. Human play has the special quality of human freedom, which is not simply the freedom of randomness or caprice, but is a freedom that involves the intentional self-restrain that goes along with any effort to accomplish something. It involves what Gadamer refers to as a profound commitment.[76]

With Guston, one can replace Vilaheur's term "rule" with the notion of restricted means. It is by pushing against these limits that Guston's narratives build. There is an intensity of commitment to every line and gesture that makes each object tremble with the marks of time. Through repetition and return, Guston's objects become heavy with the weight of experience as time and events stack up within the forms. If Guston was seeking an "anxious fix" within each painting, he also creates instability and uncertainty through the promise of the objects' return. As meanings become ungraspable through the slip and slide of shifting connections, these become images to worry over. Denied resolution, Guston's anti-linear scenes are restless in expectation.

Notes

1. Interview with Fiona Mathison on 20/10/2011.
2. Keith Johnstone, *Impro: Improvisation and the Theatre* (London: Methuen Drama, 2007).
3. J.G. Ballard as quoted in "Speculative Illustrations: Eduardo Paolozzi in Conversation with J.G. Ballard and Frank Whitford, 1971," in *Eduardo Paolozzi: Writings and Interviews*, ed. Robin Spencer (Oxford and New York: Oxford University Press, 2001), 199.
4. Ibid.
5. Eduardo Paolozzi, Ibid.
6. Hannah Arendt, *The Human Condition* (Chicago: University of Chicago Press, 1998), 2.
7. Johnstone, *Impro: Improvisation and the Theatre*, 142.
8. At the conference, *Eduardo Paolozzi: Re-Readings*, held at Manchester Metropolitan University in 2011.
9. Fay Ballard shared her recollections at the conference, *Eduardo Paolozzi: Re-Readings*, held at Manchester Metropolitan University in 2011.
10. Lev Manovich, *The Language of New Media* (Cambridge, MA: The MIT Press, 2001), 78.
11. Ibid., 36.
12. Ibid., 325.
13. Marshall McLuhan, *The Gutenberg Galaxy* (London: Routledge & Kegan Paul, 1971), 5.
14. Eduardo Paolozzi, "Paolozzi Explains About BASH, 1971," in *Eduardo Paolozzi: Writings and Interviews*, ed. Spencer, 219.
15. David Egan, "Playing Well: Wittgenstein's Language-Games and the Ethics of Discourse," in *The Philosophy of Play*, ed. Emily Ryall, Wendy Russell and Malcolm Maclean (New York: Routledge, 2014), 56.
16. Ibid., 57–62.
17. Eduardo Paolozzi, "Notes from a Lecture at the Institute of Contemporary Arts, 1958," in *Eduardo Paolozzi: Writings and Interviews*, ed. Spencer, 85.
18. Eduardo Paolozzi, "Waste, 1982," in *Eduardo Paolozzi: Writings and Interviews*, ed. Spencer, 258.
19. Eduardo Paolozzi, "Artificial Horizons and Eccentric Ladders," in *Eduardo Paolozzi: Artificial Horizons and Eccentric Ladders* (exh.cat.) (London: British Council, 1996), 11–12.
20. Ibid.

21. Eduardo Paolozzi as quoted in "Speculative Illustrations: Eduardo Paolozzi in Conversation with J.G. Ballard and Frank Whitford, 1971," 206.
22. Here the question of power is key: in other words, whose images, and what context. The use and misuse of the *Mona Lisa* is obviously quite distinct from processes of cultural appropriation, where cultural elements from a minority or denigrated culture are removed from context without acknowledgement by a dominant culture for profit. And, indeed, Paolozzi has been accused of a colonial approach to culture on other occasions, namely his 1985 exhibition, *Lost Magic Kingdoms and Six Paper Moons from Nahuatl*, staged at the Museum of Mankind using the museum's ethnographic collection. For a detailed discussion of the critical responses to Paolozzi's exhibition *Lost Magic Kingdoms and Six Paper Moons from Nahuatl* (1985–7), see Lisa Maddigan Newby, "Lost Magic Kingdoms: Eduardo Paolozzi's Assemblages at the Museum of Mankind, 1985–87," in *Eduardo Paolozzi* (exh.cat.), ed. Daniel F. Herrmann (London: Whitechapel Gallery, 2017), 236–43.
23. Eugen Fink, *Play as Symbol of the World and Other Writings* (Bloomington: Indiana University Press, 2016), 19–20.
24. Mieke Bal, *Narratology, Introduction to the Theory of Narrative* (Toronto and London: University of Toronto Press, 1985), 6.
25. Ibid., 7.
26. Ibid., 26.
27. Ibid., 74.
28. Mieke Bal, *Louise Bourgeois' Spider, the Architecture of Art Writing* (Chicago and London: University of Chicago Press, 2001), 31.
29. Ibid., 8.
30. Ibid., 49.
31. Ibid., 77.
32. Ibid., 78.
33. Eduardo Paolozzi, "The Wealth of Nations, 1993," in *Eduardo Paolozzi: Writings and Interviews*, ed. Spencer, 325.
34. Fink, *Play as Symbol of the World*, 21.
35. Martin Heidegger, *Basic Writings* (London: Routledge, 1993), 356.
36. Ibid., 173.
37. Ibid.
38. McLuhan, *The Gutenberg Galaxy*, 42.
39. Philip Guston, "Interview with Jan Butterfield, 1979," in *Philip Guston, Collected Writings, Lectures, and Conversations*, ed. Clark Coolidge (London: University of California Press, 2011), 290.
40. Philip Guston, *Philip Guston: A Life Lived*, directed by Michael Blackwood. New York, NY, Michael Blackwood Productions Inc., 1981.
41. Brian Sutton-Smith, *The Ambiguity of Play* (Cambridge: Harvard University Press, 2001), 183.
42. Walter Benjamin, "The Author as Producer," in *Art in Theory, 1900–1990: An Anthology of Changing Ideas*, ed. Charles Harrison and Paul Wood (Oxford and Malden: Blackwell Publishers, 1997), 485.
43. Ibid., 487.
44. Ibid., 488.
45. Philip Guston, "Talk At 'Art/Not Art?' Conference, 1978," in *Collected Writings, Lectures, and Conversations*, ed. Coolidge, 278.
46. Philip Guston, "Talk at Yale Summer School of Music and Art, 1973," in *Collected Writings, Lectures, and Conversations*, ed. Coolidge, 223.
47. Ibid., 224.
48. Ibid., 223
49. Philip Guston as quoted in Andrew Graham-Dixon, "A Maker of Worlds: The Later Paintings of Philip Guston," in *Philip Guston Retrospective* (exh.cat.), ed. Michael Auping (London: Thames & Hudson, 2003), 56.
50. Harold Rosenberg, *The Tradition of the New* (New York: Da Capo Press, 1994), 26.
51. Philip Guston, "Conversation with Morton Feldman, 1968," in *Collected Writings, Lectures, and Conversations*, ed. Coolidge, 89–90.

52. Guston as quoted in Robert Storr, *Philip Guston* (New York: Abbeville, 1986), 109.
53. Guston, *Philip Guston: A Life Lived.*
54. Philip Guston, "Philip Guston Talking," in *Philip Guston* (exh.cat.) (London: Timothy Taylor Gallery, 2004), 36.
55. Hans-Georg Gadamer, *Truth and Method* (London and New York: Continuum, 2006), 104.
56. Ibid., 118.
57. Ibid., 109.
58. Ibid., 117.
59. Philip Guston, "Faith, Hope and Impossibility, 1965/66," in *Collected Writings, Lectures, and Conversations*, ed. Coolidge, 53.
60. Gadamer, *Truth and Method*, 129.
61. I have experimented with many different configurations of Guston's panel paintings using reproductions.
62. Ross Feld, *Guston in Time* (New York: Counterpoint, 2003), 14.
63. Stanley Kunitz, *The Dark and the Fair*, All Poetry, accessed June 18, 2018, https://allpoetry.com/The-Dark-And-The-Fair
64. Guston as quoted in Musa Mayer, *Night Studio, a Memoir of Philip Guston* (New York: Da Capo Press, 1997), 148.
65. Philip Guston, "From Panel at the Philadelphia Museum School of Art, 1960," in *Collected Writings, Lectures, and Conversations*, ed. Coolidge, 29.
66. Philip Guston, "Philip Guston's Object: Conversation with Harold Rosenberg, 1965," in *Collected Writings, Lectures, and Conversations*, ed. Coolidge, 49.
67. Guston, "Interview with Jan Butterfield, 1979," 297.
68. Philip Guston, "On Survival," in *Collected Writings, Lectures, and Conversations*, ed. Coolidge, 242.
69. Guston as quoted in Craig Burnett, *Philip Guston: The Studio* (London: Afterall Books, 2014), 28.
70. Ibid.
71. Ibid., 29.
72. Ibid.
73. Ibid., 30.
74. Philip Guston, "Piero Della Francesca: The Impossibility of Painting, 1965," in *Collected Writings, Lectures, and Conversations*, ed. Coolidge, 41.
75. Philip Guston, "Studio Notes, 1970–78," in *Collected Writings, Lectures, and Conversations*, ed. Coolidge, 314.
76. Monica Vilhauer, "Gadamer and the Game of Understanding: Dialogue-Play and Opening to the Other," in *The Philosophy of Play*, ed. Emily Ryall, Wendy Russell and Malcolm Maclean (New York: Routledge, 2014), 76.

6 Absurd Processes

A Break From the Rational

In this final chapter, I will read Guston and Paolozzi's play processes through notions of the absurd. I will move away from the definition of the absurd as a noun as it is used in the philosophy of the absurd and return to older adjectival definitions. This will allow the chapter to depart from the conclusions of a specific school of thought. I will look at how these definitions point towards connections between Guston and Paolozzi's work and that of Dada and *The Theatre of the Absurd*, but more significantly I will consider how the broader adjectival definitions may suggest a reading that offers a divergence from these two frameworks to allow the viewer to play with meaning. Merriam-Webster defines the noun "the absurd" as "the state or condition in which human beings exist in an irrational and meaningless universe and in which human life has no ultimate meaning—usually used with the theater of the absurd."[1]

The Theatre of the Absurd was a term coined by the dramatist, scholar and critic Martin Esslin in an essay published in 1960.[2] Writing in the wake of two world wars, for Esslin the playwrights of the absurd (whose primary exponents were Samuel Beckett, Arthur Adamov, Eugène Ionesco and Jean Genet) reflected a time in which previously held certainties had been blown asunder and faith destroyed. Esslin stresses the dramatists' connection to Camus' philosophy of the absurd, citing Camus' text *The Myth of Sisyphus*.[3] Ionescu is quoted as defining the absurd as "that which is devoid of purpose. . . . Cut off from his religious, metaphysical, and transcendental roots, man is lost; all his actions become senseless, absurd, useless."[4] Esslin applies Ionescu's definition broadly to the themes explored by all the playwrights. The plays lack plot and resolution and employ repetition and contradiction between word and action. These key characteristics function as metaphors for the inadequacy of language and reason.

There are obvious overlaps here with the processes employed by Paolozzi and Guston. The previous chapter examined both artists' dismissal of plot-led narrative to create structures for which there is no resolution. More broadly, throughout the book I have been exploring both artists' use of processes that break from the cohesive plan to create form for which there is no pre-ordained meaning. However, while many of the processes employed by Guston and Paolozzi would seem at first sight to parallel Esslin's analysis of the dramatists of the absurd, in fact the implications of Guston and Paolozzi's processes appear at odds with Esslin's conclusions. This chapter will explore how Guston and Paolozzi would seem to dismiss certainties and push against the limitations of rationality, not to suggest an existence without meaning, as presented by Esslin's study, but rather to present a condition in which meaning can exist even if it is paradoxical, multiple and inconstant.[5] Guston's thrill at the possibilities presented by a shuffling process serves as a key example here. If one returns to the letter Guston wrote to Bill Berkson in 1976 (quoted in the previous chapter), one can see that, for Guston, a lack of certainty points to a wealth of meaning, as opposed to a condition of meaninglessness:

> Last month, trying to select 9 or 10 paintings from about 40 for [the] McKee show, I shifted pictures around for days and nights, *reeling* from the diverse possible *meanings* the pictures possess when in different image relationships. But that is the potency of image making—it's as if we are dense—swamped—image-ridden—we teem with meanings "constantly." So the what is never settled.[6]

Guston and Paolozzi's shuffling process, used to create unpredictable results, has its precedent in Dadaist techniques that employed chance as a means to break from the limits of rational control. Additionally, Dadaist experimental theatre can be seen as a forerunner to *The Theatre of the Absurd.* It too emerged from rage against a rationale that had led to the mass slaughter of the First World War. In response, Dada sought to undermine language, to make nonsense of logic and corrupt society's established rules and structures. Rudolf Kuenzli points out that the name Dada itself points to the heart of the endeavour "in equating everything with 'Dada,' which does not mean anything, the Dadas hoped to invalidate all meaning."[7] But Kuenzli also allows us to acknowledge that right from its inception in Zurich in 1916, Dada was not a unified movement. This is a point made clear by Hans Richter, who describes Dada as a "jungle of contradictions" when recalling the differences between its founding members.[8] While Dada's most fervent publicist, Tristan Tzara, promoted a nihilistic vision for the movement, Richter recalls that for other Dadaists (such as he, Hugo Ball and Hans Arp), the destruction of meaning was a method by which to remake a new kind of order in which meaning emerged through non-rational methods. Richter recollects that for Arp the new "law" was that of chance: "How meaningful! How telling! Chance movements of his hand and of the fluttering scraps of paper had achieved what all his efforts had failed to achieve, namely *expression.*"[9]

It is perhaps, then, Arp's Dadaism that might offer the closest connection to the work of Paolozzi and Guston. Arp offers a model in which rational order is corrupted, not to offer a nihilistic vision, but to suggest a world whose laws operate beyond the limits of rational understanding. Furthermore, in Arp's use of chance, we discover the artist engage in a "to-and-fro" dialogue between contingency and control, elements that have been seen to characterise Guston and Paolozzi's play processes. So where would this leave the work of Guston and Paolozzi in relation to definitions of the absurd? To take this further, I want to move away from Camus' philosophy of the absurd to engage with Deleuze's concept of sense. In *The Logic of Sense*, first published in 1969, Deleuze distinguishes his argument from that of Camus: "[Lewis] Carroll, yes; Camus, no" is the declaration.[10] Deleuze clarifies that, for Camus, the absurd rests on the recognition of a lack of sense, while, for Deleuze, where structure is concerned there is always an excess of sense. For Deleuze, sense does not exist as an origin but as a product; the challenge he sets is to "rediscover" meaning. The contemporary philosopher James Williams writes that, for Deleuze, "meaning depends on a prior set of combinations of relations that themselves have no fixed meanings."[11] According to Williams, it follows that, for Deleuze, if meaning is an inconstant product of changing combinations and relations, then the concept of ever reaching a final truth is itself absurd: "For him [Deleuze], life is not absurd, but endlessly complex."[12] Importantly, Williams emphasises that Deleuze's position emerges from structuralism's concern with games and play, specifically the means by which a game allows for innumerable variations.

Deleuze provides another means of approaching the notion of absurdity within the work of Paolozzi and Guston. If we return again to their use of a shuffling process, their engagement with unpredictable structures and unresolved narratives, then we are provided with a condition in which multiple meanings can emerge from changing combinations. Formed from individual elements that have no fixed meaning, works such as Paolozzi's *Moonstrips Empire News* print suite (Figure 5.1) or Guston's small panel paintings (Figure 5.14) (both explored in the previous chapter) are inconstant structures that continue to produce meaning as they are reshuffled. The work of Guston and Paolozzi allows us to conceive of absurdity as the attempt to find conclusive meaning in a world that has many contradictory, inconstant meanings. Unlike Tzara's Dadaism, both artists' destruction of rational systems and heroic icons are not nihilistic acts. Belief remains, but belief that allows for cycles of confusion, contradiction, doubt and reaffirmation without resolution.

Martin Esslin had been careful to distinguish the absurd as defined by Camus from its original meaning and common usage. The *Oxford English Reference Dictionary* defines the adjective absurd as "ludicrous" and "incongruous."[13] The word "ludicrous" is derived from the term ludic (playful), while "incongruous" is defined by the online *Oxford English Dictionary* as "disagreeing in character or qualities; not corresponding; out of keeping; discordant, inconsistent, inharmonious, unsuited."[14] Together, the two terms—ludic and incongruous—may describe a territory explored in the work of Paolozzi and Guston; work formed through processes that play with the discordant and bring together that which ordinarily (or rationally) should not "fit." In the previous chapters, we have seen how Paolozzi's sculpture and print-work were created using a kit of forms that dismissed taxonomies to create connections between far-ranging material. Paolozzi acknowledged his debt to Surrealism when describing his process as the "connecting of disparate images . . . a non-stop game."[15] For his bronze sculptures created between 1956 and 1959, Paolozzi harnessed the absurdist potential within the medium of assemblage to use rubbish and junk to build the epic, the heroic and the regal in works including *Jason* (1956), *St. Sebastian I* (1957) (Figure 3.14) and *The King* (c.1956–8) (Figure 3.12). Paolozzi's symbols of power are quite literally built on waste.

Similarly, Guston's late paintings brought together an extraordinary jumble of forms, which came together in unlikely clusters and assemblages in works including *Forms on Rock Ledge* (1979) (Figure 6.1), *Story* (1978) (Figure 5.21) and *Slope* (1979). In 1968, in discussion with Morton Feldman, Guston had described an engagement with material that was animated by a collision of contrary elements:

> You see, in thinking you carry things to their logical conclusion, but when you deal with matter you deal with opposites always. Things that won't. . . . What's the word. . . . When things don't easily mix or fuse. . . . Incompatible things.[16]

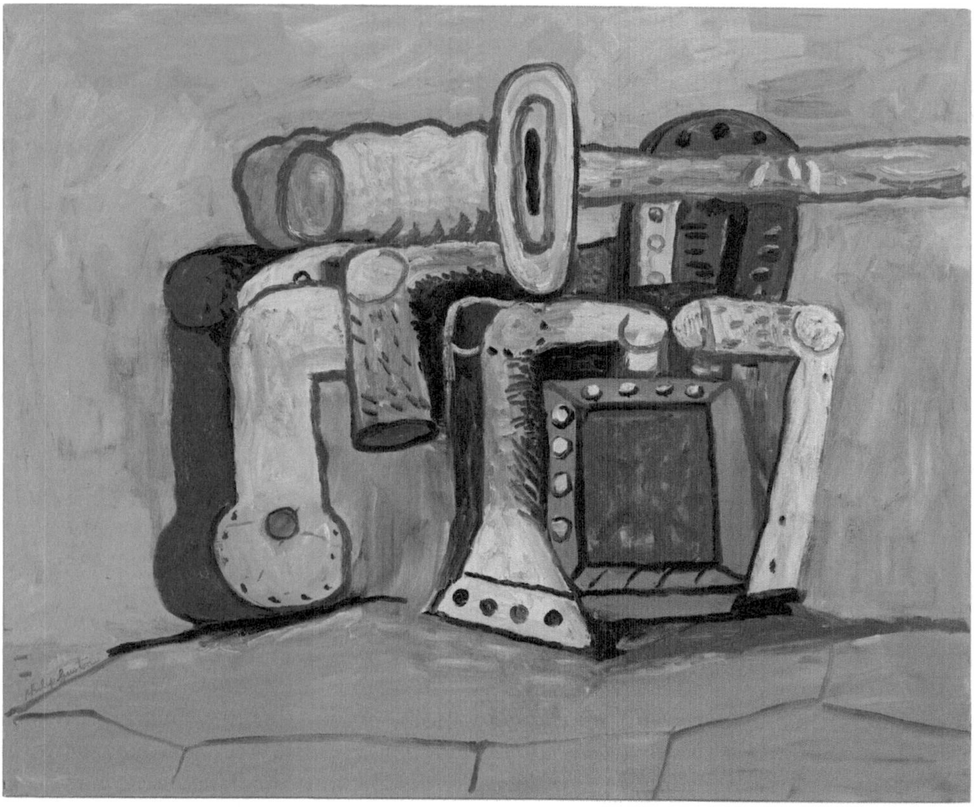

Figure 6.1 *Forms on Rock Ledge*, 1979, Philip Guston, oil on canvas, 152.4 × 182.9 cm (60 × 72 inches).

I will now consider the absurd as a play with incongruity to describe processes through which unstable connections are formed and new irresolvable meanings generated from dissonant structures.

Those other definitions of the incongruous—the "inconsistent," "inharmonious," "disagreeing in character or qualities"—re-orientate the discussion to the focus of the previous chapter. Through an examination of Paolozzi and Guston's approach to narrative, I explored the possibility that the use of conflicting elements thwarted teleological progression, to provide form with freedom from a goal. This, then, is perhaps above all what is offered by associating play with the older adjectival definitions of the term absurd; in defining absurdity as incongruity, one is able to positively dismiss resolution in order to place unresolved process at the centre of the work.

In returning to Guston's use of repetition, one can further give form to a notion of absurdity that is distinct from the concept articulated by Camus. In the 1979 painting *Forms on Rock Ledge* (Figure 6.1), a tightly knotted heap towers perilously near the edge of a precipice. The sense is of impending collapse, immanent doom. The image seems to invite the description provided by the academic Neil Cornwell in his preface to *The Absurd in Literature*, which promises "chaos will abound and the abyss will loom" in his survey of absurdist fiction and theatre.[17] With the knowledge that the painting was completed just a year before Guston's death, the painting cannot help reading as a prophecy. And yet, against the backdrop of doom (or at least a future unknown), the painting appears to stand as a challenge to create structure and meaning. But if the structure is built on the edge of collapse, perhaps the painting can also allow us to perceive meaning as unstable and paradoxical, both inchoate and on the verge of disintegration. Here it is necessary to see *Forms on Rock Ledge* as existing as part of a large series of works in which Guston heaps and piles form. In Chapter 3, I discussed how Guston identified the "pile-up" as the recurrent structure within his painting. *Residue* (1971), *Slope* (1979), *Summer* (1980) (Figure 3.7), *Pile Up* (1980) (Figure 3.8) and *Untitled* (1978) (Figure 6.2) are just a few other examples where heap

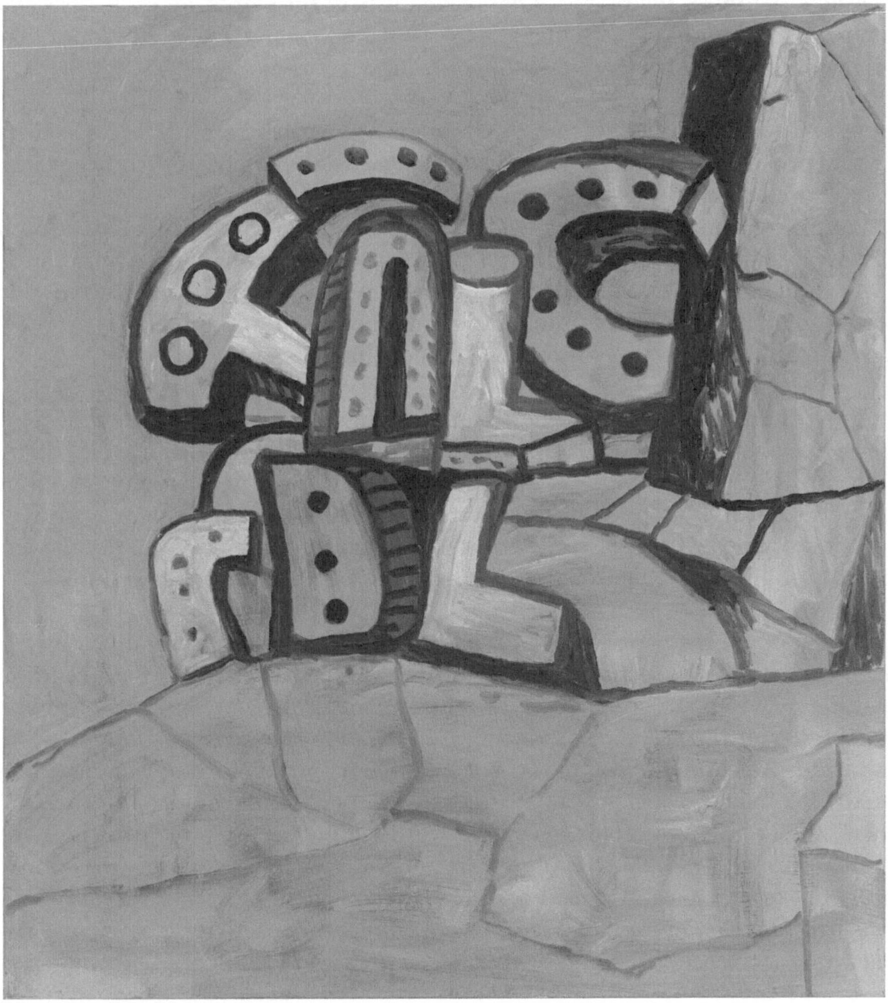

Figure 6.2 Untitled, 1978, Philip Guston, oil on canvas, 121.9 × 106.7 cm (48 × 42 inches).

structures resurface in Guston's late paintings. In regarding the structure as something that returns and mutates, the piling process was seen as an activity caught in a cycle of construction and dissolution, the building tirelessly beginning again and again. But, while this may risk sounding Sisyphean, by returning to the importance of repetition within play, one is able to formulate an alternative notion of the infinite process from that of Camus' reading of the myth of eternal punishment. Although Camus ultimately asks us to "imagine Sisyphus happy"[18] and asserts that the "struggle itself towards the heights is enough to fill a man's heart,"[19] this is a consolation. For Ionescu, repetition served to illustrate a world without meaning or purpose. But, with both Benjamin and Gadamer's notion of repetition as play, each time a "rock is rolled" the activity becomes created anew and a different meaning is produced. As Gadamer states, it is endless movement that comes to define play in all its forms, to reiterate

> the play of forces, the play of gnats, even a play on words. In each case what is intended is to-and-fro movement that is not tied to any goal that would bring it to an end; rather, it renews itself in constant repetition.[20]

But, just as the activity would now neither find nor seek resolution, the meanings might also prove provisional, and as they slip away they may in turn necessitate or provoke new structures and new meanings.

Guston makes allusions to the *Myth of Sisyphus* in the Michael Blackwood film *A Life Lived* (1981). Filmed during the installation of his retrospective at the San Francisco Museum of Art, Guston reflects on his life in painting and compares his experience to an explorer that never quite made it to the top of a mountain. However, this "failure" is seen as the source of renewal rather than despair:

> nothing is ever solved in painting, it is a continuous chain that sometimes doesn't go in one line but goes in a serpentine line or in crooked paths, detours that have to be investigated. I felt like an explorer who almost got to the top of Mount Everest and somehow stopped just short and remembered and thought well maybe I forgot some gear, I forgot some equipment. But in going down to get this equipment I took some side paths that looked exciting and full of possibilities.[21]

It is certainly possible to see Guston's repeated piling as an absurdity in Camus' sense of the term. But, where repetition and circularity are seen as a basis for reinvention and renewal, the piled-up structures seem to make an absurdity not so much of the beginning again, but of the very notion of the resolvable. In this sense, Camus' absurd can be read as just one among a multitude of possible (contradictory) meanings emerging from Guston's piled-up structures. Guston's cyclical processes, in which forms "clump together" and then "move apart," as the artist described it, offer a way to point to the potential absurdity (or limitation) of rational, goal-driven logic.[22] In their place, we have a process full of incongruous meanings, in which one activity can, through repetition, produce difference and plurality. Here, Guston's repetitive activity moves closer to the logic at work in his beloved comic strip *Krazy Kat*. Tim Blackmore points out that

> while each day for 31 years Krazy, Ignatz, and Offisa Pup closed the recurrent syntagm of the brick and the jail, the paradigm remained open and unsettled, nor has it been settled since: no one has proved successfully what the strip is about.[23]

Blackmore looks to Huizinga's discussion of the fool as a means to engage with the workings of *Krazy Kat*; for Blackmore, this allows us to see the unstable identities and systems within the strip as a means "to scramble our expectations, but not to make human endeavour seem pointless."[24] With both Herriman and Guston, we encounter a delight in the confusions repetition brings, multiplying meaning into a state of excessive abundance.

Through a game of infinite return, one encounters a process propelled by contradiction and incongruity. In Chapter 2, I saw Guston's rapid painting process as connected with definitions of play as "rapid movement."[25] However, this fast-paced action now needs to be seen as working in relation with the never-ending game. Effectively, where timing is concerned within a play process, there is a pull of opposites. In specific terms, while both Guston and Paolozzi employed processes that allowed them to make quick changes and responses—such as the shuffled elements, erasures, overpainting—both artists took great pleasure in repeatedly reworking a piece, stalling a work's conclusion by dwelling on the process itself by means of layering and scraping back, shuffling and constructing, tacking and cutting. Guston even spoke of the simple pleasure of returning to his favourite colour: cadmium red, then mixing a "mess of pink," and this being enough to make him want to paint.[26] There is a delight in the engagement with the material itself in its raw state, before a work has begun to take form. For Guston, it was vital this simple pleasure was acknowledged as central to the creative process:

> for man from the beginning, who made the line of this bull, it was a catharsis, a joy, an ecstasy, to make this line . . . you read social historians who talk about modern art, psychological motivations and endless reasons for it. . . . But the part they miss is that there's material, there's you and there's this feeling, an inchoate feeling, a raw feeling.[27]

It is this delight in the material—the colour, the smell, the mess and the feel of the material response—that enabled Guston not only to tolerate the unknown outcome, but to dwell on the process of uncertainty itself. Two apparently contradictory speeds then work together within a play process: there is an urgency to the action and yet a desire to endlessly delay its conclusion. As we have seen throughout the chapters with both Guston and Paolozzi, the finalisation of a work should be understood not as a conclusion but merely as a point of return to their kit of forms (or game elements) with their innumerable possibilities. In reading these processes through absurdity as incongruity, we could imagine the pull between rapidity and delay in terms of the "circular sense of the activity of play" articulated by Fink, which has no ultimate goal.[28] Once again, Guston's images of knotted legs and shoes charging but going nowhere, in such works as *Monument* (1976), *Green Rug* (1976) and *Night Room* (1976) (Figure 5.24), give form to the incongruous processes that sit at the centre of the dynamics of play. There is a desire to not progress beyond but rather endlessly revisit. Indeed, Guston spoke of each work emerging from a criticism of the last.[29] In a landscape of incongruity, doubt appears as a motor, with the artist's conclusions challenged by the endless complexity of a world of infinite variation. Just two years before the artist's death, Guston wrote of painting as if it were a game he endlessly needed to learn how to play:

> When I complete a painting that feels real—I think afterwards that I have found a way. . . . And my mind races on—painting pictures in my head. . . . What a

> delusion this is. . . . They all tumble down when paint is put on. And again you must learn that there is no road—no way. . . . No good to paint in the head—what happens is what happens when you put the paint down—you can only hope that you are alert—ready to see. What joy it is for paint to become a thing—a being. Believe in this miracle—it is your only hope.[30]

In the next section, we will see how this belief itself operated within a process that embraced an incongruous collision with doubt and anxiety.

Clowning With Power

In this final section, I will examine how Guston used clowning as a means to play with power. Reflecting on his "hood" paintings, created between 1968 and 1972, Guston stated that

> they are self-portraits. I perceive myself as being under the hood . . . my attempt was really not to illustrate, to do pictures of the KKK, as I had done earlier. The idea of evil fascinated me, and rather like Babel. . . . I almost tried to imagine that I was living with the Klan.[31]

In David Kaufmann's insightful analysis of Guston's late works, Kaufmann points to the importance of Hannah Arendt's writing in Guston's approach to the subject of evil.

> Guston meant something quite specific when he called his Hoods . . . evil . . . they are evil in a distinctly modern everyday way. They are banal. In this they appear to owe much to Hannah Arendt's notorious description of Adolf Eichmann, the engineer of the Final Solution. . . . In *Eichmann in Jerusalem* Arendt presented Eichmann as a ludicrous buffoon . . . a painfully ordinary man who suffered from a . . . very ordinary kind of thoughtlessness. . . . No longer demonic or wilful, modern evil—the crime of thoughtlessness—is laughable.[32]

Arendt had specifically characterised Eichmann as a "clown."[33] Arendt had looked to Brecht in advocating laughter as a reduction of the "greatness" of evil. Brecht had wanted to make a distinction in scale between a perpetrator and the enormity of their crimes. For Brecht, "the great political criminals must be exposed and exposed especially to laughter. They are not great political criminals, but people who permitted great political crimes."[34] In agreement with Brecht, for Arendt it was imperative that political criminals were depicted in ways that reduced their stature; comedy, then, not tragedy, was the most powerful tool: "No matter what he does and if he killed ten million people, he is still a clown."[35] Drawing on Kaufmann's analysis, I will examine how Guston appears to engage with Arendt's use of the term clown. This will provide a means to approach the multiple layers at work within Guston's declaration that the hoods were self-portraits. Here one finds a meeting point between a play of representation and play as process. Through definitions of clowning and slapstick, one finds Guston's need to engage with the political climate converge with his desire to create "golems"; in both cases, clowning becomes a means to undermine power.

Guston's lumbering, ragged hoods are the very image of the circus' "chief clown," as described by Caillois in *Man, Play and Games* (Figure 6.3). Here, Caillois describes

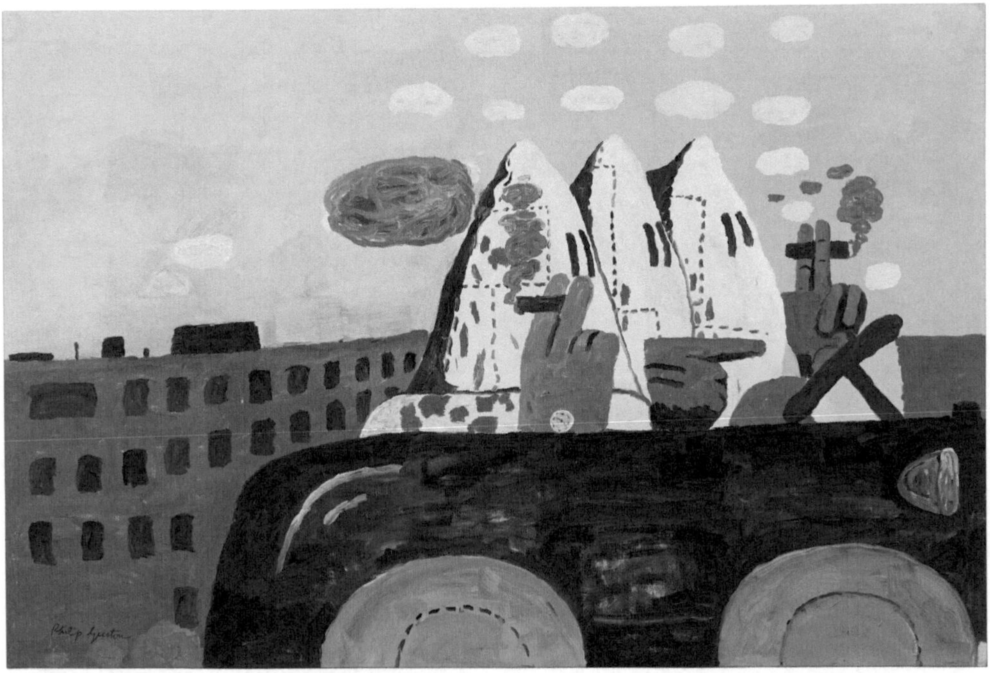

Figure 6.3 Riding Around, 1969, Philip Guston, oil on canvas, 137 × 201 cm (54 × 79 inches).

the clown's garb as "patched and ill-fitting (either too large or too small)."[36] For Caillois, "the wretch is incorrigible. Being pretentious and awkward at the same time, he tries desperately to imitate others, but only succeeds in provoking catastrophes of which he is the victim."[37] While Guston's clown thugs casually play with mindless violence and butchery, they become a symbol of inadequacy. Guston had turned to his childhood love of cartoons and cartooning for clown imagery, specifically Bud Fisher's comic strip *Mutt and Jeff* (Figure 6.4). The beefy gloved hands, cigars, roller blinds, giant shoes and goofy cars are all borrowed from Fisher. The comic strip draws upon an entire history of slapstick comedy. The rivalrous friendship between Mutt and Jeff has all the classic traits of the clowning double act, rich in status games sparked by a dynamic in which one plays the idiot while the other sees himself as superior. True to the slapstick form, almost every strip ends in vengeance and violence, whether by tripping and falling or hurling projectiles. The characters are forever trapped in a cycle of violent pranks that fail to progress. The clowning slapstick humour connects violence with incompetence. Through this lens, we see Guston's hoods' murderous games as a display of their own failings.

In equating violence with weakness through clowning, Guston's hoods produce a connection to Caillois' characterisation of the mask. Caillois describes how the mask has been used as a tool to wield political power; employed as a symbol of superiority, the mask is donned as a means to seem imbued with powers and spirits in order to inspire fear. However, for Caillois the mask is a form of fragile power.

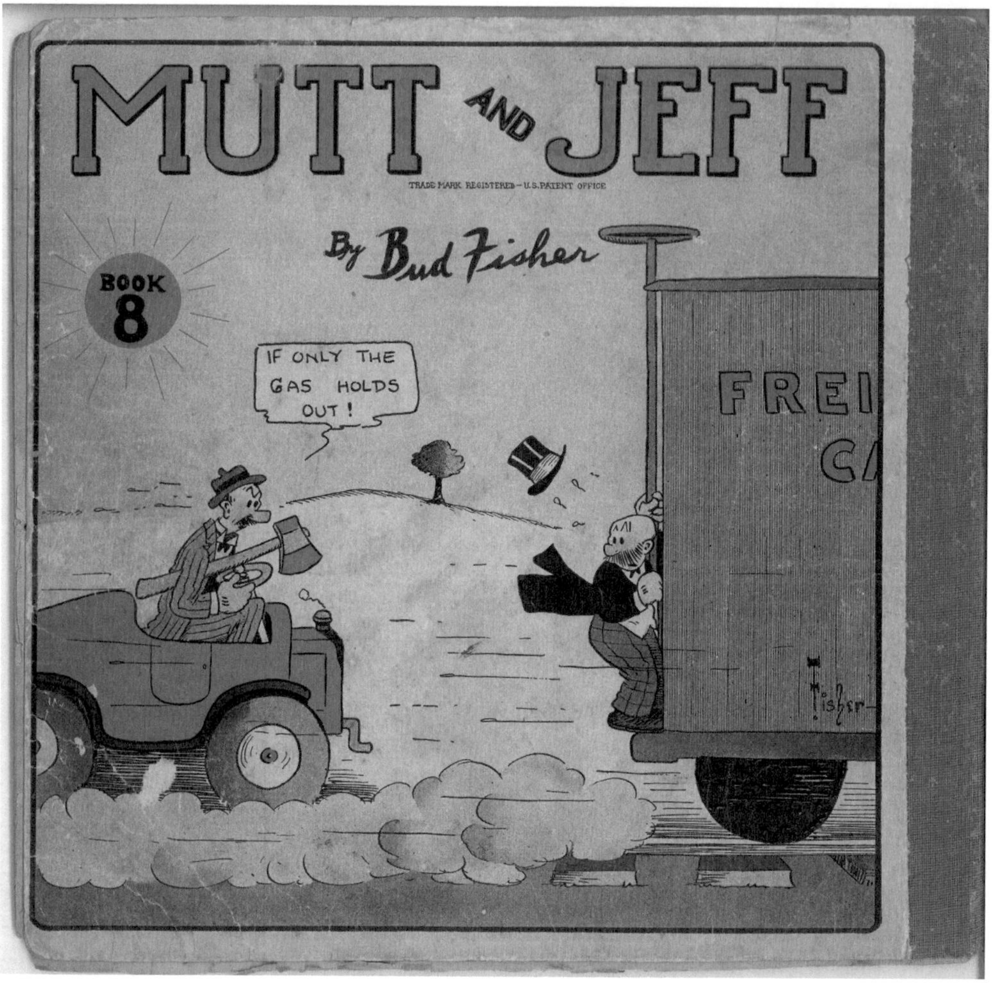

Figure 6.4 Mutt and Jeff, Book 8, 1922, Bud Fisher.

Image credit: The author.

While used to terrorise, it is constantly in danger of being revealed as merely a disguise. It is therefore in need of protection from its secret. Guston's pitiful hoods capture this fragility. The artist appears to have delighted in the reduction that the hood offered; Guston's ironically termed "pure" drawing (Figure 2.17) returns in the form of two dashes for eyes, which appear in turns witless and anxiety ridden. In *playing* the clown, Guston connected to a tradition of using buffoonery to reveal the injustices and failings of the powerful.

However, importantly, Guston stated that his favourite hood paintings were of artists. Guston had produced a series of works that satirised the art world—hooded figures are depicted attending exhibition openings, seen discussing painting and portrayed "earnestly" at work at the easel (Figure 6.5). In the most powerful work in the series *The Studio* (1969) (Figure 6.6), a hood appears blissfully immersed in work on a self-portrait. These are works that ridicule the self-absorption of Abstract art, condemning its detachment from the political turmoil of the time. Guston's hood paintings, then, are not merely concerned with pointing the finger at the failings of others. These works are as much about the failure of art to respond, while policing its own limits on creative freedom (as explored in the previous chapter). Crucially, they are also works in which Guston acknowledged his own complicity. While the mask is a device used to convey power and instil fear, it is also a means to conceal individuality in order to become part of a group. The studio, by contrast, is supposedly a place of individuality, self-expression and freedom. *The Studio*, then, can be seen as a work that provides a reflection on Guston's experience as a painter within the New York School, one in which the artist felt he had concealed his individuality to become part

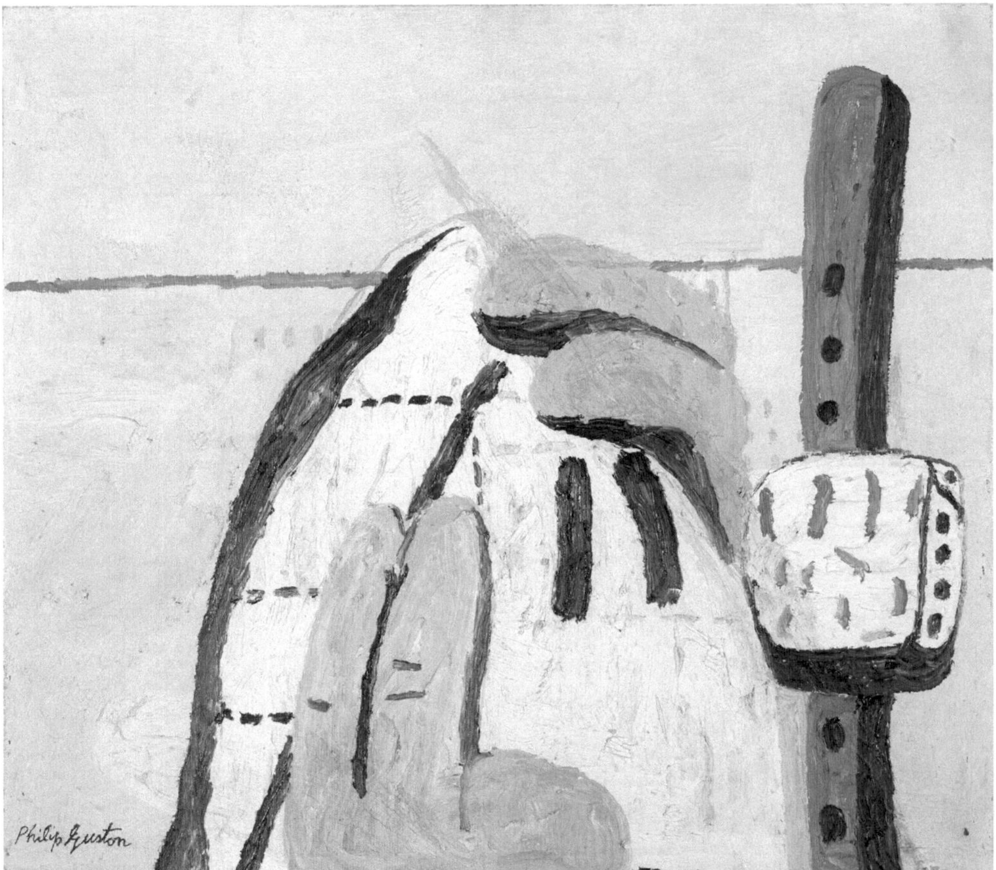

Figure 6.5 The Painter, 1969, Philip Guston, oil on panel, 60.9 × 67.3 cm (24 × 26 ½ inches).

Image courtesy of The Estate of Philip Guston. © The Estate of Philip Guston.

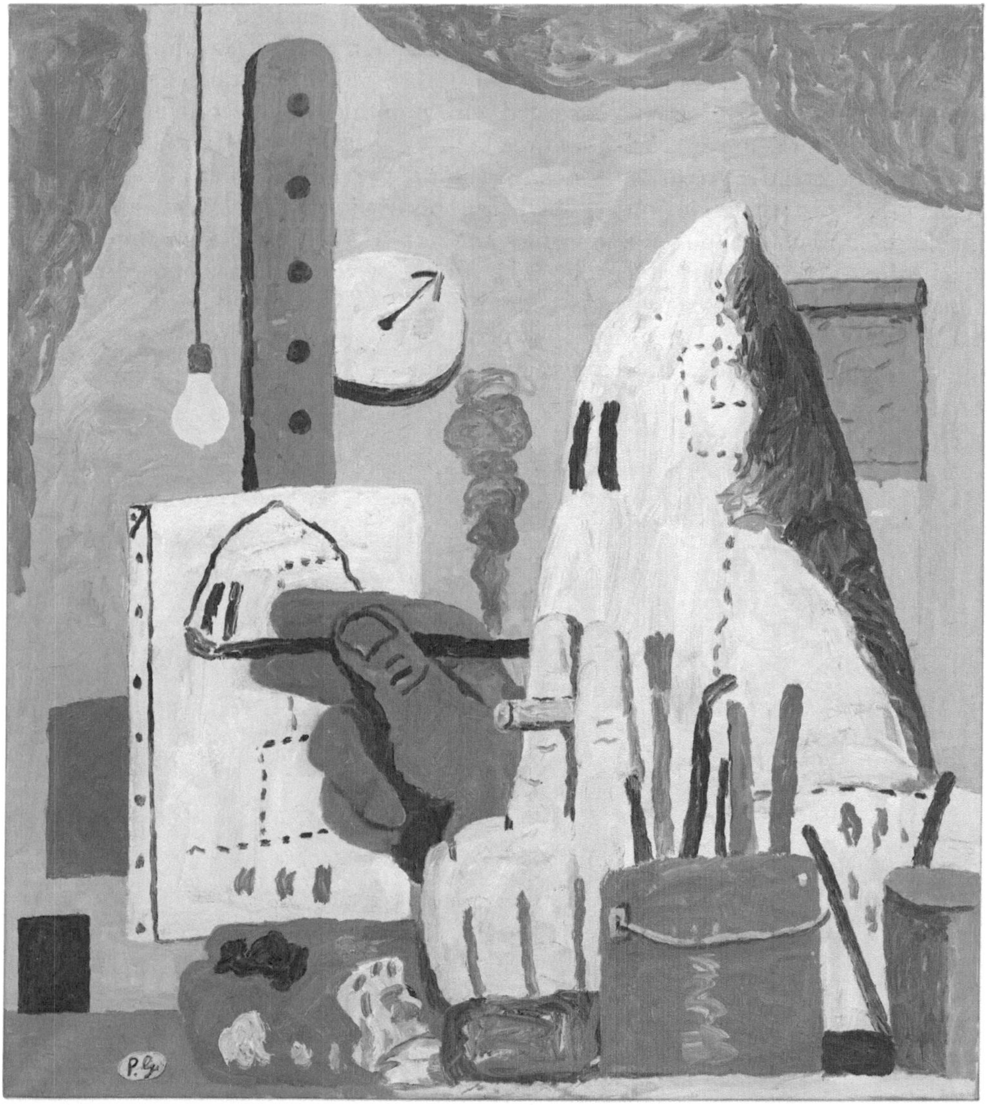

Figure 6.6 The Studio, 1969, Philip Guston, oil on canvas, 121.9 × 106.7 cm (48 × 42 inches).
Image courtesy of The Estate of Philip Guston. © The Estate of Philip Guston.

of a movement, making a mockery of the view that Action Painters unleashed their psyche on the canvas. Indeed, Guston would describe Abstract art as

> a lie, a sham. . . . A mask to mask the fear of revealing oneself. . . . It is laughable, this lie. . . . It is an escape from the true feelings we have, from the 'raw,' primitive feelings about the world—and us in it.[38]

But the *Mutt and Jeff* cartoon form also captures a sense of political impotence. The clowning allows us to question what it means to create art at times of extreme brutality. For an artist as acutely self-critical as Guston to see images of the horrors of the Shoah, the Vietnam war, police violence against anti-war protestors and civil rights activists, and then respond with a painting, however political its target, is an endeavour that necessitates a form encapsulating a sense of the inadequacy of the response. Guston's self-absorbed hoods point to an absurdity in the condition of an artist. In 1978, Guston would articulate the contradiction in his need for art that had an "involvement with the condition of the world we live in," simultaneously declaring "not that it would change anything."[39] The redemptive quality of Guston's painting emerges from the work's acknowledgement of this absurdity while expressing a continued faith in the power of the creative act.

By 1972, Guston had jettisoned the hooded figures. As Kaufmann has asserted, "a man as riven by doubt and as captivated by nuance as Guston would have found the banality of evil ultimately constricting, if only because it could yield neither depth nor nuance."[40] However, the *Mutt and Jeff* infused cartoon form continued. The mask had acted as a means to open a door on a way of working that remained connected to clowning. Here again, Caillois' writing on the chief clown, Auguste, helps to further elucidate how one may engage with Guston's approach to his creative process. For Caillois, the buffoon

> symbolizes the hero-dunce, mischievous or stupid as the case may be, who has been mocking the work of the gods by his fumbling imitation of their gestures ever since the creation of the world, and on occasion introducing intimations of mortality.[41]

It is in wrestling with a creative process that risks "mocking the work of the gods" that one finds Guston's central preoccupation in the last decade of his life.

In his lectures and writings, Guston repeatedly returned to his sense that he was making golems. Aaron Rosen importantly discusses how in later life, "rather than disguising his Jewishness, one of Guston's central preoccupations . . . was precisely how to uncover and explore his Jewish identity,"[42] having painfully regretted changing his name from Goldstein.[43] For Rosen, this "folds into the very structure of his late work; namely, in . . . attempting '*to make a Golem*.'"[44] Guston declared that his work was driven by the creation of a character that "triggers everything off," explaining:

> I like the feeling that I don't have a painting in there, I've a being in there . . . It's like making a golem. . . . The medieval rabbis made a golem. It's impossible. Only God can make life. A golem was like Dr Frankenstein.[45]

While the various narratives of the golem allow for multiple interpretations, the golem as understood by Guston is a lesson in hubris. In the legends cited by Guston, rabbis use mud or clay to create a creature in human form that is animated through incantations. Created in order to perform various tasks, the golem becomes disobedient and monstrous, increasing in size and power as it unleashes its destructive force. Guston's statement, therefore, captures an inherent contradiction and anxiety in his persistent desire to make a "living thing," acknowledging it is hubristic and an "impossibility." However, rather than dismiss these contradictory beliefs, Guston embraced the incongruous conjunction by employing a clowning idiom that gave form to this absurdity.

Guston's late painting persistently dwells on the creative act. In works such as *Paw* (1968), *Deluge II* (1975), *The Line* (1978) (Figure 3.6) and *Untitled* (1978)

(Figure 6.7), the hand of the painter is depicted in the act of creation—a parody of the hand of god, a joke used repeatedly by cartoonists, including Guston's childhood favourites, Fisher and Herriman. The paws and lumpen hands in Guston's paintings draw crude thick lines and model amorphous heaps of paint. The grotesque form mocks the artist's very attempt at creating a "parallel world,"[46] the process acknowledging its own inadequacy by playing up its "fumbling imitation," to use Caillois' term. Where the images of hooded figures had represented daemonic power by taking life, here we are presented with an anxiety in the belief in one's own creations, presented as a risible absurdity. Importantly, Rosen connects Guston's stated desire to paint "badly" with the artist's sense that he was creating golems. The original meaning of the word "golem," as it appears in the Bible, refers to formless matter. Adam is said to have been created from dust kneaded into a formless mass (golem), before being brought to life by the breath of God. In the legends of the golem, mud and clay

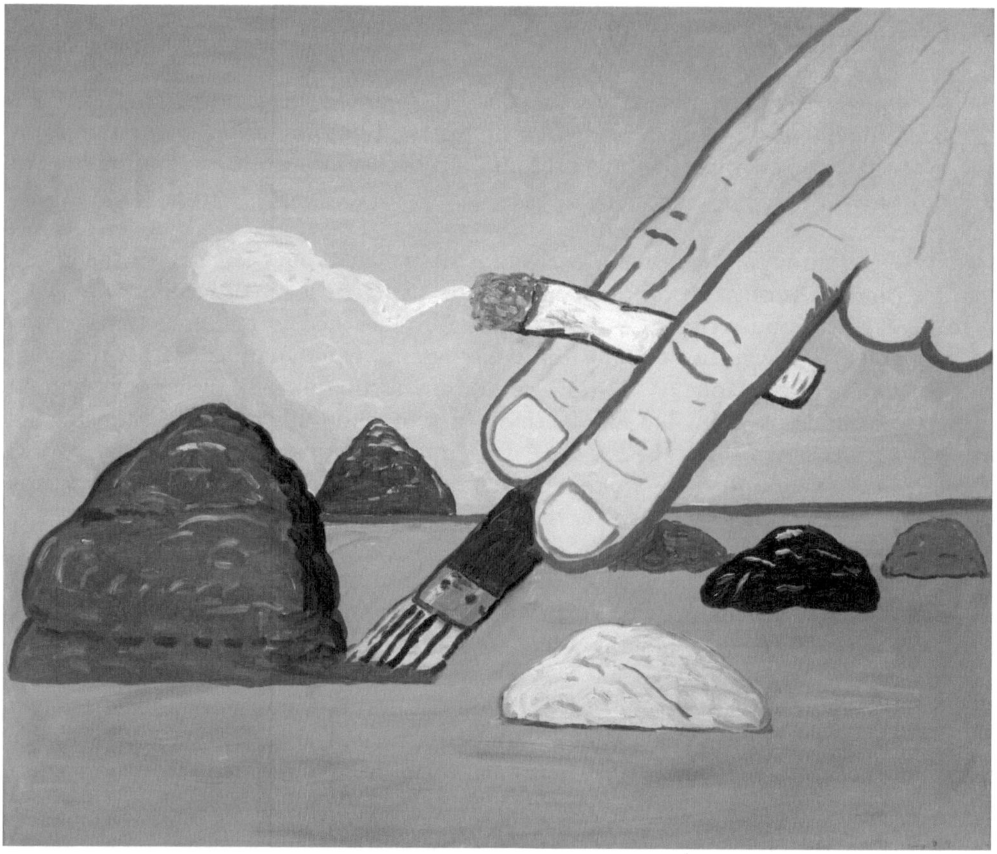

Figure 6.7 Untitled, 1978, Philip Guston, oil on canvas, 106.7 × 121.9 cm (42 × 48 inches).

are used in imitation of the act of creation. Significantly, Rosen connects Guston's handling of paint to the substance of the golem:

> By breaking down the enchantments of illusionistic space, Guston found he could instil the objects in his canvases with a more tangible magic. . . . His golems did not have to be *believed* . . . they could instead be felt in the thick, oleaginous strokes which he slopped onto the canvas.[47]

As Rosen points out, Guston's late paintings always acknowledge the material qualities of the paint and the brush. There is no smooth sheen that attempts to trick the eye; instead, there is a pronounced connection to the material properties of the artist's tools that attempt to create life from dumb matter. In Guston's impoverished world, paint remains paint, just as the golem remained mud, never succeeding in becoming human. Guston's swollen bean heads, beefy paws and clunky shoes exist as crudely shaped masses that threaten to return to formless matter.

Guston would also have been aware of the term golem as it is used in Yiddish, meaning a "fool, a clumsy man or woman, a clod, graceless."[48] Through Guston's heavy lines, thick brushstrokes and lumpen forms, we see the artist employ a process that allowed him to revel in the adoption of the clowning persona of the "graceless fool." However, as slapstick scholars importantly emphasise, here there is a paradox, in that to *perform* the necessary trips and falls, the clown's clumsiness requires extraordinary acrobatic skill. Similarly, Guston's apparently crude handling of paint belies the sophistication of the works, which are steeped in an entire history of art. However, to return to the concept of the impossibility of the golem, laughing at one's own inadequacy and hubris could also be considered empowering—a means of dismissing failure by absorbing its inevitability into the process of the work. In his publication, *Taking Laughter Seriously*, John Morreall explains:

> When the person with a sense of humor laughs in the face of his own failure, he is showing that his perspective transcends the particular situation he's in, and that he does not have an egocentric, overly precious view of his own endeavors. This is not to say that he lacks self-esteem—quite the contrary. . . . The person without real self-esteem . . . who is unsure of his own worth . . . simply cannot afford to laugh at himself whatever happens.[49]

Guston was not only able to laugh at his process but also welcomed such a response from others, stating: "If someone bursts out laughing in front of my painting, that is exactly what I want and expect."[50] This response led Guston to consider the nature of laughter by turning to Baudelaire's definition in *The Essence of Laughter*, summarised by Guston as "the collision of two contrary feelings."[51] We see this "collision" in Guston's contradiction of beliefs in his desire to make a "living thing," given expression through his cartoon-like process and informed by the clowning of *Mutt and Jeff*. Through humour, Guston allows us to emphasise, once again, the importance of the use of incongruity within a play process. Furthermore, in turning directly to the incongruity theory of humour and laughter, one can expand how one engages with notions of "the mistake" and "the contest" as factors that are welcomed into a play process, returning to the discussion introduced in Chapter 3. Here again, we are provided with a means to embrace the unexpected outcome. Morreall informs us: "for the incongruity theory, amusement is an intellectual reaction to something that is unexpected, illogical, or inappropriate in some other way . . . there is a certain duality or contrast that triggers laughter."[52] In elaborating more fully, Morreall goes on to quote Schopenhauer:

> The cause of laughter in every case is simply the sudden perception of the incongruity between a concept and the real objects which have been thought through it in some relation, and laughter itself is just the expression of this incongruity.[53]

This incongruity Schopenhauer articulates between concept and object allows us to consider again how an artist's use of a play process not only seeks the unexpected but also delights in the discrepancy between their originating concept and the resulting artwork. We could understand the laughter Guston experienced as occurring in this gap. One thinks again of the artist describing how he dismissed the notion of "the mistake" (discussed in Chapter 3). An understanding of the philosophy of comedy provides a means to add another layer to how one might think of the mismatch between a pre-visualised image and the final work, seen not as a failure, but re-imagined as a dialogue with forces of contingency and the physical properties of the world. Here, it is helpful to turn to Alan Dale's analysis of slapstick in American movies.

Dale draws on an assertion made by Jerry Lewis to define slapstick as "the idea that comedy is about getting a man into and out of trouble."[54] There is a connection that can be drawn here between comedy as a negotiation through "trouble" and game playing, defined by Bernard Suits as "the voluntary attempt to overcome unnecessary obstacles."[55] Recalling the game-playing methods by which Guston and Paolozzi welcomed in a problem through an engagement with gravity and the "mistake," with Lewis' notion of "trouble" we can now take a step back and see the comedy within these processes. These are in a sense slapstick processes, in which the artist fights not for an ideal but an acceptance of the physical world as it presents itself, together with a recognition of one's own limitations. For both Guston and Paolozzi, then, absurd processes are not merely the means by which to mock the powerful; slapstick allows us to see the comedy of these creative processes as rooted within a responsive engagement with material:

> slapstick achieves accord here on earth by a comic concession to the body at its most traitorous . . . in contrast to the pagan approach of the Olympic Games, in which athletes attempt to achieve a perfect union of body and will . . . slapstick seeks a temporal acceptance of physicality by a cathartic exaggeration of its very limitations.[56]

It is also here that one encounters a crucial paradox, in that it is in delighting in things going "wrong" that one gains the sense of the reality of one's creations. While clowning can be seen as a protection against hubris and the creation of idols, in slapstick comedy there is also a battle between human and object in which the objects very often get the upper hand. It is at these points that the objects appear sentient. Louise Peacock describes such objects as malicious props: "Such props appear to take on a life of their own, behaving in ways that neither the viewer nor the antagonist would anticipate but which serve to make objects much more dangerous—and more animate—than they should be."[57] It is through the obduracy of matter that objects begin to feel alive. In Guston's desire for a contest within his painting process, Guston repeatedly stated that he wanted to feel the "resistance of matter"[58] and the "resistance of images."[59] For Guston, it was through this resistance that he felt "free." This condition, however, was something the artist described as having to fight for, a blank canvas offering no resistance and too much freedom.[60] In a sense, Guston was searching for the point within a process in which the images appear to answer back, by providing problems, "obstacles" and limits to the decisions that can be made. As Gadamer describes of play, it is here that the game plays the player, or for Guston, that the painting starts to take control of the painter. Guston described the point of "resistance" as one in which he felt like a "victim"; for Guston, this was "a glorious thing."[61] It does not require much of a leap to think of this condition of painter as willing victim as continuous with the acrobatic clown appearing to become a victim of their "malicious props." We could think of Guston, in his desire to make a golem, enjoying the point at which his kit of forms become, to use Peacock's words, "more dangerous—and more animate—than they should be."

Clowning processes can then be seen to both enable an animation of inanimate matter, while lampooning the very attempt, providing a way to engage with Guston's sense that he was creating beings, while acknowledging this as an impossibility. Play is not only able to contain contradiction and duality but is also defined by it. One recalls that in discussing role-play, Fink described play as a doubling activity that enables two realities to sit side-by-side.[62] Role-play was central to Guston's use of the mask; as the painter described it, this was not just an image that appeared within his hood paintings but became part of an ongoing process. Through the clowning persona, one can imagine material resistance and the creative battle as means by which images become "living things." Furthermore, by engaging with slapstick processes, one can see this battle as one in which the artist mocks their original concept. Tripped up by their plans and ideals, the artist learns to revel in an entanglement with the multiplicity of the world that endlessly confounds their expectations.

Notes

1. *Merriam-Webster*, www.merriam-webster.com/dictionary/absurd
2. This was later expanded in the classic text *The Theatre of the Absurd*, first published in 1961.
3. In Greek mythology, Sisyphus was a king that was condemned to eternally roll a boulder uphill and then watch it roll down again as it neared the summit. In *The Myth of Sisyphus*, Albert Camus uses the myth to put forward his philosophy of the absurd, in which the search for the meaning of existence is seen to be eternally thwarted by a chaotic universe.
4. Eugène Ionescu writing in 1957 quoted in Martin Esslin, *The Theatre of the Absurd* (London: Pelican Books, 1968), 23.
5. Here, I am specifically referring to *Esslin's* analysis of the work of the dramatists of the absurd, rather than making broad assertions as to the playwrights' approach to meaning. Esslin asserts the following "works that are essentially concerned with conveying their author's sense of mystery, bewilderment . . . despair at being unable to find a meaning in existence." Ibid., 44.
6. Guston as quoted in Robert Storr, *Philip Guston* (New York: Abbeville, 1986), 109.
7. Rudolf Kuenzli, *Dada Themes and Movements* (London: Phaidon Press Limited, 2006), 17.
8. Hans Richter, *Art and Ant-Art* (Cologne: Thames and Hudson, 1965), 57.
9. Ibid., 51.

10. Gilles Deleuze, *The Logic of Sense* (London: Continuum, 2004), 82.
11. James Williams, "Deleuze and Structure: How Far Can You Bend It?," In *Deleuzian Events: Writing History* [conference proceedings], ed. Hanjo Berressem and Leyla Haferkamp (Berlin: Lit, 2009), 48.
12. Ibid.
13. *Oxford English Reference Dictionary* (Oxford: Oxford University Press, 2008).
14. *Oxford English Dictionary Online*, accessed January 2012, http://oed.com/
15. Eduardo Paolozzi, "Conversations between Eduardo Paolozzi and Alvin Boyarsky, May 1984," in *Eduardo Paolozzi: Writings and Interviews*, ed. Robin Spencer (Oxford and New York: Oxford University Press, 2001), 316.
16. Philip Guston, "Conversation with Morton Feldman, 1968," in *Philip Guston, Collected Writings, Lectures, and Conversations*, ed. Clark Coolidge (London: University of California Press, 2011), 85.
17. Neil Cornwell, *The Absurd in Literature* (Manchester: Manchester University Press, 2006), x.
18. Albert Camus *The Myth of Sisyphus* (Harmondsworth: Penguin, 1975), 111.
19. Ibid.
20. Hans-Georg Gadamer, *Truth and Method* (London and New York: Continuum, 2006), 104.
21. Philip Guston, *Philip Guston: A Life Lived*, directed by Michael Blackwood. New York, NY, Michael Blackwood Productions Inc., 1981.
22. Philip Guston, "Conversation with Clark Coolidge, 1972," in *Collected Writings, Lectures, and Conversations*, ed. Coolidge, 194.
23. Tim Blackmore, "Krazy as a Fool: Erasmus of Rotterdam's Praise of Folly and Herriman of Coconino's Krazy Kat," *Journal of Popular Culture*, Vol. 31, No. 3 (December 1997): 27.
24. Ibid., 22.
25. Johan Huizinga, *Homo Ludens* (Boston: Beacon Press, 1955), 32.
26. Philip Guston, "On Drawing, 1974," in *Collected Writings, Lectures, and Conversations*, ed. Coolidge, 259.
27. Philip Guston, "The Image, 1969," in *Collected Writings, Lectures, and Conversations*, ed. Coolidge, 133.
28. Eugen Fink, *Play as Symbol of the World and Other Writings* (Bloomington: Indiana University Press, 2016), 21.
29. Guston, "The Image, 1969," 135.
30. Philip Guston, "Studio Notes, 1970–78," in *Collected Writings, Lectures, and Conversations*, ed. Coolidge, 313.
31. Philip Guston, "Philip Guston Talking," in *Philip Guston* (exh.cat.) (London: Timothy Taylor Gallery, 2004), 28–29.
32. David Kaufmann, *Telling Stories, Philip Guston's Later Works* (London: University of California Press, 2010), 32–3.
33. Hannah Arendt, *Eichmann in Jerusalem: A Report on the Banality of Evil* (New York: Penguin Books, 2006), 54.
34. Bertolt Brecht as quoted in Hannah Arendt, "Hannah Arendt: From an Interview," *The New York Review of Books*, October 26, 1978, www.nybooks.com/articles/1978/10/26/hannah-arendt-from-an-interview/
35. Hannah Arendt, Ibid.
36. Roger Caillois, *Man, Play and Games* (Urbana and Chicago: University of Illinois Press, 2001), 138.
37. Ibid.
38. Guston as quoted in Andrew Graham-Dixon, "A Maker of Worlds: The Later Paintings of Philip Guston," in *Philip Guston Retrospective* (exh.cat.), ed. Michael Auping (London: Thames & Hudson, 2003), 54.
39. Philip Guston, "From Panel at 'Art/Not Art?' Conference, 1978," in *Collected Writings, Lectures, and Conversations*, ed. Coolidge, 288.
40. Kaufmann, *Telling Stories, Philip Guston's Later Works*, 36.
41. Caillois, *Man, Play and Games*, 138–139.

42. Aaron Rosen, *Imagining Jewish Art: Encounters with the Masters in Chagall, Guston and Kitaj* (London: Legenda, 2009), 180.4/430.
43. Although Guston experienced a sense of shame in later life at his decision to change his name, the Anglicisation of Jewish names was commonplace at the time. Indeed, in my own family Russian Jewish surnames were changed in an attempt to avoid discrimination.
44. Rosen, *Imagining Jewish Art*, 182.3.
45. Guston, "On Drawing, 1974," 266.
46. Ibid.
47. Rosen, *Imagining Jewish Art*, 208.3.
48. Leo Rosten, *The Joys of Yiddish* (London: Penguin Books, 1970), 139.
49. John Morreall, *Taking Laughter Seriously* (New York: University of New York Press, 1983), 106.
50. Guston, "Studio Notes, 1970–78," 309.
51. Guston as quoted in Craig Burnett, *Philip Guston: The Studio* (London: Afterall Books, 2014), 89.
52. Morreall, *Taking Laughter Seriously*, 15.
53. Arthur Schopenhauer as quoted in ibid., 17.
54. Alan Dale, *Comedy Is a Man in Trouble: Slapstick in American Movies* (Minneapolis: University of Minnesota Press, 2000), 18.
55. Bernard Suits, *The Grasshopper, Games, Life and Utopia* (Plymouth: Broadview Press, 2005), 55.
56. Dale, *Comedy Is a Man in Trouble*, 14.
57. Louise Peacock, *Slapstick and Comic Performance: Comedy and Pain* (London: Palgrave Macmillan, 2014), 32.
58. Guston, "On Drawing, 1974," 259.
59. Philip Guston, "Conversation with Morton Feldman, 1968," in *Collected Writings, Lectures, and Conversations*, ed. Coolidge, 84.
60. Philip Guston, "Interview with Joanne Dickson, 1980," in *Collected Writings, Lectures, and Conversations*, ed. Coolidge, 306.
61. Ibid.
62. Fink, *Play as Symbol of the World*, 24.

Concluding Remarks

In reading Guston and Paolozzi's work through the lens of play, I have examined the artists' studio methods in terms of games strategies. In considering the game as an engagement with "unnecessary obstacles," Guston and Paolozzi's processes can be understood to have embraced contradictory forces. It appears that for both artists, a play process was enabled through a push against self-enforced limitations. One can see that for Guston, the focus on a limited collection of objects such as shoes and books provided a productive constraint. Additionally, at breakthrough moments in the artist's career, it is the concentration on an action that propels Guston's painting in a new direction. This can be seen in the self-enforced restriction of not stepping back from the canvas when producing *White Painting* (1951), and again twenty years later, when *Flatlands* (1970) was created through a continuous burst of painting, as Guston moved from the right to left side of the canvas. For Paolozzi, it is the limitations imposed by gravity that offer his sculptures of the late 1950s a battle with contingency. Within these works, we see the artist return repeatedly to an "Alphabet of Elements." As with Guston, it is these limits that generate multiplicity. With "flexibility" provided by Paolozzi's loose kit of forms, the elements gain multiple uses within a profusion of structures. In this push and pull between limit and multiplicity, Guston and Paolozzi's work points to play as an activity that places opposing elements in dialogue. While both artists repeatedly asserted the need for the unforeseen, the unpredictable seems closely connected to elements of predictability, while change appears to be entwined with repetition. But within this slip and slide, *responsiveness* emerges as the key characteristic of the artists' play processes. Both artists can be seen to have employed methods that enabled them to respond, adapt and change paths during an unfolding process.

While this study has drawn heavily on the writing of Caillois and Sutton-Smith, both understood play as an activity that does not produce a product. Moreover, Sutton-Smith found the attempt to make broad associations between art and play problematic. According to Sutton-Smith, art results in a product, whereas play is indeterminate and inconclusive. However, this study has found that much of the work of Paolozzi and Guston appears to be concerned with a tension between finality and continuity. Both artists wrestled against the static artwork to return to a continuing process. It is through the artists' delight in the pleasure of the materials and processes themselves, together with the artists' desire to endlessly stall their conclusion, that play appears. Additionally, Guston and Paolozzi both considered destruction as a vital part of their creative process. Rather than counter Caillois and Sutton-Smith's argument in purely oppositional terms, one could say that Paolozzi and Guston's processes suggest that play occurs when one is able to *risk* producing nothing but the process itself.

While I have been examining Guston and Paolozzi processes in terms of play, their work has appeared to respond by playing games with interpretation; in effect, the material seemed to toy with me. In Paolozzi's case, the volume and wealth of material is ungraspable, while with Guston the ambiguity of the multitudinous meanings that emerge from the artist's repeated return to a limited collection of forms seems to forever defy interpretation. In relation to the shifting, self-renewing, contradictory nature of the material, the attempt to communicate Guston and Paolozzi's processes through sequential chapters seemed at times to threaten to become too formulaic. However, I have not wanted to reduce the extraordinary complexity of the artists' output to a small collection of methods. Nor would I want to suggest that play can be defined through a neat set of processes. Rather, this book has identified some methods that provide the potential for play through the work of two artists who battled against definitions and certainties.

Bibliography

Allen, Marjorie (Lady Allen of Hurtwood). *Planning for Play*. London: Thames & Hudson, Ltd., 1968.

Alloway, Lawrence. *Eduardo Paolozzi: The Metallization of a Dream*. London: Lion and Unicorn, 1963.

Alloway, Lawrence. *Paolozzi and the Comedy of Waste*. Paris: Cimaise, 1960.

Anchor, Robert. "History and Play: Johan Huizinga and His Critics," *History and Theory*, Vol. 17, Issue 1 (February 1978): 63–93.

Arendt, Hannah. *Eichmann in Jerusalem: A Report on the Banality of Evil*. New York: Penguin Books, 2006.

Arendt, Hannah. "Hannah Arendt: From an Interview," *The New York Review of Books*, October 26, 1978, www.nybooks.com/articles/1978/10/26/hannah-arendt-from-an-interview/

Arendt, Hannah. *The Human Condition*. Chicago: University of Chicago Press, 1998.

Arnason, H.H. *Philip Guston*. New York: Solomon R. Guggenheim Foundation, 1962.

Ashton, Dore. *A Critical Study of Philip Guston*. Berkeley, Los Angeles and Oxford: University of California Press, 1990.

Auping, Michael, ed. *Philip Guston Retrospective*. Fort Worth: Modern Art Museum of Fort Worth in association with Thames & Hudson, 2003.

Bachelard, Gaston. *The Poetics of Space*. Boston: Beacon Press, 1994.

Bal, Mieke. *Louise Bourgeois' Spider: The Architecture of Art Writing*. Chicago and London: University of Chicago Press, 2001.

Bal, Mieke. *Narratology, Introduction to the Theory of Narrative*. Toronto and London: University of Toronto Press, 1985.

Beckett, Samuel. *The Complete Dramatic Works*. London: Faber and Faber, 1986.

Benjamin, Walter. "The Author as Producer," in *Art in Theory, 1900–1990: An Anthology of Changing Ideas*, edited by Charles Harrison and Paul Wood, 483–489. Oxford and Malden: Blackwell Publishers, 1997.

Benjamin, Walter. *Illuminations*. London: Fontana Press, 1992.

Benjamin, Walter. *Walter Benjamin Selected Writings* (Volume 2), edited by Michael Jennings, Howard Eiland and Gary Smith. Cambridge: The Belknap Press of Harvard University Press, 1999.

Bergson, Henri. *Creative Evolution*. New York: Dover Publications, 1998.

Bergson, Henri. *Laughter: An Essay on the Meaning of the Comic*. UK: Wildside Press, 2008.

Bergson, Henri. *Matter and Memory*. New York: Dover Publications, Inc., 2004.

Blackmore, Tim. "Krazy as a Fool: Erasmus of Rotterdam's Praise of Folly and Herriman of Coconino's Krazy Kat," *Journal of Popular Culture*, Vol. 31, Issue 3 (December 1997): 19–46, Wiley Blackwell.

Blackwood, Michael, dir. *Conversations with Philip Guston*. New York, NY, Michael Blackwood Productions Inc., 2003.

Blackwood, Michael, dir. *The New York School*, written by Barbara Rose. New York, NY, Michael Blackwood Productions Inc., 1972.

Blackwood, Michael, dir. *Philip Guston: A Life Lived*. New York, NY, Michael Blackwood Productions Inc., 1981.

Boden, Margaret A. *Piaget*. London: Fontana, 1994.

Brosterman, Norman. *Inventing Kindergarten*. New York: Abrams, 1997.

Burnett, Craig. *Philip Guston: The Studio*. London: Afterall Books, 2014.

Caillois, Roger. *Man, Play and Games*. Urbana and Chicago: University of Illinois Press, 2001.

Clark, Timothy James "In Defense of Abstract Expressionism," *October*, Vol. 69 (Summer 1994): 22–48.

Collins, Judith and Paolozzi, Eduardo. *Artificial Horizons and Eccentric Ladders*. London: British Council, 1996.

Coole, Diana and Frost, Samantha, eds. *New Materialisms, Ontology, Agency, and Politics*. Durham and London: Duke University Press, 2010.

Coolidge, Clark, ed. *Philip Guston, Collected Writings, Lectures, and Conversations*. London: University of California Press, 2011.

Corbett, William. *Philip Guston's Late Work: A Memoir*. Cambridge, MA: Zoland Books, 1994.

Cornwell, Neil. *The Absurd in Literature*. Manchester and New York: Manchester University Press, 2006.

Cotton, Michelle, ed. *Nigel Henderson & Eduardo Paolozzi Hammer Prints Ltd, 1954–75*. Colchester: Firstsite, 2013.

Curtis, Penelope and Feeke, Stephen, eds. *Towards a New Laocoon* (exh.cat.). Leeds: Henry Moore Institute, 2007.

Dale, Alan. *Comedy Is a Man in Trouble: Slapstick in American Movies*. Minneapolis: University of Minnesota Press, 2000.

Deleuze, Gilles. *Difference and Repetition*. London and New York: Continuum, 2004.

Deleuze, Gilles. *The Logic of Sense*. London: Continuum, 2004.

Deleuze, Gilles and Guattari, Felix. *Anti-Oedipus*. London: Continuum, 2004.

Deleuze, Gilles and Guattari, Felix. *A Thousand Plateaus*. London: Continuum, 2004.

Derrida, Jacques. *The Truth in Painting*. Chicago: University of Chicago Press, 1987.

Edwards, Jason. "Play and Democracy: Huizinga and the Limits of Agonism," *Political Theory*, Vol. 41, Issue 1 (February 2013): 90–115, Sage Publications, Inc.

Ehrenzweig, Anton. *The Hidden Order of Art*. London: Phoenix Press, 2000.

Ehrlich, Robert. "Winnicott's Response to Klein," *Psychoanalytic Quarterly*, Vol. 73, Issue 2 (April 2004): 453–484.

Ehrmann, Jacques. "Homo Ludens Revisited," *Game, Play and Literature: Yale French Studies*, Issue 41 (1968): 31–57, Yale University Press.

Esslin, Martin. *The Theatre of the Absurd*. London: Pelican Books, 1968.

Feld, Ross. *Guston In Time*. New York: Counterpoint, 2003.

Fineberg, Jonathan. *Discovering Child Art*. Princeton, NJ: Princeton University Press, 1998.

Fineberg, Jonathan. *When We Were Young: New Perspectives on the Art of the Child*. Berkeley, Los Angeles and London: University of California Press, 2006.

Fink, Eugen. "The Oasis of Happiness: Toward an Ontology of Play," *Yale French Studies*, Issue 41, Game, Play, Literature (1968): 19–30.

Fink, Eugen. *Play as Symbol of the World and Other Writings*. Bloomington: Indiana University Press, 2016.

Flanagan, Mary. *Critical Play, Radical Game Design*. Cambridge, MA: The MIT Press, 2013.

Fogel, Gerald I. "Winnicott's Antitheory and Winnicott's Art, His Significance for Adult Analysis," *The Psychoanalytic Study of the Child*, Vol. 47, Issue 1 (1992): 205–222.

Foster, Hal. "Savage Minds (A Note on Brutalist Bricolage)," *October*, Vol. 136, Issue 1 (Spring 2011): 182–191.

Freud, Sigmund. *Animism, Magic and the Omnipotence of Thoughts, Totem and Taboo (1912—1913)*. London: Hogarth Press, 1995.

Gadamer, Hans-Georg. *Truth and Method*. London and New York: Continuum, 2006.

Getsy, David J., ed. *From Diversion to Subversion, Games, Play, and Twentieth-Century Art*. University Park, PA: The Pennsylvania State University Press, 2011.

Guston, Philip. "Philip Guston Talking," in *Philip Guston*. London: Timothy Taylor Gallery, 2004.

Heidegger, Martin. *Basic Writings*. London: Routledge, 1993.

Herrmann, Daniel F. "Bronze to Aluminium and Back Again: Eduardo Paolozzi's Use of Materials in Sculpture, c.1957–71," *Sculpture Journal*, Vol. 14, Issue 1 (2005): 71–85.

Herrmann, Daniel F., ed. *Eduardo Paolozzi* (exh.cat.). London: Whitechapel Gallery, 2017.

Highmore, Ben. "Brutalist Wallpaper and the Independent Group," *Journal of Visual Culture*, Vol. 12, Issue 2 (2013): 1–17.

Highmore, Ben. "'Image-Breaking, God-Making': Paolozzi's Brutalism," *October*, Vol. 136, Issue 1 (Spring 2011): 87–104.

Highmore, Ben. "Patio and Pavilion Revisited," *Oxford Art Journal*, Vol. 29 (June 2006): 269–290.

Highmore, Ben. "Playgrounds and Bombsites: Postwar Britain's Ruined Landscapes," *Cultural Politics*, Vol. 9, Issue 3 (2013): 323–336.

Hopkins, Brooke. "Winnicott and the Capacity to Believe," *International Journal of Psychoanalysis*, Vol. 78, Issue Pt 3 (July 1997): 485–497.

Hughes, Robert. *The Shock of the New*. London: Thames & Hudson, 1996.

Huizinga, Johan. *Homo Ludens: A Study of the Play Element in Culture*. Boston: The Beacon Press, 1955.

Johnstone, Keith. *Impro: Improvisation and the Theatre*. London: Methuen Drama, 2007.

Kaufmann, David. *Telling Stories, Philip Guston's Later Works*. London: University of California Press, 2010.

Kirkpatrick, Diane. *Eduardo Paolozzi*. London: Studio Vista, 1970.

Kitnick, Alex. "Another Time," *Art Journal*, Vol. 71, Issue 2 (Summer 2012): 32–43.

Klein, Sheri. *Art and Laughter*. London: I.B. Taurus, 2007.

Kozlovsky, Roy. *The Architectures of Childhood: Children, Modern Architecture and Reconstruction in Postwar England*. Farnham: Ashgate, 2013.

Krauss, Rosalind E. *Passages in Modern Sculpture*, London: The MIT Press, 1981.

Kubler, George. *The Shape of Time*. New Haven and London: Yale University Press, 1973.

Kuenzli, Rudolf. *Dada Themes and Movements*. London: Phaidon Press Limited, 2006.

Lefaivre, Liane and de Roode, Ingeborg, eds. *Aldo van Eyck: The Playgrounds and the City*. Amsterdam: Stedelijk Museum Amsterdam, 2002.

Lichtenstein, Claude and Schregenberger, Thomas, eds. *As Found: The Discovery of the Ordinary*. Baden: Lars Müller Publishers and the Zurich Museum für Gestaltung, 2001.

Lucie-Smith, Edward. *Movements in Art since 1945: Issues and Concepts*. London: Thames & Hudson, 1997.

Malt, Johanna. *Obscure Objects of Desire: Surrealism, Fetishism, and Politics*. New York: Oxford University Press, 2004.

Manovich, Lev. *The Language of New Media*. Cambridge, MA: The MIT Press, 2001.

Massey, Anne. *The Independent Group, Modernism and Mass Culture in Britain, 1945–59*. Manchester: Manchester University Press, 1995.

Matthews, John Herbert. *The Imagery of Surrealism*. New York: Syracuse University Press, 1977.

Mayer, Musa. *Night Studio, a Memoir of Philip Guston*. New York: Da Capo Press, 1997.

McDonnell, Patrick, O'Connell, Karen and Riley de Havenon, Georgia. *Krazy Kat: The Comic Art of George Herriman*. New York: Harry N. Abrams, Incorporated, 2004.

McGhee, Paul E. and Chapman, Anthony J. *Children's Humour*. Bath: The Pitman Press, 1980.

McLuhan, Marshall. *The Gutenberg Galaxy*. London: Routledge & Kegan Paul, 1971.
McLuhan, Marshall. *The Mechanical Bride: Folklore of Industrial Man*. London: Duckworth Overlook, 2011.
Middleton, Michael. *Art in Progress, Eduardo Paolozzi*. London: Methuen, 1963.
Milner, Marion. *The Suppressed Madness of Sane Men*. London: Tavistock, 1987.
Mitchell, Juliet. *The Selected Melanie Klein*. London: Penguin, 1986.
Mitchell, Juliet. "Theory as an Object," *October*, Issue 113 (Summer 2005): 27–38, MIT Press Journals.
Mitchell, William John Thomas. *What Do Pictures Want?: The Lives and Loves of Images*. Chicago and London: University of Chicago Press, 2005.
Moore-Gilbert, Bart J. and Seed, John. *Cultural Revolution?: The Challenge of the Arts in the 1960s*. London: Routledge, 1992.
Morreall, John. *Taking Laughter Seriously*. New York: University of New York Press, 1983.
Morris, Robert. *Continuous Project Altered Daily*. Cambridge, MA: The MIT Press, 1995.
Muensterberger, Werner. *Collecting: An Unruly Passion: Psychological Perspectives*. Princeton, NJ: Princeton University Press, 1994.
Ozenfant, Amedée. *Foundations of Modern Art*. London: John Rodker, 1931.
Paolozzi, Eduardo. "Child Art as Image, National Exhibition of Children's Art," *Sunday Pictorial*, 1959.
Paolozzi, Eduardo and Spencer, Robin. *Eduardo Paolozzi: Writings and Interviews*. Oxford and New York: Oxford University Press, 2001.
Peacock, Louise. *Slapstick and Comic Performance: Comedy and Pain*. London: Palgrave Macmillan, 2014.
Pearson, Fiona. *Paolozzi*. Edinburgh: Trustees of the National Galleries of Scotland, 1999.
Phillips, Adam. *Winnicott*. Cambridge, MA: Harvard University Press, 1988.
Piaget, Jean. *The Child's Conception of the World*. London: Paladin, 1973.
Piaget, Jean. *The Child's Construction of Reality*. London: Routledge & Kegan Paul Ltd., 1976.
Piaget, Jean. *The Language and Thought of the Child*. London: Routledge & Kegan Paul, 1959.
Piaget, Jean. *Play, Dreams and Imitation in Childhood*. London: Routledge & Kegan Paul, 1962.
Piaget, Jean and Inhelder, Bärbel. *The Origin of the Idea of Chance in Children*. London: Routledge & Kegan Paul, 1975.
Piaget, Jean and Inhelder, Bärbel. *The Psychology of the Child*. London: Routledge & Kegan Paul, 1969.
Read, Herbert. *Art Now: An Introduction to the Theory of Modern Painting and Sculpture*. London: Faber and Faber, 1936.
Read, Herbert. *Education Through Art*. London: Faber and Faber, 1961.
Read, Herbert. *Modern Sculpture: A Concise History*. London and New York: Thames & Hudson, 1996.
Richter, Hans. *Dada, Art and Anti-Art*. Cologne: Thames & Hudson, 1964.
Rose, Barbara. *American Art Since 1900*. London: Thames & Hudson, 1975.
Rosen, Aaron. *Imagining Jewish Art: Encounters with the Masters in Chagall, Guston and Kitaj*. London: Legenda, 2009.
Rosenberg, Harold. *The Tradition of the New*. New York: Da Capo Press, 1994.
Ryall, Emily, Russell, Wendy and Maclean, Malcolm, eds. *The Philosophy of Play*. New York: Routledge, 2014.
Sabin, Roger. *Comics, Comix and Graphic Novels: A History of Comic Art*. London: Phaidon, 1996.
Sawyer, R. Keith, John-Steiner, Vera, Moran, Seana, J. Sternberg, Robert, Henry Feldman, David, Nakamura, Jeanne and Csikszentimihalyi, Mihaly. *Emergence in Creativity and Development*. New York: Oxford University Press, 2003.
Schmied, Wieland. *Arche Noah*. Munich: Münchner Stadtmuseum, 1990.

Schreier, Christoph and Semff, Michael, eds. *Philip Guston Works on Paper*. Ostfildern: Hatje Cantz Verlag, 2007.
Sichel, Kim and Drach McInnes, Mary. *Philip Guston 1975–1980: Private and Public Battles*. Boston: Boston University Art Gallery, 1994.
Smith, Leslie. *Critical Readings on Piaget*. London: Routledge, 1996.
Sontag, Susan. *Against Interpretation*. London: Penguin Classics, 2009.
Spencer, Robin. *Eduardo Paolozzi Recurring Themes*. London: Trefoil, 1984.
Stewart, Susan. *On Longing*. Durham and London: Duke University Press, 1993.
Storr, Robert. *Philip Guston*. New York: Abbeville, 1986.
Stryker, Eric M. "Parallel Systems: Lawrence Alloway and Eduardo Paolozzi," *Tate Papers*, Issue 16 (Autumn 2011).
Suits, Bernard. *The Grasshopper, Games, Life and Utopia*. Plymouth: Broadview Press, 2005.
Sutton-Smith, Brian. *The Ambiguity of Play*. Cambridge, MA: Harvard University Press, 2001.
Sutton-Smith, Brian. *Toys as Culture*. New York: Gardner Press, 1986.
Thompson, D'Arcy Wentworth. *On Growth and Form*. London: Cambridge University Press, 1969.
Trotter, David. *Cooking with Mud: The Idea of Mess in Nineteenth-Century Art and Fiction*. Oxford: Oxford University Press, 2000.
Wallis, Simon. *Philip Guston*. London: Timothy Taylor Gallery, 2006.
Walsh, Victoria. *Nigel Henderson: Parallel of Life and Art*. London: Thames & Hudson Ltd., 2001.
Wardle, Louise, dir. *Paolozzi*, BBC, December 7, 2000.
Weltens, Arno. *Mechanical Tin Toys in Colour*. Dorset: Blandford, 1977.
Whitford, Frank. *Eduardo Paolozzi*. London: Tate Gallery, 1971.
Whitford, Frank. *The Keiller Collection: Eduardo Paolozzi Sculptures from a Garden*, Arts Council, 1987.
Williams, James. "Deleuze and Structure: How Far Can You Bend It?," in *Deleuzian Events: Writing History* (Conference Proceedings), ed. by Hanjo Berressem and Leyla Haferkamp, 46–57. Berlin: Lit, 2009.
Williamson, Beth. *Between Art Practice and Psychoanalysis Mid-Twentieth Century: Anton Ehrenzweig in Context*. Farnham: Ashgate, 2015.
Winnicott, D.W. *The Child, the Family and the Outside World*. Harmondsworth: Penguin Books Ltd., 1969.
Winnicott, D.W. *Playing and Reality*. Oxon: Routledge, 2005.
Winnicott, D.W. *Psycho-Analytic Explorations*. London: Karnac Books, 1989.

Index

Note: Page numbers in italics indicate a figure on the corresponding page.

For Product Safety Concerns and Information please contact our EU representative GPSR@taylorandfrancis.com Taylor & Francis Verlag GmbH, Kaufingerstraße 24, 80331 München, Germany

Batch number: 10722200

Printed by Printforce, the Netherlands